ALANNA NASH

THE
COLONEL

THE EXTRAORDINARY STORY OF COLONEL TOM PARKER AND ELVIS PRESLEY

SIMON & SCHUSTER

NEW YORK   LONDON   TORONTO   SYDNEY   SINGAPORE

SIMON & SCHUSTER
Rockefeller Center
1230 Avenue of the Americas
New York, NY 10020

SIMON & SCHUSTER and colophon are registered trademarks
of Simon & Schuster, Inc.

For information regarding special discounts for bulk purchases,
please contact Simon & Schuster Special Sales at
1-800-456-6798 or business@simonandschuster.com

Designed by Karolina Harris

Manufactured in the United States of America

10   9   8   7   6   5   4   3   2   1

Library of Congress Cataloging-in-Publication Data
Nash, Alanna.
The Colonel : the extraordinary story of Colonel Tom Parker
and Elvis Presley / Alanna Nash.
p.   cm.
Includes bibliographical references and index.
ISBN 0-7432-1301-7
1. Parker, Tom, 1909–   2. Presley, Elvis, 1935–1977.
3. Impresarios—United States—Biography.   I. Title.
ML429.P33N37   2003
782.42166'092—dc21
[B]   2003045538

ACKNOWLEDGMENTS

T H E English writer Richard Holmes described the crafting of biography as "a haunting, an act of deliberate psychological trespass, a continuous living dialogue between subject and author as they move over the same historical ground."

That analogy seemed apt as I readied this manuscript, since I haunted the streets of Tom Parker's past, and he haunted my daylight and my dreams. Many times, we seemed to do battle as I struggled to decode the cryptic actions of his life. For a man who lived eighty-seven years, he left remarkably few words on the major events of his nine decades, neither writing a tome of his own, nor cooperating with journalists, as if daring a biographer to create an accurate account from stony silence.

Judith Thurman, reflecting on the French writer Colette, the subject of her own biographical work, has said that during this mysterious process of committing a life to the page she felt at some level Colette "was waiting for the recognizer—someone who would see through her poses and her masks and her reticence and describe her to herself." But Colette would not collaborate with her: "She wanted to control the narrative."

At the most difficult juncture of researching this biography, Parker seemed to do the same—to taunt me, to invite me to explain him, if not to himself, to others. But then just as quickly, he, like Colette, attempted to exercise control, erecting one hurdle after another.

If I succeeded in capturing him, in pinning him to the ground like Lemuel Gulliver in the land of Lilliputians, it was only with a great deal of help, beginning with Michael Korda and Chuck Adams at Simon & Schuster, who understood the project in a way that almost no one else did.

Beyond those who helped with the mechanics of turning a manuscript into a book are the people who offered the information that made the story live and breathe, all of whom knew a different Tom Parker. Without them, he would never have arrived between these covers with his complexity intact. I owe tremendous gratitude to the following:

In Holland, many people worked diligently to help me shed some light in dark corners, beginning with Parker's family—his sister, Marie Gort–van Kuijk; his niece, Maria (Mieke) Dons-Maas; and her husband, Ted Dons. They opened their homes and their hearts to me. I will always cherish them for that singular experience, and for their friendship. Parker's refusal to acknowledge these very loving people in his latter years was to deny himself an extraordinary gift.

I am also exceedingly grateful to Angelo Somers and Hanneke Neutkens, who champion Parker's legacy in his native country, and to Parker's nephew Ad van Kuijk Jr., for sharing precious family documents.

A number of Dutch lawyers provided essential information, including Erik M. J. Thomas of Schoenmakers & Thomas, Breda, Holland, and Pauline Reitsma, who midwifed the legal process of examining old police reports. Additionally, several archivists worked cheerfully to marshal dates of births, deaths, and marriages, including Mevr. M.-L. van den Wijngaard, City Archives Section Head, and C. J. J. Biemans-Voesenek, City Archives, Breda, Holland. A profound thanks goes to Amnon and Lynn Shiboleth and Lilyan Wilder for serving as vital contacts to key figures of this group.

Although he left his native Holland long ago, Lee Wulffraat set me straight on so many aspects of Dutch life, educated me about the kinds of boats that likely transported the future Colonel Parker to America, and offered countless translations of important articles, documents, and letters. He was a constant friend, always willing to try to do the impossible. His brother, Tony Wulffraat, still residing in the Netherlands, was as giving and helpful, spending his Christmas holidays taking photographs that helped me understand one part of the story so well. Lee's daughter, Karen, proved the important link in our fortuitous meeting, and in fact, the book seemed to become a Wulffraat family project, as Elsa and Wim van Pelt, Lee's sister and brother-in-law, and Ine Wulffraat, Tony's wife, also helped decipher antiquated texts and speed the translations.

No amount of thanks can convey my deep appreciation to the Dutch journalist Constant Meijers, who shared both his keen insights into Parker's personality and his transcripts of interviews from his documentary film *Looking for Colonel Parker*. In the darkest days of this project, his shared belief kept me going.

I'm grateful also to the Holland Society of New York; Professor David van Kuijk; Tanja Eikenboom Warren, for translations of crucial Dutch periodicals; Adriaan Sturm and Willem Kaauw, for magazine articles and photographs concerning Parker's origins in the Netherlands; and to E. A. van den Enden–v. Meer, Harry van den Enden, and Ad van den Enden, for clues into the fundamental mystery at the heart of this saga. Additionally, Frans de Leeuw at Breda's St. Joseph School cleared up some confusion about Parker's early education.

There are others without whom this book would not have moved beyond the routine assimilation of dates and facts. Dirk Vellenga and Mick Farren, whose seminal *Elvis and the Colonel* laid the foundation for this work, spoke with candor about the still-elusive nature of the subject. In pointing me in some new directions, they provided a blueprint for my research. This book would clearly not exist without theirs.

Peter Whitmer, Ph.D., and the author of *The Inner Elvis,* supplied a plethora of original source material, invaluable psychological profiling of the Colonel, and a much appreciated analysis of Parker's letter to his Dutch nephew. He also propped me up when the going got rough.

Dick Bielen of the U.S. Locator Service worked tirelessly to find Parker's long-lost army records, which add immeasurably to the understanding of the Colonel's early years in America. Unquestionably, these records stand as the most exciting and illuminating evidence of Parker's psychological make-up.

Finally, Bolling Smith, the editor of *The Coast Defense Journal,* read the military chapter and straightened out some crooked facts, and Michael Streissguth, Eddy Arnold's biographer, helped me corral the facts of the Arnold years. He also shared his interview transcripts, made introductions, and offered support for an often sagging morale.

While everyone interviewed for the book contributed in ways he or she can't imagine, several sources were indispensable and gave generously of their time and treasures, from photographs to historical records. I will never be able to express my gratitude to Byron Raphael, Gabe Tucker, Sandra Polk Ross, Bob McCluskey, and Larry Geller. All were of such glorious help that I don't know if I could have done the book without them. Chick Crumpacker also deserves extra mention, not only for his written responses to questions and his phone interview, but for his dogged research on my behalf in the RCA archives.

The following are some of the many people who helped in significant ways: Cindy Adams; Gaylen Adams; Steve Allen; Kathy Allmand; Chet Atkins; Marjorie (Mrs. Ollie) Atkins; Kevin Atkinson; M. R. Avery,

D.V.M.; Duke Bardwell; Georganne La Piere Bartylak; Armand and Marde Baum; Linda Bayens; John Berry; Frances Bevis; Sharon Bevis; Freddy Bienstock; Steve Binder; Barbara Boger; Frank Bogert; Jenny Bohler; Charlie and Mary Lou Boyd; Don Bradley; Harold Bradley; Terry Bream; David Briggs; J. W. Brown; James L. Brown; Tony Brown; Don Burch; Bob Burris; Sam Bushman; Albert Buys; Noble Case; June Carter Cash; Harriet Chalfant; Dick Clark; President William Jefferson Clinton and Daniel W. Burkhardt, Special Assistant to the President; Barry Coburn; Steven Cohen; Dick Contino; Janet Costner; Dr. Susan Cottler; Lance Cowan; John Craig; Mike Crowley; Marc Cummings; Susan Darnell; Larry Davis; Oscar Davis Jr.; Cartha "Deke" DeLoach; Bill Denny; Alice Virginia Dodd; Ann Dodelin; John Dotson; Jackie Dowlen; Louise Draper; Tommy Durden; Al Dvorin; John Eastman; Alan Eichler; Allison Elbl; Joycelyn Engle; William Ervin; Sam Esgro; Donna Fargo; Art Fein; Lamar Fike; Bob Finkel; Larry Fitzgerald; Tom Flagg, University of Nevada at Las Vegas; Ed Fleck; Kira Florita, Sandy Neese and Kevin Lane, Mercury Nashville; D. J. Fontana; Trude Forsher; Richard H. Frank Sr.; Tillman Franks; Anne Fulchino; Joe Galante; Jan Gay and Judy Burkley; Robert Gregory Gibson; Paul Golden; Charlie Gouvenia; Scott Gray; Charles Grean; Tony Greaves; Tom T. Hall; Maxine Hansen, Executive Assistant to Gene Autry; Buddy Harman; Summer Harman; Andrew Hearn; William Helfand; Sharon Henry; Leonard Hirshan; Randy Holmes; Sue Horn; Terry Houck; Richard Hull; Nick Hunter; Janis Ian and Patricia Snyder; Tormod Lunde Idsø; Mel Ilberman; Clancy Imislund, Director of the Midnight Mission, Los Angeles, California; Joyce Jackson; Ron Jacobs; Jackie Jett; Van Joyce; Norman Kaye; Frances Keanan; Lydia (Mrs. Pee Wee) King; Buddy Killen; Bill Kimbro; Otto Kitsinger; Dorothy Koenig; Bob Kotlowitz; Betsy Kronish; Marty Lacker; Charlie Lamb; Dick Lane; Jane Lane; Bob Leoni of the Songwriters Hall of Fame; Pam Lewis; Horace Logan; Charlie Louvin; Sandy Lovejoy; A. C. Lyles; Peter Maas; William C. MacGregor; Diana Magrann; Benny Martin; Kathy Mattea; Mary Matthews; Helen McCloud; Brad McCuen; Joyce McMakin; Hal and Vi Moldenhaur; Chips Moman; Bob Moody; Bob and Kittra Moore; Scotty Moore; Erin Morris; Joe Moscheo; Bitsy Mott.

Also Nick Naff; Tracey Nathan; Ken Nelson; Tracy Nelson; George M. Newill; Hugh O'Brian; Brent Olson; Frank Page; Patti Page; Richard Palmer; Ben Payne; Federico Pollicina, M.D.; C. J. Pressma; Mark Pucci; Norman Racusin; Bill Rains; Michael Ravnitzky; Jere Real; Raymond Richardson; Don Rickles; Libby Riggins; Steve Rinaldi Sr.; Jordan

Ritchie; Dennis Roberts; Dale Robertson; Cathy Hetzer Rogers; Dusty Rogers; Monsignor George W. Rohling; Robert Kenneth Ross; David Rothel; Ronna Rubin; Leon Russell; Tommy Sands; Karen Schoemer; Walter Seltzer; Joe Shane; Andrew Shankman, M.D., Marva (Mrs. Lloyd) Shearer; Jim Sherraden of Hatch Show Print; Joan Shoofey; Evelyn Shriver; Clare Simpson; David Skepner; Todd Slaughter; Steve Small; Mary Smiley, the pride of Toledo, Ohio; David C. Smith of the Southern California Miniature Horse Club; Jon Guyot Smith; Rosalie F. Sochinski, Executive Director, Variety Clubs International; Stan Soocher; Kathie Spehar; Gordon Stoker; Lisa Stout of the Nashville Metro Medical Examiner's Office; Joe Sullivan; John Szabanowicz; Preston Temple; E. Parry Thomas; Dr. and Mrs. John B. Thompson; Mel Tillis; Pam Tillis; Anna Trainor; Justin Tubb; Tanya Tucker; Dana Tumpowsky; Jenifer van Deinse; Wes Vause; Ken Vrana; James Wade Jr.; Michael Wallis; Diane Warren; Dr. David Weide, University of Nevada at Las Vegas; Cheryl Weinstein; Allan Weiss; Kay West; Christie Mullins Westmoreland; Kathy Westmoreland; Kay Wheeler; Roy Wiggins; Paul Wilborn; Dorothy Wilder; David Wilds; Don Wilson; Amy Wimberly; Elaine Tubb Wingerter; Charles Winn of Spring Hill Cemetery and Mausoleum; Mac Wiseman; Irv Woolsey; Marvin Worth; Jules Wortman; Don Wrege; Mark Wright; Mary Yandell; James Harvey Young.

Thanks also to John Agan, LouCeil Austin, Debbie Germany, Jackie Lawton, Tommy Overstreet, and Angela Snyder for help with the Gene Austin period.

The following also provided essential information:

For help with the presidential connections, Lynda Johnson Robb; George Reedy; Bill Moyers; Mike Parrish and Claudia Anderson, Archivists, Lyndon Baines Johnson Library, Austin, Texas; Lisa Vitt, Archivist, Ronald Reagan Library, Simi Valley, California; Mary Finch, Warren Finch, and Sam McClure at the George Bush Library, College Station, Texas; Kathleen A. Struss and Bonnie Mulanax at the Dwight D. Eisenhower Library, Abilene, Kansas; Raymond Teichman, Supervisory Archivist, Franklin D. Roosevelt Library, Hyde Park, New York; Dennis E. Bilger, Archivist, Harry S Truman Library, Independence, Missouri; Albert Nason, Archivist, Jimmy Carter Library, Atlanta, Georgia; Geir Gundersen, Archivist, Gerald R. Ford Library, Ann Arbor, Michigan; the archivists of the John Fitzgerald Kennedy Library, Boston, Massachusetts; and Pat Anderson of the Nixon Presidential Materials staff of the National Archives.

In California, a number of people were instrumental in helping me trace the intricate business and personal relationship of Hal Wallis and Parker, beginning with the staff of the Margaret Herrick Library, Center for Motion Picture Study at the Academy of Motion Picture Arts and Sciences: Linda Mehr, Barbara Hall, Faye Thompson, Bonnie Daley, Marcelle Angelo, Eddie Baker, Sue Bulden, Galen Wilkes, Andrea Battiste, Jonathan Wahl, Matt Poodiack, Scott Curtis, and Kristine Krueger of the library's National Film Information Service. Larrian Gillespie not only worked alongside me there, but offered room and board and showed me the sights of L.A. She was a true friend when I needed one.

And in Nashville, Kent Henderson, Ronnie Pugh, Alan Stoker, Paul Kingsbury, John Rumble, Dawn Oberg and Kyle Young of the Country Music Foundation gave aid and comfort at every turn, Kent going on to pore though government documents outside the office.

Thanks additionally to David Millman, Nevada State Historical Society and Museum, and to Frank Gorrell for his expert tutelage in the art of gambling and his recollection of Parker's personal history in the Las Vegas casinos.

As usual on any project, my fellow journalists bolstered me with facts, interviews, and long-distance hand-holding. I'm especially indebted to Moira Bailey and Kristen Kelch of *People* magazine; Bill Bastone of *The Village Voice;* Ted Bridis, Ed Staats, Lisa Holewa, and James Derk of the Associated Press; Andrea Campbell; Roger Capettini; Floyd Martin Clay; James P. Cole; Patsi Bale Cox; Don Cusic; Joe Delaney, Ruthe Deskin, Dee McConnell, and Merilyn Potters of *The Las Vegas Sun;* Jim Dickerson; Joe Elliott, WHAS Radio, Louisville, Kentucky; Pat Embry of *The Nashville Banner;* Jim Emerson; Ralph Emery; Todd Everett; Chet Flippo of CMT.com; Stephen Fried; Peter Gilstrap; Vernell Hackett; Michael Hall of *Texas Monthly;* Stacy Harris; Leland Hawes of *The Tampa Tribune;* Jack Hurst; Chris Hutchins; Beth Johnson of *Entertainment Weekly;* Deborah Evans Price, *Billboard* magazine; Danny Proctor; Tamara Saviano; Tom Scherberger of the *St. Petersburg Times;* Elizabeth Schlappi; Bob Schulman; Steve Simels; Panky Snow; Linda Upton; Bill Willard; E. Bingo Wyer; and especially Beverly Keel, who turned her reportorial skills to my cause, and not just because her journalist father coined the term "Elvis the Pelvis."

Thanks also to Marsha Mercer of Media General News Corp.; Margaret Schmidt of *The Jersey Journal,* Jersey City, New Jersey; the library staff of *The Louisville Courier-Journal;* David Valenzuela, Carolyn Marlin, and Anita Coursey of the library staff of *The Nashville Banner;* and

Kyle Neiderpruem, Freedom of Information Committee, Society of Professional Journalists.

Additionally, I am grateful to my tireless researchers: Jim Cole of the Mississippi Valley Collection, University of Memphis; Pam Courtney; Juliana Hoskinson; Art Nadler; Nancy Randle; Margaret Shannon; and Lynn Waddell. Judy Raphael not only did research, but also introduced me to the book's single best source, her brother, Byron. And Charlene Blevins accepted a records-checking task that tested her both as a journalist and as a thespian, and proved her equally skilled at both.

Thanks also to the following, who helped with a myriad of special collections and archives: the staff of the American Film Institute; Manny Arocho, Librarian, Special Collections Department, Tampa-Hillsborough County Public Library System; Art Bagely, Special Collections, University of Tampa; Carol Butler, Salvador Dali Museum; Dean DeBolt and Benita Fox, University Librarians, Special Collections and West Florida Archives, John C. Pace Library, University of West Florida, Pensacola, Florida; William B. Eigelsbach, Manuscripts, University of Tennessee Libraries; Ed Frank, James Montague, and Sharon Banker of the Mississippi Valley Collection, the University of Memphis; General Library and Museum of the Performing Arts at Lincoln Center; Sharon Johnson, Special Collections Librarian and Archivist, Autry Museum of Western Heritage; Ashley Koostra, Archivist, Mississippi Department of Archives and History; Lois Latimer of the Tampa Historical Society; Laura Lupole and June Miller-Spaan of the Chautauqua Institute; Robert A. McCown, Special Collections Library, State University of Iowa; Sally McManus, Palm Springs Historical Society; the staff of Profnet, for Internet search queries; Dr. Richard Ranta, the University of Memphis; Cheryl Rogers-Barnett, Director of the Roy Rogers–Dale Evans Museum; Ed Schreiber and Michelle T. Rogers, for copies of letters Parker's office sent to fans; Phyllis Stinson, for sharing her incredible archive of Parker memorabilia; Robert Vay and Paul S. Koda, Special Collections and Archives, George Mason University, Fairfax, Virginia; Mark Weitzman of the Simon Weisenthal Center; and Travis Westly, Reference Specialist, the Library of Congress.

For help with the Albert Goldman archives, Jere Herzenberg, Carolyn Krupp, and Jane Krupp.

And for additional assistance with obtaining and interpreting information regarding Parker's army years, thanks go to Colonel Gregory Belenky, Walter Reed Army Institute of Research; J. Earle Bowden, historian and former editor of *The Pensacola News-Journal;* Leah Dickstein, M.D., Director of the Division of Attitudinal and Behavioral Medicine, University of Louisville; Thomas M. Fairfull, Chief, Museum Division, U.S. Army Museum of Hawaii, Schofield Barracks, Hawaii; Donne Florence, University Relations, Media, and Publications, University of Hawaii; Judith A. Bowman, Assistant Curator, U.S. Army Museum of Hawaii; Lt. Col. Allen Frenzel, U.S. Army, Professor of Military Science, University of Hawaii; Jerry Goodson, Reno Veterans Affairs Office; Susan Heffner, Director of Library and Archives, American Psychiatric Association, Washington, D.C.; Wendy Hollingsworth, Assistant Branch Chief in the Records Reconstruction Branch at the National Personnel Records Center, St. Louis, Missouri; David J. Johnson, Museum Technician, the Casemate Museum, Fort Monroe, Virginia; Lt. Col. Richard S. Johnson; Earl Kilgus, for sharing memories of Fort Shafter, and his grandson, Robert H. Egolf III, for the photograph of the 64th Coast Artillery; David P. Ogden; Al Reynolds, Reference Librarian of the Walter Reed Army Institute of Research Library; David A. Ross, Curator of the Air Defense Artillery Museum in Fort Bliss, Texas; Bud Smyser of *The Honolulu Star-Bulletin;* Mr. and Mrs. Clifton E. Sprinkle Jr., Raymond Willis Sprinkle, and Scott Sprinkle, for help with the Fort Barrancas years; and Dr. Sheila A. Schuster, both for help with interpretation of Parker's army papers and for the loan of an audiotape transcriber.

For help with Parker's early years in America, Allen "Slim" Binkley; Paul E. Mix; the Tom Mix Museum, Dewey, Oklahoma; Merle "Bud" Norris; Dr. Richard F. Seiverling; and Debbie Taylor of the Tampa Bay Humane Society.

Parker's immigration history and illegal alien status were especially difficult to track. My thanks to the following for assistance: Robert Ellis of the National Archive; Linda Kloss of the FBI's Freedom of Information Privacy Act Section, Washington, D.C.; Diane Biggs Korwin, Gary Baude, and Marian Smith of the Immigration and Naturalization Service; the Honorable Ron Mazzoli; Margaret Roman of the U.S. State Department; Lily Talapessy of the Dutch Consolate, New York; and Blanchard E. Tual.

For insight into the carnival years, Jack Bennett; John Campi; Cheryl Collins; Fred Dahlinger Jr., Director, Collections and Research, Circus World Museum, Baraboo, Wisconsin; Larry Davis; Bruce Feiler; James E. Foster, editor, *The White Tops;* Chappie Fox; Ken Fox, Magic Makers Costumes, Huntington, West Virginia; Dave Friedman; Bob Goldsack, publisher, Midway Museum Publications; Ward Hall; Minnie Heth; Allan C. Hill; Joseph G. Hoffman; Bob Jarvis; Don Marcks of *The Circus Report;* Joe McKennon; Harley Newman; Fred D. Pfening Jr., editor, *Bandwagon* magazine; Maggie Riley; Judy "Rustie" Rock; Renee Storey of the Clyde Beatty/Cole Bros. Circus; Jeanie Tomaini; Hoxie Tucker; Ernie Wenzik; Bettie Siegel Whittaker; Safari Pete Wood. And for foot-long hot dog research: Chris Brian, Bill Dryden, Rick McCarty, and Kenny Vincent.

On such a project, photographs are especially important, and while many people contributed, I owe a round of applause to Jeff Burak, Time Pix; Kelly C. Hill, Photography Research Manager, and Angie Marchise, Curatorial Assistant, Elvis Presley Enterprises Inc.; Steve Buchanan, President, Grand Ole Opry Group, and Barbara Turner, Gaylord Entertainment Group, for assistance with the Gordon Gillingham photo collection; Maria Columbus; James Forsher; Tony Davidson; Trish McGee, the Ryman Auditorium; John Mott; Elizabeth Odle, The Nashville Public Library; James R. Reid; Michele Romero, *Entertainment Weekly;* Robin Rosaaen; Karen Silverol, the Las Vegas News Bureau; Marsh Starks and Rebecca Bagayas, *The Las Vegas Sun; The Tampa Tribune* library and photo departments; Richard Weize and Heidi Cordsmeier of Bear Family Records; and the incomparable Al Wertheimer.

A very special thanks to Greg Howell, former exhibitions and collections manager of Graceland; to Paula B. Kennedy and Joan Buchanan West, of the E. P. Continentals Elvis Fan Club, who helped me unearth a key part of Marie Parker's past; and to Mark North, who gave me an extraordinary tour of Parker's former home in Madison, Tennessee.

And for care and feeding of the author, Elizabeth Thiels and Ellen and Bill Pryor in Nashville; Ted Dons and Maria Dons-Maas in Holland; Barbara Shircliffe, Sandra Polk Ross, and Frances Keenan in Tampa; and in Memphis, Charles and Virginia Overholt, who at the directive of Diana Magrann, kindly let me stay in Vernon Presley's house. My Memphis cousin, DeAnna Mooneyhan, was brave beyond all measure.

On a technical note, it's impossible to properly thank Jerry Maskalick and Dan Coddington of Dr. Dan's Computers, as well as Brian Arnold, for modifying my word processing for this project, and for gluing it—and me—back together when my system crashed, and crashed, and crashed.

Finally, I haven't the words to thank my parents, Allan and Emily Kay Nash, who gave me bottomless financial and emotional support during this long and difficult journey. No mother and father could have done more. Judy F. May, Elizabeth Clifford, and Robert Morse also deserve my deepest gratitude for always being there, as does Carolyn Shircliffe, who transcribed nearly all of the hundreds of interviews I conducted for the book. Her family—Mary Jo Shircliffe, Barbara Shircliffe, and the late Montgomery Shircliffe—did so much in innumerable ways to make this book see the light of day, and served as my guardian angels on a constant basis. Additionally, Robin Rosaaen supervised all critical Elvis sightings, and Bill and Connie Burk performed Herculean deeds, especially on our joint trip to Holland. Bill also fact-checked the manuscript.

Warm thanks, too, to Bobbie Ann Mason and Frances Zichanowicz, who kept me buoyed during the last half of the writing. And I'm especially grateful to Phil Collier of Stites & Harbison for extraordinary legal magic, and Hugh Wright, Leslie K. Hale, and Missy Coorssen of National City Bank.

In many ways, it is astonishing that this book survived the many setbacks that threatened its publication, but then it had many shepherds along the way. Joyce Engelson, as always, offered sage advice and enthusiasm when I needed it most, as did Regula Noetzli and David Black.

But it was Sam Hughes and Bob Solinger of the Dickens Group Literary Agency who lent a peerless stewardship. Sam was the one who strongly encouraged me to do the book, since I had met with the Colonel on three occasions in Las Vegas and had written about him in my two previous books on Elvis. She was always the one with the clearest vision for it, never giving up when others, including myself, lost faith.

Sam and I labored through some wrenching times in the six years it took to bring the book to completion, and at one dark juncture, we not only split our business association, but also dissolved our deep friendship. Two years went by before we reconciled, and she set me back on course to continue the writing, working several miracles along the way. "It just looks as if we were meant to be together," she said, and I knew she was right.

The day after Simon & Schuster agreed to acquire the book, Sam became ill with pneumonia. Two weeks later, she died, at the age of fifty-five, leaving a crater in my heart and an unfillable void in the lives of her family and clients. After that, not a day went by that I didn't feel her sitting next to me at the word processor, suggesting a word here, elaborating on an idea there. Now a project that started out as one kind of haunting had turned into another. Here's to you, Sam. I'll be seeing you.

For Maria Dons-Maas,
who searches still for her
Uncle Andreas

CONTENTS

Cunning and deceit will serve a man better than
force to rise from a base condition to great fortune.

—*Niccolò Machiavelli*

THE COLONEL

PREFACE

N O sane person goes to Memphis in the month of August, when the air, rolling off the hard-by Mississippi River, hangs sticky sweet and damp, and the simplest inhalation feels like breathing through burlap. But on August 17, 1977, nothing would have kept me from this place. The day before, Elvis Aaron Presley, the greatest entertainer of the twentieth century and a social force beyond measure, watched his life ebb away on the bathroom floor at his beloved Graceland.

Now I stood only yards below that bathroom window, numb with confusion at the surreal events that had brought me to the grounds of the most private of rock and roll estates. At twenty-seven, I had been reviewing pop music for *The Louisville Courier-Journal* for only a few months, but my fanatical interest in the subject dated to Presley's first appearance on *The Ed Sullivan Show* in 1956. How could the King of Rock and Roll be dead at forty-two?

I stepped to the edge of the press pool and gazed down the long driveway. There, to the soft sounds of crying, scores of fans who had succumbed to heat and grief lay prostrate on the grass. Behind them, thousands of mourners stood in line behind the famed gates that bore the resemblance of the man who lay in his casket inside Graceland's foyer. All of us were waiting to hear the same news—the hour when the public visitation might begin.

It was then that Dick Grob, head of Presley's security, walked out of the house and stopped where I was standing with John Filiatreau, a respected *Courier-Journal* columnist who had flown down with me on the company plane.

Grob raised his bullhorn: "Any members of the press who want to view the body, line up behind these two," he announced, and put his hands on our shoulders. The single rule: no lingering—the line must move at all times. I turned to John. "You first," I said, and he obliged me as we made our way inside.

There before us, in a large copper-lined casket, lay a swollen figure dressed in a white business suit, a blue dress shirt, and a silver tie, his skin a white and waxy hue.

A woman cried out: "He looks like a tub!"

Not to me, he didn't. But he also didn't look like Elvis Presley. I went through the line again, my mind racing with the possibilities of a hoax, a plausible explanation for the unthinkable. When I tried to ease my way through a third time, a guard pulled me out. "You've been through twice," he said. "Only get one shot."

Today, I have no doubt that Elvis Presley occupied that coffin. But in 1977, as eager as I was to gaze once more at that famous face, one man refused to look at all.

"It's so strange," remembers Larry Geller, a member of Presley's entourage who styled Elvis's hair for his funeral. "We all wore our black suits. But Colonel Parker wore a Hawaiian floral shirt and a baseball cap. And never walked up to the casket. Very strange. Very strange, indeed."

INTRODUCTION

"**D I D** you see it?" the old man asked, shifting his mountainous heap of flesh to the edge of the chair, his eyes open wide and twinkling. "What a hell of a thing! Unbelievable!"

It was June 18, 1994, the day after O. J. Simpson's infamous Bronco run, and Colonel Tom Parker, with his attentive wife, Loanne, at his side, held court for two visitors at the N'Orleans Restaurant, a meat 'n' two joint in a run-of-the-mill strip mall named Lucky's on the outskirts of the gambling capital of the world.

Like the rest of the country, Parker had been mesmerized by Simpson's bizarre highway chase. But now his reaction, with his face momentarily frozen in awe, spoke silently of something else—not of a fascination with sports or the subtleties of race relations, but of a sort of perverse pride, perhaps, in an elite and remarkable fraternity of rogues. Or at the very least, in a man who had taken a terrible risk, and managed to beat the odds.

This was my second of three visits with Parker, whose own survivor instincts so defied description that many thought him indestructible. Yet less than three years later, also in Vegas, far from his birthplace of Breda, Holland, where he first learned the art of the hustle as an errand boy in Dutch fairs, circuses, and carnivals, he succumbed to the complications of a stroke at the age of eighty-seven.

A master illusionist in business and in the business of life, Tom Parker made things appear and disappear at will, and created something very great out of nothing—including himself. Out of respect for that, if nothing else, I went back to say good-bye.

..

The giant marquee outside the Las Vegas Hilton was both sweet and succinct (FAREWELL, COLONEL PARKER), but not everybody knew what it meant.

"You here to gamble?" asked my taxi driver, who had shuttled me in from the airport on a late January day in 1997 and who had uttered not a word until tip time.

"No, I'm going to the memorial service for Colonel Parker."

A beat. "Dat the fried chicken guy?"

At least one cynical obituary writer, Serene Dominic, seconded that thought in a *Phoenix New Times* article headed "Cooked the Colonel's Way—Colonel Tom Parker Has Kicked the Bucket, and the Original Recipe for Rock 'n' Roll Rotisserie Goes with Him." But the 160 mourners who filtered into Ballroom D saw him as one of the last giants and true iconoclasts of the century—a penniless immigrant who slipped into the country, befriended U.S. presidents and corporate CEOs, created both an icon and a $4-billion business, and never let any of it get in the way of what mattered most—playing the game.

Through it all, he remained as individualistic, as shrewd, rude, crude, and fun-loving as ever. At his death, he still delighted in practicing what he called the art of "snowing," the exquisitely performed act of separating people from their money, leaving them with a smile on their face and melting away before they realized what had taken place.

While some would argue that Parker's very body was a temple to gluttony, greed, and feeding off the dimmer wits of others, it was the Snowman his friends had come to honor this day, his widow, Loanne, posing an intriguing question.

"I want to leave you with just one thought," she said, addressing the crowd, which had passed a lobby-card-size photo of the couple at the entrance. "If Thomas A. Parker had never existed, how would each of your lives be different today?"

One person who couldn't answer that question was Elvis Aaron Presley, whose piped-in versions of "Memories" and "How Great Thou Art" opened and closed the service with ghostly reverence. The Elvis Presley who had first come to Vegas in 1956 as an acne-faced adolescent left it twenty years later as a pathetic, corseted cartoon, his body blown from years of abuse, his spirit picked hollow.

For all of the twenty years that Parker outlasted his greatest discovery, he would also have to live with the allegations that he had destroyed him, stifling his artistry in third-rate Hollywood formula pictures, suffocating his ambition in 837 Vegas performances from 1969 to 1976, and killing his will to live by refusing to challenge him in meaningful ways—a European tour, a dramatic film role to reclaim his self-respect, a crack at a memorable song.

Whether regarded as a meretricious and evil confidence man, or as a brilliant marketer and strategist, as remarkable as the star he managed, no figure in all of entertainment is more controversial, colorful, or larger than life than Tom Parker. "He was so immense, so gigantic in his way," remembers writer Robert Kotlowitz, an RCA publicist in the late '50s and early '60s. "His style was equivalent to a great politician's, with so much flamboyance and wit and, underneath it all, cunning. He had to beat the whole world."

Yet at his death, Parker was blasted by rock critic Dave Marsh as "the most overrated person in the history of show business," and assessed by Dutch journalist and filmmaker Constant Meijers as "a nobody who needed a somebody to be anybody." To this day, a favorite debate question among pop music journalists is whether Elvis, whom the Colonel often referred to in carnival terms as "my attraction," would have remained a regional act without Parker's guidance, or if the young performer was such a blazing comet that no one could have stopped his streak across the sky.

The probability is that neither man would have been as big in his field without the other, Parker realizing, like P. T. Barnum, that the promotion of a curiosity was just as important as the curiosity itself. A chameleon who was many things to many people, Parker has his staunch defenders—as a visionary, a businessman, and a friend, even by those who got up from the losing side of the bargaining table. And while Parker probably would have referred to himself as a promoter more than anything else, having marketed the icon most recognizable in all the world after Coca-Cola, Chet Atkins, who dealt with many of the biggest artists during his tenure as an RCA Records executive, pronounced Parker "the best manager I ever saw. . . . Whatever he cost Elvis, he was worth it, because Elvis would've . . . lost that luster in no time if it hadn't been for the Colonel."

Mike Crowley, who traveled with Parker in the concert years of the '70s and is now a talent manager himself, speaks, like many, of Parker's loyalty, and also justifies his treatment of Elvis, the addict. "Nobody killed Elvis except Elvis, and nobody could have helped Elvis but Elvis. The only other thing he could have done was walk away."

Parker himself never bothered to address his critics, nor did he try to carve out much middle ground in the debate of whether he was the devil or angel in Elvis's own private hell. When pressed about his handling or mishandling of Elvis, he'd merely bristle, stamp his cane into the ground, and repeat his stock answer: "I sleep good at night."

Beyond that, the old Dutchman who understood America far better than most Americans simply threw out the line he'd used for decades to keep himself out of headlines ("Elvis is my only client and my life, so I never give out stories about myself"), allegedly because he was writing a memoir to be called *How Much Does It Cost If It's Free?* But it was an excuse he had concocted to keep others from looking too closely at the hocus-pocus of his life, and from having to explain himself, especially in light of a 1980 lawsuit in which the state of Tennessee accused him of "overreaching" in his fiduciary responsibilities to Presley.

If Elvis was unknowable by his manager's design, the Colonel was beyond knowing, even to his own family. In 1980, Parker's brother-in-law, Bitsy Mott, who spent many years on the road in the Colonel's employ, was asked to explain the man he'd known for nearly half a century. "That man's a mystery," he said, and little more, for not even he knew that Parker had a secret to protect, a secret that colored nearly everything he did.

On the surface, it would appear only that Parker had entered the country illegally and had never become a naturalized U.S. citizen. But if something darker had happened in the distant Netherlands, it must have been deep, shameful, and nearly unforgivable, at least to Parker himself. Certainly he never talked about it, or about his Dutch upbringing, to either Presley or any of his previous clients. And when the Colonel's stepson, Bobby Ross, died in 1978, it was without benefit of the knowledge that the man who had reared him from the age of ten had not been born as Thomas Andrew Parker in Huntington, West Virginia, as he always claimed, but as Andreas Cornelis van Kuijk—known as Andre to his Dutch biological family.

I first met Colonel Parker in December 1992, and I wondered then how the secret of his origins—revealed to the world at large in 1981— impacted the all-dominating decisions he made in shaping nearly every event in the life and career of Elvis Presley.

At first glance, Presley and Parker appeared to have little in common except the raging fire of ambition, shaped by a shameless ferocity both struggled to keep hidden. Yet I discovered as I began to research this book that in the strange choreography of chance and coincidence, the fates of Elvis Aaron Presley and Thomas Andrew Parker were bound by two still surging events, and the pull each incident had on both of them.

Despite the hundreds of books profiling Presley and his career, the story of the relationship between these men, I saw, had yet to be uncovered. Parker was a man of not just one, but many secrets, and the keeper of several fantastic tales he fought to preserve, with Elvis almost always paying too much of the price.

On each of my three visits with Colonel Parker, I sat across the table from him and looked into his eyes—hypnotic pools of unearthly blue— and wondered, Just who *are* you?

And so I decided to research the story chronologically, trying to find the boy who became the man. That mission took me to Holland, where I met with the kindest and most cooperative sources on this book: Parker's Dutch family, who were as mystified by his behavior and as dedicated to finding the truth as I was.

Over a period of three years, I interviewed and corresponded with several members of the van Kuijk clan, including the Colonel's ninety-two-year-old sister, Marie. And with the help of American journalist Bill Burk, I established an ongoing and treasured friendship with Parker's niece, Mieke Dons-Maas, who worked so hard in the 1990s to try to reunite her mother, Engelina, with her brother in America. Along with her husband, Ted, and friends Angelo Somers and Hanneke Neutkens, who spent years gathering materials for a proposed Parker foundation, we united as a team, chasing the apparition of a lad who had walked the Breda streets so long ago on the first leg of his remarkable journey.

In the end, my research led me to realize that the tale of Colonel Thomas Andrew Parker, né Andreas Cornelis van Kuijk, is, beneath the veil of secrecy, a tragedy, and very nearly the stuff of Shakespeare.

The following is my attempt to resolve the conundrum of his life.

—Alanna Nash

1

THE LITTLE DUTCH BOY

T O a first-time visitor, the town of Breda, Holland, is a picture postcard of European charm and character. The prettiest metropolis in Noord-Brabant, Holland's largest province, which stretches from Zeeland, a large Delta area opening on the North Sea, to within three miles of the German border, Breda was originally built as a strategic fortress at the convergence of the Mark and the Aa Rivers. The town now boasts all the ultramodern facilities as a commercial and industrial center, but the remnants of the wall that surrounded the city at the beginning of the fourteenth century, the glassy canals that run all through the town, and the old, ornate architectural façades serve as reminders of its past.

Today, the van Gend en Loos building at Veemarktstraat 66, for example, houses an upscale menswear shop, Joep Krusemeyer Herenmode. In the late 1980s, the structure was targeted for demolition, but saved because of its historic significance. Having survived some three hundred years, the building remains one of the six oldest in Breda. It was here that the man who would later call himself Colonel Tom Parker was born.

Like so much of Breda, the row-house neighborhood is a mix of old and new. Five shops down from the former van Gend en Loos building, at Veemarktstraat 52/54, there's the Spronk Muziekhandel, a record shop whose window front features a sticker with a likeness of Elvis Presley and the dates 1977–1997, a reference to the twentieth anniversary of the singer's death.

Little has actually changed here for centuries. On the Grote Markt, the the cobblestone square that serves as the vibrant focus of life in this easy-going town of some 130,000, the handsome old buildings that have housed everything from hay markets to municipal offices since Breda was granted its city charter in 1252 are still in use, as is the Grote Kerk, the impressive Gothic church with its openwork gables, crocket spires, and a baroque onion-shaped dome ornamenting its tower.

The church, which took 125 years to build and dominates the town, has stood above the Grote Markt since the thirteenth century, a silent witness to Breda's succession of feudal rulers from 1250, its Spanish conquest in 1591 and 1625, and its French domination from 1793 to 1813. Not far away, atop the Kasteelplein, where Catholics once tortured the Protestants and then burned them at the stake, looms the Kasteel, Breda's citadel, built in 1536. Today, it houses the Koninklijke Militaire Academie, or Royal Military Academy.

The military tradition of Breda, an army city where the Royal Dutch Indian Army, or Koninklijk Nederlands-Indies Leger, established their headquarters—and where, as a soldier, René Descartes first became interested in math—has long been a strong and honorable source of pride. And so, in 1887, when Adam van Kuijk was drafted into the Dutch army as a private in the 3rd Regiment of the Field Artillery, and stationed at the Seelig Barracks in Breda, the twenty-one-year-old was joining a noble and historic tradition.

The son of a working man—probably a fisherman—named Andreas van Kuijk, who hailed from Enkhuizen, about forty miles north of Amsterdam, Adam, born May 7, 1866, had grown up in the village of Raamsdonksveer, twelve miles north of Breda.

This particular branch of the van Kuijks (or van Kuyks) could perhaps trace their ancestors back to the Middle Ages, when they were a wealthy, aristocratic, ruling-class family, for more than a hundred years (from 1295 to 1428), governing the small town of Hoogstraten.

Later, when the region split in two, the southern part was assimilated into Belgium. The van Kuijks could not sustain their rule in the new political geography, and fled fifteen miles due north to the town of Breda. Their ancestors forever claimed to be related to the lords of Hoogstraten, and never forgot their sense of loss, or their sense of entitlement—no matter how tenuous it might have been.

Adam van Kuijk had joined the army for a twelve-year term. His artillery unit relied upon horse-drawn gun carriages, and Adam found he had a natural affinity for tending horses. When he was discharged in 1899, he stayed in Breda and took a job as livery man for the freight and package handling firm van Gend en Loos, the UPS of Holland. Although he had just spent a dozen years in army attire, Adam was happy to don the heavy, dark, double-breasted van Gend en Loos uniform, with its shiny brass buttons and regulation cap.

Van Gend en Loos had established their offices at 66 Veemarkstraat, a prestigious main thoroughfare in town. The company used the rear of the building to stable its ten draft horses and offered an apartment above the stables for the livery man and family.

As it happened, Adam van Kuijk did, indeed, have a family on the way. The mustachioed army man was not especially comely. He wore a perpetually stern, if not sour expression, his cheeks sunk in, his dark eyes seemed drilled in his head, and he carried the gene for the van Kuijk ear (the left one stuck out almost at a right angle), which he was destined to pass on to his first two children. His personality—rigid, disciplined, and unyielding—was also not the type to turn the head of the opposite sex, nor was his stiff, humorless voice. But while still in the service, he had begun dating Maria Elisabeth Ponsie, a woman ten years his junior. The youngest of eight children, she was also from Raamdonksveer, born September 2, 1876, the daughter of freewheeling merchants.

Whether the couple got caught up in the Christmas spirit, or in ringing in the twentieth century, sometime in December 1899, Maria conceived a child. Adam and Maria were Catholic, as were most people in southern Holland, and allowing few outlets beyond the pale of the church, their Catholicism was far more strict than the Catholicism practiced in America. With the attending guilt and sense of propriety, especially as Maria was beginning to show by springtime, the couple married on May 10, 1900. Their son, Josephus Andreas Johannes, also called Joseph, or Sjef, was born four months after the wedding, on September 19.

By the time of Sjef's birth, Adam and Maria had taken up residence in the *bovenhuis,* or living quarters above the stables, and as part of the marriage agreement, her parents, Johannes and Maria Reinenberg Ponsie, had moved in with them. The accommodations were snug: the area had a living room and a great room—the newlyweds slept in one, and the Ponsies in the other—with a loft that would double as the children's bedroom.

Maria's parents, Johannes and Maria, could not have been more different from Adam van Kuijk, except for their shared Catholicism. The Ponsies were *parlevinkers,* floating peddlers who traveled Holland's intricate river and canal system, selling and trading household goods from their barge to other travelers on the water.

Today, the family recalls that the Ponsies also owned a small store in Raamsdonksveer with the colorful name of A Thousand and One Things Bazaar. It offered both new and used items, even new Bible covers and special funeral mass fronts, which the Ponsies fashioned out of black crepe paper.

The tinker and his wife peddled these to the area churches, many of which never guessed that the books inside were the very ones they had earlier discarded. But the store generated only a struggling income, so when the weather kept the Ponsies off the waterways, Johannes loaded up a horse and wagon and took his wares to the farmers of the surrounding regions.

But the Ponsies couldn't ignore their greater wanderlust, preferring the itinerant life, drifting from village market to town fair, assimilating themselves into the merry hubhub of organ grinders and jugglers.

By the time Adam and Maria married, Johannes Ponsie was seventy years old and in poor health. The newlyweds welcomed him to their home with the understanding that Johannes and his wife would help with baby Sjef and the other children as they came along.

The van Kuijk family would expand rapidly. On March 31, 1902, Adriana Maria, also called Sjaan, was born. As the eldest girl, she would always be a "second mother" to her siblings. The following year, the van Kuijks welcomed Johannes Wilhelmus, but the boy would not live four months.

Adam and Maria planned quickly for another child, and Maria Wilhelmina, known as Marie, arrived before the year was out, on November 12, 1904. But tragedy befell the couple again with the birth of Johanna Huberdina, called Anneke, on July 22, 1906. She, too, would die in infancy. As before, the van Kuijks rushed to produce another baby, and Petronella Johanna, known as Nel, was born September 23, 1907.

Given their recent pattern of infant deaths, the family was anxious about the health of their seventh child, whom they would name Andreas Cornelis, after Adam's father and his friend Cornelis Roovers, a cobbler who accompanied Adam to register the birth at the *Burgerlijke Stand* in the town hall.

In the year 1909, the 28th of June, has appeared before us, civil servant of the county of Breda: Adam van Kuijk, age 33, profession: deliveryman, residing in Breda, who gave notice of the fact that Maria Elisabeth Ponsie, without profession, residing in Breda, his wife, on the 26th of June of this year, at 11 hours in the afternoon in this country has given birth to a child of the male sex, which child will have the names of Andreas Cornelis. This notice has been given in the presence of Hendrikus Rogiers, age 26, profession: smith, and of Cornelis Roovers, age 22, profession: shoemaker, both residing within this county.

Dries, as the family nicknamed their fifth living child, had his mother's clear blue eyes and was robust and energetic almost from birth. Much to the van Kuijks' relief, his delivery, at home above the stables, was unremarkable.

As the first surviving male child in nine years, Dries was doted on by his three older sisters. They dressed the infant like a doll and delighted in taking him for carriage strolls in nearby Valkenburg Park, and around the Begijnhof, a cheerful group of sixteenth-century convent houses occupied by the lay order of Begijnen nuns.

As he grew to a toddler, Dries appeared to be a normal and even gregarious boy in every way. But as he got older, he displayed an unusual characteristic: he slept with his eyes open and was known as the family sleepwalker. The family had to lock the doors to keep him from venturing outside in the small hours of the morning, but even that did not always deter him. One day, a neighbor, Mrs. van Overbeek, came to inform his mother that Dries had been standing in the street in the middle of the night, apparently asleep.

From the beginning, Dries was more a Ponsie than a van Kuijk. He had the Ponsie sense of humor, playfulness, and appreciation of fun, and their optimism, imagination, and daring. And in addition to his mother's eyes, he possessed her small, taut mouth (if his father's thick bottom lip), the set of her nose, her soft chin line, and her tendency toward a general fleshiness, a characteristic of the robust Ponsie family. His genetic coding dictated that by the time he reached his teens, Dries would thicken in the hips and waist in an almost womanly fashion.

Since the child spent so much time in the company of women, he looked forward to his visits at the *gasthuis* with Grandfather Ponsie. The old man was always quick with a funny story of one kind or another, especially about the gypsy life, the hustle, bustle, and magic of the little fairs, and the thrill of closing a sale to people who didn't want, and couldn't use, a wooden puppet with carved hands, or another piece of chipped crockery or tin jewelry. It was all in the presentation, Grandfather Ponsie made clear. And if you had to be just a little cunning—if you sometimes had to trick people into thinking they needed something they didn't—well, everyone was the better for it.

And despite the grandfather's rootlessness, the ancestral Ponsies, like the van Kuijks in the Middle Ages, had been people of means, he told the boy. Originally from France, they had lost their status and bearing when they fled to Holland during the Revolution. But they were well-mannered people, elitists who appreciated the best of everything and dressed in finery—even gloves!

The latter story had a profound effect on the child, for as Marie Gort–van Kuijk, Dries's sister, remembers, "Dries was very keen on his looks, and he paid a lot of attention to his clothes. When he got a little older, he would really dress up. He was a gentleman, but he could look down on people a little bit. He thought he was just better."

All this talk about traveling and freedom and fine clothes—and most of all being somebody—swirled around in the boy's head. He would come home from visiting his grandfather and soon find himself stuck between his dreams of the Ponsies' independence and nomadic lifestyle, and his father's stern sense of order, discipline, and obligation.

Adam, who performed his professional duties with military precision, hoped Dries might become a soldier like him, if for no other reason than the guarantee of work in the city. But Dries, who had a difficult time taking orders from anyone, showed little interest in soldiering.

In Adam's time, the father and the priest were law in Holland, and a clash between this particular father and son was inevitable, especially since Adam van Kuijk, who considered humility a virtue, was not one to indulge his children. He went to church daily, and saw to it that Dries, who rankled against regular church attendance, became a mass server. The van Kuijks worshiped at various churches in the area, primarily at the St. Josefkerk, situated next to the town brewery, and the Antoniuskerk, in the St. Janstraat.

According to the *Wijkregister,* or the neighborhood register kept by their priest, the van Kuijk children "performed their religious duties as they should in the period 1916–1924—all of them received the Holy Communion and were confirmed."

But Adam van Kuijk stayed close to his God for reasons other than strict Catholic obeisance. When Dries was about six, Adam was diagnosed with diabetes, and his kidneys had begun to fail. A frequent patient at the Catholic St. Ignatius Hospital, Adam feared he would not live long, but if Dries helped him with the horses and package delivery, the father might be able to conserve his strength.

Yet while Dries shared Adam's love of animals, he hadn't his father's sense of regimented order. Once the boy took several of the horses to Hendrikus Rogiers's blacksmith shop and on the return trip let them go to see if they could find their way home. Such boyish pranks did little to bolster Adam's waning health.

Still, Adam did not let his illness get in the way of duty. He rose each morning at five o'clock, readied the horses, and delivered packages until 7:00 or 8:00 A.M., when he returned home for breakfast. If he found the boys still in bed at that late hour—and Dries often was—he reddened in the face, yanked the child from his sleep, and beat him with a stick for bad children that he kept behind the door.

"When they had done serious wrong," remembers Marie, her father's favorite child, "they got serious punishment. Our parents wanted the boys to have a better job than our father had, to make easier money and not have to work so hard."

The family was poor, but it was not by any means considered low-class. Maria van Kuijk took great pride in the fact that once the girls reached age twelve and finished primary school, they went to work as live-in maid servants and nannies to some of the finest families in Breda. A young girl who served with such a respectable family was recognized as good lineage herself. And if it was an irony that the van Kuijks themselves had a maid, Maria reconciled the expense by remembering that both the van Kuijks and the Ponsies had once been aristocracy.

In recent years, accusations have arisen that Maria, to put on airs and earn more money for luxuries for herself and parochial schooling for her children, forced her husband to work long overtime hours for van Gend en Loos and to moonlight at a variety of jobs—shining the boots and belts of Breda's police force, peddling postcards to the soldiers at their barracks, and dealing in secondhand furniture and household items.

It was precisely the way her father and brothers had always made a living, so why shouldn't it be a supplemental form of income for Adam? Besides, now there were other children in the fold. Engelina Francina, called Lien, was born November 13, 1910, followed by Adam Franciscus, or Ad, on September 21, 1913. Two more children would round out the family to eleven, or nine surviving, the last two named in honor of those who died: Johanna, born May 8, 1916, and Johannes, or Jan, on October 1, 1918. Maria managed to find a pillow and blanket for all, and Adam provided an extra place to sleep by sweeping up at a small auction house and taking a bed that hadn't been sold as payment for his work.

As the children were growing up, their mother, who practiced as much religious discrimination as others in Holland of the time, restricted their playmates—no Protestants or low-class families—and strictly forbade them to go into the music hall next door.

Whether her mother thought Marie was too drawn to the sound of music and laughter, in later years she convinced the girl to join the St. Josef convent in Etten en Leur for Franciscan nuns, a move that was perhaps a comment on married life from a woman who was forced to marry. "I was never happy at the convent," says Marie, who spent eighteen years in servitude, "and I told my mother I wanted to leave there. But she said it was probably best that I stay."

Maria would expect much of Dries, too, when he grew older. For now, she was content to let him be a child, and argued with her husband when Adam required too much of his time in the stables. By age seven, Dries had already been slipping away by himself to explore Breda's streets and alleyways with his best friend, Cees Frijters, and schoolmate Karel Freijssen, and to visit Grandfather Ponsie and absorb himself in fantasy.

The stories about the small fairs and village markets only heightened the child's anticipation of *kermis,* or the large fair, which came to Breda on the third Sunday in October after the last mass. Situated at the Grote Markt, its tents and brightly colored awnings spread out through the neighborhood, down Halstraat, then across Oude Vest to the Kloosterplein, and up Dries's own street, Vlaszak. *Kermis* was a major event in Breda, a week of renewed good spirit, laughter, and optimism, when the adults drank too much and threw caution and Catholic reserve to the wind, and the children finagled ways of earning money for exotic treats, mechanical attractions, and games of chance.

Dries was no exception, and using the techniques his grandfather taught him, he hustled a few guilders whenever the opportunity arose, mostly trading or running errands.

To Dries, *kermis* was a nearly delirious escape from the glum world of his father and the nonsense of school. Apart from the circus—which brought the clowns and larger animals, like elephants, to the Gasthuisvelden—*kermis* was the child's favorite thing in all the world. When either was in town, the boy would vanish before daylight and not come home until the moon shone bright in the sky.

When his parents figured out that his fascination had turned into something of an obsession, they strongly suggested that the boy spend more time on his studies and less on dreaming of fly-by-night pleasure. However, it is doubtful that their words carried any weight. Dries didn't tell his mother that when *kermis* rolled around, he regularly cut school to be at the head of the line to ride the merry-go-round, since the first round was free. Getting something for nothing seemed to thrill the child, and when Dries realized that being paid to be part of the fair was more fun than simply watching it, at nine, the enterprising boy became what Americans would call "a carny"—literally, someone who works in a carnival, a term considered pejorative by some.

It started out small—an offer to help a vendor nail the boards together for his booth in exchange for a candied apple. From there, he was promised free admission for helping the roustabouts raise the tents. His mother somehow found out that he intended to aid in the building of the viewing stands and thwarted his plans. But she couldn't stop him from hiring out as an advance man, bumping along the cobblestone streets of Breda on a high, old-fashioned bicycle with a sandwich board hung over his shoulders.

Before long, he was working shoulder to shoulder with the principals, first as a circus water boy—following along after the clowns and smoking the butts of the cigars they threw on the ground—then as a feeder and caretaker of animals. And when he got a little older, as a barker.

"I worked for a gypsy and stood in front of her tent," he once said. "I waved my cane and called to people who passed by, 'Have your fortunes told for fifty cents.' I would get to keep twenty-five cents." Then came the day when he told a fortune himself and "got to keep the whole fifty cents."

With that marriage of commerce and con, and the promotional, marketing, and image-making tricks he was starting to pick up about how to sell a show, the spirit of Tom Parker was beginning to take form in the body of young Dries van Kuijk. Everything that he would ever be would have its genesis in Breda, in the swirl of noise and color and excitement of the fairgrounds and the circus, and in his search for the biggest attraction of all. That quest would ultimately end with a kid from South Memphis, in Tennessee, in another land, far across the ocean.

As an individual whose entire life was built on lies and fabrications, two key features of Dries van Kuijk's personality were starting to emerge: his need to hustle as opposed to earn honestly or by merit, and his delight in the con as the highest form of creative achievement.

Although that is not to say that Dries ever lost his generous streak, which could show itself when least expected—but almost never when called upon by others. As an adult, his largesse had to be spontaneous and self-generated—he intensely disliked being asked for charity—and if possible, involve somebody else's money. If that proved impossible, the next best thing was to ask a company for free goods, which he would then pass on to promote a good image for himself and to reap the glory of magnanimity. That pattern—which culminated in his frequent donning of a Santa Claus suit, Christmas or not, and dispensing candy to children—apparently began in Holland.

Each Friday a farmer from the northern village of Teteringen would come to the van Kuijks' to collect some horse manure and bring fresh straw and hay. He would leave his bicycle parked near the front of the stables. One Friday, he returned to his bicycle, hoping to be home for his noon meal, only to find his transportation missing. Dries had taken the bike to ride to the home of his friend Cees Frijters, who lived on the Ginnikenstraat.

On the way over, the boy began thinking about the Teteringen farmer and concocted an intricate ruse. Dries and Cees would ride the bike in tandem back to Teteringen, but to visit yet another farmer, one who was unknown to them, who sold fruits and vegetables. Once there, Dries would pretend that he was from England—making up a foreign language out of English and French—so the farmer would give the boys bags full of apples as a token of hospitality.

The trick worked, and loaded with booty, the boys rode to the Teteringen orphanage. There, according to Engelina, "the orphans stood in a row of twelve, and Dries gave them each an apple." The rest he took home to his mother.

Adam van Kuijk was so angry at his son that when the boy finally arrived at the stables that evening, his father sent him straight to bed without any supper, giving the farmer his dinner instead. Later on, Maria, grateful for the fruit for her family, slipped her errant son a sandwich, as she almost always did when Adam sent him upstairs without supper.

"He would scheme, but always in a good way," says Mieke Dons-Maas, Engelina's daughter. "Some people might have thought he was a terrible guy. But others had to laugh because they had fun with him."

Through childhood and adulthood, "fun" was uppermost in Dries's mind. From as long as anyone can remember, the quick-witted boy used his imagination to entertain his younger siblings, making a dull, dreary morning an event to remember.

The child was so accomplished at storytelling, in fact, that the van Kuijk children began looking forward to bedtime. "They all slept in the loft, the boys on one side and the girls on the other, with a door and some curtains separating them," Mieke Dons-Maas remembers her mother saying. "They'd get ready for sleep, and lay in their beds, and the girls would call out, Okay, Dries, . . . tell.' And Dries would open the door and tell his stories. He was unique in all the family."

Indeed, he seemed to be driven by something that the others weren't. "He never hurt anyone, but he was always up to something," remembers sister Nel. "He did everything that the others didn't dare."

And seemed to relish it. When his father was away delivering packages, he even risked leading the other children in play in the stables—an area off limits for such antics—and always assumed the starring role. On rainy days, he began by closing the big stable door and pulling out the spare carts and the *karos*, or horse-drawn coach, and letting the children jump gleefully among them. When they tired of that, he climbed to the top of the silos where the hay was dropped down to the horses, and repeatedly slid down the big copper pipe.

For his big finale, the young performer would walk on the backs of the horses, doing tricks and balancing acts as he jumped from one to the other—"even on the back of the meanest horse," says Mieke Dons-Maas; "the stallion who stood apart from all the others in another box."

Dries had no fear of the stallion, nor of most creatures. From the age of seven, he had begun putting on little tent shows and charging admission, and he was prone to take all sorts of animals into the living quarters and let them run free. But when he impetuously sold the goat to the circus for one guilder and the promise of free tickets for all the van Kuijks the week the big top was in town, the boy got a beating.

Dries's clashes with his father became more routine as he grew older, more independent, and headstrong. As the instigator of the children's more outlandish games, he was considered mutinous, and his father began to punish him in ways that seemed overly severe.

The breaking point came shortly after Dries began working for a small local circus on the Kloosterplein, run by a family named van Bever. The van Bevers couldn't compete with the big European outfits; all they had to offer was a trumpet-playing clown, a dancing midget, and a wild donkey that bucked like a bronco ("Stay on his back five minutes and win five guilders!"). But Dries was guaranteed work there every season, and the little circus had something that stimulated his drive and imagination: Madam van Bever was a skilled and accomplished horse trainer, with a desire to work a string of elegant Lipizzaner stallions into the act.

Each day as Dries helped Madam van Bever with these horses, he was struck by how graceful and romantic they were in comparison to his father's plodding work animals. And then it hit him: Why couldn't he train his father's horses to do some of the same tricks?

On Sundays, Dries was appointed to mind the stables. With no deliveries scheduled that day, there wasn't much for him to do except sit and nod off to the occasional sound of a swishing horse tail. On these Sunday afternoons, the story goes, Dries would spread the children's blankets on the stable floor to muffle the sound of hoofbeats, so that his mother wouldn't hear upstairs. Promising his siblings that he would have a big surprise for them in a few weeks if they simply left him alone, he would lead two horses from their stalls and train them to trot in a circle while he stood on their backs. After several sessions, he could straddle the two in an act as precise as any he had admired at the circus.

Finally, the Sunday came when Dries was ready to share his secret. He called for his brothers and sisters, invited a few neighborhood children, and showed them where to stand along the stable walls. Then he moved easily among the big horses, untying first two, then two more, and leading them out of their stalls.

Now Dries positioned the horses around him in a ring. Drawing himself up with the bearing of a ringmaster, he cracked his father's long, thin wagoner's whip, and as if by magic, the tired, old workhorses snapped to attention, rearing on their hind legs, pawing the air, and then prancing around the stables as if they'd been grand and glorious show animals all their lives.

Just as Dries was bringing the beasts to a kneel-and-curtsy farewell, his father burst through the big double doors with a force that froze every child in his place. He stood with his hands behind him on the latch, his face twisted in anger. Dries's antics not only endangered the valuable animals—what if they'd injured their backs?—but threatened the family's very livelihood. If the firm were to hear of this, Adam could lose his job and be tossed out on the street with nowhere to live, his reputation forever sullied.

"Andreas van Kuijk!" he bellowed. "You will never amount to anything!"

With all the children looking on, Adam methodically unbuckled and removed his thick harness belt, then commanded his wayward son to bend over a chair. Dries van Kuijk would get the whipping of his life— one that would surely knock this circus folly out of him for good.

The story of Adam's beating the boy while the others watched would go a long way to explain the origin of a third key trait that showed up in Dries's personality in adulthood: his need to humiliate others around him, especially those in subordinate positions.

Whether the story of the horses is rooted in truth—some of the siblings believe it to be a fabrication—certainly the boy's relationship with his stern, authoritarian father left a scar on his psychological make-up. With his mother, who nurtured and forgave him, he could be himself. But his father made him feel only like an unlovable failure.

And so, until the boy could physically get away from the grim side of his home life, he would begin to learn how to suspend his tender and affectionate feelings, to be resilient and strong in the face of adversity, while acting as if nothing were wrong. He also began to retreat more into himself, to compartmentalize his life, and to live several lives at once, one at home, and another while he was away. Finally, he learned to show the people in each life only what he wanted them to see. In some ways, he grew to be as inscrutable, obdurate, and obstinate as his father.

Secrecy had been part of Dries's personality since the age of five, but now the pattern became more pervasive, even with his mother. For example, Engelina remembered that Maria had given each of her children a drawer—a place for himself—in a big hutch, where they kept small treasures.

"You could close the drawer, but my brother's had a lock on it so that nobody could get into it," she said. But as Marie remembers, "our mother was clever. She drew out all the drawers so that she could get in and discover all our secrets." The result was that Dries began to feel as if no one could be trusted.

If ten-year-old Dries could not get the attention and respect he craved at home, he found it in actions that were valued by his peers, winning approval and admiration from his fellow students by acting out.

Maria van Kuijk could have placed her son in a free school for the children of the poor. But her pride and Catholic propriety directed that she pay the equivalent of fifty cents a week for Dries to go to the all-boys St. Antoniusschool, run by the friars of the order of Huijbergen, and located on the Karrestraat.

From the beginning, Dries chafed against the rigid rules of the Huijbergen brothers, who corrected wayward students with harsh, punitive, and often sadistic methods, including the smart sting of a strap.

As the class clown, the boy was often in trouble, making jokes about the teachers or the subjects of their lessons, proving himself someone to be contended with, and trying the friars' mercy. Then came the day when he scored a 3 out of 10 on an exam, and was ordered to take the paper home and get his father's signature. But Dries was either too ashamed or too afraid to show it, and so he forged his father's handwriting. He was found out, and the brothers doled out a distinctly Dutch punishment, making him kneel with his knees shoved into a pair of wooden shoes until he could no longer tolerate the pain.

Yet even that did not deter his mischief, and so the van Kuijks enrolled him in the public elementary school, the Openbare Lagere School, on the Boschstraat, near their home. Dries didn't settle in to the new school any more easily than the first, and was often truant, leaving school anytime he took a notion. He spent such afternoons rambling around, looking for adventure down at the Prinsenkade, where he watched the ships, visiting an uncle on his boat at the inland harbor of Oosterhout, hanging out at the abandoned World War I defenses at the Nonnenveld, and hitchhiking to any nearby village when a circus or fair was in town.

The child thought he wanted to escape Breda and his family altogether. But at eleven, that was impossible. Still, he made a halfhearted attempt at running away from home, sneaking aboard the passenger train to Rotterdam, where he was caught and turned over to his father.

His schooling came to an end in the fifth grade, after a typical adolescent prank on the birthday of one of his teachers. The man had been cursed with a generous and unfortunate nose, the object of much ridicule among his students. This day, when the teacher was called out of the classroom, Dries rose from his seat, walked to the front of the class, and wrote, "Long live the nose!" on the blackboard. His classmates jeered and giggled, but on returning, the infuriated teacher expelled the boy on the spot. It was just as well—Dries no doubt would have quit the following year, at the end of primary school.

For a while, he spent his days helping his father. In the last ten years, Adam's health had steadily declined. Now, in addition to his diabetes, he suffered lung problems, rheumatism, and a swelling in his feet that sometimes made it difficult for him to make his rounds.

But after Dries injured his hand—one of the heavy coaches slipped while he was greasing a wheel, and his mother had to rush him to the doctor—the teen began looking for someone else to assist his father.

Away from the stables, Dries's first jobs were menial, at best. For a while, he went down to the train station each day and carried luggage for busy travelers. Then he got a job as a delivery boy for a grocery store, but was soon let go, and from there went to the same jam factory where his brother Sjef had once worked. Both jobs should have pleased him, since food was like gold to him. But he found these tasks boring.

He much preferred the kind of pickup work he got when the dog show booked several days at Breda's Concordia Theatre. Unlike a thoroughbred kennel show, this was an exhibition of performing dogs who did tricks on command—hounds who hopped like rabbits, poodles who danced the cancan line on two legs—much like a canine circus. There he would feed and groom the animals, and receive the handsome sum of five guilders for his trouble. Better still, he would learn more about the training of dogs.

The lad found regular employment again selling and checking tickets on a trolley that ran between Breda and Oosterhout. But the bitter wind whipped through the trolley, and after a while, he decided he'd had enough.

Finally, at fifteen, things began to look up when he went to work for a barber and his wife who ran a shop on the Oude Vest. The couple, who had no children, pampered the boy as their own, paying him ten cents a day. They made excuses for their young assistant if he left customers with soap in their hair when he heard music out in the street or, for a lark, shaved half a man's face and let him walk out with the other half still covered with stubble.

Despite such behavior, the barber and his wife wanted to adopt the teenager and bring him into the business full-time. Maria didn't like the idea of her son living elsewhere, but with Dries's combative attitude toward his father, she advised him to take advantage of his opportunity. In the end, however, Dries wasn't interested. He wanted only to be his own boss, to make his money on his own time, in his own way. And he harbored resentment toward those who had "made it."

"Possessing money was very important for him," remembers Marie. The family knew one thing for certain: "Don't touch his wallet."

One of the reasons Dries wanted money was to buy fine clothes. Engelina recalled that "he was very conscious about how he looked," and Marie remembers that "if Mother didn't iron his collar properly, he would throw it away and not wear it."

At sixteen, the boy was growing up and now requested that he no longer be addressed by the diminutive name of Dries, but by the more proper sounding Andre. Still, he didn't seem to be concerned with much of a social life. Other than his friendship with Cees Frijters, he almost insisted on a kind of apartness from the rest of the world. Even the idea of getting together in a crowd and sharing a few brews didn't appeal to him, after he experimented with beer early on and found that it made him a violent drunk. Later, in middle age, he would drink perhaps half a bottled beer in social situations, but no more.

"He would never drink a complete beer," remembers Joe Esposito, foreman of Elvis's Memphis Mafia. "He told me, 'I can't drink. I completely change when I drink, my personality does. I get very mean.'"

Above all in his teen years, he seemed completely disinterested in any attachment to the opposite sex. "I'm sure that by the time he was seventeen, he still had not been with a girl," says Marie. "He had no sexual interests whatsoever." While that may have been normal for the culture of the times, the boy may have also felt trapped by the dangers of dependency. But whether he was truly asexual, or if there was perhaps some sexual squeamishness among several of the van Kuijk children—Marie volunteers that she and her husband lived as brother and sister for fifty-three years—Marie says she can't imagine why her brother eventually married, unless it was to be cared for.

For now, Andre van Kuijk had other, more important things on his mind. In his work with the circus and the dog show, he had met people who whetted his appetite for adventure beyond the walls of Breda. He was also desperate to leave the confines of his immediate family unit and to break free of all the rules and ties that led back to the church. He began to tell his siblings that he would move to the big city of Rotterdam. There he would work on the harbor and hear the stories of the sailors who had traveled the world and seen the things he had only imagined. He could live with the family of his uncle Jan Ponsie, his mother's brother.

Rotterdam, while only a distance of some twenty-five or thirty miles, would separate mother and son, and Maria was heartsick. She was the sort of woman easily terrified—by thunder, which sent her scurrying to hide under a blanket and make the sign of the cross; by anything that suggested the work of the devil; and by the predictions of fortunetellers. Only recently, a "naturopath," or *paragnost,* from Heberle had told her that her husband would die within the year. And now, late in the spring of 1925, Adam was white as an angel and confined to St. Ignatius Hospital. With two of the younger children away in Catholic boarding school, to lose Dries to Rotterdam just now would be difficult.

But once Dries had his mind set on something, Maria might as well have tried to change the flow of the tides. She asked only that he go to the hospital and seek his father's permission. Adam, too, saw the staunch determination in his son's eyes and, too weak to protest, realized that there was nothing he could do.

From the hospital, Andre traveled to the town of Etten en Leur to visit his sister Marie, who was by now living in the convent. He told her that their uncle in Rotterdam had a good job in the shipping office in a large boat company and that he was planning to move in with him and start a new life.

"He came to say hello and good-bye," she remembers, "not just to me, but also to a rector in the convent. Dries had been a mass server with this priest when he was little."

When Marie had her formal admission ceremony that August—a very proud day for a family in a country where everyone does his best to honor birthdays, anniversaries, weddings, and graduations—Dries was the only one not to attend.

By that time, Andre was a regular on the foggy docks of Rotterdam, watching the great ships pull out to exotic ports and searching for his destiny.

2

BEHAVIOR MOST STRANGE

A T nearly sixteen, Andre van Kuijk did not appear to be a happy lad. In a photograph from the time, his pouty mouth sets firm on a sullen countenance, refusing to smile for the camera. His eyes, eerily cold and blank for one so young, stare out from beneath heavy brows, and his round face tends toward puffiness in the jowls.

Given his demeanor, it is unlikely that anyone told the boy he was handsome, even though he is well dressed in a suit, with a perky bow tie adorning a starched collar, his dark hair slicked down and parted just off-center to the left. Big for his age, he is stuck in the gawky years of his teens, neither child nor man.

The source of his petulance could well have been his move to Rotterdam. He had come to the world's largest port city full of excitement about his new life only to find that while his surroundings were different, some of the more irritating aspects of his home life were no better here. Uncle Jan did not berate him in the stentorian tones of his father, but there were rules and regulations in the house that he was expected to follow. As before, he was pinned under the thumb of an elder.

Jan Ponsie and his wife lived on Spanjaardstraat, situated on the west side of town, within easy walking distance of the Rotterdam harbor, with its large river berths for oceangoing passenger ships, tankers, and freighters, and smaller ports and docks that served the canal barges. Several small shipyards and ship repair shops dotted the area at the mouth of the Nieuwe Maas River.

Because the docks were the life of this rough, worker city, the residents of the neighborhood were considered middle class, blue collar. In Andre's time, Spanjaardstraat comprised four-story brownstone row houses, each dwelling two windows wide and three rooms deep. The street stretched from the Hudsonplein to the Schiedamseweg, a shopping district. Several small parks offered respite from the cobblestone hardness and the noise from the streetcar that ran through the middle of the thoroughfare. Where the road ended at the Hudsonplein sat the Café Hudson. All the seamen knew the little bar, says one, since they considered it a point of honor to frequent every waterfront saloon in the city.

Andre still demonstrated little interest in socializing at such places, preferring at first to spend his evenings with the Ponsies. After dinner, the family sat in the living room, and Andre usually turned to his cousin, Marie, for a game of checkers or other benign amusement. Slightly older than Andre, Marie thought he viewed her as something of a big sister. She, on the other hand, saw him only as a dreamer. "He never told me what he wanted out of life," she remarked years later, "but I knew he was busy making plans all the time. He wanted adventure."

Rotterdam is Holland's second largest city, and for a time, Andre seemed lost, both geographically and emotionally. He hadn't yet learned his way around the streets—how the sprawling city was linked by tunnels, bridges, and public transportation—and with poverty more rampant in Rotterdam than in Breda, he hadn't found the locales to hustle the pocket change and pickup work that had sustained him at home.

For a time, Andre tried the usual assortment of odd jobs but discovered that steady work was difficult to find, other than in retail or on the docks. His uncle put in a word for him at Spido, a maritime freighting company where he worked in the shipping office.

Spido, which was already in operation before the big bridges were built, made package deliveries to ships. It also operated a river taxi, or ferryboat, for passengers, mostly laborers, who needed to move handily back and forth across the Nieuwe Maas.

Andre apparently worked on both the river taxi and the delivery boat, although presumably at different times of his Rotterdam stay. Given the choice between jobs, he probably would have opted for the delivery boat, since he would have gone on board other ships and engaged the crewmen in conversation, however perfunctory.

On the ferry boat, however, the endless repetition would have been deadly dull. The only saving grace: financial reward. Aside from nice things for himself—he enjoyed such treats as eating in cafés, where he especially liked the Indonesian fare, with its hot pepper sauces, and the *rijsttafel,* the huge rice table meal with up to forty or more dishes—he wanted to send money home to his mother.

Maria van Kuijk was in dreadful straits. On July 6, 1925, Adam van

Kuijk died at the age of 59. Death, which had quietly hidden in the sheets and blankets of his life for so many years, finally made a hushed leap and filled the room with silence. Six months later, in January 1926, Jan Ponsie became guardian of the six minor van Kuijk children, including sixteen-year-old Andre. With its livery man gone, the van Gend en Loos firm had almost immediately evicted Maria, then forty-eight years old, and the children. She had been forced to move to a smaller house, one without many comforts, on the Boschstraat, around the corner from Vlaszak.

But without Adam, Maria was neither emotionally nor financially equipped to care for her children. She had lost her husband, her status, her income, and as far as she was concerned, her life. There was nothing left. Eventually, the family would fragment. In a few years, she, Engelina, and Johanna would live together in another house in town, and later she would move to Eindhoven with Nel. As she had cared for her children, her children would care for her.

Andre, whose father's death made him ineligible for the draft, was now expected to show some responsibility for his mother and the other children—a frightening prospect for a boy who shied away from serious threats to his independence.

Nonetheless, he returned to Breda on holidays and the occasional family birthdays, sometimes coming by boat, other times hitchhiking or taking the train. Holidays or not, his visits were cause for celebration. He sometimes got up and sang with a Rotterdam accent, and he never came home without presents for the others.

The family was proud that Andre worked at the same fine company as Uncle Jan, but he soon left Spido and hired out to a skipper who sailed to Raamsdonksveer.

He was always thinking, scheming, of other ways to make money, either for himself or for Maria. For a time, he worked on a ship that moved from port to port on a twenty-four-hour schedule and rotated the lower ranks on day and night shifts.

Once he knew everyone on board, he hustled the crew with the idea of affordable laundry service, which he chartered out to his mother. The proposition paid double dividends: Maria made money, and Andre got his washing done free. His letters home referenced his fine new clothes.

Back in port, Andre had a habit of disappearing overnight, much to the worry of Jan Ponsie. When his uncle questioned him about it, Andre explained that he was moonlighting on the docks. But when Andre began to stay away for days, Ponsie grew angry and reminded him that he was still a minor and legally in his care. As long as he lived in the Ponsie house, he had to abide by the curfew.

With that, seventeen-year-old Andre van Kuijk announced that he was now a sailor for the Holland America Line. After a year, he no longer had need of the Ponsie hospitality. He was setting off to seek his fortune, leaving Holland far behind, perhaps even going to America.

Jan Ponsie was completely taken aback. Andre had not talked about leaving Holland—not to him, and not to his daughter, Marie. Nor had Andre said anything to his siblings, and certainly not to his mother.

Whether his sense of adventure or his uncle's code of conduct figured into his decision, he certainly would have realized that his chances of making a living were slim in the poor southern provinces of Holland, especially with the things that stirred his imagination. And now he·had the additional burden of contributing to his mother's upkeep.

Mieke Dons-Maas believes her uncle's motivation was more personal than that. "He wanted to be *somebody*," she says. And he wanted his family to know of his quest. In the spring of 1926, he sent word to his sister Marie in the convent, saying he was going to another country.

However, he did not say which one, perhaps because being seventeen, with little education, no papers (the family is uncertain if he had a passport), and not the slightest command of the English language, it would have made more sense for him to go to Italy or to France than to America. Or maybe he kept quiet because he knew that the Holland America Line sailed to the United States with stops in Boulogne, France; Southampton, England; and once across the Atlantic, Halifax, Nova Scotia. He might have signed on board to swab the decks and then jumped ship in any one of those ports.

The Holland America Line has no record of Andre van Kuijk, as either a crew member or a passenger. Could he have been hired on a temporary basis, which prevented his name from showing up on the roster? Or had he embellished his plan to his uncle, claiming to work for the distinguished passenger line when he knew he would cross the ocean on a far less glamorous tramper or freighter?

Years later, after Andre had become Tom Parker, he told his friend Connie B. Gay, the country show promoter, that he had sneaked into America through Canada. And, indeed, Halifax, Nova Scotia, was Holland America Line's last port of call before the great ships arrived in the United States and docked at Hoboken, New Jersey.

Yet there's another reason Andre van Kuijk's name might not have shown up on the Holland America Line crew roster, one the family wholeheartedly believes to be true: Andre may have made his voyage not as a crew member, but as a stowaway.

Might a boy as large as Andre—and one who so loved to eat—really have risked life and limb, crammed in a tiny hole for a two-week crossing to America? Certainly he could have easily found his way on to the ship if he were working for the Holland America Line. But even if he weren't an employee, sneaking aboard wouldn't have been difficult. The docks were not particularly secure, and Andre would have welcomed the challenge.

Still, there was the problem of going through customs and immigration without papers, since as a minor he was not yet eligible for a Dutch passport without his guardian's signature. But it is possible that he simply greased the right palm, or that he got off the ship in Nova Scotia and made his way into the United States either through the Canadian mainland or directly by smaller boat.

Or there is a third possibility, and the most plausible. If Andre had attached himself to a family on board the big passenger ship—perhaps a Dutch family who lived in America—they could have easily vouched for a "misplaced" passport.

Whether that actually happened, Andre somehow managed to ingratiate himself into a Dutch family who lived in Hoboken, where the Holland America Line docked. He moved in with them, and seemed to take root in their living room.

Hoboken, a working-class town on the Hudson River, was "the roughest spot in the United States" in the late '20s and early '30s, according to the city's most famous son, Frank Sinatra. That was precisely the time when Andre van Kuijk saw it as his introduction to America. But unlike Sinatra, who grew up on the hard side of a tough town, Andre had the good fortune to be bunking with well-to-do folks.

His new family took a shine to the big Dutch kid who knew little English and almost never left the house. In many ways the arrangement was precisely as it had been with his uncle in Rotterdam. The New Jersey family even had a daughter, although unlike Andre's cousin, she was still a child, only ten. As he had done with the Ponsies, he spent an inordinate amount of time with them because he didn't know the territory, and because he could count on them for regular meals. The teen was perfecting the rudiments of sponging—a skill he would raise to a fine art.

But where before he had kept at least some of his ties to his Breda family, he now refused to write to anyone in Holland, an odd turn of events for a boy who had carted presents home and written frequently to his mother in the months just before his departure. It was as if he had been reborn in the womblike hold of the big passenger ship.

The family pressured Andre to let everyone know that he was all right. But he had no interest in that, and finally just gave them the Ponsies' address, rather than his mother's, so they could do the job for him. The mothers of his adopted families began a spirited correspondence, and while the letters disappeared in the shuffle of time, Marie Ponsie remembered some of their contents.

"Dries must have been talking about me, because the woman wrote, 'I hear you have a nice daughter; could she come to America, too?' I guess the woman was homesick and missed Holland. That must have been why she let Dries in."

But before any plans for Marie's visit could be arranged, Andre simply vanished. One day he had been the family's adored surrogate son, and the next day, it was as if he had never existed. Whether Andre felt they were becoming too attached and dependent on him, or if it was simply time to go and he didn't know how to end the relationship, he disappeared. The New Jersey family was more concerned about his welfare than angry that they had been forsaken.

The woman sent passionate letters across the seas to the Ponsies. "Have you heard from him? Do you know where he might have gone?" She herself suspected the U.S. Army, because he has occasionally talked of that. But back in Holland, they thought it more likely that he might have tried to join a circus.

Andre had not joined a circus, but he had hooked up with a different kind of traveling show—Chautauqua, at the time a phenomenally popular movement for education, culture, and entertainment. By 1926, when he went to work for the Des Moines, Iowa–based booking agency Traver's Chautauqua Shows, the Chautauqua phenomenon was fading— so much so that the previous year, George W. Traver's partner Ray Newton left the company to try to bond with the remaining outfits as United Chautauquas. Traver, meanwhile, continued to call his outfit a Chautauqua, but his three-railroad-car operation was more like a carnival, replete with midway. Since carnivals were banned in many towns and considered a corruptive plague on the morals of the young, he made sure to hang on to enough of the old Chautauqua staples to stay in business.

At its height, Chautauqua offered escape in every dramatic style from Shakespeare to Broadway, and featured a staggering variety of talent: teachers, preachers, scientists, explorers, politicians, singers, yodelers, whistlers, dancers, pianists, accordionists, humorists, jugglers, magicians, opera stars, and Hawaiian vocal groups. On the Traver's show, however, the "Hawaiians" were thoroughly bogus. The show's general agent, L. Harvey "Doc" Cann, called it a Hawaiian show because the banners for such an act were the only ones not in use, and achieved his effect by throwing together a Salvation Army bass drum, a couple of dark-skinned Caucasians, and a palm frond.

On the legitimate side of the operation, two programs in particular reminded Andre of home. The first was "chalk talks," given by artists who used large blackboards to explain how they created sculpture or other visual art. While this was similar to "movies" Andre had put on for his brothers and sisters, the animal acts pleased him more, since they featured performing canines like Wonder Dog, a German shepherd who demonstrated feats of mathematical genius.

Just exactly what position Andre filled on Traver's Chautauqua is anyone's guess. At the start, he may have simply worked with the tent crew, helping to raise the huge brown canvas as he had back in Breda, perhaps later migrating into food concessions, or distributing advertising cards while gleaning more about the marketing side of the business.

Whatever he did, the Chautauqua experience was a wonderful introduction to small-town America, especially for a lad who was just learning English and too often answered "Ja, ja" when asked a question.

For Andre, the only trouble with Chautauqua was that it was strictly a summer event. In the winter, he hoboed around the country, getting to know the various hobo jungles and the crusty old vagabond characters. He learned their lingo and their habit of carving the face of a smiling cat on the fence post outside a home where they found kindness and nourishment, alerting fellow travelers that a generous and compassionate "touch" lived within. And he loved their wild freedom, later bragging to his family that he'd hung under trains, risking all for a free ride and a chance to see the whole of America.

Andre's hobo experience ultimately left two indelible imprints: a romantic fondness for slumgullion, a boiled meat stew that hobos prepared in a large pot on an open fire, and a respect and sentimentality for hobos. In the 1950s, when Elvis Presley was a rising Hollywood star, Parker cajoled the studio commissary to make up dozens of sandwiches, which he took to the hobo hangouts at the Los Angeles train stops.

But on this, his first trip to the United States, he was on the receiving end of charity more often than not. When he reached Los Angeles, he had no compunction about taking sustenance at the Midnight Mission. There, after vowing to welcome Christ into his life, he would repeat a religious mantra and be rewarded with a hot meal and a hard bed.

Years later, he would tell the story and end it with a funny punch line: "If you're going to stay at the Midnight Mission, be sure you get there by seven o'clock." It was true—the dinner hour was from five-thirty to six, and the beds were likely filled by seven. But the statement also served as a metaphor for his deeper beliefs—that to succeed, you had to stay one step ahead of everybody else, know how to manipulate the system, and dig for everything you got.

Nonetheless, to everyone's surprise, Andre showed up back in Holland on his mother's birthday, September 2, 1927, after being gone nearly a year and a half. Had he saved his second summer's wages from Chautauqua and bought a third-class ticket home, as his sister Nel believes? Or had he simply been caught and deported, even though the U.S. Immigration and Naturalization Service has no record of it?

However he made passage back, he timed his arrival in Breda for nine o'clock in the evening, when the family had gathered for Maria's celebration. Stylishly dressed in an American suit and long, striped tie, his arms full of presents for all, he knocked on the door of the little Boschstraat house. At eighteen, Andre seemed every inch the successful prodigal son. But no matter how hard the family begged and pleaded, there was one thing he wouldn't talk about: exactly what he had been doing in America.

For the next two weeks, he seemed happy to be home. When his eldest sister, Adriana, married a mechanic named Antonius H. W. "Toon" van Gurp on September 15, Andre was the life of the party.

Demonstrating both the spirit and the theatrics of Chautauqua, he jumped up on a table, threw his arms out like an experienced orator, and launched into a poem about a smart but lazy lad who squandered his future and ended up as a bellhop. From there, he danced a funny, one-legged jig. And then he finished entertaining the crowd with a short concert of songs, including one that was so risqué that members of the family stole a sideways glance at Maria.

But within a month his mood had darkened again. Breda was no longer the place of his youth. Many of his favorite haunts had been torn down. He kept to himself, rarely looking up his old friends Cees Frijters and Karel Freijssen. For a young man who had tasted the excitement of

New York, tent Chautauqua, and hanging under trains, Breda was sorely lacking.

And as Europe was sliding toward a depression, the odd jobs were more difficult to come by. According to his sister Nel, he served a short stint with the river police during this time.

Finally, he took a job with a shipping company called Huysers on the Prinsenkade, loading and unloading barges on the waterfront. Huysers, later the maker of Jansen boats and automobiles, was an old customer of van Gend en Loos, and Andre probably got his job by reminding the owner of the days when he and his father had delivered the company's packages. Now he would be doing the same thing, only carrying heavier packing cases and parcels on and off the boats in numbing repetition— and he had to be at work at 6:00 A.M.

Andre wouldn't have tolerated such a job before his trip to America, but now he saw it as a means to an end. Huysers also owned the *Stad Breda,* which made a daily run between Breda and Rotterdam, and as soon as the ship needed a deckhand, Andre would arrange for the transfer.

When the day came, he moved back to the port city, but instead of living with his uncle, he opted for a bunk at Huysers's rough-and-tumble employee hostel on the top floor of the office. He stored his good clothes and a few personal belongings in a locked trunk, which he positioned near his cot.

Andre had no trust for the sailors, who knew better than to invite him for a night of drinking, or offer to introduce him to a girl. Now, at nearly twenty, he had turned into a good-looking, bright-eyed lad with a slim face and an impish smile. At times, he could look almost sensual, like a dreamy young poet. The fact that he'd rather take long walks by himself than spend the evening in the company of a pretty girl was the subject of comment among the others.

Then one day in May 1929, Andre failed to show up for work. His fellow crewmen thought he was just late, or maybe sick. But Andre would never step foot on the boat again. Somehow, at some time, he had quietly slipped away. No one seemed to know why, or where he had gone.

Two months later, in July, Huysers returned Andre's trunk to Maria van Kuijk's house on Boschstraat. The family opened it to find three of his treasured suits, a rosary, a Bible, his identification papers, and a small purse containing what appeared to be his savings. He had taken nothing with him but two shirts and two pairs of undershorts. Why had the boy who so adored dressing up left behind his expensive clothes? Even more perplexing, why had someone who so valued money abandoned his hard-earned gains, especially if he was planning to move halfway around the world? He had even left behind his unopened birthday presents, which the family had sent for his special day in June.

On one of his last trips home to Breda, he had dropped by Adriana and Toon's upstairs apartment on the Haagdijk. "I remember it like yesterday," Adriana said nearly fifty years later. "We were standing in the kitchen. He gave my little son, who was just born, a hand, and then left for Rotterdam."

It was a long time before the family heard from him again.

Finally, a missive arrived, written in English, simply saying their brother had gone away. The family was bewildered. And he had signed it with the most quizzical name: Andre/Tom Parker.

"He just changed identity," says Marie, who believes he chose the name Tom Parker in homage to a stowaway who was thrown overboard. "He wanted to remain unknown." There would be more sporadic letters, and after awhile, he would sign them solely with his new moniker.

Usually, he gave no return address, offering just enough information to let the family know he was all right. The letters were carefully worded, teasing almost, more for what they didn't say than for the news they conveyed. Sometimes he sent photographs that suggested he was having a ball—a small black-and-white snapshot in which he stood next to a large American car in some tropical setting, and another one of himself by a swimming pool. The family thought he must be a chauffeur for a very rich man.

Then came a third, provocative photograph that placed him between two other men, sitting on a beach in an old-fashioned one-piece bathing suit, his legs drawn up and his knees together, his hands crossed in front of him in an almost feminine pose.

Just where was Andre, and what was he doing? And who in the world was this Tom Parker, who had such a strong hold over him?

Thirty-one years would pass before the family would learn that answer.

3

"ALL GREAT NEPTUNE'S OCEAN"

Will all great Neptune's ocean wash this blood
Clean from my hand? No; this my hand will rather
The multitudinous seas incarnadine
Making the green one red.

—*Macbeth*, ACT 2, SCENE 2

I N 1957, Colonel Tom Parker was riding cross-country, returning to California from his home in Tennessee. Behind the wheel was twenty-three-year-old Byron Raphael, a William Morris agent-in-training that Parker plucked from the mail room a year earlier to become the first of his Morris-paid assistants. The "Parker School for Trainees" would become part of Hollywood legend for both the rigor and the humiliation that the manager foisted on his "students." But at the time, Raphael only knew that he loved and feared the man he called Pops.

Parker, whose marriage was childless, would tell the young man he thought of him as his adopted son. Whether that was entirely true, certainly on that 2,000-mile road trip, he trusted Raphael enough to share one of his closest secrets.

"We were driving through Hobbs, New Mexico," Raphael begins, "and it was snowing. I couldn't keep the car on the road—we were sliding everywhere—and we stopped at this little motel. There were very few rooms available, so I had to share a room with him that night.

"He started out by telling me about how he was made a colonel by the governor of Louisiana. And then he said, 'Where do you think I was born?' I said, 'Well, I guess Tennessee.' And he just told me the story. He said he made a deal with somebody to come over, and he worked in the kitchen of the ship, as a dishwasher, I think.

"The way he arranged it, he was supposed to stay sixty days and then go back. And he said they were going to give him a paycheck when he landed, but he didn't want to get the check, because he felt they might find out where he was. So he never picked it up, even though he had no money. All he wanted to do was get to this country and disappear into the heartland to start working in carnivals."

His route, from what he told various sources, was through the island of Curaçao, in the Dutch West Indies, via England. From Rotterdam, he sailed for one of the British ports, probably Southampton, with a possible stop in France to pick up cargo. If he took a passenger ship to England, he likely would have jumped to a tramper or a freighter for the run to the Dutch West Indies, since the passenger ships concerned themselves with North Atlantic trade.

Eventually, he wrote home that an English friend had given him the papers he needed—presumably a passport and visa—to enter the United States. But whether the friend arranged for him to "become" Tom Parker during his layover in the British Isles or, as Nel believes, while Andre was still in Holland, is unknown. And if he already had a Dutch passport, as several members of the family believe, the more curious question is why he needed another in a different name.

Whatever the answers, he seemed to be going to a lot of trouble. In Curaçao, he apparently changed boats again and quickly moved on.

From here, the picture of Andre van Kuijk, just weeks away from his twentieth birthday, begins to blur. In all probability, he entered the United States through the gulf port of Mobile, Alabama, although the names recorded in the ships' manifests for that year fail to bear witness to Andreas van Kuijk or Thomas Parker. Dirk Vellenga, the journalist who chronicled Parker's Dutch origins, first for the Breda newspaper *De Stem* and later in a biography, *Elvis and the Colonel,* speculates that Andre came in on a rumrunner, a boat transporting illegal liquor to America. According to Lloyd Shearer of *Parade* magazine, Parker himself said he gained entry through Mobile on a Dutch fishing boat. Either way, that would have been the boat that issued the paycheck he never picked up.

For some reason, those events were on Parker's mind in 1957, the morning after his late-night disclosure to Byron Raphael in a roadside motel.

"That's when he told me the rest of the story—how fearful he was that he might be deported, or if he ever left the country, that he might not be able to get back in.

"He said, 'You know, Byron, we're never going to be able to take Elvis abroad to do personal appearances.' By that time, Elvis was already the biggest star in Japan, and also in Germany. And the offers from Europe were for many millions of dollars, even then."

Since Parker's personality was so forceful ("He gave you the feeling that he was omnipotent," says Raphael), it never occurred to the teenager to ask him why he didn't call on his powerful friends to solve his passport problems, especially given his celebrity and wealth.

But now the answer seems obvious. It wasn't that Parker *couldn't leave* the country. Through the years, he accumulated many influential friends in all ranks of government—including President Lyndon B. Johnson—who could have solved his problem with a single phone call. The truth of the matter was that Parker *didn't want to leave* the country. And not even the promise of money beyond his wildest dreams could stir him from his spot.

For a man who judged the worth of every deal by money alone, such virulent aversion to international travel begs two nagging questions: Why had he never registered with the U.S. government, bypassing, as late as 1940, the safety net of the Alien Registration Act, which required all aliens to comply with the law, but did not discriminate between legal and illegal residents? And what was outside the refuge of the United States that frightened a man who otherwise seemed afraid of nothing?

"The Smith Act, or the Alien Registration Act of 1940, wouldn't have necessarily made him legal," explains Marian Smith, historian at the Immigration and Naturalization Service in Washington, D.C., but as an overstayed seaman, Parker could have registered and applied for certain kinds of relief. "And I am curious as to why he didn't," she muses. "Failure to register was subject to punishment, but I'm sure he could have later just paid a fine. It's very odd."

The search for his mysterious truth spawned a host of imaginative explanations through the years. The first is the theory that he might have been a low-level government spy, or carried papers for the leaders of a radical social movement. But although the U.S. government used Dutch citizens as drops in Nazi-occupied territory in the years before World War II, Andre was long gone from Europe by then. Besides, his family says he demonstrated no political agenda, and the selflessness of such an act—even if paid—doesn't fit his psychological make-up.

The second tale—that he fled Holland after "knifing a man to death in a fairgrounds brawl"—sounds more plausible. The alleged incident was reported in 1997 in the British tabloid *The People,* as an introduction to a memoir by reporter Chris Hutchins. But, alas, Hutchins says he has "no recollection of such a story," and furthermore hasn't the faintest idea how it landed atop his published piece. The FBI, credited as the source, is equally unaware of such occurrence.

However, the third story is harder to shake off. If true, it could answer every question about the enigmatic behavior of Colonel Thomas Andrew Parker.

In the days just after Elvis Presley's death in August 1977, Dirk Vellenga was sitting at his desk at *De Stem* when he received an anonymous phone call. It was a man's voice: "Do you know that Colonel Tom Parker comes from Breda? His name is van Kuijk, and his father was a stable-keeper for van Gend en Loos on the Vlaszak."

While this information had been published before, first by Dineke Dekkers in the fan club magazine *It's Elvis Time* in 1967, and then in Hans Langbroek's 1970 eccentric booklet *The Hillbilly Cat,* Vellenga thought it only rumor. His curiosity now piqued, he began poking around in the ashes of Parker's early years, interviewing his family and schoolmates, and soon began to sift out the fragments of the life of Breda's most famous nonresident. The first of Vellenga's splashy articles appeared in the newspaper in September 1977 and started the taciturn reporter on a quest—perhaps an obsession—that drives him still today. Even though he long ago left reporting to become an editor, he has continued to file stories on the subject every few years, even as late as 1997, twenty years after he began.

At the end of one of his pieces, Vellenga posed a question: "Did something serious happen before Parker left that summer in 1929 for America, or maybe in the 1930s when he broke all contact with his family in Breda?"

One reader thought he knew the answer and in 1980 mailed a letter to Vellenga at the newspaper. The document had a hushed, dark-alley tone, as if its author were afraid that someone might be reading over his shoulder. It carried no signature, but the urgency and gravity of the words made it seem somehow real, as if the author experienced an unburdening in the telling:

Gentlemen:
At last, I want to say what was told to me 19 years ago about this Colonel Parker. My mother-in-law said to me, if anything comes to light about this Parker, tell them that his name is van Kuijk and that he

murdered the wife of a greengrocer on the Boschstraat in Breda. This murder has never been solved. But look it up, and you will discover that he, on that very night, left for America and adopted a different name. And that is why it is so mysterious. That's why he does not want to be known. But believe me, this is the truth and nothing but the truth. It has been told to me in confidence. I have been carrying it around with me for years, and am glad now that I can tell you what happened. This is the truth. Thank you.

At first, Vellenga hardly knew what to think. Could it be true? The reporter was intrigued to find that, indeed, there had been such a murder. Anna van den Enden, a twenty-three-year-old newlywed, the wife of the potato trader Wilhelmus "Willem" van den Enden, had been bludgeoned to death in the kitchen of her home behind the shop. The crime was what the Dutch call a *roofmoord,* a murder with intention of robbery, since the bedroom and bathroom had been ransacked in an apparent search for money.

More surprising, the date—May 17, 1929—coincided with Andre's sudden disappearance.

Today, a careful reading of the original police report—handwritten in Dutch and numbering more than 130 pages—reveals a woefully inadequate investigation of the crime. The murder weapon, possibly a crowbar, was never positively identified. No background check was done on the victim. And once several witnesses reported seeing Anna's brother-in-law, Jan van den Enden, a contractor, near the shop that morning, police focused solely on him, detaining him as a suspect. Eventually, however, he was released, and no one was ever brought to justice for Anna's murder. The crime remains unsolved to this day.

There is not a single shred of evidence to tie Andre van Kuijk to the murder of Anna van den Enden. His name does not appear anywhere in the police report, and until the anonymous letter arrived at the Breda newspaper fifty-one years after the fact, no one in Holland had spoken of his name in connection with the crime.

Yet a set of circumstances makes it impossible *not* to speculate that Colonel Tom Parker in fact may have gotten away with murder.

Although Andre had been living in Rotterdam and America for several years, it was almost certain that he knew Anna Cornelia Hageners before she married, either in childhood or during his return to Breda at age eighteen. Only three years apart in age, they apparently attended the same church, St. Josefkerk. Andre also knew her husband's family. Johannes van den Enden ran the café where Adam van Kuijk spent his Sunday afternoons, and the elder van den Enden's home on the Beyerd was just around the turn from the van Gend en Loos stables. Furthermore, Anna's twenty-four-year-old husband, Willem, was fond of *kermis,* or fancy fair. Like Andre, he traveled as far as Oosterhout when the *kermis* came to town.

And there was another connection. The van den Enden greengrocery was located at Nieuwe Boschstraat 31. Nieuwe Boschstraat is merely the continuation of Boschstraat, where Andre went to public school. What schoolboy, and especially one as fond of fruit as Dries, would not have stopped off at the market for an apple after school?

Certainly he would have known the shop, even if it had been in the hands of a previous owner when he was a child. And he would have remembered that of the two doors in the front, only the middle door led inside the shop. Then, too, the van Kuijk family is unsure which grocer employed him for deliveries when he first left school. Had this been the one?

Boschstraat is also where his mother moved after van Gend en Loos evicted her from the stables. It was that house that Andre visited whenever he returned home to Breda after the age of sixteen. And he was likely in town the weekend Anna was murdered. She was killed on the Friday before Whitsunday, or Pentecost—to Catholics, an important high church occasion accompanied, like Easter, by a longer school holiday, which made it a good time for travel and spending time with family. Surely Andre would have come home rather than spend it alone in the dreary hostel above his Rotterdam employer's office.

Anyone familiar with the habits and interests of both Andre van Kuijk and the older Colonel Tom Parker will find several small points of the police report most absorbing. Witnesses described seeing a man in a "fancy costume . . . a dark fantasy jacket costume" come out of the shop at the hour the murder was committed, though one thought he recognized him as Jan van Enden. Another talked about seeing a well-dressed man "in a gray-colored overcoat and fancy trousers, and I do believe a black hat." And still another described a man leaving the shop who wore a "light yellow" raincoat.

Any of those outfits might have belonged to Andre: a "fantasy jacket" reflects his obsession with *kermis.* He wore a gray suit to his father's funeral, and in a letter he wrote to his mother when he first moved to Rotterdam, he talked about his plan to buy a raincoat and hat. And in the 1950s, when his closet held a variety of large overshirts, worn loose and over the belt, the majority of them were his favorite color—light yellow.

In the days after the murder, another witness, a meat delivery boy, came forth to testify seeing the same man in the yellow raincoat exit the fruit shop around the time Anna was killed. Shortly after, he encountered him again, this time elsewhere in the neighborhood, in a "conflict of words" with a woman approximately sixty years of age, "pretty chubby around the hips and a very slim face. She had gray hair which she wore in a twist on the head." With the addition of eight years, that description fits Maria van Kuijk to perfection. Had she had an altercation with her son, a young man who had changed so much during the years he was away that he might not be immediately recognizable to others?

And perhaps a matter that most puzzled the police, according to the report, can be easily explained. Whoever snuffed out Anna van den Enden's brief life sprinkled white pepper around her body and then left a "very thin layer of corresponding gray dust"—again pepper—on the floor going into the bathroom, as well as "on the marble top of both drawers in the bedrooms, and in the hall from the bedroom to the stairs and descending into the hall which led from the shop to the kitchen." A young man who had worked with the training of dogs surely knew that police used German shepherds in the tracking of criminals, even in the Holland of 1929. And he also might have thought that a snout full of pepper would have prevented them from picking up a scent.

But even more coincidental is the fact that the author of the anonymous letter referenced 1961 as the year he was told this story. That was the year that Ad van Kuijk, Andre's younger brother, flew to Los Angeles and met with the man who called himself Colonel Tom Parker. It was the first time anyone in the family had seen him since 1929. And yet when Ad returned to Holland, he refused to talk about his trip, arousing suspicion with his siblings that he had either been bought off or threatened.

The more important question is whether the letter writer really knew his facts, or if he was simply reporting a rumor that had, through the years, become "truth." In 1982, Parker claimed he came to America in 1928, a year before these events. Was that to cover his involvement in the murder of van den Enden, or could the anonymous author just have been wrong?

There is no way of knowing whether Andre van Kuijk visited the fruit shop on the morning of May 17, 1929. But if so, had he merely meant to rob Anna, to knock her cold and steal money to return to America? Was that the money Andre left behind in the trunk? Had he been too scared to change the guilders to dollars after things had gone so wrong? Once inside the building, the intruder had locked the door between the shop and the living quarters. Had he not expected to find anyone there—Willem was out with his cart making deliveries—and panicked when he saw her?

Standing at the sink, she was struck several times from behind and hit with such force that, as the police report vividly put it, "part of the brain came through the right ear." Immediately, the burglar realized his awful mistake and attempted to bind her wounds with a piece of material torn from clothing later found in the hall. But the housewife was dead where she fell, her slippers askew on the coconut mat by the sink, a dark puddle under her head.

Yet was Andre truly capable of such a brutal deed, a sudden psychotic act? And one so bold?

"I really don't think there was a murder in him," says Todd Slaughter, who as president of the official Elvis Presley Fan Club of Great Britain, grew to know Parker well in the last twenty-five years of his life. "He was a noisy character, but I don't think there was any brute force within his psyche at all." But others disagree.

"I don't think there's any doubt that he killed that woman," asserts Lamar Fike, a member of Elvis' Memphis Mafia, assigned to the Colonel in the 1970s. "He had a terrible temper. He and I got into some violent, violent fights. We fought all the time. When we started arguing, people would get up and leave the table. Everybody was just a nervous wreck."

"I never saw him hit anybody, other than to shove his assistant [Tom Diskin] one time," remembers Byron Raphael. "But he did have a violent temper and a terrible mean streak, and it took very little to set him off. In those fits of rage, he was a very dangerous man, and he certainly appeared capable of killing. He would be nice one second, and stare off like he was lost, and then—boom!—tremendous force. He'd just snap. You never saw it coming. Then five minutes later, he would be so gentle, telling a nice soft story."

Such fury is often triggered by frustration, and Anna's killing seems too horrific and personal to have been done by a mere burglar. Had Andre just learned of her five-week-old marriage and gone to the fruit market for a confrontation, perhaps after a night of drinking? Might she have said something that unleashed a torrent of emotion, something that drove the humiliated Andre, in a flash of anger, to pick up a heavy tool and strike all sense out of her, then rob the house to mask his motivation? Only Andre and Anna know that now, speaking the truth with no tongue, no mouth, and no throat, nestled in the cool, dark folds of death.

On a purely emotional level, Parker's family in Holland refuses to entertain thoughts of Andre as a murderer. His sister Marie, the former nun, says it could not possibly be true. Besides, she adds, Mother would have known.

And yet this odd tale had a postscript, some fifty-three years after the fact. In the course of his research, Dirk Vellenga wrote to the American journalist Lloyd Shearer for help in piecing together the facts of Andre's strange odyssey to America. Shearer had at least a working relationship with Parker, who had refused to reply to Vellenga's letters, and Vellenga hoped that Parker would answer some preliminary questions if they were put to him by someone he knew.

To Vellenga's delight, he soon received a telephone call from Lloyd Shearer. At first, the men chatted about the weather and exchanged pleasantries. But as Shearer talked on, Vellenga noticed that Shearer spoke with a familiar accent—something about the way he pronounced his *R*s and *J*s—and that he seemed hoarse, like a man who might be trying to disguise his voice. Vellenga dismissed those thoughts momentarily, as Shearer was most intrigued by the Dutchman's questions about Parker's past, and the two journalists agreed to correspond about the matter.

Vellenga kept his end of the bargain, sending letter after letter. But he never again heard from Lloyd Shearer—lost today to the ravages of Alzheimer's disease—or, for that matter, from Colonel Parker. Or did he? Today, Vellenga is convinced it wasn't Shearer who called him after all, and Mrs. Shearer agrees. That phone call was between two Dutchmen, both wildly curious about an investigation into the murky life of one Dries van Kuijk.

4

MISSING IN ACTION

W H E N Andre returned to America in the late spring of 1929, much had changed in the two years since his first trip. Chautauquas were now almost exclusively a thing of the past, soon to be finished off by the October 29 stock market crash, which would plunge the American economy into the Great Depression, with its accompanying unemployment, homelessness, and starvation. Everywhere, the talk was doom and gloom. But for a young man who had already led a marginal existence for years, it hardly mattered.

Almost immediately, Andre left Mobile, Alabama, where he had sneaked into the country, and headed out to find work with a carnival on its summer route. Occasionally when he earned money, he managed to send some to his mother, but always without a return address—he was moving too fast.

Throughout his carny life, Andre would hook up with some eight traveling outfits, from the lesser-known Bruce Greater Shows, Dietrich Shows, and the L. J. Heth Shows, to the prestigious Royal American Shows. But for now, with little command of English and scant experience with American carnivals, Andre would settle for employment almost anywhere.

"When he got off that boat," says Gabe Tucker, a musician and talent manager who was associated with Parker on and off for some twenty-five years, beginning in 1939, "he got on the first carnival he come to, up in West Virginia." Carnivals were the perfect blind. In an atmosphere that attracted people on the run, nobody cared if you had a passport or not. Better yet, the hustlers and the cons of the carnival protected one of their own if somebody came asking questions.

The carnival that likely took Andre on was Rubin & Cherry Exposition Shows, a highly successful company that loftily referred to itself as "the Aristocrat of the Tented World." As for which West Virginia town Rubin & Cherry was playing at the time Andre signed on, no one knows for certain. But a good guess would be Huntington, where the carnival pitched its tents at the end of May through early June 1929—precisely the time Andre is thought to have arrived in America. By the 1940s, the man who called himself Thomas A. Parker always listed Huntington, West Virginia, as his birthplace, as good a town as any to be "reborn" in.

In 1929, the American carnival was thirty years old, with some two hundred outfits plying the circuit. Each moved on as many as forty railroad cars, eager to set up their midways on the cow pastures and fairgrounds around the United States and Canada. Many of those shows carried an elephant, the world's largest land mammal.

Long known as premier symbols of strength and power, elephants, which can weigh as much as seven tons and stand as tall as twelve feet, did more than simply perform in the carnival. They carried the support poles to set the show tents and often helped the horses pull the wagons. But the elephant is also a grand arbiter of fortune. With his trunk raised, he is said to forecast good luck; with it down, a turn of the fates. Naturally, the elephant captivated Andre's attention.

Indeed, his brother Ad van Kuijk said in 1961 that Andre started his career in America "working in a circus by lying on the ground in front of elephants," a reference to that part of an act in which the great beast demonstrates both his gentleness with humans and his control over his massive bulk.

In 1994, Colonel Tom Parker gave a list of his career affiliations to the Showmen's League for a tribute page in their annual yearbook. Nowhere did he mention a specific circus, only carnivals, though he would announce at a 1988 Elvis Presley Birthday Banquet that he had worked for Ringling Brothers for "about two years when I was sixteen years old." But he would allude to elephants and circuses again in a 1994 letter to Pam Lewis, then the co-manager of country superstar Garth Brooks. "Please tell [Garth] . . . I enjoyed the television show on NBC," Parker wrote. "When I saw him on the high wire flying in the air, it reminded me of my circus days when I floated on top of an elephant."

In all probability, Andre joined a small, one-family circus or a carnival, and not a grand independent outfit. But whether he thought it sounded more impressive than a carny (circus performers traditionally look down their noses at carnival workers, whom they consider merely cheap hustlers), he was far more modest in recounting his pachyderm past to Byron Raphael in the late 1950s.

"Colonel never invited questions about his past, but he would bring it up on his own," Raphael recalls. "He would go into these periods of melancholy where all of a sudden he'd drop his aggressive business stance and become very soft and sentimental. Several times, Colonel said he was the guy who washed the elephants. He used to water them and take care of them, and he used to give kids elephant rides. Then he would bring it back and tie it up by the foot and wash it down.

"He was pretty much of a loner, and he told me that he would be there with his elephants, or moving hay or dung around, and he would eavesdrop and listen in—what the carnies call 'staying on the earie.' That's the way he learned a lot, just by listening to people."

But Andre the elephant groom was also already honing his entrepreneurial skills. "The story I heard," says Mac Wiseman, the bluegrass star whom Parker booked in the mid-'50s, "was that the Colonel was smart enough to get the carnival owner to give him the elephant manure that they normally hauled away. He processed it and sold it as fertilizer, or took what everybody else considered trash and turned it into money. That sums up the Colonel to me."

While in many ways Andre's association with the big "rubber cows" was reminiscent of his work in his father's stables, he nonetheless found a great affinity with the elephant. More than that, as Tom Parker he seemed to form some sort of primal bond with the creature. He would more quickly cry over the fate of a doomed elephant than he would over the end of a human being.

"Colonel was very loyal to his friends, and he didn't forget," offers Sandra Polk Ross, his daughter-in-law in the 1970s. "His memory was as long as an elephant's."

Predictably, the Colonel's detractors would find less flattering comparisons: the elephant's enormous bulk and compulsion for food; its thick hide, which makes it impervious to barbs thrown its way; and especially its dangerous behavior when enraged.

"He was like a giant elephant standing on flat ground," says Memphis attorney D. Beecher Smith II, estate and tax counsel to Elvis Presley near the end of the singer's life.

A 1993 made-for-television biopic carried the symbolism further, opening with a scene in which Parker demonstrates how to train an elephant by placing a rope around its neck when the animal is young. As the elephant grows larger, it can easily break away, but without the intellect to overcome its early training, it remains a passive captive. The scene was meant to foreshadow Parker's command over Elvis, who could have broken off his relationship with his manager at any time, yet remained under his control.

Whether Parker agreed with that characterization, during his days with Presley, he festooned his offices at the various movie studios with elephant memorabilia, from canes with elephant heads worked into their knobby tops to stools disconcertingly made from an actual elephant leg—a big, stubby foot with huge, splayed toenails. "The place looked like a carnival midway," remembered Alan Fortas, a Presley entourage member.

From his first weeks in America, then, on this, his second and final trip, Andre the elephant handler had found his personal totem. But he had yet to reinvent himself in the full persona of Tom Parker. For that, the young man with no education, no legal papers, and no real job prospects would need to slip away somewhere, to sequester himself where he could sharpen his language skills and have some time to think. At the same time, he would need to draw a modicum of pay, enjoy free lodging, and receive his required three squares a day. On the eve of the Depression, the solution seemed obvious. He would go for the security of his father's early calling.

On June 20, 1929, Andre made his way to Fort McPherson, southwest of Atlanta, Georgia. There, the boy who had wanted nothing to do with military life, drill, or taking orders back home joined the army.

Or so he would later claim. On May 18, 1982, in legal papers filed in answer to a lawsuit brought against him by RCA Records, Parker contended:

> After I left the Netherlands and emigrated to the United States, I enlisted in the United States Army in or about 1929, in which I served until I was discharged in 1933 or 1934.
>
> In connection with my enlistment, I was required to and did willingly swear allegiance to the government of the United States of America. I did not seek or obtain the permission of the Dutch government to serve in the United States Army either prior to or after my service. As I am now informed, my failure to seek and receive such permission effected an automatic forfeiture of my Dutch citizenship. I am not a citizen of the United States, having never become a naturalized citizen of this country, or of any other country.

He later told the lawyers for the estate of Elvis Presley that he enlisted in the army while a minor, and reenlisted after he attained his majority.

Did Parker truly serve in the U.S. Army? There are several reasons to believe that he did. To begin with, he occasionally sent a brief note home with a photograph of himself in what appeared to be an army fatigue uniform. Certainly he could have lied about his military service and, as the illusionist he was, merely posed in a borrowed uniform to fake the images.

But that explanation seems too easy, especially in light of a second set of supporting evidence. From January 1930 through February 1932, Maria van Kuijk received monthly allotment checks sent directly to her bank in Breda from a military finance office in either Washington, D.C., or New York. Because the death of her husband rendered Maria nearly helpless in some situations, Engelina went to the bank to collect the money. The seventeen receipts she saved through the years from Frans Laurijssen, Bankier, in Breda, show that at first, Andre, who voluntarily had the money deducted from his pay, sent home $5 each month, later increased to $7—a generous sum at the time.

Another reason to believe Andre served in the U.S. Army is that he regularly exchanged letters and photos with his old school friend Cees Frijters, who was then stationed on Java, in Indonesia, with the Dutch army. Unlike the van Kuijk family, Cees had an army postal address for Andre, whom he still called Dries.

"I had ten or twelve pictures he sent me in those days," Frijters said in the 1980s. "Dries was in the U.S. Army; he was in Hawaii."

And from the photographs, the story checks out. In one, he wears tall army boots and a Smokey the Bear–style ranger hat, and appears to be in a rocky location, such as the foothills of the Koolau Mountains. In another, he poses in front of an American army tent. In two others, he seems to be in a tropical area and wears a work uniform and tie that match the uniforms in archival photographs of other army personnel stationed in the territory of Hawaii at that time.

Perhaps the most clinching of the photographs is one in which Andre stands next to a large number 6, with the rest of the photo cut off, and another in which he appears smiling, sitting in front of a wooden structure with his hand on a fire bucket. The bucket is the clue, for there, painted on the side is the code "A-64," which would indicate that Dries was part of Battery A of the 64th Coast Artillery Brigade Regiment, an antiaircraft unit stationed at Fort Shafter near Honolulu.

This, then, would seem to settle things. Except for one nagging problem: the name Andreas Cornelis van Kuijk does not show up in the mainframe records of the U.S. Army, nor do nearly twenty variations and spellings of that name. While a Captain Thomas Parker appears to have been a staff officer in the Coast Artillery stationed in Hawaii in 1930, the forty-two-year-old captain was Thomas R. Parker, from Nebraska, who died in an accident at Fort Hood, Texas, in 1945.

Might the captain have been the man who interviewed the young Dutchman when he first arrived in Hawaii? Dirk Vellenga thinks he was. If so, Andre simply appropriated his name and changed the R of his middle name to A, for Andrew, the American version of Andre. But Thomas A. Parker, and even the more generic Thomas Parker fails to show up in several checks of computerized army files and databases.

Complicating the mystery is the fact that Andre wrote to Cees saying that he was part of the Mountain Guard, and sent along a photo of himself with a hiking stick against a hilly background. But Thomas M. Fairfull, chief of the U.S. Army Museum of Hawaii, which maintains an archive on the Hawaiian Coast Artillery, says that Hawaii had no Mountain Guard at any time in its history.

Just as strange is the fact that as the manager of Elvis Presley, Parker never reminisced about his army days. While he lined the walls of his offices with pictures of himself with movie stars and carnival pals, he displayed no such photographs of himself from that era.

Even more perplexing is the fact that the music publisher Freddy Bienstock is certain Parker said he was in the U.S. Navy, not the army, and that Parker told his brother-in-law, Bitsy Mott, that he was in the merchant marine: "He used to tell me some of the stories and the places he would go. You can name almost every country there is, and he hit the port."

If Parker had been in the merchant marine, why would he have told the lawyers for RCA that he had served in the U.S. Army? And why would he have been so secretive about this period of his life at all?

Perhaps Andre did not use his own name for two obvious reasons: his underage status and his illegal entry into the United States. And the reason he failed to ever become an American citizen is as easily explained. A requirement of foreign nationals serving in the U.S. armed forces was a legal declaration of their intention to become a citizen. Such citizenship was not automatic, however, and Andre never followed through with the official naturalization process, perhaps for a more unsavory reason.

By forfeiting his Dutch citizenship and by never becoming a naturalized American, Andre could argue, if pressed, that he was not subject to the laws of either country, especially any laws that governed the extradition process. In fact, perhaps that is the very reason Andre enlisted in the army—to *lose* his Dutch citizenship. That position might have worked well for a man suspected of wrongdoing at home, especially of anything as heinous as the bludgeoning death of a greengrocer's wife. And if such a thing did occur, it could certainly explain why Andre suddenly changed his name in America, even in the U.S. Army, where foreign nationals served with regularity.

"Looking back from 1982, when he declared in legal proceedings that he wasn't a citizen," says Constant Meijers, a Dutch journalist who produced a documentary film about Parker, "you would almost think that he had figured it out by 1932. Because he had already changed his name to Tom Parker. Why would he do that in the first place? Unless he understood that one day when he had to deal with the law, it would come in handy if he were not naturalized."

In 1973, a fire destroyed many of the U.S. Army files stored in the National Personnel Records Center in St. Louis, Missouri, the primary repository of individual military histories. But ancillary records scattered in archives throughout the country show that during his interview at Fort McPherson, Andre claimed to be one Thomas Parker (no middle initial), and was issued the service number of 6363948. He reported that he was both a sailor and an orphan (and hence got around the question of why the recipient of his allotment had a different name from his own), and he volunteered to serve in the territory of Hawaii, then a little-known locale in a forgotten part of the world.

But if America was halfway around the globe and almost inaccessibly remote to a Dutchman of the 1920s, Hawaii must have seemed even more impossibly isolated. A recruit could choose a tour of duty of either twenty-four or thirty-six months, and Andre opted for the longer stay, signing up for a three-year hitch. After thirty days aboard ship—departing from the Brooklyn Naval Yard, traveling through the Panama Canal, stopping in San Francisco to replenish the boat, and then sailing the waters of the Pacific Ocean—he arrived at Honolulu, and finally at Fort De Russy in the heart of Waikiki on October 19, 1929. There, among a boatload of others, he received a week of instruction before being transferred to Fort Shafter, three miles northwest of Honolulu at the base of the Koolau Mountains.

As part of Battery A of the 64th Coast Artillery (AA) Regiment, Private Parker and his fellow recruits were expected with numbing repetition to man the three giant, sixty-inch searchlights in defense against attack by sea.

"We didn't have much to do," remembers ninety-two-year-old Earl Kilgus, a Pennsylvanian who served along with Thomas Parker as one of the unit's forty-five privates. "It was mostly drilling, training, listening to speeches—what to do in emergencies or whatever. We wore our fatigues instead of our uniforms almost every day. But you're not talking about anybody working too hard."

The initial months of Parker's military service appeared to have a profound effect on his development. According to photographs, he was in the best physical shape of his life. While most of his letters home perished during the German occupation of Holland during World War II, in one that survived, his handwriting and grammar had obviously improved, although he continued to write without regard to a flow of information. The family remembers he was still signing his letters "Andre," but often just "Tom Parker."

As he ended his two years in Hawaii with a transfer back to the mainland in the fall of 1931, Andre seemed to be thinking more of home and informed the family of his change of post. He was now part of Headquarters Battery of the 13th Coast Artillery, stationed at Fort Barrancas, just outside Pensacola, Florida, only fifty-five miles from where he had come ashore at Mobile. As proof, he sent along a photo of himself in a Florida setting, dressed in the civilian attire of a baggy suit and bow tie. His sister Marie recalls that their mother sent him clothes occasionally, for which she received a brief thank-you note after a long silence.

Sometime in the following months, Andre would say, he injured his right foot in an accident while on duty, and supporting records show that he, indeed, spent $1.50 at the post cobbler. Whether his injury contributed to the painful gout he suffered in his later years, the immediate result, he told his brother Ad in 1961, was an early discharge from the service and a small pension for life.

Yet Jerry Goodson of the Reno, Nevada, office of the Department of Veterans Affairs says there is no record of Andre van Kuijk or Thomas Parker ever collecting such a pension in any of the four states—Florida, Tennessee, California, or Nevada—where he lived.

How is it that a man who routinely drove miles out of his way to promote a free meal in years to come failed to take advantage of a lifelong military pension?

In 1982, Colonel Tom Parker came as close as he ever would to offering up his secrets, when the Nevada federal court, in connection with the RCA Records suit, ordered him to submit to a deposition on the issue of his claim as a stateless citizen. On October 25 of that year, lawyers planned to question him concerning all of the events that caused him to leave the Netherlands and take up residence in the United States. And, they wrote, "We should also be entitled to question him about his enlisting and re-enlisting in the United States Armed Forces."

Yet in the end, the old Dutchman decided the truth was too great a price to pay. As a lifelong carny, Parker took pride in being able to talk his way out of a tight place, and even enjoyed the challenge. But now he realized he was in a spot from which not even the great Harry Houdini could escape, and so he settled the case before he could ever be deposed.

"We were never successful in finding his army records," reports Blanchard E. Tual, the former guardian *ad litem* for Lisa Marie Presley, who set the lawsuit in motion. The answers to the puzzling questions about Parker's military life would sleep silently with him in the grave.

But a nearly two-year search for Parker's army records, aided by the Freedom of Information Act, finally yielded a glimmer of what Parker feared would be known. While the information is incomplete, at best it offers a vital key to understanding not only his army experience, but also the psyche of Tom Parker himself.

Parker's principal personnel file no longer exists, having either been destroyed in the 1973 fire or otherwise "lost." But in June 1982, when he needed to prove his military service in the RCA court proceedings, his lawyer, Jack Magids of the Memphis firm Krivcher & Magids, contacted W. G. Seibert of the National Personnel Records Center.

At Magids's request, and based on details supplied in the lawyer's written communication and in a supporting letter from Parker himself, Seibert began compiling a reconstructed file of Parker's military service. The discharge document and final pay vouchers contained in that file, combined with ancillary records (such as morning reports and unit rosters found elsewhere) begin to frame a far clearer picture of Tom Parker than anyone has ever seen. And also far darker.

Judging from the morning reports and rosters from Fort Shafter, Parker fulfilled his tour of duty in Hawaii without incident. And for nearly a year after he arrived at Fort Barrancas on October 24, 1931, things seemed to go fine. He enjoyed a sixty-day furlough beginning in March 1932, and when his three-year hitch was up on June 19, he collected $95.51 in wages, travel, and clothing pay, and re-enlisted the next day. Then on July 18 of that year, he enjoyed a promotion to Private First Class, an honor that certainly would have pleased his military-minded father.

Parker, like most recruits, had every reason to be content. Fort Barrancas, located on Pensacola Bay, was regarded as one of the prettiest bases in the country. "The men who served here in the thirties loved it," says Coast Artillery expert David Ogden, a park ranger at Gulf Island National Seashore.

But Private First Class Parker did not love it. Behind his controlled army demeanor, Parker was deeply restless. He had stuck with the military—an institution directly at odds with his willful and autonomous personality—longer than he had committed himself to anything else in his twenty-three years. And perhaps he had followed orders until the thought of one more command—one more deafening, bone-rattling blast of the big guns that guarded the mouth of the harbor—made him want to run screaming into the night.

Precisely what drove Private First Class Parker to desperate straits is lost to the blur of time. But Tuesday, September 27, 1932, a day after seven of his fellow soldiers had departed the base on furlough, the perfect soldier calmly and quietly walked out of Fort Barrancas. Whether he had been denied furlough and refused to accept the ruling isn't known, but that evening the army marked him AWOL, or "absent without leave." A week later, on October 4, he was reduced in rank to private, and after thirty days, on Halloween, Private Parker was officially classified a deserter. If he did not return within six months, the Department of Defense would refer the matter to the FBI.

Desertion! It was the one offense that overshadowed all others. In the army, Andre, crisp in his uniform, had played a grown-up, the child imitating the father, the son becoming the father—the two were interchangeable in his mind. But he could never really *be* the father any more than he could ever really be a soldier. And when the stresses of that conflict mounted with those that only he knew for certain, the little boy that was still Andre fought to escape.

But where did Private Parker go when he left the serenity of Fort Barrancas? Almost certainly back to a fantasy world where he finally felt superior—if only to the marks he outsmarted. For a check of the local newspaper turns up the fascinating fact that the Ringling Brothers and Barnum and Bailey Circus, with its "50 big and little elephants, 700 horses . . . 100 hilarious clowns . . . and a whole congress of freaks," arrived in Pensacola for two performances only on September 27—the very day Private Parker went AWOL. Was this what Parker had alluded to later in life, bragging about the days when he "floated on top of an elephant"? There, under the "big top," in the lights and the noise, it didn't matter what you'd done on a nearby army base, or halfway around the world, or even if you lied every time you spoke your name. For the next day would bring a new identity and a new town. In this case, Tallahassee.

Parker arrived at Fort Barrancas in the fall of 1931 as one of two privates transferred from Fort Shafter. Had he brownnosed his senior officer in Hawaii specifically to be transferred to the Coast Artillery in Florida, just to be close to the headquarters of the biggest traveling shows? Is that why the allotment checks stopped going to Holland? Had Parker been hoarding his money for escape?

Whether law enforcement or the military found him there, or whether he turned himself in, when he returned to the base on February 17, 1933, he had been missing for 140 days—nearly five months. Desertion was an offense punishable by court martial, and Parker pleaded for leniency, officially rejoining his unit the next morning.

But to a man with wanderlust in his blood, the punishment ultimately meted out was worse than any dishonor a court martial could have delivered. Records show that his commanding officer marked his 140-day AWOL as lost time without wages. Then he added sixty days more: for two months, Private Parker would be placed in solitary confinement in the guardhouse jail on the post. There, he would ponder his actions until he could be rehabilitated and restored to duty.

By the time Parker was taken from confinement on April 18, his speech was an incoherent rush of sound, punctuated by terrifying bursts of paranoia and rage. The army doctor had seen this kind of psychotic breakdown before and, suspecting schizophrenia, had Private Parker moved to the guarded lockup ward at the base hospital for observation and treatment. Two months later, after the patient showed no improvement, the doctor knew only one thing for certain—he could do nothing to help this soldier.

On June 19, 1933, Private Thomas Parker, having taken leave of his senses, was removed from the guarded lockup ward and sent to Walter Reed Army Medical Center in Washington, D.C. The hospital had no locked psychiatric ward, or even a mental health facility—neuropsychiatry became a board-certified specialty only that year. But Walter Reed did reserve a wing for solders whose behavior was unpredictable, and Parker may have been kept there if the doctors thought he was no real danger to himself. The likelihood, say army historians, is that he was transferred to St. Elizabeth's Hospital, a "government hospital for the insane," as it billed itself, or transported there daily as one of Walter Reed's pseudo-psych patients.

No longer a federal institution, St. Elizabeth's is now run by the District of Columbia and houses such patients as John Hinckley Jr., the would-be assassin of President Ronald Reagan. However, no records exist to support treatment for Parker other than at the army medical center, where the staff guessed that it was not confinement that caused this state, but rather a long-standing, pervasive psychotic process. Before his breakdown, Private Parker had likely suffered a persistent personality problem, marked by impulsive acts and disregard for the rights and feelings of others.

The army doctor wrote out a vague but serious diagnosis: "Psychosis, Psychogenic Depression, acute, on basis of Constitutional Psychopathic State, Emotional Instability."

On August 11, 1933, after two months of treatment, a medical board consisting of three army surgeons decided that Private Parker was ready to rejoin society. However, he would never again be fit for military duty. They prepared his certificate of disability, repeating the diagnosis—"Constitutional Psychopathic State"—that would forever stigmatize him as a mental patient.

Eight days later, Private Parker received his separation papers. The Walter Reed personnel concluded that since his desertion had been brought about by illness, his discharge would be honorable.

On August 19, 1933, twenty-four-year-old Thomas Parker, a civilian now, pushed open the doors of Walter Reed Army Hospital and walked out into the summer sun of Washington's Georgia Avenue. In his pocket was his final paycheck of $117.57. Across town, a new president, named Roosevelt, sat in the White House.

Just exactly where Parker went when he left the hospital corridors is unknown, but once again, a sixty-seven-year-old photograph holds a clue. One of his favorite pictures shows him as a handsome, thin young man, well dressed in a dark casual jacket and light pants, and adorned with a snappy hat and tie. He is posed with several ponies, one with a spider monkey riding its back. The group, which includes a German shepherd, stands on what appears to be hay, in front of a large movie poster for the Christmas 1935 release *Home on the Range*, starring Jackie Coogan, Randolph Scott, and Evelyn Brent.

The horses suggest an explanation for an employment entry in his 1994 salute in the Showmen's League yearbook: Silver's Ponies. Today, no one recalls ever hearing of Silver's Ponies. But Slover's Ponies was a popular kiddie ride outfit in the 1933 season of the Johnny J. Jones Exposition, which enjoyed winter dates in Tampa, Florida, that year.

Tampa, the winter quarters of several carnivals and the hub of off-season carny life, would be Andre's new home. And it would also be the place where the newly reinvented character of Tom Parker would mold itself, starting with his early job of promoting Bert Slover's ponies. Parker had once again allied himself with the carnival world, integrating himself into a social network that at times was as intricate and as furtive as any underground railroad.

But an odd thing happened once Andre left the army. His letters home, which had never arrived with frequency, slowed to a trickle. He said nothing to his mother about his awful ordeal or what had so occupied his time. Finally the letters stopped coming at all. In his last missive, Andre wrote in an especially emotional tone that he had very little money, was without a job, and was struggling to eke out a living in a tough but vibrant America. As a boy he had dreamed of greatness, he said, and he expressed his belief that he could still make his dream come true—that out of nothing and with his own hands and ingenuity, he would build a career as he saw it in his imagination back in Holland.

After that, the family heard only silence. It seemed as if Andre had been swept from the world and drowned in the vastness of America. On April 4, 1935, when a member of the Breda municipal government inquired about Andre's whereabouts for a routine matter—taxes, or census, or the Dutch welfare pension, perhaps—Maria van Kuijk reported with a leaden heart that Andre was not coming home. Across from his name on the van Kuijk family Register of Birth, the government worker wrote "Ambtshalve," meaning it had become apparent to him in his official capacity that this citizen had "gone to America." Andre was now removed from the family record and, in effect, written out of their lives.

The van Kuijks never stopped searching for answers. During World War II, Andre's sister Johanna carried his picture, showing it to American soldiers when they reached Holland, pathetically hoping they might know him, or perhaps had seen him somewhere and could report that he was all right.

After the war, when they had still heard nothing, Maria van Kuijk tried to remain optimistic about his return. But when another decade passed in which she waited in vain for a letter, she figured her son was dead. Still, she lit candles for him at church, prayed for his safekeeping, and whispered the secret language that exists between extraordinary mothers and extraordinary sons. When she died in 1958, the same year as the death of the mother of another famous man—a singer whose name would always be linked with that of her son—it was without the knowledge of Andre's remarkable life in America.

"She was for me a very kind, easygoing woman," remembers her granddaughter Mieke Dons-Maas. "But she had a sadness pain because of Andre. And it never went away."

Unless Andre had, indeed, died, the family couldn't conceive of such cruelty, especially since Andre and his mother had once been so close. But for reasons of shame, or confusion, or the continuing effects of his illness, perhaps, Andre van Kuijk had no grieving mother in Holland. For that matter, Andre van Kuijk did not exist at all. Tom Parker, an orphan from Huntington, West Virginia, had taken his place. And Tom Parker, lost and alone, grew almost frantic to find his place in America.

5

TURNING THE DUKE

B Y 1933, just as Tom Parker joined the Johnny J. Jones ranks, the future of "the Mighty Monarch of the Tented World" was in grave doubt. At the end of the 1930 season, with the Depression signaling a steady decline of customers, Jones, who had been regarded as a genius, found himself heavily in debt. Then on Christmas Day, he unexpectedly died of uremia at the age of fifty-six, leaving his thirty-one-year-old wife, Hody Hurd, to carry on. Now Hurd had suffered a nervous breakdown, and with her finances equally exhausted, she would sell the once-great carnival to E. Lawrence Phillips at the end of the disastrous 1933 season.

If the majority of the Johnny J. Jones troupers were downhearted, Tom Parker couldn't have been happier to be among them. And while showing Bert Slover's ponies at a Tampa movie theater was a natural assignment for him, he was willing to get up at 5:30 A.M.—which became his lifelong habit to be part of the action.

From the beginning on Johnny J. Jones (where he was an independent contractor and not a salaried member of the staff), Parker set his sights on making the most money, just as he had as a young dockhand in Rotterdam. That meant working the front end of the lot, or concessions, a broad-based term that covered food, merchandise, and gaming booths, but with one important difference: merchandise and game operators bought their booth space by the foot; food worked on a percentage basis.

"He started out in a candy stand, making candy apples and popcorn," says Larry Davis, owner of California's largest outfit, Carnival Time Shows, who came to know Parker well in the early '70s through the Showmen's League of America, the venerable outdoor fraternal organization. From there, Parker told Davis, he floated throughout the carnival, doing whatever he could—shaving ice for snow cones, running the merry-go-round, anything—trying to stay alive.

"I knew him as a concessionnaire," says Joe McKennon, a carnival historian who worked on the shows. By the time McKennon met him, Parker had several small concessions, adding a game or two to his food stand, which immediately made him suspect to the other showmen. Concessionaires who ran games were often crooks specializing in "flat stores," or games of chance that offered no winning numbers. As "gentlemanly agents" who sold "conversation" and bragged about "turning the duke"—not just hustling the customer out of his money, but shortchanging the count with a skilled slip of the hand—they were a disgrace to the honest men among them.

In those first years, the young Tom Parker kept his nose clean and stayed out of trouble. In fact, "he just didn't make an impression," according to McKennon. But one thing McKennon does remember about Tom Parker: he went by yet another name. "I used to know what it was, but it wasn't Parker," he begins. "At a showmen's convention about fifteen years ago, he was the speaker, and I had to introduce him. I said, 'He was just a so-so concessionaire until he found that boy from Memphis and went into the business of creating names.' And I used that name he had on the Jones show. Afterwards, Parker came up and said, 'I didn't know you knew that, Joe.'"

Parker may have felt compelled to use another alias during the AWOL and desertion period of his military service, and perhaps carried it over to the early part of his Johnny J. Jones days. But to carnies such as Larry Davis, Parker's decision to hide his true identity simply isn't worth noting.

"You could know a guy ten years in that era and not know his real name," offers veteran concessionaire John Campi.

Indeed, Jack Kaplan, Parker's best friend throughout his carnival years and an associate for decades to come, never felt the need to ask his true identity. The two slept next to each other in railroad cars for months on end, but Kaplan had no idea what Parker did before the carnival, or even where he came from, although he noted that "in 1933, he was [still] talking like a Dutchman: 'Brassa, was ist los, ja, ja, ja'" Parker's refusal to elaborate on his past was considered neither mysterious nor unusual. It was simply part of the carnies' silent understanding.

For those who did feel a need to shield either their identity or their predilections, the carnival offered a perfect place to hide. It was also fraught with danger, a situation that tends to bend the mind-set of the fraternity.

In the Depression years of the '30s, especially, those who worked the carnivals trusted no one, and the strain of always having to watch their back often led to frayed nerves and sometimes tragedy. Stabbings on the lot were not uncommon, nor was a callous attitude toward death and the survival of the fittest. It was all a part of business as usual.

Parker so identified with that lifestyle that he sought out the company of concessionaires, midway operators, and sideshow performers long after his carnival days were over.

"When we were traveling across country," says Byron Raphael, who frequently drove Parker in the late '50s, "he often took me to these little carnivals that were so small they didn't even have a big tent. He knew where they were, all through the states, and the first thing he would do was to search out the midgets and the freaks.

"In California, between Barstow and Bakersfield, there were billboards every hundred yards, 'See the Thing! Half Man, Half Animal!' He took that really seriously. We'd stop and go in there, and it would be very dark, very eerie, and 'the Thing' would be this poor pathetic black person on his hands and knees in a low cage. He had a tail on him, and long hair, and when he would growl, it was really frightening.

"The Colonel loved that, and at these little carnivals, he loved the fat lady, and the bearded lady, and he would sit and talk with them for hours. He was a very superstitious person. I remember him being very respectful of the Tarot reader. Every place we stopped there was always one woman who would sit in a little hut and read your fortune. He would say, 'This woman is very good. She can read the crystal ball.' Then he'd go spend time with the cooks who were making the hot roast beef sandwiches. They all knew him. These were people that he had worked with."

Until his death, Parker remained active with the Showmen's League of America, contributing generously to their causes. "He did a lot of good work for the Showmen's League," remembers Campi, who first met Parker in the '40s. "He was a beautiful guy, a good man, and a friend. Of course, he was an enemy if you were his."

But the code of the carnies directed that even his enemies had to concede one point: "I think that everyone in our show business world considered Colonel Parker a great man," assesses Larry Davis. "He was just about the best there was at thinking and figuring things out. I've never met anyone who thought as deeply as the Colonel."

In the winter of 1933–34, only a few months past his awful ordeal at Walter Reed Army Medical Center, Parker probably still had enough of his army discharge pay, sizable for the times, to see him through the winter. But his compulsion to take to the streets to finagle money or promote a free meal had not dimmed since his childhood. The elderly locals of the area remember him from those days as someone who did what the carnies called "rough hustling"—hawking candy apples, popcorn, or whatever he could—on the streets of Tampa. Joan Buchanan West grew up in the area hearing her mother tell stories of how Parker sold potatoes and onions off the back of a pickup truck between carnivals, traveling to the little agricultural communities of Ruskin and Plant City and dickering with the farmers, saving enough beans and tomatoes to keep himself from starving along the way.

It was during this period that Parker met Louis "Peasy" Hoffman, a special agent for Rubin & Cherry Exposition Shows. Hoffman, a short, portly man with an ever-present cigar setting off a face framed by rimless eyeglasses and a seasoned hat, was a legend in the carnies. Before moving over to Rubin & Cherry, he had carved out a solid reputation as an expert public relations, advertising, and advance man for Johnny J. Jones, Lackman Exposition Shows, and Cetlin & Wilson.

Tom Parker may have shared much of the flair and philosophy of P. T. Barnum, but if he ever had a hands-on mentor and guide, it was Hoffman, who had started out as a well-finessed and friendly but persistent game operator. By the time Parker met him, Hoffman was a front-office man in his late forties who dressed impeccably in a three-piece suit and carefully knotted tie. What's more, noted the young Parker, who had developed a prominent stutter in his transition from Dutchman to homegrown American, Hoffman could speak smoothly and glibly about nearly anything. One of the most crucial lessons he passed on to Parker was the importance of getting to know every influential man and woman in even the smallest of burgs in the South and Southeast, long the provincial heart of the carnival circuit. That was the way the world really worked, he told him.

Yet if the show needed to get a carny out of jail, or if a bribe was required to set up on the grounds or to run unlawful games, another man, the "fixer"—also known as the "legal adjuster" or "patch"—would step in.

As the promoter Oscar Davis remembered, Parker paid close attention to such ways of dealing with authority, knowing that like almost everything else he learned on the carnival, they would become useful in other negotiations in life.

Parker understood that the real clout in the carnival lay in the front-office positions like Hoffman's. He aspired to such a job himself, where he could be a big shot and dress in a fine tailored suit. He admired how Hoffman could handle almost any situation with grace and aplomb, certainly a prerequisite for any front-end employee. But it was Hoffman's skill at selling advertising that Parker coveted most, and so he offered to chauffeur Hoffman on his local rounds in exchange for tutelage. At first, the lessons were slow in coming—Hoffman was still on Rubin & Cherry, and Parker on Johnny J. Jones, and so they met up in Tampa in the winter. Before long, they were teaming to work the smaller "turk," or non-railroad shows, in the off-season.

Soon, Parker was emulating Hoffman in almost every fashion, and from all appearances stood out as the very model of the well-dressed front-office agent. A photograph of him from the time shows an eager would-be promoter in a dark suit, white dress shirt, and dotted tie, a fedora on his head. The cigar, which not only gave him an air of grit and confidence, but took a stranger's eye away from his weakening chin line would come soon afterward.

"You could say he patterned himself after my father a bit," says Hoffman's son, Joey, also a carnival man. "But later on, he attributed all of his dirty tricks to my dad. Parker was a big, likable Dutchman and a nice fellow, but he was really nothing but a half-assed promoter who eventually lucked into a hot property."

In his second winter with Hoffman, Parker bragged about several stunts he'd originated on the Jones show, such as a public wedding ceremony. In this stunt, staged on Saturday night for optimum effect, Parker and a girl off the show—allegedly two carny kids in love—"married" on top of a Ferris wheel. Soon the public wedding ceremony was a staple on carnivals across the country, and its success filled Parker with the hope that he would be rewarded with a front-office job. Instead, tough carnival owners and managers regarded him as a renegade who happened to hit with a good thing.

"He always had quick ideas," remembered Jack Kaplan, Parker's chief crony of the time, "and he was quick on talking. He wanted to be a big man in this country. He always said, 'Them dummies can do it. Why can't I?'"

If Parker had not yet earned the respect of management, he found in Kaplan the first of a long line of flunkies who would eventually make up a sort of entourage—men who would work cheap for the privilege of being around him and his milieu, be on call twenty-four hours a day, suffer silently any form of verbal or emotional abuse, and never question his authority. Usually, like Kaplan, they were younger men and of small stature, intimidated by Parker's size, girth, and aggressive personality. They were yes-men to the extreme, perfectly suited to his deep-seated need to control, subjugate, and bully. Parker hoped having a subservient gofer like Kaplan would boost his profile with the carnival brass and dignitaries—men who had the title of Colonel in front of their names to designate them as important figures.

By 1934, Parker was on and off the Jones show, hopscotching from one carnival to another to make a season's work. The smaller the show, the more corrupt, and most of the little outfits were so undercapitalized that sometimes they couldn't afford enough tires to simultaneously move all the trucks to the next town.

Understandably, with such limited prospects, Parker was hoping to worm his way into a job like Peasy's. Hoffman got him a break at Rubin & Cherry, but a front-office job remained beyond his grasp. Back on the Jones outfit, he talked his way into selling a few ads, yet the front ranks seemed closed to him there, as well.

And so he scrambled to do what he could, including "cherry pie," or jobs wheedled out of his fellow showfolk, even something as menial as guarding the railroad cars. All the while, he indoctrinated himself further into the closed, secret society of the carnival, he and Kaplan resorting, when they needed to talk business in front of the townies and not be understood, to the gibberish of carny lingo.

For a time during this early period, the young Parker moonlighted as a pitchman on a sideshow—in part to lose his stutter and Dutch accent and learn to talk "American." He also ran a "mitt camp," or fortune-telling booth, tracing his customers' occupations by the calluses on their hands. He could look into the eyes of the gullible, read the life history on their face, and communicate with them silently, almost controlling the very words they said.

6

DANCING CHICKENS, TOOTHLESS
LIONS, AND RODEO COWBOYS

CARL J. SEDLMAYR was indisputably the man to see. In just twelve years, the success of his Royal American Shows, headquartered in Tampa, had made him the modern "King of the Carnivals." The Nebraskan, a former fountain pen salesman, had ventured into the carnies in 1907 as a talker on a sideshow. In 1921, he purchased the Siegrist & Silbon Shows, and after two years, changed the name to Royal American—"Royal" to appeal to Canada, where he hoped to take his outfit for part of the season, and "American" to rouse the patriotism of those back home.

Sedlmayr, whose fierce eyes and formidable, turned-down mouth hid a kind heart and a genuine liking for his employees, was a man of honor. He had built the Royal American Shows' reputation by carrying nothing less than clean, high-class entertainment and by creating the extraordinarily diverse "World's Largest Midway" that treated its customers as patrons, and not as "marks."

The skilled showman also knew the supreme selling point of meeting personally with the fair committees who might book his outfit exclusively on their grounds. By this method, he managed to replace Johnny J. Jones as the resident show at the Florida State Fair and establish decades-long relationships with other fairs and venues throughout the country. The Memphis Cotton Carnival, where a teenage Elvis Presley would win a stuffed teddy bear at a baseball concession in the early 1950s, was among them.

In 1925, Sedlmayr upped his ante by partnering with the equally respected Curtis and Elmer Velare, a brother team who started as acrobats with the C. W. Parker Shows and who would go on to help found the Showmen's League.

When the Velares joined forces with Carl Sedlmayr, who early on saw the potential of outlining the carnival rides with neon tubing, their fellow troupers correctly forecast that they would mold the Royal American into the greatest collective amusement organization in the world. In 1933, the show pushed all larger competitors aside to reign as the leader in the industry ("a mile of magnificent, stupendous midway!"), with more than a thousand workers boarding the Royal American's seventy private red-and-white train cars each spring.

Tom Parker, whose frustration over his stalled career mounted daily, knew that a position on the Royal American would do wonders for his reputation. And so he approached Sedlmayr, asking to represent the carnival in an office-echelon job. He knew all about publicity, press agents, and advertising, he said. Peasy Hoffman had trained him.

Sedlmayr recognized an overly zealous hustler when he saw one. And so he turned Parker over to the harder-hearted business manager, Elmer Velare, who noted Parker's fractured English, wondered how solid a character he was, and delivered the word that the front office didn't need a new man just then.

"The Colonel told me that Velare didn't think he could handle it," remembers Larry Davis. "The shame of it is that the Colonel had a lot to teach the carnival, rather than learn from it."

But for now, either no one at Royal American realized Parker's worth, or the Velares considered his brash enthusiasm a vulgarity better-suited to running a mitt camp. Yet Sedlmayr admired the young man's moxie, and told Curtis Velare, the concession manager, to put him in an ice cream booth. Parker soon worked his way into other concessions, running wooden sticks through candy apples for Ruby Velare in her cotton-candy stand and cutting a deal with her during the off-season to provide the treats he sold on the streets of Tampa.

Over the next few years, Parker tried nearly everything to break through at the carnival—even volunteering his services with an old, toothless lion whose sore gums had set him on a hunger strike. According to a story Parker later recounted with great fanfare, he fashioned a set of false teeth for the beast, smearing the choppers with mustard when it came time for the big cat to go on show. The spicy condiment irritated the lion's tender palate but guaranteed an authentically fierce roar.

Such a story has the decided ring of fiction, if for no other reason than its inherent cruelty. As someone who often treated animals with more dignity than he showed to humans, he would not have tolerated such behavior, much less initiated it.

That rationale is precisely why one of the most famous stories attributed to him—that of the "dancing chickens"—also proves apocryphal. According to legend, Parker carried a hot plate, a gramophone, and a cage of assorted fowl—hens, roosters, or turkeys—with him on the carnivals, a practice that supposedly lasted well into his early days of touring rodeos with country singer Eddy Arnold in the 1940s. Whenever the concession business turned slow or, in Arnold's case, if a fair slapped an amusement tax on an act without a livestock exhibit, Parker simply covered the hot plate with straw and set it in the cage. Then he plugged it in, dropped the gramophone needle on a fast little number, and gathered the crowds as the poor chickens high-stepped around the cage to keep from burning their feet.

The great cowboy star Gene Autry swore that the story was true, and that it led to a friendship that endured until Parker's death. But Gabe Tucker says it never happened with Parker, who merely appropriated the tale and passed it off as his own. According to Tucker, the real perpetrator was Dub Albritten, who told Tucker about it in 1945, and it was a dancing duck, not a chicken.

By the time Parker started telling the story to others in the Elvis era—usually flourishing a chicken leg at lunch to bring the tale full course—he'd worked out a kicker. "I'd start each week with seven dancin' chickens and finish with just one," he'd say, pausing for dramatic effect. "A fella's gotta eat!"

Despite his obvious aptitude for myth making, in the 1930s, the Royal American brass still found Parker beneath consideration as a press agent or, for that matter, any job of authority. And so his years there would never amount to anything beyond the camaraderie and pride he enjoyed in being associated with the most celebrated carnival of its day.

The sting of that early rejection—so reminiscent of Adam van Kuijk's reinforcement of failure—left a permanent welt on Parker's consciousness. Long after he attained a measure of wealth and fame that would have staggered Carl Sedlmayr and the Velare brothers, Parker returned to the carnival time and again to brag and gloat and seek approbation.

Ernie Wenzik, who operated a Pitch 'Til You Win game on the Royal American midway in the 1950s, remembers that Parker kept up with the carnival's schedule. "He used to come and visit Mr. Sedlmayr every time he was in the neighborhood," says Wenzik.

But it was more important that he confront the Velares, who continued to be active in the business well into their elderly years, introducing the ninety-foot-high double sky wheel when most men their age had long since retired. In 1972, Parker finally got his chance, when he spied Elmer Velare at the Showmen's League convention in Las Vegas.

"Mr. Velare," he began. "I'm Tom Parker. I used to work for you on the Royal American. I manage Elvis Presley. I'm a big promoter now."

"Yes, indeed," said eighty-eight-year-old Elmer Velare, graciously trying to soften the moment. "Why didn't you do that when you were with us? If I'd known you had this ability, I would have put you to work a long time ago."

"Oh, but Mr. Velare," countered Parker, twisting the knife. "I asked you tens of times to let me be a promoter back in the thirties, and you people wouldn't let me. You remember that, don't you, Mr. Velare? I told you I could do it."

Parker had managed a miraculous journey from his days with the carnival, but he never got past his need to boast of his accomplishments, or of his relationships with famous people. From nearly his first major interview in the Elvis years, Parker crowed of his friendships with cowboy stars Tom Mix and Ken Maynard, although none of the Mix biographers or Maynard experts can document an association. Maynard and Parker might have made a passing acquaintance when Maynard played the smaller circuses in the 1930s and '40's, but there is one other possible explanation, hidden in the details of an embarrassing promotion.

"One time, Colonel produced a show at some ballpark, where he advertised somebody's famous white horse," Alan Fortas remembered. "I'm not sure whose horse this was, but it might have been Ken Maynard's horse, Tarzan, or this big cream-colored horse that Tom Mix had, Comanche. Anyway, something happened, and they couldn't get him. So Colonel said, 'Hell, just take that black one over there and whitewash him,' which was an old circus trick. But just as they were bringing him across the field, damn if it didn't start rainin'! By the time they got to where they were going, that horse was coal black."

He was "always intrigued by cowboys and cowboy stars," Parker's friend Oscar Davis observed. His fascination with all things Western never wavered, and resulted in his hiring Nudie Cohen of Nudie's Rodeo Tailors to create Elvis Presley's famed gold lamé tuxedo.

More important, the infatuation was behind his insistence that Presley make such Western-themed pictures as *Love Me Tender; Stay Away, Joe;* and *Charro!*

If the Western image appears to be a curious choice for a man of his background, somewhere in his psyche, Parker seemed to believe he was a product of that pioneering spirit of the West, seen in his fondness for cowboy hats, and the logo of an old-fashioned covered wagon ("We Cover the Nation") that adorned his business stationery. During the 1964 U.S. presidential campaign, he "loaned" the logo to Lyndon Johnson, gifting him with a thirteen-inch, hand-carved wagon that doubled as a lamp and carried the words ALL THE WAY WITH LBJ on its cloth tenting. Parker hoped it would inspire a promotional giveaway to symbolize Johnson's Texas fortitude.

Yet if Parker did not genuinely embrace the romance of the Old West, it was a perfect ruse for an illegal alien. What could be more American—and by extension, *patriotic*—than a cowboy, a figure who stood for all things good and virtuous? Certainly not his antithesis, the outlaw. It was always a white hat Parker wore, never a black one.

7

ONE BORN EVERY MINUTE

I N February 1935, when the Royal American Shows played the Florida State Fair at Tampa's Plant Field, Tom Parker sauntered up to the Hav-A-Tampa cigar stand with his mind on free samples. Marie Frances Mott, a dark-haired beauty queen with something of a racy reputation, took one look at the well-dressed man with the strange blue eyes and was only too happy to comply. She parted her Kewpie doll mouth and flashed a smile of even white teeth, and then sweetened her cracker's drawl with the honey of seduction. "You work on the carnival?" she asked, stringing the words out to lay a hint of promise in between. Suddenly, Parker was interested in more than just stogies.

Tom Parker had perhaps shown no interest in girls to his friends back in Holland, but on the Johnny J. Jones show, said Jack Kaplan, he demonstrated that the old circus maxim—"a pussy pulls stronger than an elephant"—was true. Like any good con man, Tom Parker was a charmer, and what he didn't see at first was that Marie Mott, in laughing at his jokes and complimenting his clothes, was conning him right back. Three months away from her twenty-seventh birthday, and a full thirteen months older than Parker, she, like him, had a secret in her soul.

Born in Pembroke, Florida, on May 18, 1908, she was one of six children of Susie Ardelia Woodard and Elisha Mott, a rough-hewn Spanish-American War veteran who plied his trade as a blacksmith and iron worker, and subsidized his meager income as a dirt farmer. The family picked up and moved whenever the land played out.

Unlike her more sedate sisters, Lula Mae and Gertrude, Marie was a high-strung, hyperactive child, and already something of a wildcat by her teens, much to the consternation of her uneducated but moral-minded mother. Although she retained some of the tenets of her hard-shell Baptist upbringing (shunning alcohol, for instance), the high-spirited Marie could turn the air blue with her language.

"She was a piss cutter, and Granny Mott couldn't do a thing with her," says her daughter-in-law, Sandra Polk Ross. Still, her natural beauty was enough to see her run for queen of the Gasparilla Parade—part of an annual celebration to salute buccaneer Jose Gaspar and re-create the invasion of Tampa—and ride triumphantly on the lead float. "Colonel fell in love with Marie because he liked her spirit—and she had that flash in her eye, too," according to Ross. "He thought she was the prettiest thing he ever saw."

Marie Mott was not only pretty—she carried the exciting stigma of a divorcée. Where Tom Parker was still relatively inexperienced in matters of sex ("I knew he had a girl for a short while in North Carolina," said Jack Kaplan), Marie had deserted her husband, Willett Man Eagler Sayre, in Jacksonville only a month earlier. Furthermore, she had another husband, Robert Burl Ross, in her past and, on the day she first met Tom Parker, a nearly ten-year-old son, Robert B. Ross Jr., to raise.

And the comely Marie held yet another surprise. Asked in 1983 about his sister's family, Marie's younger brother, Elisha Mott Jr., known as Bitsy, said, "She had two children by Ross. The other one died at birth. We have no record of it."

The last statement may have been true, but the second certainly wasn't. Bitsy Mott had full knowledge of the survival of William Ross, who was born July 4, 1928, in Tampa. Billy had arrived with the deformity of a clubfoot, but was otherwise a startlingly beautiful child.

The Rosses had already split by the time of Billy's birth, and whether Marie believed that having a handicapped child hurt her chances of landing another man, in 1929, she packed Billy, then a year old, off to the Florida Children's Home, where he was adopted two years later by a Plant City farming family, used and abused as a field hand—and as a kind of "play toy" for their older son.

With Marie off living the wild life, Granny Mott reared Bob Jr. with the help of her husband Bitsy, who was only seven years older, and viewed Bobby as a younger brother to mentor and protect. The boy was still living with his grandparents when Marie married for the second time and moved to Jacksonville with Sayre. But soon she was back in Tampa, and in a matter of months—shortly after meeting Parker—she phoned Sayre to tell him it was over and found only his mother at home.

"She said she was in love with another man," Mrs. W. S. Sayre reported to the court. But Marie never brought action for divorce, leaving it up to Sayre to file. The court found her guilty of "willful, continuous and obstinate desertion of the complainant," and granted Sayre the final decree on March 18, 1936.

Marie Mott Ross Sayre was then free to marry Tom Parker. But what was it that really drew them together, apart from Parker's realization that having an American wife and stepson could come in handy if he were ever in trouble with the immigration officials?

"I believe they were in love, plain and simple," says Sandra Polk Ross. "He was a fine cut of a man in those early pictures. And she was such a handsome woman and so trim. Marie was a hot number when she was young, and he had her on a pedestal."

Whether or not Tom and Marie enjoyed a vigorous sex life, after years of struggling on his own, Parker needed a woman to take care of him. At his lowest point—when the Velares and Sedylmayr continually turned him down—he craved the reassuring words that might have come from Maria van Kuijk, who always comforted him after confrontations with his father.

Marie, whose name so resembled his mother's, and who was older than he and more seasoned in various ways of the world, was a perfect choice for a surrogate mother and lover. And she had one more irresistible quality: Marie Mott was an exceptional cook, specializing in the heavy Southern fare that Parker had become accustomed to in his travels. Surprisingly, he let Marie all but rule him.

"I think he loved her as much as he could love any woman," says Byron Raphael. "But later on, when I knew him, I got the distinct impression that he might not have liked women sexually. In fact, I was certain that the Colonel was asexual. He couldn't relate to a soft, romantic woman, but he could somehow relate to this bossy kind of lady. She had a coarse, dominant quality about her, and that apparently attracted him."

To Marie, an uneducated woman with a child to support in the heart of the Depression, any man who took a genuine interest in her must have seemed like a lifeline on the open sea. And with Marie's appetite for adventure, Parker would have seemed an appealing companion for a life that broke with conventional tastes, regular work hours, and confinement to a single location. In short, they made a good team.

And so they married, as Parker would tell the Associated Press, "in 1932, while wintering with a carnival in Tampa."

Or did they? As usual with the saga of Tom Parker, the most mundane of facts often prove to be illusions. Parker was still in the service in 1932, stationed at Fort Barrancas. Certainly he might have married Marie during a furlough, or in his months of desertion from the army. But the

Florida Office of Vital Statistics, checking the years of 1927 to 1946, finds no record of marriage between the two.

Bitsy Mott says his sister and Parker married in Alabama in 1935, a date Parker has also cited. But Mott doesn't remember the ceremony ("I guess they went to a justice of the peace or a judge, and a party was too much money"), and documents prove that Marie was not divorced from Willett Sayre until 1936. There is no marriage license on file for them in any state in which they lived or visited for any length of time.

Parker was inordinately skittish of legal documents throughout his life, fearing, perhaps, that they might lead to a discovery of his alien status. For that reason, the couple may not have officially tied the knot.

But both Byron Raphael and Gabe Tucker feel certain that Marie and Tom were legally married, since Parker was adamantly opposed to couples living together out of wedlock, a view that may have harkened to his parents' forced marriage.

The best guess, then, is that the Parkers simply laid their hands on the Showmen's League Bible, said a few somber words, and entered into a "carny wedding."

Whatever their situation, the two soon grew inseparable, and Marie proved an asset on the carnival, putting her natural good looks to advantage as a bally girl on the various revues, or "gal shows." There, she would wear a skimpy costume—little more than Egyptian veils and a few strategic beads and feathers—and sway provocatively to the music.

Often, Parker would be the talker on these shows, and Marie, as one of the line girls out front, would catch the eye of the yokels who gathered round the platform and excite them to lay down their money to go inside. But once beyond the bally platform, the pretty girls disappeared, leaving the less attractive girls to strip for the customers. In between shows, Marie helped Parker deliver the apples to Mrs. Velare, and worked as a short-order cook in several food concessions he operated on the midway.

Perhaps the most famous tale from the Parker carnival lore is the foot-long hot dog scam, which dates from this time. In this story, Parker found his niche in the shadow world of the carnival advertising foot-long hot dogs, which had just made a hit at the Chicago World's Fair. What the customer got, however, was an appropriate size bun with a smidgen of frankfurter tucked in each end and a middle generously filled with slaw and onions. Whenever a sucker wised up to the gyp and returned demanding his money, Parker, who presumably ate the middles himself, feigned surprise and pointed to a hunk of meat carefully arranged on the ground in front of the booth. "You just dropped your meat, son," he said calmly. "Now move along."

Such a stunt, worthy of the best W. C. Fields routine, is merely myth, say Parker's cronies. But Bobby Ross always swore it was true, adding that the Parkers also manned a hamburger booth where the meat was so stretched with sandwich loaf and food coloring that "by morning, you could have sold those burgers for pancakes, there was so much bread in them. They were basically bread on a bun."

By the time Bobby was twelve, he spent his summers working on the carnivals with Tom and Marie, mostly as a shill. The Parkers advertised a daily "free" drawing for a ham with purchase of one concession item, but the pork only served as a prop before landing on the Parkers' own table. Each afternoon, Tom slapped a big ham on Bobby's shoulder and had him walk the fairgrounds like an excited schoolboy. "Look what I won!" the child would cry. "If *I* can win a ham, anybody can!"

Soon Bobby would leave Granny Mott and travel with Tom and Marie full-time. Parker, only sixteen years older than the boy, treated him as a combination of son and friend, especially as Bobby grew older. He looked after him on the carnival and tried to steer him away from the heavy grift and gambling, warning that a gambler's dollar was greased. For that reason, Parker kept Bobby out of the pie car when he and Marie took it over as a privileged concession. The dining car on the show train, the pie car was also a kind of rolling casino, with slot machines and games of chance for show people only. It was here, and in the after-hours gambling tents, or "G-tops," that the carnivals carried for their private use, that Tom Parker indulged his new fascination with gambling, which would grow into an obsession throughout his life.

For a while, with Jack Kaplan's help, Parker found a solid bit of luck promoting Coca-Cola throughout Florida. But when that job played out, he was back to taxing his imagination—booking magic shows and even staging a pie-eating contest by advertising the chance to go up against the fattest man on earth, a sideshow performer hired out from Johnny J. Jones's Congress of Fat People. The carnival had taught Parker the importance of "now" money—getting it square in your hand at the time of the deal, even up front, if possible.

Occasionally, he still hooked up with Peasy Hoffman to sell ads. But the notion of making an honest dollar through the regular channels of advertising and sales didn't deliver the zing that Parker got from artfully adding a bit of humbug to his whirl of fast promises. He was particularly proud of the time he talked the owner of a funeral home into letting him bury a human being alive, drilling peepholes in the earth so the curious and macabre could talk to the man—the unfailingly cheerful Kaplan— who said he'd never been more comfortable than he was at that moment in a "breathable" straw casket.

Just to what extent Parker had become a perpetually scheming promotion machine shows up in the way he turned Franklin Street, the main drag and shopping hub of downtown Tampa, into a virtual carnival lot— selling the staid Jewish proprietors of a furniture store, for example, on a public sleep endurance contest, promising they would keep a throng of people at their display window.

At Maas Brothers downtown department store, which was the biggest and most elegant store in town—recognized as an emporium of good taste—Parker cultivated the friendship of Isaac and Abe Maas. There he hired on as Santa Claus for the Christmas shows, standing out on Franklin Street in the fluffy red-and-white suit, enticing the children of Tampa's well-heeled citizens upstairs into Toyland. He also convinced the Maas brothers that running pony rides in front of their Franklin Street store would add immeasurably to their business.

Working a deal with Bert Slover to "borrow" four carnival ponies and a small track, Parker then ambled into Rinaldi Printing Company on Tampa's Howard Street and asked about having tickets made on credit. For the loan of $5 during the Depression, Parker would reward Clyde Rinaldi in the 1960s by insisting that RCA use the small Tampa firm for much of the massive Elvis printing.

"He made Mr. Rinaldi rich," says Gabe Tucker. But Parker also forged an intimacy with him that he extended to few: Clyde Rinaldi was among the handful of people Parker told about his Dutch origins. The men remained close until Rinaldi's death in 1988.

Meeting Clyde Rinaldi was one of the rare breaks Parker got in the off-season months of the 1930s, which marked the bleakest period of an already desolate existence. Marie struggled to feed the three of them on fifty cents a day and woke up many mornings wondering how she would do it. On March 6, 1937, both she and Tom registered for Social Security and were assigned numbers just one digit apart. Parker's original application, which he filled out in ornate, European handwriting, marks the first official appearance of the middle name Andrew. He wrote that his present employer was Park Theatre, a popular movie house located at 448

West Lafayette Street. His birthplace, he claimed, was Huntington, West
Virginia. And in listing his parents, he gave life to two people who never
existed, Edward Frank Parker and Mary Ida Ponsy (sic). He signed the
form at the bottom with great, self-assured flourish.

In the fall of 1937, Parker suggested to Marie that they send Bobby
back to Granny Mott for a time and travel the country. They would hobo
when they had to and stay with carny friends when they could. Somewhere along the way, they would find a warm hearth, a bountiful table,
and the smile of good fortune.

Instead, Parker told his brother Ad three decades later, he found a
country more paralyzed by economic hardship than he had imagined.
For months on end, he and Marie lived on a dollar a week and often slept
in horse stables. In the great Southwest, they took shelter on Indian reservations, where Parker, "the big, wise white man," told fortunes to the natives and sold sparrows he painted yellow and passed off as canaries.

During such difficult times, Parker told his brother, he often thought
of the family back in Holland. Yet he still stayed silent. "I didn't want you
all to know what I was doing," he admitted. "In fact, usually I couldn't
afford the writing paper or stamps."

When the couple returned to Florida, they moved in with the Motts,
but Parker never treated his in-laws to a story about his mysterious past,
not even when he sometimes spoke in a foreign language that Bitsy mis-
took for Yiddish.

By now, Parker's desperation led him to draw a thinner line between
outright corruption and the petty larceny of the carnival. In a scam that
was vaguely reminiscent of his grandfather Ponsie—and that would later
serve as the basis for Joe David Brown's novel *Addie Pray,* adapted for
the 1973 motion picture *Paper Moon*—Parker traveled the neighboring
states posing as a Bible salesman.

"He would go into a town and read the obituaries and then have the
names embossed on a box of Bibles that he got in other cities by doing
work for churches," Byron Raphael remembers him saying. "He always
chose men's names, because he figured the widows were soft touches.
He'd walk up and ring their doorbells, ask for the husband by name, and
then pretend he didn't know he had died. And then he'd say, 'That's such
a shame, because he'd ordered this Bible and paid five dollars on it.'"

More often than not, the grieving widow, struck by her late husband's
devotion to the Lord and his eerie premonition of death, gladly forked
over the balance owed as a last fulfillment of his wishes. But if she didn't,

Parker would sometimes be "visited" by the voice of the dearly departed ("Is that my Helen there?"). A guy had to be careful, though, and save that gimmick as a last resort. "He had no conscience," says Raphael. "He thought it was funny."

Both Tom and Marie continued to dupe the unsuspecting in bolder and more blatant ways as hard times wore on. As with the Bible scam, Parker would brag about his survival methods in years to come. In the 1960s, he showed Gabe Tucker how he would walk through a marketplace and eat enough produce on the spot to make a meal. Likewise, Marie would pilfer, or "cloat" in carny language, a bag of flour from the concessions stands to carry them through.

But Marie would not be able to stop with a mere bag of flour.

"The truth is, Marie was a kleptomaniac all of her life," says her daughter-in-law Sandra Polk Ross. "I'm not sure when it started, but she was good at it—whatever she could palm or pocket. When I first met Bob, and Marie would say she wanted to go shopping, Bob would tell me to take her and keep an eye on her, and pay for whatever she took, and Colonel would reimburse me."

In the carnival years, the showman who had spent his life treading the line between deals and ideals found it increasingly difficult to tell the difference in the kind of cleverness and deceit born of need and the shameful violation of others.

During the late 1950s, in his early Hollywood days with Presley, Parker stunned the old-guard studio heads when he suggested how they could really make money on their pictures: charge the audience $1.50 to get in and another $3 to get out. It was exactly what he had done in the carnival when he staged a tent show in a cow pasture, far away from the midway, and designated one flap as the only exit. Once outside the tent, the furious patrons had a choice of walking a quarter of a mile through a field covered in cow manure or renting one of Parker's ponies to carry them through. Parker, like most of the carnies of the era, saw nothing reprehensible about it.

In the spring of 1954, when RCA Records sent the Colonel out to tour some of its hillbilly stars as the RCA Country Caravan, Brad McCuen, one of the company's Southern field men, was assigned to accompany the prickly Parker on the road.

As part of their conversations during the long drives, Parker regaled McCuen, a child of the Depression, with the hijinks of his carnival life in the 1930s. He shared the details of how he and two grifting confeder-

ates—known in the trade as the "broad mob"—would set up the unsuspecting mark for crooked game operations, staging the three-card monte,
in which a shill makes a bettor think he can win by cheating the dealer, or
the shell game, in which the pea under the shell was actually under the
table. As he told McCuen, you had to know how to choose your sucker,
see when he was just about to buckle, and seize the psychological moment. To know when it arrived . . . Ah! That was the art of grifting!

According to Byron Raphael, Parker thought there was no finer
practitioner than Jew Murphy, an old-fashioned peddler turned flim-
flam man.

"The Colonel took me to this one little carnival in Louisiana just so I
could see him," remembers Raphael. "Murphy would stand by this
wagon full of shiny objects, and he'd start by saying, 'Who'll give me a
dollar for one of these beautiful lighters?' And people would crowd
around and give him a buck.

"The Colonel would turn to me and say, 'Now watch how he hypno-
tizes people.' And it was the most amazing thing. Murphy would give
somebody a clock, and thirty or forty people would start waving five-
dollar bills over their heads. His assistant would rush through the crowd
and pull that money right out of their hands." Everyone received a piece
of merchandise, but it was always a "lumpy," some substandard item,
never one of the beautiful clocks from the first row of the wagon.

Raphael believes that Parker gleaned much of his skewed business philosophy from Murphy and the older confidence men of his ilk: in the real
workaday world, you either conned somebody, or you got conned. It was
as simple as that. "He told me that was what life was about, and he
meant it," says Raphael. "He treated everything like a carnival."

8

DEEPER INTO AMERICA

I N 1938 Parker was running a penny arcade on the Royal American, selling picture cards of movie stars, cowboys, and sports heroes, dispensed in sliding slot machines for one cent apiece, when he met Gene Austin, the first of several men who took his bravado seriously.

The popular singer was working the theater circuit to support his first and only Western film, *Songs and Saddles*. Parker, smitten with the notion of meeting a living legend—the high-voiced crooner was known far and wide as "the Voice of the Southland"—approached him and told him of his background in carnivals, "starting as a boy with his family," as Austin would remember. The carny laid it on thick, promising that as a "crackerjack press agent and manager," he knew every important contact in the region.

Austin had no need for Parker's services just then, but the singer took his address and noted that Parker was "a great salesman who had the ability to back up his conversation." Several months later, Austin got in touch.

In his prime, Gene Austin had been a sensation beyond all imagining. The best-known singer of the late 1920s, Austin became not just the first crooner, making way for Rudy Vallee and Bing Crosby, but the first true pop star, with the attendant fame and adulation that would later grace the careers of Frank Sinatra, Elvis Presley, and the Beatles. From 1924 to 1934, he sold an astonishing 86 million records—5 million alone of "My Blue Heaven," an upbeat ballad that celebrated the domestic bliss of "Just Molly and me/And baby makes three." Grown men blubbered.

Austin's first royalty check from RCA Victor Records totaled $96,000, an almost unfathomable sum in the pre–income tax years of the '20s. But soon that and the $17 million that followed disappeared like a wispy dream, squandered on nights of carousing with famous friends like

Louisiana politician Huey Long and jazz great Louis Armstrong, and on the buying of cars, mansions, and speakeasies.

By the time Austin hooked up with Tom Parker in the late '30s, it was all but over. The '29 crash had nearly buried the entertainment industry, and when it recovered, Bing Crosby had eclipsed him in popularity. Austin, a two-fisted drinker who had begun to experience throat problems ten years earlier, doubted that his voice would hold up much longer.

On the night he chanced to meet Parker, Austin, then thirty-eight years old, was just about to headline a tour of the Star-O-Rama Canvas Theater, a traveling tent show that traversed the rural South in nine large trucks. That's when he sent a wire to Parker, who agreed to meet him in Atlanta and showed up with Marie in tow. On the surface, Gene Austin and Tom Parker—or Tommy, as he called him—made an odd couple, the tuxedoed toast of the town and the coarse young carny with his righteous disregard for Middle America's social norms and etiquette. But Austin took an immediate liking to Parker, who loved to hear about the grander escapades of Austin's career, when as a young heartthrob, Austin would return to his hotel room to find women hiding under the bed. Parker was enthralled; what he wouldn't give for an act like that!

For now, Parker busied himself with the job at hand, which was to help Austin's new manager, Jack Garns, secure bookings for the tent show and to promote them with the carnival techniques he'd learned from Peasy Hoffman. Driving an old panel truck with its best days behind it, Parker traveled the backwoods towns of the South to stake out a prime lot for Hoxie Tucker, the boss canvas man responsible for hauling and maintaining the three-ring tents. Then he set about securing permits, lining up sponsors, scheduling advertising, handing out flyers, and finally billing posters, plastering the paper sheets on anything that didn't move, using a glue made out of flour and water. In essence, his job was to do almost anything he could to drum up business, ballyhoo the star, and diddle the townsfolk into a close approximation of frenzy.

That included the restaurateurs, from whom he not only solicited tie-in advertising, but also promoted free meals, hinting that the troupe might want to eat there every night, never mentioning that the Star-O-Rama carried its own cookhouse.

"It was obvious Tom knew his business by the way he went about things," the singer wrote in his autobiography, *Gene Austin's Ol' Buddy.* "In a short while, he had the show going full blast. It looked like we would never know anything but success and money."

Such sweet victory convinced Parker, with his almost maniacal need for control, that he, and not Jack Garns, should guide Gene's career. In becoming an important manager, Parker saw, he might attain a level of power, fame, and wealth on his own. As he told Gabe Tucker years later, "The stars come and go, but a manager can work until he dies."

Little by little, Parker began to find reasons to circle back to the show, to get closer to Austin and to ease out the hapless Garns, much the way he would outmaneuver others in the early days of Elvis Presley's career.

Whether Parker actually became Austin's manager during those years, as he later claimed, is open to dispute. But the two became fast friends, and whenever the opportunity allowed, they headed for Hot Springs, Arkansas, to sample the glamour of the fast life—of racetracks and night life and illegal gambling, a smooth sleight of hand practiced in elegant casinos that doubled as meeting places for big-name entertainers and notorious racketeers.

The giddy atmosphere of Hot Springs clearly agreed with him. In a picture taken there in 1939, a grinning Parker strolls down the sidewalk arm in arm with Hoxie Tucker, and in his hepcat sunglasses, two-tone shoes, and combed-back hair—thinning dramatically with each passing year—Parker was the very definition of the confident con on the make. Walking the streets of Hot Springs, Arkansas, that summer day, Andreas van Kuijk unmasked Tom Parker for what he was, the hustler extraordinaire. Never again would he allow himself to appear so slick and unguarded.

At the season's end, Austin crowed about his "proud, bulging bank account." But it was then that Austin learned that the government was attaching most of the show's profits for back taxes. Now Parker was forced to be creative in keeping the show up and running. When the troupe played Tupelo, Mississippi, he found prophetic good luck in the hometown of then five-year-old Elvis Presley. "We sold out and made enough money to get out of town," Parker remembered years later, speaking in that same small town, and adding how he'd left the tires off the truck as collateral for the grocer, "which we did in a lot of small cities in those depressed times."

However, when the outcome was different and they still owed a local hotel, Parker would string up a big banner—HELD OVER BY POPULAR DEMAND!—and the show would stay on until the bill was paid.

The Star-O-Rama Canvas Theatre continued to limp along for several months, but only through Parker's reliance on human nature. Before he took to the road each time, he'd have Austin sign a fistful of checks, which he presented at gas stations with his usual pomp and flourish, telling everybody how grand it was to work for the great Gene Austin. "That's a real autograph there—you might want to hang that on the wall!" he'd suggest to the owners, since each check framed meant one fewer cashed, a stunt he would repeat with Elvis in the mid-'50s.

Finally, though, there was no stopping the inevitable, which arrived during a tour of Virginia in 1940, when a marshal attached the gate receipts and equipment.

In the bleak days of 1940, with a family to care for and no money coming in, Parker found it more difficult to believe that things would soon get better, especially for a Dutchman whose accent sounded vaguely German as the country inched closer to conflict overseas.

On September 1, 1939, the citizens of Tampa unfolded the *Morning Tribune* to find the banner headline of WAR and the chilling news that German planes had just bombed Warsaw.

Within a year of that terrible day, two events transpired that might have dramatically altered the fate of both Andreas van Kuijk and Thomas Parker.

The first was the congressional passage of the Smith Act, or the Alien Registration Act of 1940, which required all non-U.S. citizens to register with the federal government.

Fathered by Congressman Howard Smith of Virginia, the act was aimed at curbing subversive activities. But in forcing all aliens to register, at its heart, the act worked to offer legalization to millions who had not followed proper channels to remain in the country. Instead of being deported, as dictated by previous laws, an illegal alien would now be allowed to stay if he could prove five years of residence with good moral character, or if he showed that deportation would result in serious economic detriment to a spouse, parent, or minor child who was a U.S. citizen or a lawfully permanent resident.

The Alien Registration Act of 1940 should have thrilled Andreas van Kuijk. Not only did it offer amnesty for his eleven years of illegal residency, but as with his U.S. Army experience, it could set him on a path to become a U.S. citizen. Yet as Tom Parker, he had a decidedly strange reaction to this extraordinary opportunity—he ignored it. And in doing so, he passed up a chance to easily resolve his illegal status.

The irony, says Marian Smith of the Immigration and Naturalization Service, is that "as an overstayed crewman [from 1929], after three to five years, he might have been nondeportable, in that the statutes of limitations would have run out on that offense. But to not register at all [in 1940] was a big violation. And yet we have no record of him."

Why would Parker be so reckless? His reaction to the second important event of 1940, that of the first peacetime draft law in U.S. history, was just as strange.

For on October 16, when Thomas Andrew Parker went to local board 1 in the First National Bank Building to fill out his registration card and establish a classification record, he made no mention of prior service in any branch of the armed services. By using his new middle name, he silently insisted that it was Thomas Parker who had served in the U.S. Army, not Thomas *Andrew* Parker. Tom Parker dared not chance resurrecting old ghosts from his past, especially one from 1933 who had undergone a particularly horrific stay at Walter Reed Army Hospital.

Perhaps because the Parkers never stayed long in one place, in filling out the registration card, Parker gave the Motts' address—1210 West Platt Street—as his own. And in big-shot style, he named Gene Austin, 181 South Poinsettia Place, Hollywood, California, as his employer.

Parker's real source of income during this time was far less glamorous than any alliance with Hollywood. After the heady experience of guiding Austin's career, Parker was now reduced to tending animals at the fairgrounds, where he also ran pony rides, employing a string of six ponies he'd bought in Kentucky while scouting locations for Austin.

Aside from the ownership of the horses—which he got neighbor children to groom by pretending to name one after each of them—he was no further along than when he first came out of the army.

Now that the off-season had arrived, Parker struggled to make ends meet, and as usual in such dire situations, turned to a scam. He dug a hole in the front yard, erected a three-foot-high tarpaulin wall around it, installed one of the ponies in the hole, filled dirt in around the animal's feet, and covered its legs with straw to make it appear shorter than normal. Then he hammered a sign into the ground: SEE THE WORLD'S SMALLEST PONY—ONLY 10 CENTS! The neighbors reported him to the authorities, who threatened to haul him in.

Yet just as Parker's days of working his beloved ponies appeared at an end, he received perhaps the keenest stroke of good fortune of his thirty-one years. In the late fall of 1940, he heard about an opening for a field agent at the Hillsborough County Humane Society, the shelter for homeless animals.

The Humane Society position seemed custom made for Parker's unusual background—a job that allowed him to indulge his love and understanding of animals while calling on his skills as a promoter. In between rescuing mewing kittens hung in trees and caring for the occasional stray cow, Parker was to spearhead fund-raising drives that would bring the shelter into the black.

The job paid a salary, of course, the first steady paycheck Parker received since the early months of the Gene Austin tent show. But it was the perks of the job that turned Parker's head, especially the furnished, rent-free apartment, which ran the full length of the second floor of the Humane Society, located in a pretty, ornate building festooned with Spanish accents at 3607 North Armenia Avenue, then a remote area of West Tampa.

The apartment was large enough for Tom, Marie, and fifteen-year-old Bobby—certainly bigger than any living quarters the family had occupied before—and if it bothered Parker that the arrangement was eerily reminiscent of the van Kuijk family's rooms over the van Gend en Loos stables, he quickly dismissed such thoughts upon learning what else the job had to offer. Should he convert his automobile into an "emergency ambulance" for the transportation of animals, for example, the shelter would furnish his gasoline and tires, even if the country entered the war and such commodities became rationed.

In this fashion, Parker could feed his insatiable lust for free goods and services, as well as gloat that he had been able to manipulate the system as never before. The job gave him the appearance of a county official, with a status and authority that elevated him, if only slightly, above the average citizen. He would wear a furnished uniform of light shirt, dark pants, and official cap and visor, which delighted him beyond reason.

From the outset, Parker tackled the job with gusto, setting up a meticulous log of every ambulance run and rescue mission. In November 1940, he recorded in precise handwriting, "Beating pony. Columbus Drive. Complaint settled," and, "Goat no water. Okay. McBerry St." Later, he turned more loquacious: "Horse with no shoe pulling ice wagon. Sixth Avenue. Man warned to get shoes on horse." And, "Boys shooting birds. Belmont Heights. Field agent gave boys lecture."

The Hillsborough County Humane Society was in desperate need of an image boost and makeover, and the new field agent started out with a myriad of plans for raising money. He first asked local businessmen to donate money for pet supplies, but that stopped when the word got out that Parker had traded cases of animal food for tuna fish and prime cuts of meat that the Parkers would eat themselves. Then he staged a dog's "fall" into a deep but narrow hole so he could take up a collection to hire a midget to crawl down for the "rescue." Few who came to the Humane Society for any reason left without a pet, and within a year of Parker's appointment, the Humane Society was solvent. What nobody understood, Parker thought, was that he didn't really give away fluffy kittens and snowball pups. He sold magic.

In seeking frequent newspaper coverage for the shelter's activities, Parker also made himself a familiar figure in the community. He delighted in dressing up as Santa and giving puppies away to children at Christmas. And by donning the Santa Claus suit—which he reprised at the Maas Brothers department store to earn money for the pound—Parker, in essence, wore yet another "uniform," casting himself as the compassionate philanthropist, a figure to be loved and trusted. He would return to the role each December throughout his life, both because he enjoyed giving presents to children and because the persona made him out to be a star. In his hungrier moments, he sometimes asked the children if they wouldn't like to take Santa out for a hamburger afterward.

Parker's assistant during the Humane Society days was a twenty-three-year-old flunky with the unlikely name of Bevo Bevis. Mildly mentally retarded from birth, Jason Boyd Bevis Jr. had lost his father, a Phenix City, Alabama, undertaker, at age twelve, and moved to Tampa with his mother and brother shortly thereafter. In regarding Parker as a surrogate father, even calling him Pops, Bevo, with his simpleton's stare, was all too happy to carry out any request.

The field agent treated Bevo almost like a child, using him to do a lot of the grunt work that Bobby or Marie wouldn't tackle without a fuss. Bevo's family resented how Parker took advantage of the boy's disability to assign him the most undesirable tasks, but in the presence of others, Parker referred to him as Mr. Bevis.

Bevo came in particularly handy when Parker set up one of his most inspired and creative moneymaking schemes, that of the pet cemetery. First, Parker called for a "high-level conference" with Bevo in the large yard that ran behind the building and the wire pens out back, telling him they were about to embark on a "great adventure." Then he instructed him to cut down the overgrowth, pick up the broken bottles and debris, and manicure the grass.

"As you know, Mr. Bevis," he explained, "we have many important people coming out here. We're going to start a new project, and you will be meeting some of the leading citizens in the course of it. I want them to address you by your new title, General Manager of Perpetual Care for Deceased Pets."

As Bevo readied the lot, Parker visited a monument company and talked the owner into making a free doggy tombstone (HERE LIES SPOT, A BELOVED AND FAITHFUL COMPANION), promising that many of Tampa's bereaved pet owners would soon set their precious dogs and cats to eternal rest behind the shelter. Bevo dug a small hole in the backyard, pushed up a mound of dirt, and placed Spot's marker at the head.

Parker was pleased with himself. No pet lover could resist it. He'd pay the monument company $15 and charge the owners $50. But why stop there? "Bevo," he called across the yard, "can you make little coffins?" Bevo was hardly a carpenter, but he told Pops he would try, and soon Parker figured he could hike the cost of a Fido funeral up to $100 with the casket and a promise to decorate the grave with fresh daisies, castoffs he got free from the neighborhood florists.

If a pet owner happened to stop by and express surprise at the condition of the flowers, Parker would frown and shake his head. "I wish you could have been here yesterday when we placed them. They're a bit wilted now, but they looked sensational then. Isn't that right, Mr. Bevis?"

Bevo Bevis would thread his way in and out of Parker's life until his death at age sixty-two in 1980. Their relationship was always marred by mutual frustration, and during that forty-year span, Parker fired him almost as many times as Bevo quit and went home to Tampa. As time went on, Parker treated him with increasing cruelty, making him the butt of jokes and placing him in countless humiliating situations.

"Colonel took care of Bevo, but he was rough on Bevo, too," remembers Parker's friend Al Dvorin. "He made Bevo the fall guy."

Despite all of his shortcomings and annoying faults, the pathetic Bevo was, in essence, the first in a long line of younger associates on whom Parker conferred the title of son. Through the years, there would be at least a dozen such young men—from Byron Raphael, to the actor George Hamilton, to the concert promoters Mike Crowley and Greg McDonald, to country music's LeGarde twins, Ted and Tom.

Just why Parker needed so many surrogates, especially since he already had a stepson in Bobby Ross, begs the question. And since Parker, from all reports, adored children, the fact that he and Marie had no offspring of their own sets up another debate.

Certainly the Parkers were devoted to each other. At the Humane Society, Marie helped him care for the animals and marshaled the book-keeping records. She would work right by Parker's side through the Eddy Arnold era. And though the world of country music and rock and roll was a hotbed of sexuality, no story ever circulated of Parker having affairs, at least not in the years when Marie was vital and healthy.

"He was always so crazy about Marie in the days that I was around him," says music executive Buddy Killen, who first met the Parkers in the early '50s. And then came that weird exchange during the Country and Western Disc Jockey convention, when Killen walked out of Nashville's Andrew Jackson Hotel just as the Parkers walked in.

"Marie yelled, 'Hey Buddy!' And she held her arms out and I ran over and hugged her and kissed her on the cheek. And Tom said, 'Hey, boy, stop that! Don't do that anymore!' And he was very serious. I was just a kid, so I wasn't interested in his wife. But he didn't like anybody kissing on her, even a little peck."

In Killen's estimation, the Parkers had a fabulous marriage. But the union may have been based more on the practicalities of partnership, Parker's display of jealousy notwithstanding. "I know he and Marie weren't happy at home, or at least not as the years went on," says Gabe Tucker. The main problem, both Tucker and Bitsy Mott assert, was Parker's domination. "As for kids," says Tucker, "he liked kids, but he didn't want them around too long."

Parker's perceived fear of emotional intimacy, except with select friends through the years, seemed to spill over into a fear of another kind. Whether rooted in anger or in his need to control, Parker often had a violent reaction to being touched, especially by a woman. Someone as non-threatening as a coffee shop waitress, taking his elbow as she poured a cup of coffee, could raise an outburst in him that ruined the day.

Agreeing with Byron Raphael, psychologist Peter Whitmer believes Parker was simply asexual. One family member believes he was sterile, the aftereffects of mumps he suffered from at age nine.

Instead of having his own children, then, Parker found it more desirable to choose them, as with his surrogate sons, who tended to revere him as a heroic figure, and most of all, wouldn't think of drawing too much attention to themselves in Parker's presence.

Bobby Ross's refusal to adhere to Parker's notion of the father-son alliance was at the core of a relationship that became difficult over time. Bobby looked at Parker more as an older friend than as a father, and

Parker, who never legally adopted him, seems to have held him at emotional bay.

By his high school years, Bobby had begun to exert his independence, finding employment first as a delivery boy for a local drugstore, and then at Tampa Shipbuilding, saving enough money to buy a used car. The youngster either earned, or was provided with, whatever accoutrements he needed in those crucial years of peer pressure, dating, and social growth, and Bobby proved to be a popular boy at school, his senior class voting him the "most athletic" with the "ideal senior smile."

But Parker apparently resented the handsome teen's popularity, as well as his ease with women, for the quick-witted Bobby had inherited his biological father's striking good looks and appetite for the opposite sex. In his job as the drugstore delivery boy, he'd sometimes get a call for a quart of ice cream, be invited inside by the lady of the house, and "and be there long enough for the ice cream to melt," says Sandra Polk Ross. "Colonel suppressed Bobby, because he didn't want him to have the attention. All of the girls thought he was wonderful."

One girl had found Bobby irresistible since the age of twelve. Marian DeDyne, a petite, dark-haired beauty, was Bobby's constant companion during high school, and on August 18, 1944, two months after Bobby graduated, they married.

In a photo taken at a family picnic in 1943, Bobby beams to have her beside him, as a pudgy but youthful Parker, dressed in Bermuda shorts, dives into an enormous bowl of ice cream. Such indulgences were not lost on the shelter's occasional volunteers, who harbored resentment over Parker's exacting standards for cleanliness and order, and for his strange and endless requests to be addressed as "Doctor." Whether anyone had the nerve to say it to his face, secretly they referred to the ever-ballooning Parker with a more sardonic nickname: "Tiny."

9

NASHVILLE'S NASAL WHINE:

JAMUP AND HONEY,

EDDY ARNOLD, AND HANK SNOW

D U R I N G his years of caring for Tampa's displaced pets, Parker spun off the career that would eventually lead him out of Florida and up to Tennessee—that of a country music concert promoter, booking Grand Ole Opry stars out of Nashville. He started in 1941 as the nation went to war, mostly to earn money for the Humane Society. Parker knew nothing about country-and-western music, with its predominant themes of Mother, death, and the lamentable wages of sin, preferring the sentimental crooning of Gene Austin to the nasal whine of Nashville. But he'd had it on good authority that hillbilly was the music of the common man, in this case, the Florida farmers and working class, who revered the Opry stars as something close to demigods. And so, with a sliver of the proceeds going to the war effort, Parker and two partners rented the great, sprawling Fort Homer W. Hesterly National Guard Armory, a recently completed WPA project on Howard Avenue.

Parker's first venture into concert promotion starred the future "King of the Hillbillies" (later changed to "the King of Country Music"), Roy Acuff, and a new comic named Minnie Pearl, who had just joined the Grand Ole Opry in November 1940. That December, she started on the road with Acuff at $50 a week, but only under the directive that she abbreviate her opening patter: "How-dee! I'm just so proud to be here! I'm so proud I could come!" Acuff, the son of a Baptist preacher, got drunk on occasion, but once he became the Opry's first network radio host in 1939, he kept his professional image clean as a cat's paw. And so he took his "extra added attraction" aside and spoke in low tones. "Minnie, you'll have to leave off that last part. It's just too suggestive."

A twenty-nine-year-old college-educated actress, Pearl, née Sarah Ophelia Colley, was the daughter of a prosperous Tennessee lumber man who'd lost his fortune in the crash of '29. Although the cultured Colley had traveled the Deep South organizing amateur productions of drama and musical comedy—that was where she'd gleaned the inspiration for the character of Minnie Pearl, the country girl in the Mary Janes with an eye toward "ketchin' fellers"—the country music world seemed like a sideshow in comparison. Pearl could hardly believe the lackadaisical way the community lived and conducted its business.

"When I came along," she remembered, "nobody owned their home. They lived in trailers or rooming houses. Nobody had any insurance, and very few of them had bank accounts. They carried all the money they had with them. When one of 'em got ready to buy a house, the real estate man would say, 'How do you intend to take care of this?' And they'd say, 'Will cash do?' They had no idea how big this thing was going to be."

In contrast, Pearl discovered, Parker was oddly shrewd about how the music could bring in the dollars. For his first country show, he lined up a promotion with a grocery store chain to sell discount tickets with a newspaper coupon. As Pearl remembered, the audience was large enough to fill the house for several performances.

"It was the first time we had any connection with anything like that," she said. "The store paid for the advertising, and many more tickets were sold, because every [grocery] cashier in a three-county area was working what amounted to a box office. The man was thinking even then."

The success of the Roy Acuff concert spurred Parker to expand his involvement in the country music milieu, and now he approached Acuff about becoming his manager. But Acuff, whose sister, Sue, lived in Tampa and knew his reputation ("You don't want the *dogcatcher!*"), found Parker's techniques far too radical for the Opry's staid image.

Acuff, the biggest star on the Opry other than Bill Monroe, saw that Parker was right when he told him he needed to gauge his fee to a percentage of whatever the promoter took in, plus a guarantee. But no one else in country music was doing it, and it just didn't seem the Christian way. Besides, Parker wanted complete control of Acuff's career, which the stony-faced bandleader found intolerable.

Yet for a brief period, the two men discussed Acuff's invitation for Parker to move to Nashville. But when Parker told the star he wanted him to leave the Opry, which paid only scale, for more lucrative personal appearances, the management deal died on the vine. Still, Parker hung tight as an Alabama tick, and to try to ease him out gently, Acuff let him book the dates he still had open, and arranged for him to market his new Roy Acuff Flour throughout Florida.

Before they parted, Acuff gave the budding entrepreneur one piece of gold-plated advice: Eddy Arnold. Now, *that* was a young man to keep an eye on. The smooth-voiced singer was the featured vocalist for Pee Wee King's Golden West Cowboys, and he "could charm the warts off a hog's back." It was only a matter of time before a talent like that went solo. Any record company would fall over itself to snag him.

In 1942, Parker and his partners branched out their country concert promotions, not so much to benefit the Humane Society, but to benefit themselves. More and more, Parker began distancing himself from his duties at the shelter to learn more about the Nashville way of doing business. As Acuff had advised him, he kept the name Eddy Arnold fresh in his mind.

Away from his job, Parker now began to wear a string tie to accentuate his new persona as a Southern eccentric. He also worked to make his speech more folksy and smoothed some of the rough edges off his accent, although he would always retain a hint of a lisp. When he got nervous, which was rare, he lapsed into a strange linguistic valley between Dutch and English, and involuntarily substituted the word *me* for *I*, as in, "Me got to go now." Whether he intended it, the slip only served to make him seem more of an insular, small-town character.

Soon Parker was booking shows in tandem with two of country music's best promoters, the congenial J. L. Frank and Oscar Davis. Parker shared an immediate affinity with the latter. The gravel-voiced Rhode Islander had come to concert promotions from a career in the carnival, where he toured a girl "frozen alive" in ice, going on to present her at the 1939 New York World's Fair. Like Parker, Davis never really left the carnival, and his signature slogan—"Don't You Dare Miss It!"—was straight out of carny parlance.

Parker saw that Joe Frank was a valuable ally for a variety of reasons, but he also had a hidden motive for wanting to cultivate him: Frank was Pee Wee King's father-in-law and managed King's Golden West Cowboys band. That put Parker one step closer to the young Eddy Arnold.

By 1942, Parker must have marveled at the twists of fate that had delivered such events in his life. In the last two years, the thirty-three-year-old had moved from near destitution to a position of relative prosperity. Now his sideline of concert promotions not only offered a new challenge and an avenue back into show business, with its all-important contacts, but also dramatically altered the course of Parker's life. The concerts proved more lucrative than he imagined, even as the profits were split among his partners. He saw how independent promoters and managers such as Joe Frank and Oscar Davis had been sharp to recognize the nearly limitless potential of the burgeoning country music business, and he intended to claim a large piece of it for himself.

However, Parker's rash of good fortune also triggered a potential problem in the form of an Internal Revenue Service audit. For an illegal alien who had refused to comply with the Smith Act, the demand to appear before an agent of the federal government must have been terrifying.

And so Parker approached the IRS situation as he would every other tight spot of his life—with a snow job. He began by putting a false bottom, about four inches deep, in the kind of small trunk that show people carried, and then gathered every bill that he could find. Outside the auditor's office, he carefully arranged a wad of papers so that several poked out of the lips of the trunk and, once inside, dumped the lot on the agent's desk with a ceremonious *whoosh!* Then, like a magician, he continued to make them appear—from his pockets, his hat, his pants legs—in a dazzling display.

To Parker's extraordinary luck, the auditor happened to have a thundering headache—the staid IRS agent had uncharacteristically tied one on the night before.

"Tom said the guy started pacing back and forth, just holding his head," remembers Gabe Tucker. "And Tom told him, 'Hell, let's count 'em up and see if I owe you something. If I do, me'll pay it. But I can't be up here all week.' It didn't take him long to get out of there, and after all that, he didn't owe a damn thing."

But trouble with the IRS would remain one of Parker's biggest fears, and in the future, he would do almost anything to avoid the tax man's scrutiny and suspicion.

He had gotten an even bigger scare in January 1942, when he received the draft board's questionnaire to determine his classification for military service. As before, the record shows that he made no mention of his previous army experience, but with Bobby then still at home, he argued that he should be classified 3-A, or "deferred for dependency reasons." The board accepted his claim.

In March 1944, the draft board came calling again, reclassifying Parker as 1-A, or "available for military service." With that, Parker, whose weight already exceeded that of most healthy males of his height and age group, began piling on food in an effort to have himself reclassified 4-F. Soon, with a stack of three chins bobbing on a thick stalk of a neck and his great protuberance of a belly expanding from his imposing waist, he swelled to such proportions as to resemble his personal totem, the elephant. But it did the trick.

To those around him, Parker undoubtedly appeared to go through the war years without showing the slightest hint of concern about the European front or the effects of a bombing campaign on neutral Holland. But at the same time that his sister Johanna, hoping to learn some word of him, was passing his photograph among American soldiers liberating the Netherlands, Andreas van Kuijk, dressed in his dogcatcher's uniform, sat at his desk in the Hillsborough County Humane Society, writing secret missives to a soldier wearing the uniform of the Dutch army in the city of Tilburg, some fifteen miles east of Breda. The soldier, who was serving in the Prinses Irene Brigade, a Dutch unit attached to the U.S. Army, was sorry to report before the war's end that the woman about whom his correspondent inquired, Maria Ponsie van Kuijk, had died. To the recipient, half a world away, the news was stunning. It would take a gathering around God's table before Andre would see his mother again.

"When I heard that Mother was dead," he told his brother Ad in 1961, "for me, Holland was also dead. She was my only real tie to Holland." But it wasn't until that late date of 1961 that Andre learned that the sad news from the Dutch soldier had been a tragic misunderstanding. Maria van Kuijk had, indeed, lived through the war, but she had also hurled herself into her grief—surely her son himself had not survived, or he would have sent some sort of sign. Now she lay under the good earth with an inconsolable heart, never knowing that her Andre was still alive in America, evolving into the Someone he promised he would be.

In August 1942, Parker became fixated on the name of a man he thought might help him attain that dream. A Warner Bros. film crew came to Tampa to shoot a war movie called *Air Force,* and the production staff asked if the Humane Society could bring a couple of appealing dogs to Drew Field. Parker was only too happy to be around big-name show people again and held a laughing canine to pose with actor Gig Young for a *Tampa Tribune* photographer.

"Who is the head man here?" Parker had demanded on arriving. "The director is Howard Hawks," he was told. "Yes, but who is the very top man?" "That would be Hal Wallis." The producer was in California, and unable to go to Florida. But Wallis would be the name Parker remembered.

Other film crews would come to Tampa, drawn by the city's balmy weather and the long hours of daylight. The following winter, MGM brought Spencer Tracy and Irene Dunne to town to make *A Guy Named Joe*. The Humane Society was again called on to provide animal costars, and Parker, desperate to make the acquaintance of anyone in the film community, invited the camera crew on a family outing.

Still, he obsessed about Wallis. In the old days, the pickpockets, grifters, and gamblers who traveled by rail often had their victim marked before they ever boarded the train. And so was it with Parker and Wallis. The producer could be his ticket in Hollywood.

The same summer that Wallis's crew came to town, Parker was so heady with success that he made a wild decision. The man whose mission seemed to be to bilk anyone and everyone out of as many goods and services as possible, moved his family out of the free apartment over the Humane Society and into a ranch home at 4218 San Pedro in the newly developed Palma Ceia area of South Tampa.

For the time being, Parker tried to restrict his promotions to three key Florida cities—Orlando, Daytona Beach, and Jacksonville, where he would hire a woman named Mae Boren Axton, who did promotion and publicity to offset her occasional songwriting—and listed himself as a "traveling agent" in the Tampa directory. Working out of the San Pedro house, he called his new venture Tom Parker's Hillbilly Jamboree and had a box of business cards printed for Ottie P. Johnson, "advertising manager" for press and radio.

In early 1943, through an arrangement with J. L. Frank, Parker booked Pee Wee King and His Golden West Cowboys into a Tampa hotel for a Humane Society show and dance. From there, the band played three weeks of theater dates for him throughout Florida, most of them by the bicycle method, an exhausting practice that required them to play two theaters in the same night, running back and forth between the venues while a movie showed. Joe Frank had praised Parker's style to his son-in-law, and King understood why—Parker was one of the most energetic men he'd ever seen.

"Regardless of how big the advance sale was, he always tried harder to get bigger crowds, and he was always very good to the entertainers," King said.

Parker, who had a tin ear and cared nothing about music or individual performers other than how many tickets they sold, brought King's band to Florida for two reasons: first, to flatter Joe Frank by booking his son-in-law and, more important, to get a good look at Eddy Arnold.

He assessed Arnold's square-jawed profile and liked what he saw. Then he wondered if the tall twenty-four-year-old with the full-throated baritone could be the heir to the kind of fortune and record sales that the faded Gene Austin had known in his heyday and, better still, if Arnold had the screen presence to carry a Hollywood film. But he made no move to offer a management contract once Arnold left King's band that May: Marie was adamantly opposed to pulling up stakes and moving to Nashville, and Parker feared that Joe Frank would want to keep Eddy in his personal stable.

The next time Parker and Arnold met was the fall of 1943. By now, Eddy had assembled his own band, the Tennessee Plowboys, and the foursome, dressed in country gentlemen attire, picked and sang live each morning for the farmers and early risers over Nashville's WSM radio. Arnold also occasionally appeared on an early-evening show that was produced out of the WSM studios before the Opry. One such Saturday night, Arnold was tuning up before that show when Parker, who happened to be in Nashville on one of his talent-scouting trips, heard Arnold's name on a station promo and rushed over to catch the singer before he went on the air.

"He introduced himself to me," Arnold remembered, and started with the homespun patter that he'd refined to seductive art—said he'd heard a lot of good things about Eddy since he'd gone out on his own, had just seen the profile of him in *Radio Mirror* magazine, and hoped they'd work together soon. Then he lit into his management pitch.

Arnold smiled a toothy grin and thanked him but explained that he was already in negotiation with Dean Upson, the WSM Artist Service Bureau chief, about that very thing.

"Well," Parker added, "I manage Gene Austin, you know." Arnold's face lit up, and the Tampa dogcatcher knew he'd rolled a lucky seven. Gene Austin had long been one of Eddy's inspirations. And so it was with two agendas that Parker took Austin backstage at Nashville's Ryman Auditorium for a Grand Ole Opry performance not long after that meeting with Arnold at WSM. Austin had filed for bankruptcy the previous year, and if Parker could get him on the Opry to do a song or two, maybe book some club dates out of it, he'd be only too happy to help an old friend. If in the process Parker should just happen to give Eddy Arnold the thrill of his life by introducing him to his hero, well, certainly there'd be no harm in that.

Arnold recalls that when they talked in earnest, Parker didn't mince words. "Tom was obviously interested in finding a new, young artist," Arnold says. "Seemed like he knew what he was talking about. And I was a hungry boy."

After that, Parker began to pop up more and more around Nashville, getting in Eddy's face whenever possible. Sooner or later, he would find a way to woo the Plowboy.

Parker's frequent trips to Nashville reminded him just how much he missed the traveling and the exhilarating cadence of the wheels rolling beneath him. For that reason—and to study the mind-set of the typical country musician, whose generally honest and unfettered psyche he had yet to fully grasp—Parker signed on as Pee Wee King's road manager for the bulk of the 1943 season. Then, as King remembers, Parker was always eager to play cards and shoot dice with the band to kill the long hours on the drives between dates, keeping a $100 bill in his wallet for gambling emergencies.

When the tour ended, he returned to Florida and booked personal appearances for newcomer Ernest Tubb. Parker was one of the best promoters there was, in Tubb's estimation, but he told his son, Justin, that he'd never use him on a long-term basis because "he'd constantly try to put one over on you—that was the life he'd led as a carny."

Parker saw the extreme advantage to staying on good terms with a rising star like Tubb. Soon Parker surprised Justin, then almost nine, and his younger sister, Elaine, with the magnanimous gift of two ponies: a black-and-white paint named Honey for Justin, and a smaller Shetland and buckboard for his sister.

The Tubb children, not knowing that Parker needed to unload the last vestiges of his kiddie ride concessions, were thrilled at such benevolence, even if Elaine's pony, Trigger, was, in fact, both old and blind. But their father suspected that Parker seldom did a favor without expecting one in return, and that while he gave the children the ponies because he hoped they would enjoy years of pleasure with them, he also planned to use the gifts as leverage. Indeed, Parker had plans for expanding his relationship with the lanky Opry star.

Since 1941, the WSM Artist Service Bureau had been commissioning a series of summer tent shows that took the Opry from its base in middle Tennessee and out into the rural South. Parker had tossed his hat in the ring as the booker and advance man, or "general agent," for the Jamup and Honey tent show of 1944, which would go out that April, taking country music to audiences that couldn't travel due to wartime restrictions on tires and gasoline.

The Jamup and Honey show, he told Harry Stone, WSM's general manager, held special interest for him. Aside from the blackface comedy duo, who'd heard about Parker's prowess as a promoter from Roy Acuff, the show starred old-time banjo player Uncle Dave Macon, Minnie Pearl, and Eddy Arnold, the rising performer who, in his first year on the Opry, was already being considered to host his own segment. With Stone's and Acuff's recommendations, Parker got the job.

On the day that the Jamup and Honey tent show opened a five-day run in Mobile, Alabama, the rain came down with such velocity that great tongues of water lapped at the slopes of the taut canvas tent, finally seeping through and dripping down below. By the time for the first of two shows that evening, the ground under the tent brimmed like a river, so much so, as Gabe Tucker, then Eddy Arnold's bass player, remembers, "We performed barefooted, it was so bad. And God, it rained every day."

Still, the April showers could not deter the throngs of people who came not just from Mobile, the Azalea City, but from the outlying rural areas, eager to plunk down their hard-won, wartime cash of twenty, thirty, and thirty-five cents a head—even the top ticket price of $1—to hear and see the Grand Ole Opry under canvas. For hours, they stood in a great snake of a line, the men in suits and ties, the women in Sunday dresses and long coats to keep off the spring chill, hoping to be among the lucky 1,500 to crowd into the 80-by-220-foot tent.

For Tom Parker, who had traveled the back roads of the central South and Midwest as part of the booking agent, bill poster, and advance-man crew, the choice of Mobile was not by happenstance. In selecting the spots where he would recast his life once again, following the WSM radio clear-channel signal, he returned to the city where he most likely came ashore in 1929 and reshaped himself into an entirely new entity.

Now, as the tent show got under way for the second week, Parker doubled back to Mobile to see if he had delivered what he'd promised both WSM's general manager, Harry Stone, and Lee Davis "Honey" Wilds, the owner of the show, whose daily operating expenses reached nearly $600 ("Everybody said we were crazy," admitted Wilds), and who paid the radio station a weekly commission for using its call letters and the name Grand Ole Opry. Almost always along the route of one-night locales like Caruthersville, Missouri; Harrison, Arkansas; and Meridian, Mississippi—the idea was to pick little towns that didn't have auditoriums—Parker would discover with great satisfaction that the shows sold out, often with monstrous crowds still waiting at the door. Sometimes nearly the whole town showed up: in one Oklahoma berg of 1,500, 1,100 people turned out to sit shoulder to shoulder, ten to a row, in sections marked by lines of slender poles. Word quickly filtered back to Nashville.

"Even with the tent shows," says Pee Wee King, "Tom seemed to know how to put them in the right place at the right time. Some of us would go out on the road in Georgia, Mississippi, and Alabama and have rain. And Tom would be in Illinois and Indiana and Iowa, maybe also having rain, but still drawing crowds."

As the poster of the 21-by-28-inch signs (HEARD THEM ON THE AIR! STARS IN PERSON! MAMMOTH TENT THEATRE!) that brought folks flocking to a tent illuminated by dangling lightbulbs and thrown up in the middle of a farmer's pasture, Parker traversed the country in a well-worn International panel truck, painted a somewhat sickening shade of yellow and festooned with bright red letters boasting WSM, GRAND OLE OPRY, ADVERTISING.

"They furnished him that ol' truck and gave him Green Stamps for gasoline," says Gabe Tucker, who first met Parker on the show, having admired his promotional skills since the Gene Austin days in the late '30s. "He slapped them big posters, the three [30-by-60 pictorial] sheets, up on the sides of barns with flour and water, and oh God, that truck smelled awful, just sour as hell. And he slept in it every once in a while out there on the road. I felt sorry for him, dressed like a tramp in them awkward-lookin' shoes with his britches halfway down 'em. Marie was in Tampa, and he was so damn lonesome. It was pretty rough living."

But being attached to the show brought Parker in close proximity to Eddy Arnold. The singer's management contract with Dean Upson wasn't due to expire until October 1945, yet Parker wanted to lay the groundwork now. Both Tucker and Little Roy Wiggins, the eighteen-year-old who played steel guitar in Eddy's band, remember seeing him standing in the shadows, watching, only the red glow of his cigar giving him away.

The tent show was a perfect vantage point from which Parker could talk to Arnold, persuade him, and learn more about him. To achieve that, he needed to be around the singer often enough that Arnold would feel

comfortable with him and seek his advice. Even though Parker felt superior to most of the troupe, particularly with his shrewdness about money,
he also wanted to make a favorable impression on the people around
him, both by his actions and results as an advance man, and by the sheer
force of his personality. Since he was not just establishing himself, but
still recreating himself as a country promoter, he hoped to bolster his own
reputation and to further his education in the hillbilly ways. He knew the
way to win their confidence was to gain popularity.

And so at least once a month, or every ten days if he could manage it,
Parker made a point of circling back to the show on the pretense of working out a problem or to pick up his pay.

"He was trying to make friends with everybody that was there, because he didn't know who was heavy [with power] and who wasn't,"
says Gabe Tucker. Since Parker envied Tucker's proximity to the star, "we
got along just fine. But back then, he could get along with anybody. He
was the nicest guy in the world when he needed you."

Before long, Parker was traveling in the car with the eccentric,
whiskey-nipping Uncle Dave Macon—who in 1926 became a corner-
stone of the Opry as the first individual featured performer—and his
handsome son Dorris, who accompanied his father on guitar.

A plus for Parker when he accompanied the troupe was that although
they traveled at night, while it was cool, and arrived in the wee hours of
the morning, he got to sample the downy comfort of a real bed, rather
than sleep in the truck, even if the accommodations were, as Honey
Wilds remembered, "little wasp-nest hotels."

Although Jamup and Honey wrote and performed comedic songs,
their primary act was a lively amalgamation of Southern humor, drawn
from the nineteenth-century minstrel tradition and mugged in blackface
as tribute to the Negro culture.

With his sulfurous sense of humor and appetite for the practical joke,
Parker was more naturally drawn to comedy than he was to the home-
made music of the rural Southeast, with its reliance on story songs chock
full of drunks, disappointed love, and deferred dreams. And perhaps because a joke about a bumpkin farmer from small-town Tennessee was
not so different from a joke about a farmer from a small village in Holland, Parker reveled in the stories about rube hillbillies, ethnic immi-
grants, and the hayseed who got the best of the city slicker that made up
the country comic's stock-in-trade.

Whether he realized it, Parker's six-month excursion in the company

of country comedians had a profound effect on his thinking and entrepreneurial style. In years to come, he would often book a comic on his
shows, whether the headliner was Hank Snow or Elvis Presley, and even
when such opening acts were no longer fashionable or appropriate.

Out on the road, Parker spent long hours with the troupe, sharing
meals, leisurely telling stories, strolling around the town with them before packing up the cars and heading out to the tent grounds for the performance. Yet when Minnie Pearl, who had known him from his earlier
days in Tampa, tried to engage him in intimate conversation about his
youth and growing-up years, the usually gregarious promoter turned
silent. As she said years later, "I was with him for months at a stretch, and
he never even slipped and mentioned anything about his background."

Pearl was mystified, since "Southern people talk about their grand-
mother, their great-grandmother, what their daddy did, what their grandfather did. They're involved in background and family." The rumor,
which she believed, was that "the enigma," as she called him, was born
down around Lawrenceburg, Tennessee. But no matter how hard she
tried to confirm it, Parker refused to divulge a single detail.

However, he seemed to enjoy a more relaxed rapport with Honey
Wilds. While Parker naturally would have tried to cultivate the show's
owner—the man who hired him "right out of that dog pound," as Honey
remembered—the towering Wilds was not the easiest man to know. Like
many comedians, the off-stage Wilds was frequently difficult and unpleasant, with a streak that ran close to morose. He also gave off an air of
danger. Wilds routinely carried a pocket knife, which he always prided as
the sharpest in the room and, on the lot, a ten-inch crescent wrench,
which he brandished like a weapon. For the countless miles of travel, he
armed himself with a pistol, sometimes shooting it within ten feet of
someone just to get their attention.

The basis of his bond with Parker, concludes David Wilds, Honey's
son, "was that what each did appealed to the other. My father was a total
creative rebel. He was a lot like Tom in that he was a very intelligent guy
who worked really hard to either dominate a situation through any
means necessary, or pretend that he wasn't as shrewd as he was. Tom's
thought process was just constantly evolving, and Daddy had a tremendous appreciation for his ability to get things done."

As the nights turned nippy and the tent show ended its season that fall
of '44, Parker threw a big dinner for the troupe in Tampa. In retrospect,
say members of Arnold's band, such uncharacteristic generosity came

more from Parker's hope to impress Eddy than anything else, since Eddy still hadn't made up his mind about this uneducated hustler with the faulty English.

Parker was already full of plans on how to make Eddy a major name, even outside the confines of the Opry. But until he was able to snag the singer's management contract, Parker hired on with J. L. Frank as a stump man, a combination of promoter, road manager, and advance agent, keeping Frank's acts working in the South and Midwest.

At a time when most country acts booked dates and tours from their home telephone, and the switchboard operator at the Grand Ole Opry acted as an answering service for the few personal managers working out of Nashville, Parker ran his business out of the lobby of Nashville's Andrew Jackson Hotel, making use of its free wall phones and letter desks.

"He used to tell people in New York, 'Call me in my office at two o'clock,'" remembered Parker's carnival friend Jack Kaplan. "He'd sit there and wait on it, just so everybody would think he had a big office in Nashville."

Primarily, Parker handled a tour of several hundred dates for Ernest Tubb. With a huge hit like "Soldier's Last Letter" and a pair of quickie movies, Tubb was now a big enough star to headline a package of Opry newcomers, including comic Rod Brasfield and, as an extra added attraction, the Poe Sisters, real-life siblings just barely into their twenties who used the stage names Ruth and Nelle.

As usual, Parker traveled two weeks ahead of the dates, booking auditoriums and theaters, billing posters, arranging for newspaper ads and hotel accommodations, and in keeping with Joe Frank's brand of broadcast promotion, setting up fifteen-minute early-morning radio programs for the troupe to come in to advertise the show.

Somewhere along the route, Tubb would get a telegram from Joe Frank telling him where Parker would catch up with him, usually in one of Tom's favorite diners. There, Parker would fill him in on what he'd lined up, writing it all down in his meticulous, methodical handwriting and passing the schedule sheet across a table ladened with double orders of chicken-fried steak served on green, sectioned plates, with plenty of sweet tea to wash it down. Afterward, Tubb would silently lay a deck of cards or a pair of dice on the table, and he and Parker would adjourn to get up a friendly game. "He'd take a chance on anything," says Gabe Tucker.

In contrast to his shabby, vagabond appearance with the Jamup and Honey tent show, Parker, as an agent for the distinguished Joe Frank, dressed in the kinds of clothes that had once delighted the young Andreas van Kuijk.

"He would always wear a white shirt with a nice sport jacket and slacks," recalls Nelle Poe. "He was already heavyset and balding, but he really looked like a gentleman. He traveled so hard and fast promoting us that he would have a whole suitcase of white shirts, but he wouldn't have time to get them laundered. He'd say, 'I'm sending them home for my wife to do them. I'll pick them up on the next trip.'"

Parker was in unusually good spirits on the tour, and soon he grew so bold as to insinuate himself into Tubb's stage act, impersonating the comedian Smiley Burnette and his character Frog Millhouse, Gene Autry's faithful sidekick. With his penchant for costumes, Parker had acquired an outfit similar to Burnette's signature look of checked shirt, loose black kerchief draped at the neck, and a floppy black hat turned sideways.

Nelle Poe remembers that Parker, who had studied Burnette's moves and could mug his poses, was able to play the comic with unnerving accuracy. "As soon as Ernest walked out on the stage," says Poe, "Tom would start down the aisle, brushing people's shoulders off with a little broom. He would do that on both sides of the audience, and Ernest would just stop and stand there with his guitar and look through the crowd like he didn't know what was going on. Of course, Ernest couldn't sing, because people were just howling at this big commotion of Tom's. He was really hilarious."

The heady reception fueled Parker's honeyed dreams of fame. "He always said to me, 'I'm going to Hollywood someday,'" Poe adds. "He had big ambitions, and he was sure he was destined for great things."

Yet Parker surely knew that his best chances of succeeding in Hollywood were not as a performer, but through his management of an alter ego. To that end, he continued to keep a vigilant watch on Eddy Arnold, who had just been tapped to host Ralston Purina's "Checkerboard Square" segment of the Grand Ole Opry, a plum spot.

As Eddy began to rouse the attention of national advertisers, Parker repositioned himself to strengthen his relationship with the budding star. Working with freelance promoter Jim Bulleit, who had headed the Opry Artist Service Bureau before the war, he booked Eddy for two weeks of theater dates in Florida during the winter of 1944–45. The idea was to show Arnold that he could bring him up a level, to get him away from the little piss-ant county fairs Eddy had played with Pee Wee King, where the people came up to grab a piece of the star or get an autograph. Once he was able to manage a top-notch act like Arnold, Parker vowed, he'd take him only to the bigger rodeos and fairs, and restrict that kind of fan access. To get the crowds lathered up, and then declare his star untouchable, was to rend him a god.

In the fall of 1945, Parker made a handshake deal with Arnold for exclusive representation. It was not the clear, round tones of Eddy's baritone that called to him, nor the Western bent of the tenor end of Eddy's register, reaching to surreal high yodel. With the understanding that Parker would take 25 percent of Arnold's income and Eddy would pay the expenses, Parker was not even overly concerned with the money he hoped to realize in bringing Eddy to prominence, although his funds were so tight that Marie had to temporarily hock her wedding ring to finance his trip to Tennessee. For him, the chance to couple his fate to Eddy's was a matter of personal power, of showing folks how to play the game.

As before, in the name of promotion, he was shameless. Joey Hoffman, Peasy's son, remembers seeing him hand out pictures in front of the grandstand at the Tampa fairgrounds to advertise Eddy's show, telling passersby, "It's free today, but the next time you see this face, you'll be paying for it!"

Yet Parker saved his boldest move for the day of the show, when he ambled down to the opening of Jack Shepherd's grocery store on Howard Avenue and approached a hillbilly band playing live on the air. Brashly, he went up to the microphone and asked the lead singer if he knew Eddy Arnold's favorite song, "Mommy, Please Stay Home with Me." The singer sheepishly said he didn't, so Parker invited the band—and the listening audience—to come out to the fair to hear Eddy sing it himself, thus wangling a free radio advertisement out of the station.

"He was a ball of fire, he worked hard, he got up early, and he was a nondrinker," Arnold says, reflecting on Parker's tireless efforts on his behalf. "He had a lot of energy. Actually, he was good at everything. He understood business, he was good with the record company, and he was good with the personal appearances. He was absolutely dedicated to the personality that he represented."

Although other managers stayed in their office and used the phone to complete their advance work, Parker crisscrossed the country setting up tours, often staying away for two months at a time, and bringing along for company either Bitsy Mott, Marie's diminutive brother, or Bevo Bevis, the twenty-six-year-old boy-man. Behind them, Parker towed a humpbacked trailer emblazoned with cartoonish renderings of Eddy's face, and filled it with posters, fly sheets, signs, pictures, and banners—anything to spread the word that "Eddy Arnold, the Tennessee Plowboy and His Guitar," as the trailer boasted in foot-high letters, was coming to town.

"When he was settin' up a tour," says Gabe Tucker, "he'd try to get enough money from whoever was promoting it, and, hell, he would go back to the same places sometimes two or three times if it was necessary, makin' sure folks knowed Eddy was a-comin.' And he'd tell the promoter, 'Put it on the radio. My boy can't draw you no people if they don't know he's gonna be here,' see. He would work on it and stay on it. That's one reason Eddy got in the bracket that he did, 'cause Tommy worked his ass off. If he was awake," adds Tucker, "he was preachin' Eddy Arnold to anybody that'd listen."

And like a member of any secret society, Parker knew just where to go when he needed help, back to the place and the people who still churned in his blood. To promote Eddy's early records, especially, Parker went home to the carnival, where the bearded ladies and the sprightly midgets and the fixers in their pinstripe suits and diamond rings took him in, blaring Arnold's songs over their loudspeakers as a favor to one of their own.

Yet "Tommy's boy," as the carnies affectionately called the singer, was embarrassed by such display and, on tour, quickly tired of the out-of-the-way drives to thank a hard-bitten carny manager for playing and selling his records.

"We got somebody up at this turnoff we need to go see," Parker would begin, driving out in the middle of the pitch-black nowhere, on a night pierced only by the light of the stars. Eddy, knowing what was coming, and chagrined about having to meet some leopard-skinned strongman with a neck like a pillar, finally began to voice his discontent. "Tom, do I have to? Do I have to . . . ? "

Eddy was not the only one who chafed at some of the new manager's methods of doing business. Almost immediately, Parker began to expand Arnold's tours beyond the bankable South and Southwest, taking the band and the opening act, the straw-hatted comedy duo of Lonzo and Oscar, as far north as Pennsylvania. He also stepped up the schedule, booking more dates than they'd ever played before, which meant they performed five nights during the week, drove all night Friday to get home by Saturday to play the Grand Ole Opry, and then left again on Sunday.

"It was really too much," remembers steel guitarist Little Roy Wiggins, who had played behind Paul Howard at fourteen and Pee Wee King at fifteen before joining the Tennessee Plowboys. "I told Parker he was queer for that white line in the middle of the highway, because he just had to run up and down that road like crazy."

Once, after Eddy got rolling a little bit, Parker booked him into the city auditorium in Chattanooga, where the promoter had a reputation for not paying the artist. Parker had already gotten half of his money in advance and intended to collect the remaining half in cash before the show started.

"Tom came back backstage while the musicians were standing there, strumming their guitars, waiting," Eddy recalls. "And he said to me, 'Don't you hit a lick until I go [waves his hand].' That would mean he had gotten the money. Well, he went to this gentleman [the promoter], and he said, 'You know, those singers, they're funny. They won't sing a note unless I wave my hand.' A couple of minutes later, I peeped through the curtain and he waved at me, and we did the show."

Despite Arnold's cachet as an RCA Victor recording artist and a member of the Grand Ole Opry, in the early days the idea of playing any city auditorium would have been a mere pipe dream for Arnold, whose tenure with Parker got off to a modest start. Bitsy Mott remembers the dates included towns in Texas that were so small and remote that the show was literally staged in a barn.

"We used to play all those places," he says, "and sometimes you had to kick the debris out of your way before you could let people come in— cows had been in there, you know. We set up wooden benches, and it was 'A dollar a ticket, sit where you like.' I used to hear him say that all the time."

The early tours were heady experiences for the young troupers, who were constantly learning something new about the business, and about each other. Parker vowed to always carry a fresh cigar, so that when the negotiations started and the questions came, he could light the stogie, puff some fire through it until he coaxed an orange hue at its end, and set it up for business in the corner of his mouth. By then, he'd had time to consider his answer.

Parker's habit of seeing how much he could get for as little as he could give reached new heights of audacity as Eddy's career heated up. The manager found it increasingly necessary to remain in Nashville when the group came in off the road. As he had done from the beginning, Parker took it for granted that he was welcome to stay with Eddy and his wife, Sally, a Kentucky girl whom Arnold married in late 1941 while performing with Pee Wee King.

One guest in the house had been enough for the Arnolds, who tried to keep their business and home life separate. But now Parker brought the hapless Bevo, whom Parker called Arnold's "tour manager" in the press, and Marie, who exuded a certain chilliness to both Sally and Roy Wiggins's wife, Joyce. And before long, Bobby Ross, who hoped to become a manager or promoter after apprenticing with Parker (he would eventually handle Slim Whitman and assist the Colonel in winning Whitman's first record contract), came up from Tampa and moved in right along with them. The foursome stayed anywhere from three or four days to nearly a month.

This parasitic arrangement fit the pattern of Parker's freeloading days of old, and seemed not to bother the thrifty Dutchman in the slightest, no matter who it inconvenienced. Eddy and Sally had recently bought a five-room redbrick bungalow in Madison, about seven miles west of downtown Nashville. But since Eddy's mother, Georgia, often lived there, too, and the couple welcomed the birth of daughter Jo Ann in December 1945, the house was full.

Fifty years later, Sally Arnold still rolled her eyes when the subject came up, too much of a Southern lady to say more. At the time, Eddy managed to keep his composure, until Parker also took over Arnold's newly rented office in the upstairs of a Madison real estate firm.

"Tommy told him, 'Plowboy, you need a place where you can store all of your songbooks,'" Gabe Tucker remembers. "And hell, he just dropped the shuck on him then. Eddy paid for the whole thing, and Tommy had a bigger office than Eddy did and never paid a nickel on it. Eddy started to say something to him about it, and Tommy said, 'Well, me taking care of you. Give me a better place to do it.' He never paid for office space, nowhere, his whole life."

It was at this point, after the Parkers had imposed on the Arnolds' hospitality for a particularly long and grating stay, that Eddy prompted one of Parker's most famous lines. As the singer wrote in his autobiography, "I said to him once when he was managing me, 'Tom, why don't you get yourself a hobby—play golf, go boating, or something?' He looked me straight in the eye and said, 'You're my hobby.'"

The Arnolds found relief only after Parker bought a small but stately fieldstone home nearby on Madison's Gallatin Road.

By the time Parker assumed Arnold's management, the Tennessee Plowboy, who would become one of the most prolific hit-making artists of all time, had made his first indelible mark with "Each Minute Seems a

Million Years." The song rose to the number five spot in *Billboard*'s tabulation of best-selling "folk" music.

To move beyond any initial blush of success, however, Eddy needed an energetic team working in tandem. While Steve Sholes, the heavyset and avuncular head of RCA Records' country and R&B divisions, was already in place, Tom Parker would head that team and rely on it for his own advancement in the industry. Eventually he would bring all the players to the group that would later figure so heavily in taking Elvis to the top, most prominently Hill and Range music publishers Jean and Julian Aberbach, and Harry Kalcheim and Abe Lastfogel of the powerful William Morris Agency. Nearly every major career move he guided for Arnold—a string of chart-topping records, the judicious use of early television, a foray into Hollywood movies, and even engagements in Las Vegas—served as the blueprint for Parker's plan with Elvis.

From the instant he took over Arnold's career, Parker began building momentum, not just for Arnold, but for himself. In what would serve as his lifelong pattern of artist and record company relations, he kept his client as isolated from the record label as possible. By appearing to make himself indispensable to both parties, he hoped to increase his importance and clout, while manipulating his client's knowledge of the intricacies of the deals.

Above all, it was imperative that the record label executives—and others in the trade—see Parker as a figure of equal or greater stature to his artist. In magazine and newspaper advertisements he coupled his name with that of Eddy's—UNDER EXCLUSIVE MANAGEMENT OF THOMAS A. PARKER—in letters nearly the same size as those employed for Arnold's. The idea was to convey not only Parker's insistence that they were a team, but that Parker was a deal maker worthy of celebration and reward. Already he was having large studio portraits taken of himself, in which he smiled broadly from within the proud confines of an expensive pinstripe suit. He signed them "the Gov."

Three years later, in October 1948, Parker seized the opportunity to obtain a more prestigious title on a trip to Baton Rouge, Louisiana. With Gabe Tucker in tow, he called on an old carny acquaintance, Bob Greer, then an aide to Governor Jimmie Davis, who'd had an earlier taste of fame as a country singer and the cowriter of "You Are My Sunshine." Parker and Greer carried on about their old shenanigans—"cutting up jackpots" in the carny vernacular—and Tucker, amused by Parker's outrageous stories of the showman's swindle, declared that anyone who could snow with such velocity should have a title, and put the request to Greer. Thrilled at the prospects of such an inspired con, Parker refused to leave town until the document, which commissioned him as a Louisiana colonel, with all the rights, privileges, and responsibilities thereunto appertaining, was in his hands.

Until now, Parker had requested that the members of Arnold's band refer to him as Popsy, a feigned intimacy designed to wheedle favors out of them. ("You like your room? Buy Popsy a cigar.") But things had changed.

"He turned around," as Tucker remembers, "and said, 'In the future, Mr. Tucker, you will make sure that everybody addresses me as Colonel.'" And so the former army deserter now carried what many construed as a military title.

In his early years with Arnold, Parker was dictatorial in the extreme, laying down the law with theater managers over concession rights, and stripping Arnold's band members of the songbook sales they shared in arrangement with Eddy. Now the old carny kept the songbook money for himself and his family, sending Bitsy and Bevo out in the aisles with their arms loaded up with books, pictures, and programs, and installing Marie at a table in the lobby.

"The specter of Tom selling pictures and records down the aisles of a venue was one to behold," says Bob McCluskey, former general promotion manager for RCA Victor. "That, to my knowledge, no pop manager had ever done."

But it also sent a seething shiver through Little Roy Wiggins. Parker delighted in stirring up trouble among the band members, who, before his arrival, had enjoyed an easy camaraderie. Since they never seemed to have an argument when he wasn't around, eventually they recognized it as a control mechanism, Tucker seeing how Parker loved it when "all of us would run to him so he could be the great fixer," and how the tales of internal bickering gave him a window onto everything that went on with his star.

When Eddy told Parker that Wiggins was irate at the loss of $100 a week in songbook commissions and intimated he might quit, Parker sent the message that he didn't care what Little Roy did. "Coinnal," as Wiggins mocked the way Parker pronounced his new title and his inability to say r's, had decided that's the way it was going to be.

With pressure building, an altercation was inevitable, and it came one night in El Paso, Texas, when Eddy played a private party there. Afterward, Wiggins, drinking a beer, headed for the bus to take him to the hotel.

"Where do you think you're going with that beer in your hand?" demanded one of Parker's staffers. "You're not getting on this bus with that beer."

"Just who in the hell says I'm not?" countered the five-foot Wiggins, empowered by the brew.

"The Colonel says you're not."

"Well, fuck the Coinnal!" Roy cursed in anger, and then went to Eddy and explained what happened. "I'll kill that big, fat, sloppy mother," he spewed. Eddy calmed him, said Parker was wrong, and he would speak to him about it tomorrow. But back at the hotel, goaded on by Vic Willis of the Willis Brothers, a featured act on Arnold's shows, Wiggins could stand it no longer, remembering every slight he'd endured since Parker came on board—how he'd advised Arnold to take the band off a percentage basis and put them on salary, and how he'd cut them out of Arnold's record royalties, something Eddy promised when he formed the band in 1943. Finally, Wiggins picked up the phone and called the Colonel himself. "It's one of the things I am proudest of in my life," says Wiggins. "I cussed him for thirty minutes—at least thirty minutes—until, well, he got to cryin', really."

A tearful Parker tried to explain about the beer. "Don't you know about insurance?" he said.

"Don't run that 'snowplow' at me," Wiggins retorted. "I ain't drivin' that damn bus."

For three days, the men saw not one glimpse of each other. Then Wiggins was on the hotel elevator when it stopped on Parker's floor. "Woy," said Parker, standing in the door and waiting to get on, "I want to talk to you. Everything's all right between me and you, except one thing. Did you say, 'Fuck the Coinnal?'"

"I had embarrassed him in front of his flunkies," remembers Wiggins. "I think that really got through to him."

In time, the enigmatic Parker held himself above almost everyone—certainly the powers at RCA—in a nearly Machiavellian thirst to seize and hold power. That obsession, unencumbered by the usual ethical, moral, or social values (even his brother-in-law, Bitsy Mott, felt compelled to call him "sir"), would grow in direct proportion to Parker's success, first with Arnold, whom he elevated to the number-one-selling country artist, and later with Elvis. Parker saw it only as maximizing the opportunity, both for his client and for himself.

Perhaps Parker's earliest test came in his negotiations with Jean and Julian Aberbach, the Viennese Jews who would become an essential spoke in the wheel that drove Eddy's career.

In 1944, only five years after Jean immigrated to the United States to work for Chappel Music, the Aberbach brothers founded Hill and Range Songs, Inc., a Los Angeles and New York–based company that specialized in C&W tunes.

By the end of 1945, when most New York publishers saw no percentage in country-and-western music, the visionary Aberbachs had three songs at the top of the charts and $50,000 in the bank. Not surprising, then, the Aberbachs took keen notice of newcomer Arnold and particularly of the success that publishers Fred Forster and Wally Fowler enjoyed when the young singer recorded their songs. To sew up a rising star like Arnold—to have him predisposed to select songs from their catalog— would be a fine thing. And so before Eddy's recording session in early 1946, Jean and Julian, at Sholes's invitation, met with Arnold, Parker, and the RCA producer to present songs and perhaps work out an agreement.

In the immediate years to follow, the Aberbachs—shrewd, sophisticated, fastidiously dressed, and displaying such cultured accents and gracious European manners that some pronounced them "oily"—offered an array of incentives to induce label executives, artists, and managers to do business.

Thus, before Arnold's first session of 1946—his third session with Sholes and his fourth overall—the Aberbachs presented Eddy with a check for $20,000, a substantial amount of money for the time, but perhaps not so large considering what they hoped to get in return.

"It was really for nothing, you see," explains the erudite Julian Aberbach. "We promised Eddy that every good song that we had we would submit to him first before we went to any other artist. Then we tried to get the best songs that we had that would fit Eddy Arnold."

Beginning with the March 1946 recording session, where Arnold recorded two Hill and Range songs, the uptempo "Can't Win, Can't Place, Can't Show" and "Chained to a Memory," which climbed to number three on the *Billboard* chart, most Eddy Arnold sessions included at least one tune published by Hill and Range. For a time, says Bob Mc-Cluskey, "almost every release of any importance was a Hill and Range song."

To McCluskey, it was almost certain that Sholes, a family man, was secretly on the take, and that Parker, who exploited the greed of others, knew it. "If Eddy got the twenty grand, what do you think Sholes got? [They] obviously owed [their] soul to Hill and Range after taking the money. Once it's in your pocket, there is no turning back, because they have you and they can talk."

According to Aberbach, Parker, as Arnold's manager, received 25 percent of Eddy's $20,000, "which was more than justified, because he had [only] one artist. He always had a deal, and he was without any doubt an excellent deal maker and skilled negotiator. But he was honest."

Honesty, like beauty, is in the eye of the beholder. As the Aberbachs' cousin, music publisher Freddy Bienstock points out Parker always had side deals, too, and especially with RCA Victor, where in a very real sense, he was the client, not Eddy Arnold and, later, not even Elvis Presley. From the beginning of his association with the label, it was obvious to Parker that there was plenty of money to go around, especially for the man who had the gumption to speak up and demand it, a man whose key to survival, as Gabe Tucker asserts, was always to have something better than a contract—maybe a little something to remind a guy about when the circumstance demanded.

Arnold, while grateful for the astonishing level of success he found under Parker—by 1952, he was no longer the hayseed Grand Ole Opry performer, but the star of his own network television show—chafed at certain aspects of the Colonel's flamboyant style.

Indeed, Parker seemed to want to control every facet of Arnold's life. ("All Eddy takes care of is his toothbrush and his drawers," the Colonel crowed.) The two men clashed about the direction of Eddy's music—the singer, who now hated the "Plowboy" moniker, hoped to embrace a more sophisticated sound—and Arnold was continually embarrassed by Parker's shabby dress, his braggadocio ("Which one of our planes did you come down in today?" he'd ask Eddy in a crowded elevator), and his use of carny promotions, such as parading an elephant through Nashville's downtown streets to advertise Arnold's appearances.

Yet far more troubling to Arnold was Parker's alleged involvement with the careers of other performers. The familiar rumor that the Colonel sold Hadacol—the patent medicine made up mostly of ethyl alcohol—or secretly booked the entertainers for the Hadacol Caravan appears not to be based in fact. But Parker was working with Hank Snow and Tommy Sands through his new company, Jamboree Attractions, which rankled

Arnold down deep. Together, they'd sold nearly 30 million records, and the way Arnold saw it, the 25 percent he paid Parker was for exclusivity. Then in the summer of 1953 came an embarrassing blowup in Las Vegas.

According to Roy Wiggins, Eddy, then playing the Sahara Hotel, was alone in his room when the phone rang, and the caller, thinking he had Tom Diskin, Parker's new lieuenant, on the line, said, "Tell the Colonel that show we got together with Hank Snow is doing okay." Arnold, angry and shaken, went down to the coffee shop to confront the Colonel and saw him hide something under the table—Parker would later claim it was an ad he had taken out to surprise his client—as he approached. An argument ensued outside, "and by the time I walked up," remembers Wiggins, "they were at it pretty good." Eddy drew back his fist—"Don't hit him!" yelled a frightened Marie Parker—and the singer later sent a telegram that informed his manager he was no longer in need of his services.

The firing left Parker humiliated and deeply wounded, and for a short while he moved out of music to manage wrestlers, particularly Roy and Bill Fryman, who were invariably billed as "the Fryman Brothers with Manager Col. Tom Parker." However, there was no money in small-town gymnasium wrestling, and the stress of it all so unraveled him that shortly after, the Colonel suffered the first of many heart attacks. Although his weight, which had hovered dangerously around three hundred pounds, dropped dramatically during his recovery, he told almost no one about his illness, afraid that the clients like Snow, and Rod Brasfield, and Mother Maybelle and the Carter Sisters—who were beginning to come to him and Diskin, for bookings, if not always for "direction," as he called it—would desert him.

Worse, he feared he would lose his power at RCA, as Sholes, shifting his allegiance to Arnold, "treated him like a flea-bitten alley dog, and him and Sholes was never the greatest of friends after that," Gabe Tucker recalls. Immediately, he put the squeeze on Sholes and Singles Division Manager Bill Bullock—who was being whispered about as "the Colonel's guy"—to let him manage the upcoming RCA Victor Country Caravan, a package tour designed to showcase the label's country stars, with Hank Snow headlining.

Set for spring of '54, the Caravan was the brainchild of Bob McCluskey, who'd gotten $50,000 allocated for it, and was now being pressured to involve Parker. McCluskey said that the Colonel could help with some of the dates, but he didn't want him in control of the money, "as he'd already gotten a reputation that was quite unsavory, and I was responsible for all that dough." The next thing McCluskey knew, he was out of a job, and Parker was in charge of the venture. "He got the money up front," says McCluskey, "and I was told that the money he didn't spend was his, as no one would ask for it to be returned."

Next Parker moved to bolster his standing with the William Morris office—with Hollywood—where, despite the two dreadful B Westerns, *Feudin' Rhythm* and *Hoedown*, Eddy Arnold made for Columbia Pictures in 1949, Parker had hoped to wield as big a stick as he had in the music business. He'd check into the Hotel Knickerbocker for a month at a time, trying to appear the part.

Now, all he could think of was something that occurred on his first trip to New York to meet Harry Kalcheim, who worked in the personal appearance division of the agency's Gotham office. On the plane, Parker struck up a conversation with a man who bragged that he'd just made a big deal with William Morris. By coincidence, Parker noted, they were staying at the same hotel. But when the plane landed, the Morris office had a gleaming black limousine waiting for its important new client, while Parker was left to take the bus.

Several days later, Parker was having breakfast at the hotel when he looked out the window to see the big shot sitting on his suitcase. Now it was he who waited on a bus. "Where's your limo?" Parker asked. "The deal fell through," came the reply. Parker never forgot it, and it served as a harsh reminder of a very real truth: the minute you no longer had something the power brokers wanted, you were out.

"As the last of the carnies to really make it in Hollywood," says Byron Raphael, "the Colonel was extremely jealous of the very well bred Jewish guys at William Morris. He resented them, and yet he also needed their respect. So although he made fun of the fact that he was accepted by what he considered to be the cream of New York and Hollywood, secretly he desired it terribly."

Eventually, Parker would strike a deal with Arnold to handle at least a portion of his bookings, in part to save face with the Morris agency. But for the time being, he took another kind of solace.

"Plowboy," he drawled into the phone, knowing how the name would irritate Eddy, "we've got to talk. You sent me this wire that said we was through, but you never said nothin' about settlin' up."

"What do you mean?" Arnold asked.

"Well, if you're not happy with me, and you don't want to be associat-

ing with me anymore," Parker said, "then it's gonna cost you $50,000."
Arnold, conservative about nearly everything, and especially about
money, swallowed hard and reminded Parker that they never had a contract, just a gentleman's agreement. "No, Plowboy, there's more to it than
that," the fat man said, and Arnold suggested they meet with his
Nashville attorney, Bill Carpenter.

On the day of the appointment, Parker arrived at Carpenter's office
with an old leather bag stuffed full of papers, which he emptied into a
small mountain on the lawyer's desk—the IRS trick redone. As the lawyer began sifting through the pile, Parker took a folded paper from his
pocket and started reading aloud from the last contract he'd negotiated
for Arnold with RCA, one that gave the singer five cents a record, the
largest royalty rate possible, equal to that of Perry Como.

Furthermore, Parker explained, the most favored nation clause dictated that if anybody negotiated a higher royalty rate in the future, Eddy
got that, too. The agreement was good for seven years, Parker reminded
them, and it carried his signature, not Eddy's. Now, didn't $50,000 seem
reasonable, stacked against 25 percent of whatever royalties Arnold
made for the remainder of those seven years? The singer sank deep in his
chair. "Eddy," Bill Carpenter said flatly, "pay him."

For a man who had shied away from contracts, Parker had become
exceptionally skilled in using them to his advantage. "Colonel Tom got
me out of a contract one time that I didn't want to be in," recalled the
country star Marty Robbins. "He did it as a favor. I was really hung up
bad. Colonel Tom said, 'Do you want out of that contract?' I said, 'Yes,
sir.' And sure enough, he got me out. I would have been hung up for six
years at a big percent." Robbins subsequently turned down Parker's offer
to sign him to Jamboree Attractions, but in pledging to work for the
Colonel anytime he wanted, Robbins forged the kind of contract Parker
liked best—an unwritten one.

And sometimes two contracts were better than one. Hank Snow, who
became a partner in Jamboree Attractions in late 1954, lining up package
tours for himself, Bill Haley and the Comets, Andy Griffith, Elvis Presley,
and others, found out just how learned, and treacherous, Parker had become in early 1956, when the Colonel returned to Nashville from a trip
to Memphis with dual contracts in his pocket.

The purpose of the trip had been to sign twenty-one-year-old Presley
to a management deal. Gladys Presley distrusted the Colonel from the beginning, and Parker had called in Snow, one of her favorite singers, to

sweet-talk Elvis's mother into giving her approval. Now, if on the advice of his mother, Elvis balked at the first contract, which Parker carried in his left coat pocket, he had another one ready in his right. What Snow didn't learn until later was that the only difference in the contracts was that one bound Presley to Hank Snow Enterprises–Jamboree Attractions and the other strictly to Parker, as the "sole and exclusive Advisor, Personal Representative, and Manager in any and all fields of public and private entertainment." It was the latter contract that Presley signed, forever cutting Snow out of the most lucrative deal in all of show business.

10

THE MAN IN THE SHADOWS

JUST how and when Colonel Tom Parker first took note of Elvis Presley will always be one of the unanswerable questions in the history of rock and roll. Not surprisingly a handful of men take credit for informing Parker about the combustible "Hillbilly Cat" who, starting in late 1954, performed regularly on *The Louisiana Hayride* radio program, broadcast out of Shreveport over KWKH, a powerful, 50,000-watt station that sent its signal across and beyond the southern United States.

The likelihood is that Presley's appearances on the *Hayride* and in supporting tours throughout Texas made such a stir that Parker, desperately on the lookout for another artist with the potential of an Eddy Arnold, began hearing about him from a number of sources, including Texarkana deejay Uncle Dudley (Ernest Hackworth) and Gabe Tucker, who had left Eddy's band to play local clubs and do radio work in Houston.

What really turned his head, though, was a report from his old friend Oscar Davis. In October 1954, Davis, on a trip to Memphis to do advance work for Parker for an Arnold appearance at Ellis Auditorium, dropped by WMPS radio to record his advertising spots for the show. There, disc jockey Bob Neal played him "Blue Moon of Kentucky," the first single by the teenaged Elvis Presley, who, Neal told Davis, packed a local dive, the Eagle's Nest, night after night with screaming women.

That evening, Davis went out to the club with Neal, who was booking Presley around the region. "I said, 'Bob, this guy is incredible. I'd like to meet him,'" as Davis recalled. Neal brought him over to the table, and the following Sunday, when Elvis came backstage at Ellis Auditorium to talk further with Davis and meet Eddy Arnold and his backup group, the Jordanaires, the faded impresario made a tentative deal to take over Presley's management from his guitarist, Scotty Moore.

That Monday, Davis returned to Nashville, and drove out to Parker's house. He found the Colonel sitting outside his office on that warm fall day, enjoying an informal lunch with Charlie Lamb, a former carny who now worked in the country music business as a journalist and advertising agent.

"It was really Oscar who found Elvis," Lamb says. "He came over and said, 'I saw the darnedest act you ever imagined, this kid who does this twisting around and so forth.' The Colonel's eyes popped open, and he said, 'Where was he? Who is he?' And he got up from the table and pulled his car out and left. He still wasn't back when I went out the next day."

Was Parker checking out Oscar's discovery? If so, Parker kept it to himself when he returned to Nashville. But suddenly, as Elvis's drummer, D. J. Fontana, remembers, Parker began turning up at Presley's show dates in Texarkana. "We would see him walkin' around, hanging back in the shadows, but he never would say nothin'. A lot of people just didn't want to deal with him."

Bob Neal, who assumed Presley's management duties on January 1, 1955, most certainly wanted to deal with Parker, hoping this "razzle-dazzle character, but honest and very sharp, shrewd dealer," as he later called him, would put Elvis on the package tours that Parker took out to other parts of the country.

On January 15, 1955, Parker and Tom Diskin traveled to Shreveport to watch Elvis—decked out in a rust-colored suit, a black-dotted purple tie, and pink socks—perform three songs for the *Hayride* audience. Afterward, they met with Neal and worked out an arrangement by which Parker, as an agent of Hank Snow Attractions, would handle Elvis's bookings, which Parker promised would likely include "one of the big resort hotels in Nevada."

By now, Parker was already scheming to take total control of the new sensation. But until Neal's management contract expired the following year ("I always felt that Elvis was going to be a big artist, but I never would have believed how big, so I just preferred to drop out of the scene," Neal said later), the Colonel was careful not to tip his hand, not even to Oscar Davis.

Parker respected Davis enough to lend him money on occasion— "Oscar lived high, wide, and handsome," remembers the Nashville attorney Richard H. Frank Sr.—and the two were bound beneath the skin by their carny experiences and their fondness for illegal gambling. They also shared a curious mind-set that let them find a way to always justify their actions, even if it meant disposing of people without ever once looking back. Years before, like the Colonel's own Marie, who had given away the clubfooted baby, Davis had simply walked out on his wife and five-year-old son, never to see or acknowledge them again. "He was a deserter, plain and simple," says Oscar Davis Jr.

The Colonel had little compunction about how he counseled Davis, who'd lost his last big client, the great Hank Williams, to an overdose of hooch, chloral hydrate, and fame. Now, only two years after that fatal incident—Parker himself had booked Hank for one night in Texarkana—Davis made no secret of the fact that he hoped to take over Presley's management. "The guy will get nowhere on Sun Records," Parker began, and rolled out a host of other objections. The two argued, Parker told his friend he'd gotten "too excited" over this Presley kid, and "I became completely discouraged about the whole thing," Davis said.

Parker was a skilled tactician who approached any negotiation with the forethought of a master chess player, knowing all the possible strategies and the likelihood of how the moves would play out. Brushing aside Davis more easily than he could dispense with Hank Snow or even the easygoing Neal, Parker turned his attention to Sam Phillips, who operated the Sun Records label. Without foundation, Parker started the rumor that Presley's contract was for sale. Phillips, stunned to learn of the gossip, struck back with the breathtaking demand of $35,000.

"I thought, hey, I'll make 'em an offer that I know they will refuse, and then I'll tell 'em they'd better not spread this poison anymore," Phillips remembers. "I absolutely did not think Tom Parker could raise the $35,000, and that would have been fine. But he raised the money, and damn, I couldn't back out then." Parker sent him a $5,000 deposit, with RCA later paying Phillips his asking price, plus a $5,000 bonus for Elvis.

All $40,000 would be recoupable against royalties, but still the label was nervous. "We must have met for a half hour before I put my approval on it," remembers Norman Racusin, RCA's chief financial officer at the time. "It was a lot of money, but Steve [Sholes] was so aggressive about this, he would have gone over my head if I turned him down anyhow." Later, Sholes watched Carl Perkins come on strong with "Blue Suede Shoes," and phoned Phillips to ask, "Did I buy the wrong boy?" No, Phillips assured him, he did not. By that time, the company had refunded the Colonel's deposit, but Parker forever insisted it was his money that bought the contract and his money that was at risk.

Yet it wasn't until Presley's appearance in Jacksonville, Florida, in May 1955, before 14,000 fans, that Parker fully realized what he had.

"Girls, I'll see you all backstage," Elvis joked at the end of his show, and about half the crowd broke through the police barricade, a throng following him into the dugout locker room, trying to tear off his clothes. "He was on top of the showers, trying to get away from people—guys and girls trying to grab a shoe or just anything," remembered fellow performer Marty Robbins, who'd joined the bill as a way to repay Parker's favor of the year before.

As a carnival man who only understood things in dollars and cents, Parker knew what brought 'em into the big tent. In a real sense, Elvis was just a male version of Marie and all the other thinly veiled dancing girls who tantalizingly promised the big striptease but never quite paid off. But now Parker realized that Elvis's popularity could go beyond even that, to the kind of riots that Frank Sinatra had inspired in his heyday. And from then on, when he went to Elvis's shows, it was the crowd Parker watched, not Elvis. That emotion could make him a very rich man, almost overnight.

Once Parker created his grand marketing plan, enlisting the full help of RCA Victor and the William Morris Agency, it would take no more than a year to make Elvis the biggest-selling artist in the music business and the highest-paid performer on TV. And when he accepted a nearly $40,000 advance from the Beverly Hills movie merchandiser Hank Saperstein to turn Elvis into a brand name, licensing seventy-eight different articles, from Elvis charm bracelets, Elvis lipstick in "Hound Dog" orange, and Elvis scarves, dolls, plastic guitars, and glow-in-the-dark busts, Parker's entrepreneurial vision raked in some $22 million, apart from what the fans spent on concerts and records. No artist had ever exploded on the scene with the volcanic impact of Elvis Presley in 1956, and no manager before Tom Parker had ever been so brilliantly, or blatantly, capitalistic. At a time when most managers did little more for their artists than book concert dates, Parker perpetually figured out new ways to exploit his star.

"Perhaps it is to lighten our burdens that the Lord sends us from time to time gay and imaginative men like Colonel Parker, who realize that life is a great big hilarious fruitcake loaded with potential profits," Look magazine said in 1956.

In truth, Parker's most important place in music history may be as the man who almost single-handedly took the carnival tradition first to rock and roll, and then to modern mass entertainment, creating the blueprint for the powerful style of management and merchandising that the music business operates by today. By merely applying the exploitationist tactics of the barker to his own client, he drew a straight line from the bally platform of the old-time carnival to the hullabalooed concert stage.

Yet, as long as they were associated, Parker, who preferred the bubbly champagne music of Lawrence Welk, never understood the artistic genius of Presley's surreal hiccups and king-snake moans, his seamless blending of country, pop, and rhythm and blues. Nor could he truly appreciate the elegant electricity of his aesthetic romp. In fact, Parker, who didn't know a good song from a bad ("He really was tone deaf," says RCA's Joan Deary), often made derisive comments about Elvis's music. "The first time he heard 'I Want You, I Need You, I Love You,'" Byron Raphael recalls, "he laughed, and said, 'Can you imagine the kids are going to buy this stuff?'"

Certainly neither Parker nor anyone else had the vision to see what a seismic force Elvis would become, as perhaps the most influential cultural figure of the twentieth century. But a decade earlier, Parker watched Dick Contino wrangle and hump his accordion as the teenagers went crazy. Now he began to fathom that Elvis could combine the threatening sexuality of Marlon Brando and the confused, sensual tension of James Dean and, in the process, give voice to a powerful, rising youth movement, one ravenous and itchy for change and prominence. Its purchasing power—some $7 billion in 1956 alone—would triple the sales of the American recording industry and make Elvis Presley the first RCA artist to gross more than $1 million from a single album.

However, on the day he first met Presley, Parker was preoccupied with two other performers. His choices reveal how inept he was at judging mainstream taste and in guiding unknown talent.

Still smitten with the icon of the American cowboy, Parker approached Eddie Dean, the B-movie Western star, who had appeared on the country music charts with "One Has My Name (the Other Has My Heart)" and "I Dreamed of a Hillbilly Heaven." Parker told him he could score big as "the Golden Cowboy" and, in a foreshadowing of Elvis's famous stage ensemble, suggested Dean invest in a golden suit or two.

Since '52, however, he'd been consumed with the idea of managing Tommy Sands, a *Louisiana Hayride* alum who had just entered his teens when Parker first saw him perform at Cook's Hoedown Club in Houston. Soon he had the boy opening dates for Eddy Arnold, who resented his manager's personal and professional interest in the kid.

Sands, whose parents were divorced and who rarely saw his own father, found a surrogate daddy in the strange, funny man who seemed to be grooming him more for the movies than a singing career. One day, he made the teen throw dirt on himself and walk several miles to a diner, where Parker waited and posed as an unassuming customer. Sands would pass his "acting test" if he stood at the window and looked hungry enough that the management brought him in and gave him a free meal. "My boy," Parker told him about this and other stunts, "this is all just part of your education."

"Actually," says Sands, "he wanted me to be Roy Rogers—the next big cowboy movie star. That's what he saw for me." And so Parker outfitted the youngster with string ties, cowboy hats, and all manner of Western wear. But Sands didn't want to be Roy Rogers ("I thought I'd have to be Mr. Clean, married with a family, and I'd never be able to have any girlfriends"), even though he loved Parker and "worshiped the ground that he walked on."

And so Parker switched gears and set about getting Sands a recording contract, instructing the teen to send a sample tape to RCA's Steve Sholes late in 1954 or early '55. Sholes took a perfunctory listen and immediately returned the tape to the young singer, but when Parker ran into a temporary snag prying Elvis loose from his commitment at Sun Records, he had Diskin get in touch with Sholes. "Since Elvis Presley is pretty securely tied up," Diskin suggested in a letter, "it might be possible to come out with something in that vein by Tommy."

Sholes wrote back and tactfully stated that Sands would not be a suitable replacement for Elvis, but, in a move probably meant to appease the Colonel more than anything else, offered the "possibility that we could record Tommy on some of the Rhythm and Blues type Country and Western music." Several years earlier, Parker had flown Sands to New York and Nashville to record, as he recalls, seven songs, "but my voice hadn't changed yet, and nothing sold." His producer, Chet Atkins, puts it differently: "He was just one of those pretty faces."

Parker saw his inability to develop Sands into a major artist as a singular defeat. ("The fact that he didn't make a winner out of Tommy was a burr under his saddle—God, he couldn't stand to be a loser," says Gabe Tucker.) And so he refused to relinquish hope, picking up Sands in the summers and driving him wherever Parker had a show going, "priming me for whatever the next move was going to be," Sands says.

Finally, in 1957, Parker found his vindication when NBC's *Kraft Television Theatre* produced "The Singing Idol," a drama closely based on

Elvis's story, with the Colonel portrayed as a twisted psychopath. Kraft had wanted Elvis for the role, but Parker turned them down and recommended Sands, going so far as to call Tommy's manager, Cliffie Stone. As Sands remembers it, Parker paid for his plane ticket for the audition.

The show was an enormous hit—even Elvis was impressed—and critics raved over the newcomer's acting and singing. Within the week, Sands, who had signed with Ken Nelson at Capitol Records on the strength of the Kraft contract, saw his single "Teenage Crush" go to number three on the pop charts and sell 800,000 copies.

"That really made him," recalled Stone. "In six months he'd become a fantastic star—*The [Ed] Sullivan Show, This Is Your Life,* and all the rest." Only then, reports Gabe Tucker, was Parker able to loosen that burr from his saddle, boasting about how he was being consulted about "the actor who is going to play me" in the 1958 theatrical version, *Sing, Boy, Sing.*

Parker's initial failure to launch Sands, coupled with his eagerness to shine again in the eyes of the William Morris Agency, was no small part of his drive to make Elvis America's number-one attraction.

But while the Morris office denies it today, in 1955, no one at the agency, in either New York or California, put much faith in Presley's ability to last beyond a quick, if bizarre, blaze of fame.

Parker began campaigning to interest Harry Kalcheim in Presley months before he finally got the singer signed on the dotted line, and while Kalcheim politely responded that Elvis had "a very special type of voice," he didn't seem overly impressed, noting in a February 1955 letter to Parker that he had mislaid Elvis's photograph. Parker wrote back in March that he felt certain Presley could succeed if he was "exploited properly," and stayed on Kalcheim even as the RCA deal had yet to close.

It was Hollywood that most occupied Parker's thoughts, and even as he knew he'd have to build Elvis into a national phenomenon before he could move him into motion pictures, his desire was so strong that he couldn't help but plant the idea with his William Morris contact.

Kalcheim, located in the New York office and more involved with television than motion pictures, eventually responded that perhaps Elvis could make a Hollywood short. On November 14, 1955, the day before RCA gave Sam Phillips the $35,000 to buy out Presley's Sun contract, Parker told Kalcheim that he was "interested in making a picture with this boy. However, we must be very careful to expose him in a manner be-

fitting his personality, which is something like the James Dean situation."
Perhaps, he added, in the wake of Dean's tragic death in a car accident
two months earlier, Warner Bros. had a shelved film property that might
work well for Elvis.

"Believe me," Parker said, "if you ever follow one of my hunches, follow up on this one and you won't go wrong."

On November 23, 1955, eight days after RCA secured Elvis's recording contract, Kalcheim wrote to Sam Fuller of NBC to inform him that
the label had "just tied up a youngster, Elvis Presley, a sensational singer
very much on the order of Johnnie Ray." Kalcheim was hoping that
Fuller might make room for a Presley appearance on an NBC-TV show
and notified Parker he'd gotten the ball rolling.

But secretly, Kalcheim had little faith that anything of importance
would happen for Parker's new charge. In 1955, Byron Raphael, then
a new William Morris employee, happened upon a memo from Harry
Kalcheim, addressed to all of the members of the West Coast office.

"Essentially," remembers Raphael, "it said, 'We've signed a new act,
Elvis Presley, who's managed by Colonel Parker, who had Eddy Arnold.'
And it went on to say, 'We've surveyed all our agents on the East Coast,
and our opinion is that Presley's not going to make it. At most, he'll simply be a passing phenomenon. So get him as much work as you can, and
as fast as you can.'"

Parker never saw that memo, but he knew that the deals that the Morris office was pursuing were not in Elvis's best interest. It was also clear
that Kalcheim didn't share his enthusiasm or his timetable for establishing Elvis as a national artist. When Kalcheim suggested that Parker book
Elvis on a series of dates in New York and New Jersey to increase his exposure, Parker ignored the advice.

What's more, in a move that angered Kalcheim, Parker, who had no
written contract with the Morris agency, entered into a deal with an independent agent, Steve Yates. Beginning in January 1956, Yates booked
Elvis for four consecutive weeks on CBS-TV's *Stage Show,* the popular
Saturday-night vaudeville program hosted by jazz greats Tommy and
Jimmy Dorsey. There Elvis would debut his first RCA single, "Heartbreak Hotel," with a bump-and-grind musical backing that was not
much different from what Presley's drummer, D. J. Fontana, played in
strip joints.

When Kalcheim learned of the *Stage Show* bookings, which stretched
into six appearances, he fired off a blustery note. Parker answered with a

convoluted letter that tap-danced around his use of Yates and chided Kalcheim for simply sending out letters and waiting for a response.

"I don't think this artist was pitched full force," he barked, often lapsing into run-on sentences and the peculiar sentence structure of a man who learned English later in life. "You know as well as I do offering a new artist is one thing but selling one is another. If I waited for some-one to call me with deals all the time, I would have to start selling candy apples again."

The upshot was that on January 31, 1956, the Morris office prepared a memo that gave the agency the exclusive right to represent Elvis with the American Federation of Musicians, the American Federation of Television and Radio Artists, the American Guild of Variety Artists, the Screen Actors Guild, and for "general services" and "general materials and packages."

That memo, addressed to Colonel Parker, gave the manager "final approval of all contracts to be entered into for Elvis Presley during the term of the respective exclusive agency agreements." Two signatures appeared at the bottom: Nat Lefkowitz, of the Morris agency's contract department, and Elvis Presley, who signed his compact autograph in blue fountain pen ink. In agreeing to such an arrangement—six weeks before he signed a final contract with Parker—Elvis effectively granted the Colonel total control over almost every facet of his career.

What Parker didn't tell the agency was that even though he knew the power of television could make Elvis an immense star all across the United States, he, too, privately feared that Elvis's fame would be fleeting, admitting as much to his stepson, Bobby Ross. And so, Parker rationalized, drawing again on his carnival past, he would give the people just enough to whet their appetite and fire their imagination—book him on all the top television programs, including *The Milton Berle Show, The Steve Allen Show,* and the most prestigious of all, *The Ed Sullivan Show*—and then perhaps never let him appear on television again. Certainly, he would limit his exposure to the press.

By not allowing Elvis to be seen or heard in interviews, Parker made him into the object of nearly limitless romantic fantasy, from a pious innocent who loved his mama and his Lord to a wiggling, greasy god of sex. Controlling his interviews would also make Elvis more exotic and mysterious, and obscure the fact that the young man who proved so effortlessly hypnotic in performance was, in real life, an immature and underdeveloped personality, a sort of charming "idiot savant," as the songwriters Jerry Leiber and Mike Stoller would dub him.

Early on, Parker had warned him to cut the comedy from his stage act—a familiar staple of hillbilly music shows of the time, but almost painful to hear today in the recording of his 1956 Las Vegas debut. Dutifully, after making an off-color remark about marriage ("Why buy a cow when you can steal milk through the fence?") at a high school concert in Alabama, Elvis complied. Yet it was nothing for him to belch on stage, and in private his sense of humor, played out with his cousins and cronies, who traveled with him as a pack of good ol' boy playmates and protectors, continued to run along the lines of stupefying juvenility, even as Presley eventually cultivated a margin of wit and sophistication.

The portrait of Presley as he really was at twenty-one—acne-scarred, sweet-natured, and simple, except in his music and his peculiar relationships with women (already three at a time during his *Louisiana Hayride* days) and his parents (whom he affectionately addressed as his "babies")—was either too dull or too scandalous for Parker to let out.

By the following year, the manager was still taking no chances. When *Time* magazine's Bob Schulman tried to go backstage with other reporters at Elvis's 1957 performance at Seattle's Sick's Stadium, he encountered the Colonel, standing fast, like a portly bouncer. "If you want to hear anything about Elvis, you've got to talk to me," Parker said, both adamant and inflexible. "There was absolutely no access to Elvis himself," Schulman remembers, "although we could see him through the open door, in this garish yellow incandescent light. He was leaning back in a camp chair, scratching his scrotum."

Because the press was usually denied an audience with Elvis, except in the occasional group interview, reporters painted the young inciter of teen frenzy as a reflection of their own reaction to his behavior. To one, especially after his appearance on the *Berle Show,* where he slowed down the ending of "Hound Dog" and punctuated the beat with pelvic thrusts, he was the devil's own sneering son; to another, he was a fighter for freedom on the staid, cultural battlefield. When the city of San Diego banned Elvis's orgasmic dancing, the media reported it with all the gravity of a national security breech.

Parker, who tied on a vendor's apron to peddle both I LOVE ELVIS and I HATE ELVIS buttons to folks who reacted strongly one way or another, didn't care what the newsmen said as long as they said it—and paid their own admission to the shows. Not even an "Elvis is queer" story got his feathers up. When Gabe Tucker threw just such a magazine piece on his desk, Parker didn't say a word until his friend stopped sputtering. "Well," Parker finally said, "did they spell his name right?"

To the press, then, it was almost as if there were no Elvis, except what the Colonel made him out to be. In a way, Colonel Parker *was* Elvis, and the singer, in Parker's mind, was less a separate entity, a person in his own right, than a vehicle for the Colonel's wishes, desires, and ego. When Parker, who likewise rationed his own access to the press, deemed to talk with reporters at all—"If it's a question, I'll say 'yes' or 'no'; that's all the taping I do"—he became the first entertainment manager to wrap a kind of star quality around himself. Like his title, it gave him a sense of superiority, of grandiosity, and allowed him to think of himself in the third person. Often, when he was presented with something that displeased him, he remarked, "I don't think the Colonel is going to like this," as if he were some mystical entity.

Of course, there was still another reason Parker made sure Elvis wasn't overexposed on television, and it was mostly green. "If they can see Elvis for nothing, they won't pay to see him," he declared, chewing the soggy end of an Anthony and Cleopatra. That was no way to build an empire, which was just exactly what he had in mind. With the seminal TV appearances, "Heartbreak Hotel" quickly sold more than one million singles, and continued to sell at a rate of 70,000 copies every week. Eighty-two percent of all American television sets had been tuned to *The Ed Sullivan Show* the night of Elvis's first of three guest shots, and the Colonel was able to boast that since he'd come on board, the cost of an Elvis Presley appearance had jumped from $300 to $25,000 a night, two and a half times what the current top attraction in show business, Martin and Lewis, could command.

"Colonel," the grateful but bewildered Elvis supposedly said, "you put a lump in my throat." To which Parker allegedly replied, "And you put a lump in my wallet."

The day before that first *Sullivan Show* appearance, RCA's Norman Racusin and a company attorney met with the Colonel in his suite at New York's Warwick Hotel to amend Elvis's contract, wiping out the $40,000 advance against royalties. Elvis and his cousins knocked on the door, coming to tell the Colonel they were going to Radio City Music Hall. Parker, fearing Elvis might get into a ruckus, wasn't pleased, but Presley promised they'd just see the stage show and come back. Finally, Parker acquiesced.

"Elvis was still standing there," Racusin recalls, "and Parker said, 'Now what?' " Elvis said, "I need some money." Parker reached into his pocket and pulled out a roll of cash and handed Elvis two one-hundred-dollar bills. "Now remember," he admonished, "don't do anything to draw attention to yourself." "We won't," Elvis said.

Things had moved so fast. Less than a year before, Parker had told a Texas teenager, Kay Wheeler, that she was free to start the first national Elvis Presley Fan Club. "Elvis is just one of our many attractions, and at the present time there are no fan club facilities for him, and we have no immediate plans for any," Carolyn Asmus, Parker's secretary, informed her by letter. Soon, Tom Diskin was sending her photos to mail out, and Elvis asked Wheeler, already well known as a "bop dancer," to teach him her special "rock 'n' bop" steps during a performance in San Antonio.

But when the club's membership quickly grew into the tens of thousands, Parker announced he was forming the "official" Elvis Presley Fan Club and, unlike Wheeler, charging a fee for the distribution of photographs, membership cards, and newsletters. After Elvis's national TV appearances, the money poured into the little Madison, Tennessee, post office like a slot machine gone berserk.

Bill Denny, the scion of Grand Ole Opry manager Jim Denny, who had famously turned Elvis down for Opry membership in 1954, was a Vanderbilt University student at the time. Through his father, he found a job that summer working for Colonel Tom Parker. Part of his routine was to drive a pickup down to the Madison post office "a couple of times a day" and load it up with mail, sometimes bringing along Bevo Bevis, who lived with the Parkers, to help with the bulging canvas sacks.

By now, Parker had hired Tom Diskin's quiet, loyal, and devoutly Catholic sisters, Mary and Patti. The Colonel booked them as a minor-league, supporting act under the name of the Dickens Sisters during the Eddy Arnold years, acquiring their brother, who managed them, in the deal. The sisters now worked in the shed Parker had converted to an office in back of the house, and with the help of Jimmy Rose, whom the Colonel temporarily installed as the new fan club president, they processed the astounding flow of fan mail, mostly by assembly line, dropping the money into a big metal tub on the floor. "No one really counted it, because it didn't matter," as Denny recalls. "If you were a kid someplace, and you wanted a picture of Elvis, you got it."

Within months, the task became so overwhelming that Parker paid Charlie Lamb $10,000 to take over the operation and moved the whole thing to a rented cafeteria in Nashville's Masonic Lodge Building. Lamb installed twenty-one women to assemble Elvis packages of a picture, a membership card, and a button. But almost immediately, as Lamb remembers, "this thing became a beautiful, successful nightmare." The cash came in at such a rate that Lamb couldn't deposit it fast enough and asked the bank to send an armored car to collect it. Finally, after Presley's first appearance on *The Ed Sullivan Show* in September 1956, Parker made a deal with Hank Saperstein, the merchandiser, to assume the fulfillment through his company, Special Projects.

However, Parker's idea was not to make money off the fans so much as it was to make it off deals, since he was never really concerned with selling Elvis to the public, but to the people who *sold* the public, first to the executives who controlled the television and radio networks, then the press, and soon the motion picture moguls. Above all, he enjoyed the fine art of negotiation, of winning, and of getting the best of the other man, even if it was a friend like Lee Gordon, who, along with Oscar Davis, promoted many of Elvis's early shows.

Since his days with Eddy Arnold, Parker never allowed a promoter to make more money than he did on an act. Where many promoters would hire a performer for $200 and take in $10,000 on the show, Parker, who refused to book Elvis into any venue that wouldn't sell out and leave people clamoring to buy tickets ("a real stroke of genius," says Sam Phillips), routinely adjusted the cost. That way, the promoter, who took the risk and did the real work in advancing the show, couldn't cheat him on the ticket count, but he couldn't make much profit, either. "You don't have to be nice to people on the way up if you're not coming back down," Parker allegedly joked.

From the beginning of their relationship, Parker, whose agreement with Elvis was for a 25 percent commission on all monies, royalties, or profits, also charged Elvis for any expenses, as he had Eddy Arnold. It was part of the game with the Colonel that he would pay nothing out of his own pocket, no matter how small or trivial. If he had lunch with someone, and his companion wouldn't pick up the cost of his meal, Parker later wrote it off against Presley's 75 percent, figuring Elvis was his only client, and that in one way or another, the conversation would have benefited his career.

Elvis didn't question such things, and as with the William Morris memo that gave Parker complete control over Presley's film and television contracts, the singer wasn't interested in the fine print. "As long as Elvis can write a check for something he wants, he doesn't care how much money is in the bank," Parker bragged to associates, and it was true. Elvis had put his total trust in Parker, and after a while, he never even glanced at the checks that Parker had his associates hand deliver. Shortly after they closed the RCA deal, Elvis sent his manager a telegram that pledged his absolute loyalty, in words that would later come back to haunt him:

> Dear Colonel, Words can never tell you how my folks and I appreciate what you did for me. I've always known and now my folks are assured that you are the best, most wonderful person I could ever hope to work with. Believe me when I say I will stick with you through thick and thin and do everything I can to uphold your faith in me. Again, I say thanks, and I love you like a father. Elvis Presley.

What Elvis didn't know at the time was that Parker collected money from side deals and outright hucksterism that likely never made it into his meticulous recordkeeping.

"Promoters would come in to try to get an Elvis Presley concert," remembers Byron Raphael, "and they'd ask what it would cost. The Colonel wouldn't tell them. He'd say, 'Here's what I want you to do. I want you to bring in $50,000 in cash, and I want you to put it on the bed. And if it's enough money, we'll do a personal appearance for you. And if it isn't enough money, you don't get the personal appearance, but I keep ten percent just for my time.' And people would do it."

Such chutzpah demonstrates Parker's two major rules of business: first, that everything costs—there's no free lunch; and second, always know where the money is before you make the deal.

In service to his second rule, and purely for fun, Parker, whose Madison office was in the knotty-pine basement of his home, preferred to answer his business phone himself, rather than filter the calls through his secretary. He was in his element, says Bill Denny, surrounded by his banks of phones, each with a series of buttons and lines.

"When someone would ask for Colonel Parker," Denny remembers, "he would say, 'Well, he's on the phone right now.' He'd find out who it was, and if it was someone he was in a deal with, he'd put them on hold. Then he'd come back a little later and say that the Colonel was still talking. And he'd really hammer them around. Many times I heard him trying to put a deal together, and he'd say, 'Well, if you don't take it now, the next call is going to cost you $10,000 more.'"

As a smart manager booking Elvis's personal appearances in the '50s, Parker insisted on a minimum of 50 percent to 60 percent of the money up front; often the full amount was expected with the return of a signed contract. Those promoters lucky enough to be allowed to pay on the date of the show knew to have cash, and not a check, ready before the performance, because, as Parker said, laughing, "I don't want to end up with cider in my ear."

Still stinging from the days when carnival promoters left him holding the bag, he didn't care what people thought about his tactics, preferring they found him difficult than stupid. Ninety percent of the people that he came up with in the business, he often said, were broke.

But it was not a lavish lifestyle Parker hoped to achieve. In fact, the Parkers didn't live beyond their means—they lived far below them. In full carny promotional mode, he might stroll around in fawn-colored pants, suspenders, white shoes, a pink satin shirt with ELVIS embroidered on the pocket, worn loose and untucked like a lady's blouse to cover his stomach, and either a bowler or a five-gallon hat. But aside from ordering the occasional custom-made cowhide sport jacket or white linen suit from Nudie's Rodeo Tailors, Parker kept away from flamboyant clothes. Since the Eddy Arnold years, he had often dressed like a vagrant as part of his act, hoping to appear poorer and more homespun than he really was, to throw people off and give him an edge in negotiations.

However, as Parker became more prosperous, he began to lavish luxuries on Marie. In Florida, the old-timers insist that Marie was always a rung above her husband on the social ladder, even with her impoverished origins and wild behavior. While others find it hard to believe ("Let's say she wasn't too much with the social graces—they were two of a kind, and nothing was ever going to change them," ventures RCA publicity director Anne Fulchino), Marie's union with Parker would, in time, allow her to reinvent herself, despite her husband's own rough manners.

As Maria van Kuijk had done, Marie would use the carriage of matrimony to separate from her past and rise to a higher social level, replete with the attendant costume jewelry, high-end clothing, and an endless array of shoes, remembering how, during the Depression, she'd worn cardboard liners to cover the holes in the soles. "She had a twelve-foot closet just for coats," says her daughter-in-law Sandra Polk Ross, including a full-length white mink for which she went to New York to pick out the pelts. The irony was that other than when she traveled ("She was the only person I knew who brought her whole big jewelry chest with her," recalls Ann Dodelin, whose husband, Ed, was RCA's national record sales manager), she mostly kept her finery put away, preferring a more modest way of dress in public. She was happiest, some say, playing poker with her best friend, Mother Maybelle Carter.

Parker denied her almost nothing, because, as his acolyte and friend the booking agent Hubert Long once observed, she was "the Colonel's stable base." Yet something about his psychological make-up made him unable to discard worn-out, useless objects. He directed Marie's thinking along the same lines, even to moldy food left too long in the refrigerator. On occasion, people took notice.

During his years with Arnold, Parker forged a close friendship with the well-known country disc jockey and promoter Connie B. Gay, who operated out of the Washington, D.C., area. Plainspoken and earthy (he once described Hank Williams as "a goner, just a pile of shit mixed with alcohol and pills"), Gay had worked as a huckster and street-corner salesman during the Depression, gathering a crowd by holding up a Gila monster and announcing, "I'm gonna eat this thing!"

When the Colonel first acquired Elvis, it was natural that he continue the association with his old friend. He allowed Gay to book Presley on one of his country music cruises down the Potomac in March 1956, but "It was the only time I didn't fill the boat," Gay recalled. "There was an engine problem and we couldn't take off. A lot of people wanted their money back, so I paid them and they missed Elvis."

Still, Gay's children, daughter Judy and son Jan, remember that their parents and the Parkers were so close that Tom and Marie always stayed at the house when they were anywhere near the area, and the teenagers were told that they would go live with the Parkers if anything ever happened to Connie and Hazel.

On one such visit, Judy, a huge Elvis fan whom Parker named the honorary president of the national fan club, sat wide-eyed as Marie dug to the end of her lipstick tube with a little brush. From the conversation, Judy got the impression Marie wasn't allowed to buy more until she'd used every last bit. "Later, Mother said, 'Well, if you knew Tom, you'd know why.'"

Each time the Parkers came, the Gay children saw their mother wait on Tom hand and foot, cooking the foods he liked and ate in enormous quantities. Hazel timed her banana pudding so it would be warm for his arrival, and the teenagers watched as their father and Tom, whom they remember as "an old, fat, nice guy, always schemin' with Daddy on how to make a buck with the hillbilly trade," put away bowls of the stuff, reminiscing about the early years.

"One reason Tom always stayed with us was so he could save a hotel bill," says Jan. "This one time, we'd put him up for days, and as he started to leave, he said, 'Hazel, I'd like to give you a little somethin' for your hospitality.' And he handed her a bag of all of the little hotel soaps he'd collected on his most recent swing. That was her present. Everybody liked Tom," he adds, laughing, "but he was a moocher, par excellence."

Parker's frugality is a well-known part of the Snowman's legend, and it was a favorite part of his con. But what only Marie knew was that Parker, fearing another heart attack, was terrified that he might die and leave Marie without means of support.

When the next heart attack did come, in 1956—Bitsy Mott claims it was brought on by an argument with Elvis, who "was getting a little belligerent and didn't want to show up on time"—it was mild, and Parker was merely confined to his Texas hotel room for several days.

In the future, Parker would use his heart condition as a form of manipulation, taking to his bed until Elvis capitulated and fell into line. Nonetheless, the underlying disease was real, and he unsuccessfully tried to sell Elvis's contract to both Oscar Davis and Connie B. Gay.

Parker's brushes with immortality brought all the crushing depression that often attends heart attacks, and triggered a host of old anxieties, most prominently his abnormal fear of death.

To a man like Andreas van Kuijk, with the dogma of the Catholic church still underpinning his conception of heaven and hell, the possibility of a third and fatal heart attack, coupled with the events of long ago in Holland, may have weighed heavy on his mind. But whether from honest altruism, tax considerations, or the fear of eternal damnation, beginning in the Eddy Arnold years, when he first became wealthy, Parker began making large contributions to charities, up to thirty-one separate organizations by the late '60s.

"He was never free and easy when it came to giving away money to his employees, like a bonus at Christmas," says Byron Raphael. And strangers who wrote in to the office with a hard-luck story and a plea for help received only a terse "I am so sorry" and a picture of Elvis. But although he preferred to do things to help people that didn't cost him financially—cajoling RCA's corporate office into donating appliances and television sets to philanthropic organizations and hospitals in his name, for example—at times, he dug deep into his own pocket, especially where children, unwed mothers, or crusty old carnies were concerned.

When the King's Daughters Day Home, which catered to low-income families, needed a washer and dryer, Parker told its head, the Madison society matron Louise Draper, to go pick out what she wanted. Later, he contributed a new kitchen to the center, a move that also benefited Marie, who had thrown off her carny past and attempted to reinvent herself as a cultured member of both the International King's Daughters and Sons, and the Riverside Garden Club.

While it's true that Parker often shared the credit ("Elvis and the Colonel") or insisted that his actions not be publicized ("I didn't want people comin' knockin' on the door, you know"), he often expected a favor in return, even if the arrangement was only implied. He declared near the end of his life that through the years he donated more than $500,000 to charities, two thirds of it to organizations in Tennessee, where high-powered lawyers and a succession of governors—including Frank G. Clement, who made Parker an honorary Colonel in 1953, and Lieutenant Governor Frank Gorrell—picked small, deserving groups such as the Nashville Youth Orchestra, and dispersed the monies for him. Such connections, of course, could be invaluable for a man who'd entered the country illegally and feared both discovery and deportation.

And there were other, more subtle connections. In the '50s, when Father George Rohling became pastor at St. Joseph's Catholic Church, situated next to Parker's home on Gallatin Road, the Diskin sisters, who were members of the parish, asked the Colonel if he would consider contributing to the air-conditioning for the church school auditorium.

Decades later, Parker bragged that he'd put in the whole system, "$20,000 or $30,000 worth." But the priest, now a monsignor, recalls that the church owed only $2,000 on the units and that Parker generously gave him a check for the whole amount, and followed it up with a modest check each Christmas and a miniature pony to be raffled off at a fund-raiser. The Colonel also gave Father Rohling "a small truckload of Elvis memorabilia," which the priest admits he burned, thinking anything that had to do with the pelvis-thrusting entertainer might be evil, a decision he now terms "a sad mistake."

While Parker occasionally walked over for social events, he never attended mass at St. Joseph's, nor did he ever accompany Marie to the Gallatin Road Baptist Church on Sundays. Andreas van Kuijk may have spent most of his childhood in service to the Catholic saints, but the man who became Tom Parker did not want to hear any mention of the hereafter, with judgment and retribution for earthly sins.

As Parker prepared to take Elvis to Hollywood in 1956 and began spending more time in California, his personal contact with Father Rohling diminished, especially as the priest moved on to another church in Nashville. Years later, they met again, when Marie died in 1986. Parker brought her back to Madison for entombment in the mausoleum at Spring Hill Cemetery, where, not wishing to ponder the future, he bought only one crypt.

Madison was where Marie had become a lady, an accepted member of a sometimes snooty community. But now he was worried about her soul, and perhaps his own. Would Monsignor Rohling perform the funeral, along with a Baptist minister?

"I thought it was rather unusual," says the monsignor, since Marie had never been to St. Joseph's, and, as he recalled, he'd never met her. He also thought it odd because in thirty-three years, he and the Colonel had never spoken about religion, and Parker had never told the priest he was Catholic. But Father Rohling had already figured it out. One day, when he was next door visiting the Diskins, he noticed something interesting. The Colonel, who never forgot who he was or where he came from— sending money to Holland for the flood relief in 1953—kept what the priest surmised was "pictures of family members" on his wall. The one that struck the father most was that of a nun, Parker's older sister Marie.

11

"ELVIS MAKES PITCHAS"

J O S E P H Hazen was sitting in his Park Avenue apartment, reading, one Saturday night in 1956, when the telephone rang. "Joe," said his neighbor Harriet Ames, "look at this fellow on the television, Elvis Presley. He's a terrific dancer. He's quite a character." Hazen dialed his set to the Dorsey Brothers' *Stage Show,* and, as he remembered years later, immediately called Hal Wallis in California and told him to watch the program.

Some years before, Hazen, then a lawyer with Warner Bros. in New York, had met Wallis, a Warner production chief with a long list of solid commercial films, while on a routine trip to California.

"We chatted," said Hazen, a son-in-law of Walter Annenberg, the billionaire media mogul and philanthropist who would become the U.S. ambassador to Great Britain. In time, the two worked out a 60–40 partnership to produce films independently, Wallis handling the artistic duties and Hazen the financial, with Paramount as their distributor.

The day after Presley's appearance on *Stage Show,* Hazen telephoned the William Morris office in New York and spoke with Martin Jurow, an agent in the film department, about a contract for Presley's services. Wallis, clearly smitten with Elvis's soulful stare ("There was something about his eyes, a solemn look . . . an expressive face, a new personality that I knew was definitely star material for the screen"), went to work on Colonel Parker, who told Wallis that Elvis would "probably" be out on the West Coast soon and would "consider" the possibility of a meeting.

"I knew instinctively that the Colonel was interested but playing it cool," Wallis wrote in his autobiography. What he didn't know was that Parker had set his cap for Wallis back in his dogcatching days, when the Warner Bros. film crew came to Tampa to shoot *Air Force.*

Through the years, Parker had obsessed about the producer, envying his power and his wealth. He'd followed Wallis's move to Paramount through the trade papers and fantasized about a day when he would come to Hollywood with an act so big that a man like Wallis would be eating out of his hand.

And so he planned it from the beginning with Elvis, booking him into all of the Paramount-controlled theaters in Florida and up the East Coast, where the singer packed every one he played. The word couldn't help but get back to Paramount's top brass.

But it was not just his desire to maximize his client's talents, or to make him rich and famous beyond anyone's boldest imagining. Through Hollywood, Parker, now forty-six years old, would also make *himself* powerful—more omnipotent, even, than the old-line tycoons. His aim was not only to become a figure of respect, but also to build his own legend.

He would become, in effect, too big to be touched, able to forget that he was an illegal alien with no papers. In doing so, Parker would be in his total glory, conducting his professional negotiations and personal manipulations with the outrageous, swashbuckling bravado of a pirate. At no other time would he ever be funnier, deadlier, or as obviously pathological in his business dealings.

The prime target of his discontent was Hal Wallis. Eleven years Parker's senior, Wallis was the Hollywood stand-in for Parker's own father and, in the Colonel's mind, the ultimate authority figure. To Parker, Wallis symbolized not just every wildly successful Hollywood mogul, but every Jewish son of immigrant parents who had "made it" in America. It would not be enough for Parker to be accepted as an equal by such men. He would have to needle them, bully them, and prove his superiority with whatever means necessary, including chicanery, deceit, and cunning.

When Wallis followed up to set a date for Elvis's screen test, Parker did what only came naturally: he refused to take his calls. The producer, swearing later that "nothing would stop me from signing this boy for films," telephoned and telegraphed the Colonel to the point of exasperation. Hazen, who began to envision that part of his job might be to manage the man who managed the star, likewise began a futile telephone campaign.

Finally, the Colonel entered into preliminary contractual agreements and delivered Elvis to Paramount Studios for two days beginning March 26, 1956. There, having been given the material only the night before, Presley performed two dramatic scenes from *The Rainmaker*, which Wallis was about to shoot with Burt Lancaster and Katharine Hepburn. For a musical number, Elvis lip-synched his new single, "Blue Suede Shoes," while strumming a prop guitar.

Soon after, RCA's Steve Sholes and Chick Crumpacker viewed the test in New York and were stunned at what they saw. Presley displayed both a surprisingly natural acting ability and, in the serious love scene, a directness that suggested the work of James Dean or Marlon Brando. "My God, we were agog. It was the talk of the place," says Crumpacker.

Joe Hazen was likewise startled, writing in a memo to Wallis on June 11, 1956, that Elvis's "meteoric rise is unquestionably a freak situation, but that still does not detract from the fact that as a straight actor the guy has great potentialities." Later, Hazen would reiterate with Parker that Elvis should, of course, sing in his movies, "but his dramatic abilities and talents should be carefully and steadily developed so . . . he can do strong dramatic parts as well as sing."

Nothing would have pleased Presley more. In fact, the former movie theater usher had just told Wallis, "My ambition has always been to become a motion picture actor—a good one, sir."

But Wallis had other ideas. "The idea of tailoring Elvis for dramatic roles is something that we never attempted," Wallis said years later. "We didn't sign Elvis as a second Jimmy Dean. We signed him as a number-one Elvis Presley."

Parker went along with it for two reasons: first, he saw Presley's movie career primarily as a vehicle for selling concert tickets and records, and more important, privately he had little faith in Elvis's acting abilities, even though Presley frequently recited whole scenes of Dean's *Rebel Without a Cause*, trying to convince his manager that he could carry a dramatic film.

When Elvis arrived in Los Angeles for his screen test, waiting for him at the airport were Parker, his assistant Tom Diskin, and Leonard Hirshan, the young William Morris agent who'd been assigned as Presley's representative for motion pictures. Lenny, as the guys in the office called him, was amused to see the new singing sensation step off the plane with a camera around his neck, like any other hick tourist.

Hirshan had been with William Morris just five years, but now, with Martin Jurow in New York, he was about to negotiate one of the most infamous contracts in the Morris agency's history. Acting on the advice to get Presley as much work as possible before his star burned out, Hirshan encouraged Parker to take Wallis and Hazen's best offer—a contract for one motion picture and options for six more.

On the surface, a seven-picture contract might have seemed impressive. But, in effect, it was a commitment for only one picture and amounted to a basic deal. Not only was it nonexclusive—Parker was allowed to make one "outside" picture each year with another studio—but the financial terms befitted a total unknown: $15,000 for the first film, $20,000 for the second, $25,000 for the third, and up to $100,000 for the seventh. Furthermore, it offered no billing structure, no script approval, and no perks of any kind. Nonetheless, Wallis, Hazen, Presley, and Parker signed the two-page document on April 2, 1956.

The contract, which governed the making of *Loving You* and *King Creole,* would be bolstered with bonuses and completely rewritten in October 1958. But it stuck in Parker's craw for his entire Hollywood career.

Always skittish about a situation beyond his control, and hypervigilant against deception and disgrace, Parker was paranoid that the Hollywood sharpies would shortchange him if they could. Now he was livid to discover that his own agency had made a deal that necessitated a special waiver from the Screen Actors Guild, as the terms fell below the minimum provisions—$25,000 a year salary—of the Guild contract. He was further infuriated to learn, once *Loving You* began filming, that both of Elvis's costars, Wendell Corey and Lizabeth Scott, were paid far more than Presley, and in a great display of authority that Parker would often repeat, he threatened to pull Elvis off the picture.

While Parker was grateful to Abe Lastfogel and the Morris agency for representing him through the Eddy Arnold era, he realized, in this first real lesson about the agency-studio relationship, that the Morris office gave him poor advice. ("When the Colonel demanded to renegotiate, Lastfogel tried everything he could to convince him to take less money," remembers Byron Raphael.) He also saw that a major talent agency with hundreds of clients would not risk its relationship with the movie companies over the fate of a single star.

Still, under California law, only an agent, and not a manager, could close a binding deal for a client with a studio. So the Colonel knew he needed Lastfogel for a variety of reasons, and not just to get Elvis prestige engagements like the New Frontier in Vegas, where Parker had embarrassed the agency by insisting on cash, and not a check, in advance. ("No check is good. Some are pretty good, but they got an atom-bomb testing place out there in the desert. What if some feller pressed the wrong button?") But from then on, Parker would always be wary of any Morris agent. And he would carry a special grudge against Lenny Hirshan, who would come to bear the full weight of the Colonel's revenge mentality.

Adam van Kuijk with three of his children, from left Ad, Jan, and Johanna, about 1922. He would die three years later, at the age of fifty-nine. (Courtesy of Maria Dons-Maas)

The van Kuijk family lived in the stable of the van Gend & Loos building, seen here to the right of the music hall, marked "Kon. Erk. Harmonie De Unie." (The collection of Dirk Vellenga)

Anna van den Enden was murdered in the living quarters behind this shop at Nieuwe Boschstraat 31, in May 1929. (Tony Wulffraat)

Andreas van Kuijk, aka Tom Parker, circa 1926–7, likely during his Chautauqua days on his first trip to America. (Elvis Presley Enterprises. Used by permission)

The well-dressed young gentleman, age nineteen, in the year he disappeared from his native Holland. (The collection of Dirk Vellenga)

Private Thomas Parker (seventh from left, middle row) in the 64th Coast Artillery Brigade Regiment, stationed at Fort Shafter near Honolulu, probably fall 1929. Fellow soldier Earl Kilgus stands behind him, back row, fifth from left. (Courtesy of Earl Kilgus and Robert H. Egolf III)

Cees Frijters received this picture of Andre as an American soldier, stationed at Fort Shafter. (The collection of Dirk Vellenga)

A photo Andre sent home to his family, probably in 1932, when he was stationed at Fort Barrancas, near Pensacola, Florida, in the 13th Coast Artillery. (The author's collection/source unknown)

ARMY MEDICAL CENTER,
RECORDS SECTION AND DETACHMENTS.
WASHINGTON, D. C.
OFFICE OF THE DETACHMENT COMMANDER

AGH:sjm

August 19, 1933.

201-Parker, Thomas

Subject: Discharge on Certificate of Disability.

To: The Surgeon General, U. S. Army, Washington, D. C.

1. In compliance with paragraph 16 c, Army Regulations 615-360, report that Private Thomas Parker, 6 363 948, Headquarters Battery, 13th Coast Artillery, was on August 19, 1933, honorably discharged on certificate of disability per 3rd Ind CDD Hq 3rd Corps Area, August 11, 1933, by reason of "Psychosis, Psychogenic Depression, acute, on basis of Constitutional Psychopathic State, Emotional Instability".

RECEIVED S. G. O. AUG 19 1933

A. G. HEILMAN,
Major, Medical Corps,
Asst. Detachment Comdr.

Private Thomas Parker's army discharge record, which identified him as a psychopath. (The author's collection)

Not long out of Walter Reed Army Hospital, working a movie event, most likely in Tampa, 1935. (The author's collection/ source unknown)

Late 1930s: Looking every inch the carnival press agent, though front offices jobs would always be denied him. (The author's collection/ source unknown)

Parker, as a Humane Society field agent, during filming of *Air Force* at Tampa's Drew Field, 1942. *(Tampa Tribune)*

When Hollywood came to Tampa in 1943 for *A Guy Named Joe,* Parker (back row, with ice cream) invited the camera crew on a picnic at a friend's house. Bobby Ross sits at Parker's right with his girlfriend and future wife, Marian DeDyne. Marie appears front row left. (Courtesy Sandra Polk Ross and Robert Kenneth Ross)

By 1944, Parker had signed on as the booker and advance man, or "general agent," for the Jamup and Honey tent show, where he met Gabe Tucker (right). (Courtesy of Gabe Tucker)

As the new manager of country singer Eddy Arnold (left of poster), Parker (far left) staged a 1946 promotion in Tampa to bring out the crowds. (The Country Music Foundation)

RCA's Steve Sholes (middle), with hopeful recording artist Dolph Hewitt (left), joins Parker and Eddy Arnold at an industry convention, probably 1949. (The collection of R. A. Andreas and ". . . .and more bears.")

Parker, desperate for a title and not yet a "Colonel," signed this mid-forties portrait to Bobby and Marian Ross as "The Gov." (Courtesy Sandra Polk Ross and Robert Kenneth Ross)

Elvis puts his wallet in the Colonel's pocket in this gag publicity photo from 1956. Parker's critics would later argue the image was prophetic. (The author's collection/source unknown)

Country singer Hank Snow beams beside Elvis Presley, backstage at the Grand Old Opry, December 1957. Parker had cut him out of half of Presley's management the year before. (The author's collection/ source unknown)

The Colonel helps Marie celebrate granddaughter Sharon Ross's first birthday, May 2, 1951. (Courtesy Sandra Polk Ross and Robert Kenneth Ross)

left: Elvis joins Parker, sporting fake goatee (back row), with RCA brass Bill Bullock (back row, far left), Steve Sholes (back row, center), and Hill and Range liaison Freddy Bienstock (front row, left), circa 1956. (The collection of Robin Rosaaen)

Loving You, released in 1957, costarred Lizabeth Scott as Glenda Markle, a manipulative press agent and manager who reprised a number of Colonel Parker's real-life publicity stunts. (Courtesy of the Academy of Motion Picture Arts and Sciences)

As a birthday present for Steve Sholes, Colonel Parker had an elaborate dog house built in honor of Nipper, the RCA mascot. Elvis poses in front of it with the Colonel and Marie (right) at Sholes's party at the Beverly Hills Hotel, 1957. The "Frank" mentioned in the legend over the door ("The Dog House That Frank Helped Build") is Y. Frank Freeman, the famed Paramount Pictures executive, and alludes to Elvis's films helping sell records. (The collection of Robin Rosaaen)

Parker, ever the carny, promoted *King Creole* with balloons boasting a cartoon image of Elvis. Two of the Colonel's army, secretary Trude Forsher (left) and assistant Byron Raphael (right) join him on the Paramount lot in 1958. (The collection of James Forsher)

The Colonel and Elvis make merry in a red BMW Isetta "bubble car," Presley's Christmas gift to his manager, December 1957. (Nashville Public Library, The Nashville Room)

When Texas Senator Lyndon Baines Johnson invited Eddy Arnold to entertain Mexico President Adolfo Lopez Mateos at the LBJ ranch in October 1959, Parker went along, and parlayed a meeting into a friendship. Johnson's daughter, Lynda Bird, watches at right. (Oliver Atkins / George Mason University.)

Vernon Presley, the Colonel's ally, accompanied Elvis to Germany in 1958, and conducted business with Parker in the U.S. by letter. Here, Vernon enjoys a press item with his son. (Courtesy of the Academy of Motion Picture Arts and Sciences)

Elvis arrives home in Memphis, March 1960. This is the photo that alerted Parker's Dutch relatives to his existence as Colonel Tom Parker, the manager of Elvis Presley. (The author's collection/source unknown)

At first, Parker pretended that all was well. When he dropped by the agency, he regaled the agents with his usual self-serving stories of his carny past, and recalled how, in the Eddy Arnold era, he'd sent a small boy to pick up the souvenir books that folks left under their seats at the shows. "Sold 'em again at the next stop!" Parker bragged, sliding into the line with a wink and a round-faced grin.

The William Morris agents shook their heads at such shenanigans. But sometimes, sharing the sentiments of the RCA label heads, they didn't know quite what to believe about this man to whom life seemed to be little more than a romp through a carnival fun house, filled with smoke and mirrors. The weirdest talk came from the record company, where the story went around that during his circus days, Parker had married the bearded lady. One RCA department head claimed to have seen the "full shadow of a real blue beard" on Marie, and as crazy as it sounded, nobody put anything past Parker, especially since the gossip made him seem more of an outlandish character and less an intimidating adversary.

At the least, such stories sent mixed signals, but the lighter ones hid Parker's seething animosity, which began to manifest itself in other ways, primarily in humiliating the Morris agents in public. When Elvis played the Pan Pacific Auditorium in Los Angeles in October 1957, Sam Weisbord, the president of William Morris, requested twenty-five complimentary tickets for his executives. Parker, who customarily gave no passes and despised being asked for something free if he thought the petitioner could afford it, grudgingly sent over three tickets, for Weisbord, Lastfogel, and Norman Brokaw, an up-and-comer at the agency who headed the West Coast television department.

The powerful agents, none of whom stood taller than five feet three, were shocked to discover that their seats were not in the first rows, as was customary for VIPs, but in a section far in the back.

Joe Hazen and Hal Wallis had already gotten embroiled in one of Parker's classic power plays in November 1956. As the script for *Loving You* began to take form—centering on a naïve young performer very much like Presley himself—they asked if Elvis might confer with the cowriter Herbert Baker. Parker, who had demanded early that all communication go through him, carefully keeping Elvis under wraps to the Morris agents and to the producers, insisting that Presley wanted to spare himself any business or professional contacts, sent word by Abe Lastfogel that the answer was no.

Always hot-tempered about imagined criticism or slights, Parker complained that the producers appeared to have lost interest in Presley, because no representative from Paramount had attended his show at L.A.'s Shrine Auditorium in June 1956—a time when Elvis was subjected to considerable public criticism.

Hazen responded that it was not their custom to appear at every opening of a performer they had under contract. Yet, he cited, both he and Wallis had flown to Las Vegas in April for Elvis's debut at the New Frontier, and Wallis had attempted to invite Elvis to his home for dinner several times, and to lunch at the Paramount commissary. But Parker remained adamant—the balance of power had now shifted to him.

This glimmer at how churlish and abrasive the Colonel could be prompted Hazen to memo Wallis that "Parker has a peeve about neglect." Before long, the producers would have stronger words for Parker in private, Wallis vowing he'd rather try to close a deal with the devil, and Hazen ranting, "I wouldn't be a hundred feet away from him! He's an obnoxious, terrible man. Terrible man!"

Parker doubtless took pride in such reactions, in how his irascibility provoked and exasperated others, while he was able to remain cool and in control of his emotions. But secretly he was smarting over a remark Hazen had made about *Love Me Tender,* Presley's first picture, which Elvis had made for Twentieth Century–Fox under the Wallis-Hazen loan-out clause, designed in part to let another studio test the waters.

A month before *Love Me Tender* was released, Hazen screened a rough cut of the film to see what kind of property he'd bought, and when Parker came to New York for Elvis's second appearance on *The Ed Sullivan Show* in late October, Hazen met with Parker and Harry Kalcheim at New York's Warwick Hotel.

As Elvis's first film, Hazen said, *Love Me Tender* would probably do very big business. But, he added, "very confidentially—and as man to man," neither Wallis nor Paul Nathan, Wallis's associate producer, was particularly impressed with it. In fact, they'd considered it "crap." The Colonel bristled and responded that the studio was making some changes that he had recommended. With those "methods that have been very helpful to us on personal appearances," he was certain the picture would be improved.

Parker first considered the project when he got a call from Buddy Adler, one of the last of the Hollywood power producers who had just succeeded Darryl Zanuck as Fox's top executive.

"I was in his office when the call came," remembers Freddy Bienstock, who as the Aberbachs' younger cousin became Elvis's liaison with Hill and Range Music, particularly in the movie years. "Buddy Adler told him he'd just gotten this fantastic property. He said it would make Elvis a movie star, and he'd like to send the Colonel the script. The Colonel said, 'There's no sense in sending me the script, because I can't read. The only thing I'm interested in is how much you're gonna pay me.'"

Adler countered with the fact that Elvis had never done a picture before, and the studio would be taking a chance on him: "We'll give you $25,000."

And the Colonel said, as Bienstock remembers, "'That's exactly what I want. Now, how much are you going to pay Elvis?'"

The number Parker had in mind was a staggering $1 million. No other movie star commanded anything near that salary for a single picture, but Parker was in love with the sound of the figure, with the power it conveyed, and with the audacity it took to demand it.

Adler was stunned. "Not even Jack Lemmon gets that," he told the Colonel. "Well," said Parker, "maybe he needs a new manager."

Immediately, the Colonel called Abe Lastfogel and told him Elvis needed a million up front to make Adler's picture, a Civil War–era drama with the working title *The Reno Brothers*. Secretly, he hoped for $100,000.

Lastfogel was taken aback at such moxie, but assured the Colonel that while no one would pay his asking price, he could beat the Paramount deal. Several days later, Lastfogel phoned back to say that naturally Fox wouldn't go for the million, but they'd come up to $75,000 and give Elvis top billing with his name above the title. Parker, who had begun to insist on one-page contracts at RCA and resented the studios' attempt to confuse him with talk of grosses and percentages of profits, held firm. "Better take this, Tom," Lastfogel said. "Believe me, this is as high as they're going."

"Go back to 'em," Parker barked, knowing full well that Presley's name was everything to the project, "and tell them to give the Colonel the money he wants, and they won't have to give Elvis any billing."

In the end, Elvis received the target price of $100,000 and costar credit and, at Parker's insistence, the written promise of a bonus if the picture grossed more than $5 million. Fox also took an option for two other films—*Flaming Star* and *Wild in the Country*—at $150,000 and $200,000. But Parker lived for the day when the studios would have to pay his million-dollar demand. "Elvis makes pitchas," he took to saying to himself as a sort of maniacal mantra.

Leonard Hirshan was the agent who found *Love Me Tender* and who helped finalize the deal with Lastfogel and Parker. In retrospect, he says, he ended up learning from his client's country approach to Hollywood negotiation, particularly "in getting the most for your client, not to give up early, but to hang in there. Whenever I said, 'Colonel, if we don't take this, we're going to lose it,' " he recalls, "the Colonel said, 'You can't lose it—you never had it.' "

Hirshan respected Parker, and in those days, at least, considered him good for Elvis. But what Hirshan never understood (and Lastfogel did) was that Parker saw himself, and not Elvis, as the client, and that to Parker's way of thinking, Elvis's wishes should never have been Hirshan's concern. Now Parker would insist that Hirshan, whom he considered snide, sarcastic, and contemptible, never again be allowed at the bargaining table—he got in the way of Parker's plans. In the future, Lastfogel, not Hirshan, would negotiate the movie deals based on the terms Parker laid out. Always those deals would include a number of perks for Parker, including, on *Love Me Tender,* an office on the Fox lot, a secretarial staff, and a car and chauffeur at his disposal. Such accommodations were unprecedented for the manager of a star.

From the beginning, the Colonel turned the "Elvis exploitation office," as he called it, into his own private midway, with balloons hanging from the ceiling, stuffed animals keeping watch from every corner, and Presley paraphernalia covering the walls. Hullabaloo reigned supreme. At times, Parker summoned his staff, his lieutenant, Tom Diskin, secretary Trude Forsher, and Byron Raphael, on loan from the William Morris office, with the squeeze of a toy puppy dog, one bark for Trude, two barks for Byron, and three barks for Diskin. Sometimes he did the barking himself.

Parker's main directive called for everyone to look busy at all times, even if it meant just fashioning rows of paper dolls for hours on end. Letter writing, no matter how meaningless, was a favorite preoccupation, as was the counting of the big Tennessee sausages that Parker obtained from the country comic Whitey Ford (the Duke of Paducah) and gave as gifts to every motion picture icon from Bing Crosby to Ray Bolger.

But the real order of the day was to have fun at other people's expense through a series of practical jokes. If the pompous studio heads considered him a bumpkin, walking around with a smelly cigar and his shirttail hanging out, Parker would have the last laugh. The country fool, as they initially pegged him, would soon play out a sort of down-home sting operation, in which he'd out-con the Hollywood moguls, to him the biggest sharks of all.

One morning, just after Parker had moved on to the Twentieth Century—Fox lot, he gathered his staff and told them that Buddy Adler and Lou Schrieber, who were running the studio, were coming by for their first in-person meeting with the Colonel.

Parker wanted it to be an event they'd never forget. First, he ordered a sign to read COLONEL PARKER'S WEST COAST OFFICE, which he placed over the men's room door. Then he stationed everyone in his place. Diskin and Byron were to pick up the phone and make imaginary calls, while Trude was to look studiously secretarial. Then he installed Elvis's corpulent friend Arthur Hooton, in the shower with a steno pad and a stool.

"If anybody laughs," the Colonel said to the group, "you'll be sent back to wherever you came from." With that, he unwrapped one of the Duke of Paducah's country sausages, greased the doorknobs, and disappeared into the men's room.

"When Adler and Schrieber came in," remembers Raphael, "Trude told them that Colonel was waiting for them in his West Coast office." She pointed in the direction of the men's room, and Adler opened the door to find "the Colonel sitting on the toilet with his pants down, and this gigantic fat guy in the shower pretending to take dictation. The Colonel said, 'Come on in, close the door, don't worry about anything.'"

The handsome and dignified Adler tried to pretend that nothing was out of the ordinary as he listened to a man on a toilet going on about how he intended to promote their motion picture. Schrieber, too stunned to say anything, remained mute.

"After about five minutes," says Raphael, "Adler and Schrieber started to smell something horrendous on their hands, because they'd handled the doorknobs. You can imagine what they thought, but they didn't want to embarrass anybody. They just wanted to get out of there. And the Colonel just kept talking, keeping them there as long as possible. They didn't know *what* to do. They were in shock."

Finally, Parker let them go, and the office erupted into hysterics, Byron and Trude realizing their new boss was the kind of man who left people dazed, walking around and talking to themselves. The next day, the manager of Fox's newest star called Ed Dodelin at RCA and had him send both of the executives a large cabinet television, courtesy of Elvis and the Colonel.

Parker's antics with the Hollywood power brokers brought a measure of humor to a staid and conservative industry. But the Colonel's need to diminish and degrade—to terrorize grown men all around him—also served to intimidate them into submission.

As soon as shooting started on *Love Me Tender* in August 1956, Parker sent a memo to the producer, David Weisbart. Elvis was understandably nervous about acting in a movie for the first time, the manager said, and suggested it might be prudent for Parker to be on the set, since "a familiar face will help keep this fellow settled down." Weisbart okayed it, thus giving the Colonel permission to grow bolder in his requests. A month later, Weisbart memoed Buddy Adler that Parker wanted to know if it would be possible for him to receive some kind of screen credit.

"He's been so cooperative with us on everything pertaining to Presley," wrote Weisbart, "that I thought this would not be a bad idea . . . it can read Technical Advisor . . . Col. Tom Parker." Adler, who bent over backward to make the Colonel happy after the bizarre incident in the men's room—recently giving him a pair of gold cuff links—wrote back that it was "perfectly okay," thus setting the precedent for Parker's credit on all of Presley's motion pictures.

Now Parker began flexing more muscle, asking that Elvis's visitors, including Fox executives, be limited on the set. Furthermore, Parker wanted it understood that he was the man who called the shots, and any access to Elvis would have to go through him. That went for Weisbart (and over at Paramount, Wallis and Hazen); Harry Brand, the Fox publicist; and even the people who made up the call sheets. Trude Forsher would be appointed to phone Elvis at the Beverly Wilshire with his call for the morning.

One person Parker particularly targeted was Lenny Hirshan. While Hirshan remained Presley's motion picture agent of record, Parker attempted to shut him out at every turn, working out a code with Elvis's entourage to alert him when Hirshan came to the studio. It was Hirshan who provided Fox with Elvis's exact arrival times, but Parker didn't want Hirshan or his counterpart at the agency, Peter Shaw, anywhere near his star, fearing they would try to undermine the Colonel's authority. Whenever either man suggested a breakfast meeting, Parker answered, "Sure, six A.M.," knowing that such an hour was far too early for a Hollywood agent who had been out the night before.

If Parker was always preoccupied with what he perceived as the hidden agendas of others, says Byron Raphael, at the Morris office Parker's paranoia was not without foundation. So many of the agents despised the Colonel that "if they could have stolen Elvis away from him, they would have."

Early in his association with William Morris, Parker realized that agents were encouraged to nurture strong personal relationships with the clients, both to keep the star with the agency if the client and manager split, and in case the manager became a hindrance. Too, many agents themselves became managers, and with a solid friendship in place, it was easy to wean a star away from a manager who took a hefty percentage of his earnings.

Parker, who also feared the college-educated Morris agents might influence Elvis's decisions, made sure that no one at the agency had Elvis's private phone number, even though the agents had always called such stars as Robert Mitchum and Rita Hayworth directly. And on the movie set, where he would soon spend less time on each picture, Parker encouraged Elvis's happy-go-lucky cousins and friends from home—the entourage the press would eventually dub the Memphis Mafia—to keep an eye out for anyone who tried to get Elvis alone, especially Hirshan, who insisted he was there only to make sure Elvis got everything he needed.

In time, Parker would have Hirshan barred from the set, and in the post-army years, he would be relieved as the contact altogether, "because I was developing too much of a relationship with Elvis," Hirshan admits. "Also, my thinking processes were not his in terms of the kind of pictures that I would have gotten for Elvis and that Elvis wanted to do."

To Elvis, Parker explained it differently. "You can't trust people in this town," he said. "There are Jews here, and Jews are going to take advantage of you." In the future, when the "Jewish" explanation wasn't applicable, Parker scared Elvis away from would-be advisors by insinuating they were homosexual.

Presley, who was both loyal to the Colonel and dependent on him for every professional move, remained isolated from the business dealings, both by choice and by his manager's design. Joe Hazen recognized early that Parker, who became more like a spiteful armed guard than an amiable shepherd, kept things from Elvis that he shouldn't have, and that, in Hazen's view, Parker "possessed him. If Elvis had a lawyer on his own, there would have been no Parker. No lawyer would've permitted Parker to take over a client like he did."

When Elvis signed his seven-picture deal with Paramount, he told reporters he wouldn't be singing in the movies because "I want to be the kind of actor that stays around for a long time." The way he understood it, his role in *Love Me Tender* was strictly dramatic. And so he was dismayed to learn from the Colonel that he would perform four songs, in part to allow RCA to capitalize on the movie's success—the title song, a reworking of the folk air "Aura Lee," would sell more than 2.5 million singles by Christmas—and to help Steve Sholes get out a second album for the crucial fourth quarter.

Disappointed, and then angry to realize he'd been duped, Elvis balked. Everything was happening so fast. The criticism of his stage act had actually made him cry. ("I'd sooner cut my throat than be vulgar. You've seen my folks. They're respectable God-fearin' people. They wouldn't let me do anything vulgar.") Now, with the pressure of learning how to make movies, he couldn't sleep. And the Colonel was even saying he couldn't use his band on the soundtracks, but rather studio musicians with whom he'd have no rapport.

Parker took him aside and laid it on the line. "Look," he said, "it's pretty easy. We do it this way, we make money. We do it your way, we don't make money." Presley, who as a small child promised his mother he would lead the family out of debt, and who continually heard the stern admonishment of his father not to cross the Colonel, gave in. "Okay," Elvis said, "let's make money."

Now Parker, as heady with power as any despotic dictator, was equally forceful with Fox, setting another precedent for Presley's movie years when he insisted that the songs Elvis recorded for the soundtrack be assigned to Presley's own publishing company, and not the studio's.

Through an arrangement with the Aberbachs, who organized Elvis Presley Music with ownership split equally between the singer and Hill and Range, Elvis would receive cowriting credit along with Vera Matson. In this case, the point was moot—most of the melodies were in the public domain, and Matson was the wife of the film's musical director, Ken Darby. But in the future, Parker and the Aberbachs adhered to a closed-door policy, using only those writers—primarily Otis Blackwell, Ben Weisman, and the team of Jerry Leiber and Mike Stoller—who were willing to give up a portion of their royalties in exchange for Elvis recording their songs. "For the first twelve years of his recording life," says Freddy Bienstock, "Elvis didn't look at a song unless I brought it to him."

Neither Parker nor the Aberbachs saw anything wrong with "cut-ins," as they were called. The practice was fairly common, though viewed as unethical today. The Colonel likewise considered it only good business when he and the Aberbachs later structured two of Presley's publishing companies to give 40 percent ownership to Parker, 15 percent to Elvis, and 45 percent to Parker's friends, with Parker then taking 25 percent of Presley's 15 percent as commission. After all, Parker rationalized, Elvis was his only client.

Constantly jockeying for position and control, the Colonel had much to coordinate as *Love Me Tender* began shooting. But while Parker stayed on the phone to RCA, or orchestrated his office hijinks (one of his favorite tricks was to "hypnotize" the staff to quack, bark, or dance like a trained bear when guests like Tommy Sands dropped by), his attention was sorely needed elsewhere. Elvis had reported to the lot only a week after the contract was signed, and filming began with one of the most dramatic sequences of the story, the homecoming scene in the farmhouse, which Weisbart termed "a very rough way for even the experienced members of our cast to begin shooting, let alone Presley who has yet to get his feet wet in the medium."

Although Elvis had been the producer's third choice for the lead, everyone from Frank McCarthy, Fox's director of censorship, to Presley's costar, the revered character actress Mildred Dunnock, was surprised at Elvis's assurance as an actor. Dunnock, who had coached him in the delivery of lines, praised him as "a beginner who had one of the essentials of acting, which is to believe." But the picture was on an escalated schedule, since Presley had personal appearances to fulfill, and the Morris office still thought his career might be over by the time the movie came out. And with Adler complaining that the film was over budget, Elvis was often photographed in one take, from less than flattering angles.

A responsible manager would have spoken up about how his client looked in the dailies—when the film was released, one critic compared Elvis to a sausage, another to a hunk of lamb—except that Parker didn't care about Elvis's development as an actor, only about how the film sold product and promoted the live shows.

At times, he even seemed to resent the attention that Elvis commanded. When Trude Forsher remarked to her boss that she understood all the excitement about Elvis ("He has magnetism"), the Colonel turned on her. "Magnetism?" he said. "With all his magnetism, if I hadn't taken him off that truck, he would still be driving it."

And so Parker went along with the decision to rush Elvis through his motion picture debut, and in disregarding nearly all the wishes of his client, forged the first link in Presley's long chain of artistic disappointments. But from a purely commercial standpoint, the Colonel was right. The film would make back its cost in less than three weeks.

Anticipating what the movie would mean for record sales, Parker negotiated a new contract with RCA. Elvis would receive an immediate advance of $135,000 and a weekly paycheck of $1,000, both against a 5 percent royalty. The one requirement was ten personal appearances to promote his recordings, in person, or on radio or television. Presley immediately hit the road for five cities in Texas, and the Colonel invited a host of RCA executives to Houston for the performance.

"He had an apartment down there," remembers Chet Atkins. "We were all sitting around, and he went into the kitchen and brought out a bowl. He had that accent, couldn't say *r*'s, and he said, 'The Colonel's wefidgerator is gettin' low on groceries. So I'm gonna pass this bowl around, and I don't want to hear any silver or copper fallin' in it. I want to hear paper.' So everybody chipped in a few bucks, and he sent Bevo out to get some food. He loved separating people from their money."

When *Love Me Tender* opened at New York's Paramount Theater on November 15, 1956, a forty-foot cutout of Elvis decorating its façade, nearly 2,000 fans of all ages lined up, the queue snaking all the way from Times Square to Eighth Avenue. Once the line reached the *New York Times* Building, the paper's management asked the police to redirect it across the street, where it again bottled up traffic on Forty-third Street, all the way across to Grand Central Terminal. Theater manager Charles Einfeld sent the Fox publicity department an ecstatic telegram: "Spread the news that we have a most sensational attraction!"

Parker, who had staged the gathering as a publicity stunt for newsreel photographers, handing out ELVIS FOR PRESIDENT buttons and equipping the fans with professionally lettered signs (OK, ELVIS, LET'S REALLY GO!), had his own advice for theater operators: make sure to empty the house after every showing.

Now the Colonel couldn't wait to throw it all in the face of Joe Hazen, using the film's success to sweeten the bad taste over the Paramount deal. As the studio began developing *Loving You,* Parker bragged to Hazen about his employment on *Love Me Tender.* He inquired, Hazen wrote to Wallis, "as to how much money he was going to get, indicating that he should be employed in connection with the production of the photoplay, since he knew how to handle Presley."

Hazen let the comment pass, but the Colonel soon returned to "spew" about all the deals he'd recently turned down, including $75,000 to have Elvis sing two songs in another Fox picture. His motive: to force Wallis and Hazen to adjust Presley's salary on *Loving You*. After several calls from Abe Lastfogel, the producers agreed to give Elvis a bonus of $25,000, a figure that was to include a fee for Parker's services as well. As Hazen wrote to Wallis on January 17, 1957, the $25,000 was to be "divided among them according to their own desires."

Parker, however, was now of the mind-set that any deal that benefited Elvis should also benefit him in a manner above and beyond his 25 percent commission. Lastfogel, acting on the Colonel's instructions, told the producers that Parker would have to turn over the entire $25,000 to Elvis, as he "could not or would not keep any of it personally." Additionally, Lastfogel said, Parker, who had originally pledged to remain in Hollywood throughout the production of the picture, now refused to come out to the coast unless he was personally compensated.

On February 7, 1957, Lastfogel wrote to Hazen and Wallis expressing his gratitude for "your paying Elvis Presley and Colonel Parker the additional $50,000." Parker, too, wrote to Wallis on the same day. But his letter made it clear: half of that $50,000 was for him. A second contract would be drawn "for the cooperation of Colonel Tom Parker," who would be listed as "technical advisor" on the film.

From then on, whenever Parker could justify a deal as a joint venture, where he and Elvis functioned as equal partners beyond the contractually agreed amount, the Colonel would divide the proceeds 50–50 from the first dollar. They were a team, Elvis and the Colonel, Presley providing the talent, and Parker, through persistence and ingenuity, converting that talent into one of the most lucrative careers in history. "Elvis and the Colonel," as Parker signed every Christmas card and thank-you letter, was more than just equal billing and ego. It was the Colonel's own powerful shorthand, a way of telegraphing, "I am as important as Elvis. When I say something, you must listen."

If Parker saw his job as getting the best deal for his client—and to market himself right along with Elvis—Oscar Davis questioned some of his tactics, particularly his seizing any opportunity for self-gain. Parker was taken aback. As a former carny, Davis should have known better. The Colonel exercised an honorable boldness in his bludgeoning business practices and, in that sense, never posed as anything other than what he was. Besides, loyalty was *within* the circle—outsiders were not necessarily afforded the same consideration.

"You want to tell me how I should do business?" the Colonel barked at his friend, repeating an exchange they'd once had over Eddy Arnold. "Listen, I have $350,000 in the bank. When you have 350,000 and *one dollar* in your bank account, then you can come and tell me."

Indeed, Parker was the largest single depositor at the American National Bank in Madison, Tennessee, where the Colonel still maintained his primary business office, filtering the Elvis money through his new company, All Star Shows. On one of his first trips to Nashville after acquiring Eddy Arnold in the '40s, Parker had walked into the bank and introduced himself to the owner, whom he remembered as "the only Jewish fella in Madison."

"It was a family bank, a little bank, and I wanted to borrow $5,000, because I had no money, and we needed [some for] promotion," Parker said years later. The banker asked what he had for collateral. Parker responded that he had an old car that he paid $125 for, on time at $4 a month.

"There's no value there," challenged the banker.

"Well," said Parker, "even if it was a good car, and I welshed on my pay, what difference does it make what the car is worth?" And so the banker lent him the money just on his face. "I signed the note, I paid him back in about a year and a half, and that still is my bank today," Parker said in 1993.

The Colonel, Parker would tell anyone who would listen, was nothing if not loyal.

12

DIRECTIONAL SNOWING

H A L Wallis wanted *Loving You* to be everything *Love Me Tender* was not. While the period Western introduced the singing idol to the movie audience and allowed him to learn the rudiments of acting, it did almost nothing to play on Elvis's natural charm, his exotic good looks, his provocative rock-and-roll dance moves, and the allure of celebrity life.

What Wallis had in mind for *Loving You,* Presley's first starring vehicle, was a film loosely based on Elvis's life, with a story tracing the rapid rise of a backwoods amateur (Deke Rivers) to a national sensation.

The producer was mildly concerned about how the public would react to a swiveling Elvis on the big screen, since just before Elvis's first *Ed Sullivan* appearance, Parker learned that church and PTA groups planned on filing a protest with CBS, leading the Colonel to turn down ten days of dates at $250,000 to avoid more screaming-girls publicity. For a while, he toyed with the idea of a "Clean Up Elvis" campaign—that is, photographing the singer in a series of wholesome settings. But the Colonel feared it might boomerang on him, and so he sat tight. No protests were filed after all.

Wallis wanted the script built around the formula used to sell other biopics about entertainers, suggesting that Elvis was just the modern-day Al Jolson, and his music as fun and harmless as the Charleston in the '20s. In case anyone missed the message, Wallis had it hammered home in a sequence that pokes fun at television censors, and in a scene where Glenda Markle, Deke's manager (Lizabeth Scott), appears before a small-town city council to defend Deke and rock and roll in general. It was blatant, heavy-handed propaganda—as was Elvis's line "They make it sound like folks ought to be ashamed just listening to me sing!"—but Wallis saw it as good insurance against criticism from 1950s America.

The man he tapped for the job of writing and directing was Hal Kan-

ter, who, along with cowriter Herbert Baker, fashioned the script somewhat after Mary Agnes Thompson's original story. Kanter had seen Elvis
on the *Sullivan Show* and knew that "a lot of people, hated him . . .
thought he was an instrument of the devil." Like a lot of sophisticates,
Kanter didn't much care for Presley's hip gyrations and country attitude,
and wrote him off as just a passing fancy, "a nasty little boy," as he later
recalled. Then he saw Elvis's screen test, found him "orchid-pretty," and
couldn't take his eyes off him.

To get a better feel for Presley's world, Kanter, then thirty-nine, flew to
Memphis to meet with Elvis at his new, fashionable three-bedroom house
on Audubon Drive. From there, he drove with him and his entourage to
Shreveport, Louisiana, where Elvis made his farewell appearance on *The
Louisiana Hayride*. An astonished Kanter would use on screen much of
what he saw that day, saying privately of the fan reaction, "There were
some things that happened there that I couldn't recreate, because people
wouldn't believe it."

But it was the Colonel, a "well-fed King Con," who really dazzled
him, hawking tinted photos of Elvis, souvenir programs, and even the
Duke of Paducah's smoked meat sticks at the Shreveport fairgrounds. "I
thought the colorful Colonel more interesting than his star."

Not surprising, a very Colonel-like character turned up in the film
as Jim Tallman, a portly, cigar-smoking gubernatorial candidate with
a silver tongue who sells snake oil on the side. But Kanter also wrote
many of Parker's personal traits and star-making machinations into the
script, with the Markle character playing up the singer's sex appeal ("I
like him—he's got something for the girls"), talking half of his revenue,
staging small riots, and calling her client "our gimmick."

Wallis shared Kanter's assessment of Parker, but he also had a grudg-
ing respect for him and saw in the Colonel somebody like himself—an
energetic promoter with uncanny gifts for manipulating situations to his
best advantage.

It was the other side of Parker's personality that gave the producer fits,
particularly once the manager moved into an office on the Paramount lot
before filming began, bringing his staff of Tom Diskin, Byron Raphael,
and Trude Forsher.

Parker's only female secretary in Hollywood (except for a "Miss
Wood," who was never seen, and whose signature often resembled
Parker's own), Forsher wasn't sure she wanted to go to work for the
Colonel when she met him socially through her cousins, the Aberbachs.

A freelance writer, she demonstrated both a hungry intelligence and a spirited personality. She had no intention of becoming anyone's secretary, but Parker swayed her with one comment: "Trude, if you come with me now, you're going to be somebody important. If you don't, you will have lost your opportunity."

Forsher, who was somewhat envious of her powerful relatives, found Parker's bravado exciting. And the Colonel took comfort in the thick Austrian accent she made no effort to tame. Once in a while, he'd say, "Speak German for me, Trude," finding a secret transport to a past none of his European friends detected in his speech.

Just as Parker enjoyed Byron's services courtesy of the William Morris office, he demanded, starting at Twentieth Century–Fox, that the studios reimburse him for Trude's salary. Now at Paramount, Trude, who ran the office in addition to typing letters and answering the phone, wanted a raise. Parker talked her into a title change instead, and so the lowly secretary became the more lofty sounding "promotion coordinator."

The Colonel rarely rewarded his employees with bonuses or presents, but he never wanted to look stingy, believing such an image diluted his power. One day he overheard Byron and Trude discussing the split-pea soup they'd enjoyed at the Paramount commissary and, misunderstanding, called them both into his office. "It's not good for you two to split your soup!" he said, agitated. "People are going to think I'm not paying you enough!"

Parker wanted to be thought of as successful, but it was more important to flaunt his connections than his wealth. And so in his new office dominated by a spread of Texas longhorns, shooting-gallery-prize teddy bears, winking electric signs, and a tiger skin on the floor, he made space for signed photographs of such celebrities as Sammy Davis Jr. and Cecil B. DeMille, the famed producer-director who was then at Paramount working on his biblical epic, *The Ten Commandments*. In return for such autographs, which he solicited by mail, he often sent a sausage.

At Paramount, Elvis generated so much excitement that director Kanter had to close the set to keep out the studio secretaries and wives and children of the Hollywood elite, all of whom wanted their photo taken with the young star. The Paramount brass, however, was more curious about "this bombastic, driving, one-man minstrel show," as producer A. C. Lyles called the Colonel. Even Marlon Brando, whose office was down the hall, often stuck his head in the door. The Colonel arrived at the studio each morning at eight ("Let's open up the tents," he'd say in carny talk) and stayed until six, thriving on his attention from the Hollywood royalty and the opportunity to negotiate an outrageous deal.

"That was his excitement," says Raphael, whose main job was to assist Parker in pulling off various snow jobs. "When I would see him on the phone making these deals, there would be little beads of perspiration on his face. He would sit there twirling his cigar in his mouth and be completely enraptured in what he was doing. It was very difficult for him to come down after one of those."

From the beginning, Parker saw the need to bring the Paramount suits in line, to deflate their pomposity, prove his own preeminence, and bring a relaxed humor to what he viewed as a very stuffy group. His first target: DeMille, a Hollywood god.

He saw his chance on the day he received 10,000 Elvis Presley buttons—large, metal, campaign-style badges with the singer's picture on them—to promote the new movie.

"Somehow," Raphael remembers, "DeMille heard about the buttons, and sent an assistant to get one for his granddaughter. The Colonel wanted to know why Mr. DeMille couldn't come over and ask for himself, and the assistant told him Mr. DeMille was very busy. So the Colonel said, 'Tell Mr. DeMille that I would like to get him one of these buttons, but I have to check with my lawyers first, because we're getting ready to make our merchandising deal.'"

The next day, Parker directed his staff to pass out the buttons to everyone on the lot, and then sent Trude to DeMille's office with the message that the Colonel had made a special dispensation, and that Mr. DeMille would be the only person in Hollywood with a rare Elvis button. All we ask, she said, echoing the Colonel, is that Mr. DeMille wear it himself when he goes to his set.

"When DeMille walked out of his office thinking he was the only one at the studio with that button," says Raphael, "it must have been one of the most humiliating moments of his life. Everybody from the janitors to the guards at the gates was wearing one."

DeMille never spoke to Parker again, but the Colonel took the risk of making an enemy to prove his point. Later, during the promotion of *G.I. Blues,* he talked Hal Wallis into donning a paper concessionaire's hat—perhaps meant to resemble an army cap—and called a photographer to document the moment. "He loved seeing these men that he considered sanctimonious phonies wearing Elvis paraphernalia," says Raphael, "because he got them all to be little imitation operators, straight out of the carnival world."

In June 1957, Parker inducted Wallis and Joe Hazen into his fictional Snowmen's League of America, Ltd. The best known of his nonsensical hijinks, the Snowmen's League was a takeoff on the Showmen's League, which promoted the idea of consummate professionalism among carnival workers. Parker's little club, which he established during the Eddy Arnold era, rewarded another standard of excellence: the ability to con, or "snow." Its motto: "Let It Snow, Let It Snow, Let It Snow!" The Colonel named himself High Potentate and placed an enormous stuffed snowman in his studio office, often posing with it for pictures.

With faultless attention to detail, Parker designed membership cards, certificates, a ribbon-festooned "Snow Award," and even gag wine labels (THE COLONEL'S PRIVATE STOCK—VINTAGE YEAR 1942). All were emblazoned with a cartoon drawing of a pudgy, top-hat-wearing, cigar-smoking snowman—a benevolent rendering of the Colonel himself.

Parker boasted that the nonprofit club cost nothing to get into but $1,000 to get out. With great fanfare, he inducted those with whom he had business arrangements, or whose favor he curried, such as politicians or high-profile journalists, who protected as much as publicized. Hollywood executives, says Byron Raphael, "begged to belong to that club," where they rubbed shoulders with members of Presley's entourage, and RCA reps and corporate brass. "My induction was given to me over dinner, so other people were sure to hear the presentation," remembers Charlie Boyd, a former RCA field man. "He said it was almost a secret society, and indicated it would open doors for me."

The coup de grâce of Parker's little folly was the club's slickly produced rule book, which the Colonel called a *Confidential Report Dealing with Advanced Techniques of Member Snowers,* prepared by a team "notably skilled in evasiveness and ineptitude." A slim volume filled with clever wordplay, its table of contents promised seven chapters on such topics as "Counteracting High Pressure Snowing . . . Melt and disappear technique," and "Directional Snowing . . . This deals with approach and departure simultaneously." Anyone who hoped to read such chapters found only sixteen blank pages, followed by text that ended with a "special note" on how the Chief Potentate had allegedly talked the printer into delivering the greatest number of books "at a reduced loss to himself, for which he was very grateful." As the Colonel summed up, "It is again a sterling example of a good snowman's willingness to see the other man's problems and show the greatest understanding without financial involvement."

Parker had a different snow job in mind for Hal Kanter. The director was surprised to see the Colonel frequently come by the *Loving You* set, since he had no interest in reading the script, and let Elvis speak for himself when he engaged Kanter about the kind of actor he hoped to become. To Kanter, Parker seemed to be interested only in "how much, not who, where, when, or why," and once Kanter made his presence known, the Colonel would leave. "I would never know if he was watching in the shadows or not," Kanter remembers, "but if he wasn't there, one of his minions would be. There was always somebody around."

Kanter found out what was on Parker's mind as the filming wore on. For some time, the Colonel had wanted to publish a book, *How Much Does It Cost If It's Free?*, a collection of hokum, blarney, and snow jobs extraordinaire that he would claim was his life story. He planned to insert advertising among its pages to make back its production costs. RCA, he boasted, was buying the back cover for $25,000.

Now all he needed was a ghostwriter, and Kanter seemed just the man—he could write it on weekends, Parker told him. But Kanter, who saw the Colonel as someone who "was happier fleecing the world of its money than the actual making of it," had no intention of doing such a thing, and told the Colonel to look beyond a book to a film version of his life. The manager brightened, and Kanter was astonished to hear him say that he thought Paul Newman the ideal actor to play him on the screen. Foolishly, perhaps, the director wrote in his autobiography, Kanter replied that he was thinking more of W. C. Fields. Parker's "pink face turned magenta and he never again mentioned that book in my presence."

Still, Kanter had enormous respect for what he called Parker's "genius," especially after he saw him skillfully maneuver Elvis through a frenzied throng at *The Louisiana Hayride*. Parker had once tried to work a deal with the *Hayride* and sponsoring station KWKH, offering to set up an artist service bureau for the fee of $12,000, which the show's producer, Horace Logan, found preposterous, especially as Parker planned to run it as an extension of Jamboree Productions. Now instead of booking acts on the show, Parker was stealing one in buying out Elvis's contract. With the help of Bitsy Mott, whom Parker had recently made head of security despite his slight build, the Colonel steered his client past a sea of groping arms and hands, all frantic to touch the star, get an autograph, or in the case of one overexuberant fan, snip a lock of his hair. The director thought Parker's calling for a wall of police to ring the platform shoulder-to-shoulder had been mere press agentry until Elvis got on stage, and the 9,000 in attendance sent up a roof-lifting scream that lasted the length of his performance.

Afterward, Kanter sidled up to Parker and complimented him on his call: "Now I see why you have the police there."

"That's right," Parker snapped. "If it weren't for those cops, those sweet little girls would be all over the stage and they'd tear that boy to pieces. That's why I've got to protect him. You people in Hollywood don't know a damn thing about protection."

Kanter, trying to make a joke of it, thought of the diminutive head of the William Morris Agency. "I guess Abe Lastfogel would get trampled to death in a crowd like this." The Colonel sneered: "Abe Lastfogel wouldn't know where to go to *find* a crowd like this." With that, Kanter "knew immediately what his relationship with the Morris office was."

Lately, Parker had become more disgruntled with the Morris executives, especially as they began to advise him on ways that he and Elvis might better manage their money. The Colonel should set up a corporation to shelter some of it from the tax man, they said, and in fact, they could do it for him. But the Colonel had no interest in any such thing. The Morris brass was surprised. Didn't he trust them? If that was the case, they could recommend a business manager to help him protect what he and Elvis had.

The Colonel *didn't* trust them, of course, and he'd rather have Elvis lose money than set him up with someone who might influence him in other decisions, too. Only once did he take Elvis to the Morris offices, and then just to let the agents fraternize with him a little, so he could keep them away from the movie sets. His paranoia raged to such an extent that he refused free work space within the agency, first accepting the offer and then complaining that his suite was "eight doors removed from the donniker [men's room]. It looks like the little house behind the big house." But his concerns were otherwise. What if someone should listen in on his phone conversations, maybe secretly tape him, learn of the ways he managed to take far more—sometimes in excess of 50 percent—from his deals on Elvis's behalf?

It wasn't stealing. Hadn't he chastised Byron when the younger man accidentally walked out of the grocery store with an unchecked magazine in the bottom of his cart? Hadn't he called Byron on it and made him go back and pay for it? The Colonel was an honest man. And what he took from Elvis was deserved. No other manager worked as hard.

Still, he made it clear to Lastfogel from the beginning: all checks due to

Elvis would be sent directly from the studio to Parker's office in Memphis and made out to All Star Shows, not to the Morris agency. So what if the Colonel was the only client to demand such an arrangement? Besides, the agency had no contract that strictly bound Elvis or Parker as a client; therefore, the Colonel never signed a check authorization form.

The beauty of it, as the Colonel saw, was that Presley was completely unconcerned about such matters. When Byron delivered Elvis his weekly check—which the Diskin Sisters sent to California, where Parker would sign it and put it in a sealed envelope—the singer never questioned his cut, even though the figures were seldom broken down, the expenses rarely itemized except on Parker's own ledger. In fact, Presley seldom looked at the amount. He simply pocketed it and sent it home to his father.

Lastfogel and company found Parker's arrangement perplexing, since he then had to turn around and send the agency 10 percent, which they would have deducted automatically before they sent the money on to him. They argued that it was cleaner for his IRS records to have the money come to them first. The Colonel was resolute. He feared no IRS audit, either for himself or for Elvis, he said, because he went directly to the Internal Revenue Service and asked them to calculate what they owed. In fact, Parker said, "I consider it my patriotic duty to keep Elvis in the ninety percent bracket." Remembering how he'd been stung by the surprise audit in Tampa—the IRS would also question him about the $10,000 buyout of Elvis's *Louisiana Hayride* contract—neither he nor Elvis would have any tax shelters, or dare to write off anything but the most legitimate expenses, a practice that made Elvis the largest single tax-payer on a straight income in the country. And while Parker occasionally tossed Bitsy Mott the odd $25 or $50, he was careful not to pay him any more than minimum wage, saying that the IRS precluded paying family members more than outsiders for the same work. "I love to pay taxes," he would say. "I know when I'm paying taxes that I'm making money."

The Morris accountants were stunned. Why would a man who knew the whereabouts of every penny, and went to great lengths to hold on to it, not want to take advantage of the tax breaks? Other than his home in Madison, Parker had no investments, and while the Colonel was in-formed enough to gainfully advise Byron and Trude on specific stock trades, he didn't play the market himself because he couldn't control it.

There was logic in that, the Morris accountants said, and then nodded their heads in agreement when Parker explained he didn't want Elvis to become a hapless figure like the boxer Joe Louis, losing his fortune from some obscure IRS ruling. What they didn't know was that Parker, the illegal alien, lived in fear of any government agency that poked around in his past. The IRS, says Bitsy Mott, "just scared him to death."

Already there were rumors that the reason Parker wouldn't give interviews was because there were things he didn't want the world to know, and Parker saw the suspicion on Lastfogel's face. That's why he realized, early in 1956, that he needed a snitch within the Morris agency itself. He had a certain type in mind for someone he would name as his assistant: small, young, male, quiet, and probably homosexual, someone who was easy to dominate and control, and had no marital problems.

Byron Raphael was twenty-two years old and earning $45 a week working in the William Morris mail room—the starting job for all would-be agents—on the day he messengered a script to Colonel Parker's office at Twentieth Century–Fox. He delivered it to Trude Forsher, who liked his mild-mannered personality and asked him to call back. What Byron didn't know was that the Colonel had asked her to be on the lookout. The five-foot-seven Raphael wasn't gay, but he did fit the rest of the profile: "Most of the guys he hired after me were homosexual, little, softspoken, creative, and neat in appearance."

When Byron returned to the Colonel's office, Parker immediately offered him a job, and the younger man turned it down, saying he'd planned on staying at William Morris his whole career. Parker smiled. "Well, you *will* work for William Morris," he assured him. "They'll pay your salary, but you'll come and be with me."

Raphael was already caught up in the excitement of Elvis Presley, but the Colonel, too, was compelling.

"In retrospect, I see that he had the impact of someone like Adolf Hitler, because he had an astonishing kind of mental power over the people around him. They would have done anything he asked them to do. There was no way to keep a secret from him, and I never saw him get defeated. His personality was so big, so overpowering, that when he walked into a room, he took it over, no matter who was there. They all fell under his spell."

To test Byron's loyalty, Parker put him through two trials by fire with his William Morris bosses. The first demanded that Raphael, basically an errand boy, walk into the office of the all-powerful Abe Lastfogel, sit down, and light up a stogie. Lastfogel detested the smell of smoke and wouldn't allow it around him, but he had a commendable sense of humor: "What did you do, boy, lose a bet?"

The second prank, guided by Parker's quest for revenge, was directed at Lenny Hirshan and had more serious implications. Hirshan, aloof but unctuous with stars—and so disliked by some in the agency that an assistant would eventually hide raw hamburger under his flowerpot and wait for it to rot—was an easy target. To Byron, he seemed resentful of the younger men coming up, regarding everyone as competition and scheming to keep them scared for their jobs.

Lately, he was concerned for his own. Hirshan was technically Elvis's contact at William Morris, but whenever he dropped by Parker's office at Paramount, the manager just shooed him away ("Thanks for coming over, Lenny. No, we don't need anything today"). Since Byron was the envy of the agents for his access to Elvis, Hirshan now began to pump him for information. The Colonel had a plan.

"Colonel Parker came to Trude and me and explained that Lenny Hirshan was snooping around too much," Byron remembers. "He said, 'Trude, write a note in some kind of shorthand—you know, scribble, scribble, and then carnival talk. Then say, "Leave WMA," and do some more shorthand that doesn't mean anything, and then write, "Lenny Hirshan's fault."'"

Trude took out her pad, and handled the note to Parker, who crumpled it up, stamped on it until it bore the print of his heel, and pitched it into the wastebasket.

"Now Byron," he said, his voice slipping into character as the old Colonel, his tone broadening, his pitch rising, and his accent ripening to reveal his difficulty with *h*'s and *j*'s, "I want you to call Lenny Hirshan and tell him you walked in and saw the Colonel in a meeting with MCA, and you're reporting back to William Morris."

Byron picked up the phone and sailed into the script. "And Mr. Hirshan," Byron added, measuring the agent's anxiety, "I've got this note that the Colonel left." Hirshan, mindful that Parker had no contract with the agency and panicked that he might actually leave, told Byron to bring it right over: "You did a good job. Keep spying on the Colonel for me."

The following day, Byron again dialed Hirshan's number and told him he had some terrible news: the Colonel had seen him retrieving the note, and he knew Byron had delivered it to Hirshan. Furthermore, they were coming right over.

"We burst into Lenny's office and Colonel Parker said, 'Let's get Abe Lastfogel in here, because if you're telling my guy to give you stuff from my wastepaper basket, we're through.' Of course, the Colonel had no intention of leaving—he was too loyal to Mr. Lastfogel—but he loved seeing Lenny squirm. So Mr. Lastfogel came in and said, 'Lenny, if that's true, say it.' And I said, 'It's true, Mr. Lastfogel.' Lenny looked at me and his eyes were like fire. I had betrayed him and been a traitor to the people who paid me."

Byron was about to learn a harsh lesson: if you worked for Colonel Parker, you got hurt, emotionally, professionally, or financially—and the sting never really went away.

"I never should have done it," Raphael says. "But since I idolized the Colonel, I lost my sense of reality. Everybody who worked for him wanted his approval so desperately, and when he went into that steely look, or stormed in and out of offices, slamming doors, we were also afraid of his anger. I really think he hypnotized us so that we would endure almost any kind of treatment."

Tom Diskin was foremost among them. Already in his mid-thirties, Thomas Francis Diskin revered the Colonel with a complexity of emotions that transcended any father-son relationship. Although he had reportedly been Parker's first partner in the Jamboree Productions booking agency and music publishing companies—running the Chicago office before selling his half to Hank Snow—incorporation papers suggest it was Diskin who originally owned Jamboree Attractions and later took Parker in as a partner, only to be pressured to relinquish his half when Snow and Parker joined forces.

"What he told me," says Anne Fulchino, national publicity director for RCA in the '50s, "was that Parker went to work for *him*, and somewhere along the line, Diskin ended up being his employee. I said, 'How could you let that happen, Tom?' And he said, 'You know, the Colonel's quite a guy.' Since Tom was just a nice, simple person who had the lowest expectations out of life, I could believe his story."

Short, stocky, with a crop of blondish red hair capping his everyman's looks, Diskin was mediocre in every way. He arrived for work each day on a waft of Old Spice, a yes-man in a cheap suit and washed-out tie. As Parker's $250-a-week right-hand man, he might have been expected to wield a modicum of decision-making power. But he was too sweet and meek to assert himself ("He was an angel," says RCA's Sam Esgro), and the Colonel too paranoid and obsessed with details to delegate much responsibility. The lieutenant, then, was put to work on menial tasks—writing letters to the fan clubs, taking papers to Elvis for signature, and parroting the Colonel's words to RCA. On the rare occasion, he contacted the Aberbachs in regard to a particular song, but his most useful purpose was serving as a buffer between Parker and the people the Colonel didn't want to see.

Around his boss, Diskin tamped down any resentment or thoughts of his own and remained blissfully obedient. Privately, however, he complained about being Parker's shadow, describing how the Colonel talked to him like a needful but not particularly caring parent.

On the road, at the end of the day, Diskin yearned to find a place to knock back a toddy or two and meet some nice girls, go dancing. But the Colonel wouldn't permit it, fearing it might lead to dating and marriage, and a possible end to Diskin's steadfast devotion. In the odd, Walter Mitty moment, he managed to smuggle a girl into his room, but mostly settled for the life of a eunuch, exchanging playful winks with waitresses. Eventually, he would buy the property adjacent to Parker's Tennessee home, where his boss could keep a vigilant watch.

As reward, the Colonel cut his lieutenant into a number of Elvis's business deals, including his music publishing, buying Diskin's loyalty and his silence. But while he always addressed him as Mr. Diskin in the company of others, Parker could never resist the opportunity to humiliate him, to remind him that he was not really a business colleague, but a flunky. Despite Diskin's serious-mindedness, and the thoroughness with which he attended to his duties, the Colonel found constant fault with his performance, yelling at him in front of Byron and Trude, and one day calling him in to a meeting with another talent manager and ordering him to tap-dance. Not once did Diskin ever refuse or talk back, even when Parker screamed at him with the force of a hailstorm. Eventually, Diskin's silence, along with years of hard drinking, would lead to ulcers and the surgical removal of half his stomach.

In his more benevolent moments, Parker showed strong loyalties to the people he liked. When he needed an opening act for some of Elvis's early concert dates, for example, he plucked an Irish tenor named Frankie Connors from the unemployment line, later arranging a screen test for Connors's daughter, Sharon. He also had a soft spot for Gabe Tucker, assigning him all the royalties to a song they wrote together. "There were times when he was so gentle he would go into a reverie and almost rock himself to sleep," says Byron.

When his malevolence came upon him, however, Parker spared no one's feelings, cloaking cruelty in offbeat humor. He once steered the promoter Lee Gordon into a bad business deal and later repaid him for his losses, strictly from friendship and honor. But Parker's influence had tragic results. Though handsome in his resemblance to Tyrone Power, Gordon fretted over his ethnicity. "Do you think my nose looks too Jewish?" he repeatedly asked. "Well," Parker replied, "I wouldn't eat too many bagels," and goaded him into having plastic surgery. "Something happened," Byron remembers, "and he came out looking a gargoyle, even after repeated surgeries to correct it. It was a horrible thing. But that's how hypnotic the Colonel was in his suggestion."

A more frequent target was Bevo Bevis, the Colonel's runabout. Parker looked after him, giving him a job and sending Bevo's pay home to his mother, who cared for his young daughter from a hopeless marriage. But Bevo paid dearly for the Colonel's attention. On one occasion, he was forced to stand at attention in the middle of a rainstorm, as proof of how "my people listen to me," as the Colonel snorted to cronies. When he once failed to immediately light his boss's cigar, Bevo was put out of the car on a late-night highway, told to catch up at a diner seven miles away, and waved off with the admonition not to hitch a ride, or "I'll know about it and won't even consider taking you back!"

Like Bevo, Trude was constantly threatened with termination for some imagined slight. But while the Colonel terrorized her on occasion, usually putting Byron up to some scheme to scare her into thinking she'd lost her job, the secretary almost always figured out that Parker was bluffing. "I know the inside of the Colonel," she explains today.

Trude was loyal to a fault, but she took the Colonel's teasing in stride for another reason. Caught in a crumbling marriage, the vivacious Trude simply transferred her affections to her boss. During the day, she tried to impress him with how quickly she had learned about show business, and at night, she smuggled home photographs of him, just to have him near.

She knew the relationship would never be romantic and, in fact, considered Marie a good friend, though she rankled if another woman came near the Colonel at the office. Parker noticed her possessiveness, as did her husband, Bruno, who tired of hearing her sing "Hound Dog" around the house and threatened to leave her and their two young sons, believing she was having an affair with Elvis. The Colonel was intensely uncomfortable around any female who showed any personal interest in him— he had become especially agitated on the road when a young fan repeatedly broke into his room and climbed into his bed—and never, ever demonstrated interest in another woman. Now Trude had become a threat: if Bruno didn't leave her, she would leave him instead.

In an uncharacteristically soft approach, Parker gently dissuaded her fantasy and finally appealed to what he assumed would be her European sense of hearth and home.

"He went to her," Byron remembers, "and he said, 'Trude, your marriage is going to end if you stay here. Take whatever chance you can to work it out. Otherwise you'll lose your family.' And I remember her tears. She said, 'But Colonel, you and my children, you *are* my family.'" For a while, then, the Colonel let her stay.

Parker intended to make up for more odious maltreatment when he allowed Byron and Trude to play Elvis a ballad, "Castles in the Sand," that they'd cowritten with the help of a professional songwriter. They hoped he'd record it for the soundtrack of *Loving You,* and their chances looked good: Steve Sholes was short on material for the session, and Elvis loved the song so much he sang it all night at his suite at the Beverly Wilshire Hotel. Furthermore, the Aberbachs had agreed to publish it as part of the Gladys Music catalog.

The Colonel seldom attended Elvis's recording sessions, and Presley preferred it that way. At Paramount, he'd had a difficult time getting a satisfactory take on the soundtrack's title song, and now at Radio Recorders, he welcomed no distractions in the studio, especially not from Parker, who had an irritating habit of making irrelevant suggestions or reminiscing about the Gene Austin days. Elvis called him Admiral, as a derisive play on Colonel, although it was a nickname Parker sometimes used for himself, as well as for Marie.

Lately, in private, Elvis had been more defiant with his manager, mostly out of nerves. Everything had gotten so big so fast, it made his head spin. He'd even pulled a movie-prop pistol on a marine in an argument, and gotten in a fistfight with a service station attendant, which landed him in court. In early '56, he told reporters that his success "just scares me," and that all the hysteria at his concerts "makes me want to cry. How does all this happen to me?"

Almost a year later, Elvis felt isolated and out of control. His mother, Gladys, had been in the hospital for tests. As always, the Colonel, treating him like "property," didn't approve of his new girlfriend, Dottie Harmony, a Las Vegas singer and dancer. And worse, the army was making noises about drafting him—he'd already had his preinduction physical. Everything seemed so up in the air. Soon, over Easter of '57, when he should have been enjoying his new house, a mansion with the lofty name of Graceland, Elvis would tell his minister, the Reverend James Hamill, "I am the most miserable young man you have ever seen."

And so on February 23, 1957, when Elvis arrived at Radio Recorders in Hollywood to tape five songs, including "Castles in the Sand," for the *Loving You* soundtrack, he had much on his mind. Parker forbade Byron to attend the session, but once he was there, Byron went up to Elvis almost immediately at the Colonel's suggestion. "Mr. Presley," he said, "I want to thank you for recording my song." Raphael could tell that Elvis thought the kid was trying to pressure him—why else would "Byron the Siren," as Presley playfully called him, address him so formally? Still, Elvis was polite. "Well, I wouldn't do it if I didn't like it."

From the start, the session proved difficult, as Elvis's band, Scotty Moore, Bill Black, and D. J. Fontana, struggled with the requirements of soundtrack recording—twenty-nine takes to nail "Don't Leave Me Now," and twenty-two for "I Beg of You." And RCA's Bill Bullock entered into a prolonged exchange with anyone he could about whether to include the Dave Bartholomew song "One Night," which Elvis had already toned down, changing "one night of sin," to "one night with you."

During a lull, when Elvis stepped outside to shake off some nervous energy, Jean Aberbach, the more eccentric of the publishing brothers, spoke with Freddy Bienstock, Presley's Hill and Range liaison, about getting Elvis to record a kiddie song, "Here Comes Peter Cottontail," that the Aberbachs thought would sell well at Easter. Bienstock, dumbfounded that Aberbach would seriously consider such a thing, laughed him off, so Jean placed the lyrics on Elvis's music stand. "After the break," remembers Bienstock, "Elvis came into the studio and looked at the song and said, 'Who brought that Br'er Rabbit shit in here?'"

Now the Colonel, who always moved quickly for such an obese man, came running out of the control room clapping his hands. "All right, let's get Byron's song done next." As the band readied their instruments and the Jordanaires warmed the "ooh wow wows" of their head arrangement, Elvis hesitated. Haltingly, he launched the first four bars, and then abruptly stopped. "I'm not going to do this goddamn song," he said, turning to Gordon Stoker. "I hate to disappoint Byron and Trude, but I'm not going to do it for Colonel." And then he inexplicably broke into "True Love," the Cole Porter tune that had hit big for Bing Crosby.

Steve Sholes cut a puzzled look at the Colonel, and Aberbach, who held no publishing rights to Cole Porter, rolled his eyes, bringing a palm to his forehead: "Oh my God, Cole Porter. As though he needs the money."

Never before had Elvis crossed the Colonel in public. Parker, who constantly feared the crush of another heart attack, fought to keep his emotions in check and decided to deal with it later in private. But from now on, Parker took stricter measures to ensure that all material Elvis received came solely from the Aberbachs, with one exception—"Are You Lonesome Tonight," a favorite of Marie's.

For Elvis's third picture, *Jailhouse Rock,* the Colonel exercised his outside picture clause with Paramount and moved to MGM, claiming his agreement with producer Pandro Berman—$250,000 plus 50 percent of the net profits—was "the biggest deal ever made in Hollywood."

One person who was not impressed was Kathryn Hereford, Berman's associate producer. Hereford had heard all about the Colonel's "rare" Elvis buttons, country sausage capers, and other bizarre stunts—the first day, he'd arrived at MGM in a mud-splattered car, a transparent move designed to play on his bumpkin persona. Hereford gave him the cold shoulder, advising Berman to put as much distance as possible between him and the wily manager.

In turning his attention to the development of *Jailhouse Rock,* Parker stayed in constant contact with the Aberbachs, who had pinned new hopes on the soundtrack. Jerry Leiber and Mike Stoller, both twenty-four-year-old Hill and Range songwriters who were already major figures in the R&B world, were commissioned to write four songs for the picture, including the famous production number in which Elvis distills the genius of his erotically undulating stage moves. The team, which had written the title song for *Loving You,* had a piano in their room at the Gorham Hotel in New York, and one weekend, Jean Aberbach came up and "pushed a chair in front of the door, sat down, and went to sleep," remembers Stoller. "He wouldn't move until we were finished."

Soon after, Julian Aberbach told Leiber to expect a contract from the Colonel; they intended to groom the writing team for other movies, as well. While Elvis frequently signed blank agreements at Parker's instruction, Leiber was flabbergasted to open his mail and find just such a contract and a note instructing him to affix his signature and return it at once. "I called [the Colonel] and said, 'There's nothing on it.' And he said they'd fill it in later. . . . It struck me as a great practical joke."

Breaking with his usual habit, the Colonel visited the set of *Jailhouse Rock* several times, one day bringing along Jim Denny, the powerful Nashville music publisher and Grand Ole Opry manager. Gordon Stoker, who viewed Parker as "a necessary evil," was surprised at the Colonel's audacity, knowing how painful it would be for Elvis to see the man who had once rejected him from the Opry.

Now, on the set, "Denny walked over to Elvis and said, 'I just wanted you to know that I've always had faith in you and always believed in you,'" Stoker recalls. "Elvis said, 'Thank you, Mr. Denny,' and turned around to us and whispered, 'That bastard thinks I've forgotten the way he broke my heart.'"

Denny's visit, following weeks of long hours of filming and a myriad of other problems, so upset Elvis that he asked to take the day off. The difficulties with Scotty, Bill, and D.J. in the recording studio gave rise to a host of resentments, mostly over money. The musicians worked for $200 a week on the road—$100 off—always with the promise that as Elvis became more famous, their salary would increase. Since Elvis was now the biggest star in the world, Scotty had grown impatient. Soon he and Bill would resign, but later reconsider, asking for a raise of $50 per week and a flat payment of $10,000. Colonel reminded Presley that nothing was ever put in writing ("Besides, Steve Sholes doesn't like them") and demanded Elvis cut them loose, a decision that would come to a head in a matter of months. "The Colonel had a grip on everybody but me, Scotty, and Bill," says D. J. Fontana. "He couldn't tell us what to do, 'cause we could go to Elvis, see?"

Normally afraid to question Parker's judgment, Elvis complained to his cousin Junior Smith that he thought the Colonel had steered him wrong. What the hell did that old lardass know about music? Besides, he'd also heard that Parker had blown a lot of money over a paid advertising deal gone bad. Furthermore, he hadn't liked it that Parker kept a net around him, turning down Robert Mitchum's invitation for Elvis to appear in *Thunder Road*. "He just wants to use your name," Parker said, but to Elvis, it seemed as if he didn't want him talking to other people, period, especially if they were in the business. One day, the Colonel found out that Mike Stoller was up in the suite at the Beverly Wilshire, playing pool, and ordered Elvis to ask him to leave. Jerry Leiber saw that Elvis "was trapped by his dependency on the Colonel," that "he worshiped him as a maker and savior," but "despised him because he was never able to take control of his own life."

Elvis's dissatisfaction leaked back to the Colonel, who flew into a rage and gathered his staff in his office, telephoning the set for Elvis to come at once and bellowing into the receiver. ("I don't care if he *is* shooting! Send him over!"). Elvis, shaken by Parker's fury, took a seat at the Colonel's direction. "Elvis, Trude's here, Byron's here, Tom's here," Parker began in a voice husky with emotion. "I'm saying in front of all of these witnesses that if you don't think I've done the right thing by you, you walk out this minute and you're free. Go get yourself another manager. But if you stay, you're going to do what I tell you. Do you understand me?" Elvis nodded, resigned in the future to hold his tongue. "He got me this far, made me a big star," he told his pals. "I'm going to stick with him."

Whenever anyone had the nerve to ask about such confrontations, the Colonel explained, "It's better to be feared than liked." But Parker had been decidedly on edge since learning the story line for *Jailhouse Rock,* which, unlike the sophisticated comedy of *Loving You,* traded on the dark side of Presley's rebel persona and the shadowy business practices of rock and roll.

In the role of Vince Everett, an ex-con turned rock star, Elvis began to demonstrate a formidable ability to handle dramatic material, particularly in the movie's grittier scenes. Guided by a volatile temper, Vince accidentally kills a man in a barroom brawl. Sentenced to prison, Vince meets fellow convict Hunk Houghton (Mickey Shaughnessy), a country singer who boasts of being as big as Eddy Arnold or Roy Acuff. Houghton teaches him to sing and play guitar, and when Vince's talent emerges, Hunk, who lines his cell walls with pictures of Hank Snow and Ernest Tubb, offers to become his manager ("Alone, you'd be like a lamb in a pack of wolves"). But the manipulative Hunk is still a con at heart, demanding 50 percent of Vince's money and withholding his fan mail to keep the budding star from realizing how popular he's become.

Jailhouse Rock secretly mirrors a series of events in the collective Presley-Parker past, including Vernon Presley's six-month stint in the Mississippi State Penitentiary in the late '30s for altering a check from a dairy farmer named Orville Bean, who held the Presleys' mortgage. While the references to Parker's earlier show business associates were hardly coincidental, the Colonel, who never established even the slightest curiosity in Elvis's previous motion picture scripts, seemed to have an unusual investment in this one. Before the title was finalized, he wrote a memo to Pandro Berman suggesting they call the picture *Don't Push Me Too Far* or *Trouble Is My Name.*

Had Parker identified with the character of Vince Everett, the young man who ended a life in an instant of anger? Certainly he had begun to demonstrate odd obsessions that hinted at unwelcome thoughts and deeper worries, including personal safety. At home in Tennessee, he installed iron bars on all the windows and wired the house with an extensive antiburglar system. In part, this was because Marie, who stayed behind during the early Hollywood years, was "deathly afraid to be alone," in the words of a friend, keeping the house dark with the curtains drawn in all the rooms but the kitchen, and insisting on a female companion whenever her husband was out of town.

Ordinarily, the old carny practiced a form of self-hypnotism, boasting that he could train himself to filter out certain feelings or people altogether ("Don't you know that I can put you out of my mind so I don't even know that you exist?"). But lately the stuff within him had proved bigger than his ability to handle it—he seemed eternally frustrated, unable to rest, routinely pacing back and forth in his apartment at the Beverly Wilshire—and his demons gained prominence. He fought back his anxiety with a driving need for rigidity, ritual, and control.

Where Parker had always insisted on an almost militaristic atmosphere in the office ("Like he was going to call roll," says Gordon Stoker), he now stepped up his efforts to have it run like a little Pentagon, offering a self-satisfied smile whenever anyone referred to his staff as "the Colonel's army." Since he tended to fuss if even a single item was out of place, Trude saw to it that the office was immaculate. At home in Madison, Mary Diskin knew that she might be asked to open the drawers for inspection at any time, and followed orders to make sure that all the pens were grouped together and faced the same direction, and the pencils sharpened to a rapier's point, their erasers perfect.

Both secretaries were puzzled by the secrecy with which the Colonel insisted on, typing some of his letters himself, hunched over the typewriter like a hawk, shielding the paper from view. On those occasions, the secretaries knew never to peek in the out box afterward, lest the Colonel think they were checking up on him.

What baffled Byron was Parker's habit of sitting at his desk, repeatedly stacking and centering piles of papers without apparent purpose, and his insistence on showering three or four times a day, afterward splashing on a liberal amount of 4711 cologne, the German scent that Napoleon was said to have diluted in his bath. "If we would go out for a meal, or even coffee, he would come back to the Beverly Wilshire and take a shower." Unusually preoccupied with body odor and his own feces, according to several, he had, says Byron, "an almost Macbethean compulsion to be clean." Soon, preoccupied with the notion of germs, he would drink almost nothing but Mountain Valley Spring Water.

Raphael saw even more surprising sides of Parker when he went home with the Colonel to Tennessee after filming wrapped on *Jailhouse Rock* in June of '57. In the Dutch custom, Parker put a lot of emphasis on the observance of birthdays, especially his own. For his forty-eighth, on June 26, Marie gave him a large party, and the Colonel reveled in the merriment with his Nashville cronies.

But late that night, Byron awoke to "these horrible sounds . . . like an animal wailing, the strangest sound that I ever heard in my life." The next day, over breakfast, he told Marie what he'd heard ("Maybe it was a cat outside") and asked if everything was all right. "Oh, I don't know, Byron," she said. "Elvis forgot Colonel's birthday." Raphael, mystified that such a small slight made "this powerful strong man cry all night long," went to Presley, who took off one of his rings with the instructions to tell the Colonel he just hadn't delivered it in time. Parker knew the truth, but he'd already walled off his vulnerability and repaired the cracks in his emotional fortress.

By now, Byron had married an aspiring actress, Carolyn Cline, and the Colonel and Marie invited the couple to come live with them in Madison. The Colonel had one peculiar rule for the newlyweds as long as they were under his roof: no hand-holding, which Byron interpreted to mean no displays of affection of any kind. The Parkers had separate bedrooms ("They were like an old couple, but they really weren't that old"), and Raphael was under the impression that theirs was not a physical relationship and perhaps never had been. "There wasn't the faintest sign . . . he just didn't have a physical love for any woman."

The Colonel had railed against Raphael's marriage from the start. It distracted him from his work, Parker said, and made him reluctant to take the cross-country journeys that Parker loved so well, visiting the little one-elephant carnivals and backroad diners. Raphael was always amazed to see this mellow side of him, when he told his hillbilly stories and talked about his past, a period he seemed to have enjoyed more than the present. But otherwise, Byron, who was expected to drive, hated the trips, because the Colonel inexplicably had a buzzer installed on the car that went off every time the speedometer hit 55. Now, after an argument in which Carolyn objected to Byron's accompanying Parker on a gambling trip to Las Vegas, the Colonel began working to undermine the relationship, telling Byron that Carolyn cared nothing for him, that she was just using him for his William Morris connections. Besides, in time, didn't Byron want to leave the agency and work for him? Hadn't Parker told him to call him Pops?

Within two years, the Colonel talked his young aide into divorcing ("It was something he demanded") and insisted on brokering the arrangement. So that Byron would be free of alimony payments, Marie, who was fond of Carolyn and cared about her well-being, assumed her support. "The Colonel told me not to worry about it," Byron remembers. "And as I think about it, I never saw a lawyer, never went to court. It was all just taken care of."

Parker, who had struggled to relegate his gambling to friendly pickup games and betting at the dog tracks in Florida and Arizona, began, during this period of accelerated stress, to feel the old fever and obsess about larger action. On the way back to California from their first Las Vegas trip together, Byron mentioned that he had an uncle who ran a little motel, a dump of a place called the Silver Sands, in Palm Springs, just one hundred miles south of Hollywood.

Though he had yet to make the trip, the Colonel had been hearing about Palm Springs since before World War II. Unlike Los Angeles, illegal gambling—everything from poker, to craps, to roulette—was readily available there for high rollers. "They paid the sheriff and everybody to keep it running," remembers ninety-one-year-old Frank Bogert, the former Palm Springs mayor. Three hot spots—the well-appointed Dunes Club, with its glamorous New York atmosphere; the 139 Club; and the Cove—admitted customers who weren't put off by mobsters brandishing submachine guns, and whispered the password to the hole in the door for a chance to mingle with movie stars and socialites. Palm Springs sounded exactly like everything Parker loved about Hot Springs, Arkansas, in the '30s. "Byron," the Colonel said, "Let's go see your uncle."

Parker had frequented Las Vegas since the late '40s, when Sin City was no more than a little dusty town of 10,000, and the Colonel booked Eddy Arnold into the elite, cowboy-themed Hotel El Rancho Vegas for Helldorado Days, when floats, parades, and rodeo promoted its Wild West heritage. Initially, Arnold didn't want to go ("I kept hearing stories about artists appearing out there and gambling away all their money before they left . . . I thought maybe the hotel management might expect it"), but Parker couldn't resist the lure of the green felt jungle.

"The times when I was there," remembers Gabe Tucker, "he'd say, 'Let's go down and play, fellers.' He'd give me a handful of hundred-dollar chips and say, 'Play some, Gabe, play some.' He'd take a chance on anything—covered every number on a roulette wheel. I told him,

'Colonel, you can't win playin' like you play.' But he'd just stack 'em up all over and make sure that nobody sat at that table except us. If somebody tried to muscle in, he'd have us all get out those cigars—'Now light that up, light that up!'—and they didn't stay too long. We never did play with somebody we didn't know."

With the opening of the El Rancho, built in 1941 on vacant land destined to become the Strip—at first only a two-lane highway beckoning jaded Los Angeles residents to a playground in the desert—Las Vegas began to take its first steps as a gambling mecca, followed soon by the gangster glamour of Benjamin "Bugsy" Siegel's Flamingo Hotel and Milton Prell's Hotel Sahara, the "Jewel of the Desert." Parker and Arnold were playing the North Africa–themed Sahara, where plaster camels stood as sentinels at the hotel's entrance, when the two had the spat that led to their breakup in 1953.

Prell, the first hotel executive to offer big-name attractions in Strip lounges, was one of the earliest gambling figures in the state. He'd opened Club Bingo in 1947, enlarging it in 1952 to become the Sahara, and went on to build and operate the Lucky Strike Club and the Mint downtown. But Prell had plenty of help. The Sahara was built with West Coast bookie and extortion profits, as well as Oregon race-wire money. And while the hotel would be controlled by a number of mobster families through the years, Prell himself was the front man for the Detroit branch of the Cosa Nostra. He'd given 20 percent interest in the Sahara to its Phoenix-based contractor, Del Webb, who'd also built Siegel's Flamingo, and whose company would become a major force in the gaming industry, leasing casino space.

The Colonel took a liking to Prell, a Montana native and former Los Angeles jeweler, who extended him a high line of casino credit, met him frequently for breakfast, and sat around the pool with him, deep in conversation. The two formed an intimacy unlike any other in Parker's personal history, and Prell became the one man the Colonel turned to whenever he needed a favor in Vegas.

Parker was normally too paranoid to allow himself such a close relationship. When his brother-in-law, Bitsy Mott, signed on to head Elvis's security, Parker bluntly laid it on the table: "Bitsy, I trust you more than anyone else. But you have one fault. You make too many friends."

It was imperative to Parker that he and Prell stay on the best of terms, and the Colonel went out of his way to show the hotel manager the utmost respect. When Byron told the Colonel he'd lost $100 at blackjack and written the casino a cold check—one he planned to warm up as soon as they returned to California—Parker marched his young aide into Prell's office to apologize and ask for forgiveness. "The check hadn't even bounced yet, but the Colonel made such a big production out of it that I got the feeling they had some sort of side deal, a definite connection beyond the obvious."

The Colonel was adamantly opposed to Byron's fondness for the tables ("Don't you know how stupid gamblers are? They're all nebos!"—carny talk for "dimwit" or an easy mark), and warned him against the evils of the game. In 1954, after several years of taking Marie's son, Bobby, under his wing and teaching him to become a manager for such acts as country singers George Morgan and Slim Whitman, Parker had sent him home to Tampa after Bobby developed an inordinate interest in blackjack, frequenting both Las Vegas and the after-hours clubs in Nashville. Byron was astonished, then, to see how the Colonel couldn't leave the dollar slots alone, and how he called on his "mental telepathy and perpetual perception motors" to reconcile his desire to play with his certainty that the odds were against him. "He stared at the slot machine for the longest time, then lit his cigar, and said, 'I'm hypnotizing it to pay off.' That's how confident he was that he could will anyone or anything into doing what he wanted."

Parker's increased interest in gambling and other obsessive-compulsive behaviors may have been a way to keep his thoughts from settling on the secrets of his past, including his botched army career. For the U.S. Army was very much on his mind these days, and had been since early '56, when Elvis turned twenty-one.

Certainly Elvis would be eligible for the draft, but Parker couldn't have him called up and processed like any other soldier. No, the Colonel would have to negotiate the terms of Elvis's service with the army itself, through a series of interactions that might raise questions about Parker's own tours of duty. The prospect must have filled him with trepidation, but for a man who psychologically viewed his client as his beautiful alter ego—always "Elvis and the Colonel"—any thoughts on how to handle Elvis's army career would have been a projection of Parker's own patriotism. It also would have triggered an intense desire to relive his own army experience and rectify the past. For that, Elvis would need to be the model soldier, with no blemishes on his record like AWOL, desertion, or discharge for emotional instability.

To his staff, Parker was consumed only with manipulating the situation for the greatest public relations good. What has never before come to light is exactly how he did it. In the summer of '56, he began dictating a series of letters to Trude addressed to the Pentagon, requesting that the army assign Elvis to Special Services, so that Presley might bypass boot camp and rigorous training and concentrate all his efforts on entertaining Uncle Sam's troops.

But Parker had no intention of Elvis going into Special Services. In fact, that was the last thing he wanted. At every whim, the boy would be made to perform free in front of 20,000 soldiers. The Colonel wouldn't even be able to sell programs! Worse, each appearance would be filmed and sold to television networks, with every cent going into the army's coffers. The overexposure would kill Elvis's motion picture career.

No, no, Elvis could not go into Special Services. Besides, a public hew and cry would rise up all across the land, from veterans' groups and congressmen, from mothers and fathers outraged that a hip-shaking hooligan was treated any differently than their boy. Faron Young had done it, but who cared about Faron, strumming his honky-tonk guitar for army recruitment programs? A big star who shirked his duty had hell to pay.

Why then had Parker made a request for Elvis to go into the army as anything but a regular Joe? Because the Colonel was, as usual, one step ahead of everyone. Now, in secret, he fed a story to *Billboard* magazine in October '56—more than a year before Elvis would receive his induction notice—informing the publication that Elvis would be drafted in December '57 and assigned to Special Services. The magazine telephoned Fort Dix, New Jersey, for confirmation, and learned that, indeed, Elvis was about to get a cushy deal. His hair would not be cut, and after six weeks of basic training, he would be free to resume being Elvis. All he had to do was entertain his fellow soldiers on behalf of his government.

Presley, learning of this for the first time in *Billboard,* was stunned and confused. Hadn't Milton Bowers, chairman of his draft board, promised to notify Elvis privately in advance of just such things? Bowers said yes, but the story had come out of the blue. Elvis read it again. The only people who would know the date of his induction, the magazine reported, were army personnel and Presley's "closest business associates."

For a year, Parker kept Elvis hanging, saying he would talk to the boys in Washington, see what he could do. Elvis's cronies were perplexed, George Klein, his high school friend, saying, "There's no war going on, you're sitting on the top of the world, and all of a sudden you've got to go into the army? It doesn't make sense."

Freddy Bienstock was with the Colonel in California when Parker went to deliver the unhappy news. They found Elvis in the dining room at the Beverly Wilshire Hotel, surrounded by his luckless cousins and Cliff Gleaves, a disheveled runt of a fellow Elvis met in '56 and kept around for comic relief. The Colonel said he was sorry. He had done everything possible, but Elvis had to go into the army. Elvis stared in silence, and the cousins looked away. Suddenly Cliff dropped his knife and fork. "What's going to happen to me? I've given him the best years of my life!"

Parker had outslicked them all—the army, which had long ago be-smirched his own service record, and his increasingly ill-tempered client, who needed a cooling-off period, riding around in tanks in Germany in the dead of winter. Now, he told him, Elvis must go back to the draft board and say he wanted to serve his country like any other young man, without preferential treatment of any kind.

What did it matter if Parker had, in a way, enlisted him? Elvis's service number would start with "US," the code for "drafted." He would look like a hero. And when he got out two years later, he would be visibly tamed, transformed into a pure symbol of America, a clean-cut god for the masses. No more would he personify the music of a subversive and dangerous subculture, led by wild deejays high on pills and payola.

Parker had it all figured out. But had the Colonel, in waxing nostalgic about his days as Private Parker in carefree Hawaii, granted the army a codicil, especially after backing out of the Special Services agreement? In November '57, a month before Elvis received his draft notice, Presley played two dates in Honolulu, booked by Lee Gordon, who won the honor from the Colonel on a roll of the dice. The day after the shows at the Honolulu Stadium, Elvis performed for servicemen at Schofield Bar-racks, Pearl Harbor. Thus, Elvis's last show before entering the army was a free one—hardly Parker's favorite kind. Less than a month later, he would write Harry Kalcheim at William Morris to defend his decision to stop booking Elvis for live performances, citing fear of overexposure— one of his explanations for turning down a myriad of recent offers, in-cluding tours of South America, Great Britain, and Australia. At RCA, says Sam Esgro, the story swirled that Parker must have citizenship prob-lems, because no one would turn down such lucrative dates.

Elvis, who was in constant touch with Milton Bowers at the Memphis draft board, drove down to pick up his induction notice in person on December 19. The deal was set: a two-year tour of duty and, by request of Paramount Studio head Y. Frank Freeman and Elvis himself, a sixty-day deferment to allow Presley to make his second Paramount picture, *King Creole,* which would go into production in January.

Paul Nathan and Joe Hazen had argued against putting Presley in the musical drama, based on Harold Robbins's popular novel *A Stone for Danny Fisher,* believing the story of an impressionable teen caught up in the underworld of violence and crime was too close to the feel of *Jailhouse Rock* and reinforced the image of Elvis as a troubled young man.

Wallis vetoed them and held his ground again when Nathan sent the producer a memo saying "the business of Danny using the jagged edges of two broken bottles as a weapon is unacceptable" to the Breen office, referencing Joseph Breen, Hollywood's chief censor. "Is it in the [Production] Code?" Wallis scribbled back. "If not, we will use it." Thus, Wallis ensured what became Elvis's most memorable scene. But he also directed screenwriter Oscar Saul to tone down the seamier aspects of the story dealing with mobsters and whores, and to move the setting from New York to New Orleans, with its rich musical heritage.

Although Parker cajoled Steve Sholes on occasion—for his forty-sixth birthday, Parker presented him with an enormous bead-and-gold-festooned doghouse, custom-built for Nipper—relations between them remained strained; RCA had no say about which music would be used in the movies and little input as to songs that made up the albums. Through what many at the company thought was a direct payoff to singles division manager Bill Bullock ("That crooked son of a bitch gave Elvis to the Colonel lock, stock, and barrel," says a former employee), Parker continued to wrest control from RCA. Now he dictated almost all terms with the label and determined how many singles the company released each year.

Nonetheless, the company was fired up about the idea of a Dixieland soundtrack, and a representative met with Parker and Paramount officials in California to discuss the deal. They were throwing around figures—$250,000 as Lenny Hirshan remembers it—when the Colonel stopped the meeting, saying he had someone outside he needed to bring in for an important negotiation. He opened the door to usher in a balloon salesman—a down-at-the-heels carnival supplier—and as the executives listened, the Colonel cut a deal for "a ton of balloons, cheaper than what the guy was offering them for, maybe ten cents a hundred." The men shook their heads, but the message was clear: nobody, from crusty carnies to hot-shot moguls, was going to get the best of the Colonel.

With *King Creole,* Hal Wallis gave Presley the chance to become the dramatic actor he yearned to be, matching him with respected director Michael Curtiz ("For the first time, I know what a director is," Elvis said later), and an explosive cast of Carolyn Jones, Dean Jagger, and Walter Matthau, with whom the Colonel played cards between scenes. It was the performance that would forever define his potential, both to him and to those who had never quite believed in him. "Just like in his music, he really got involved in his acting," said Curtiz. "You'd look in his eyes, and boy, they were really going."

Elvis had waited for this moment since high school, lost in the dreamy darkness of the Suzore Number Two Theater in Memphis, his arm around his girl, Dixie Locke. But now it took on new importance. Scared that rock and roll might be a fad, that his fame would fade away while he was in the army, he hoped he'd do a good enough job on *King Creole* to resume his movie career when he returned in 1960.

The Colonel sat him down and made the promise that would forever bond Elvis Presley to Tom Parker. "If you go into the army, stay a good boy, and do nothing to embarrass your country," the Colonel said; "I'll see to it that you'll come back a bigger star than when you left."

At 6:35 A.M. on March 24, 1958, the world's most famous recruit reported to the Memphis draft board, accompanied by his parents and his girlfriend, Anita Wood. He wore a wan smile and a loud plaid sport jacket over a striped shirt, and carried a leather bag with exactly what the army said to bring—a comb, a razor, a toothbrush, and enough money to last two weeks. The Colonel was already on hand, chatting with the army brass and the media, and palming off his bargain balloons—now stamped *King Creole*—to the gathering crowd. "Colonel Parker," a reporter scribbled down on his pad, "seemed happier than ever."

Before departing for Fort Chaffee, Arkansas, where he'd undergo his famous haircut, Elvis kissed his puffy-eyed mother, hugged his father, and gazed fondly at his '58 Cadillac. "Good-bye, you long, black son of a bitch," he said, drawing a laugh from his fellow soldiers. Then he climbed aboard the bus to leave behind everything he had ever known and begin life anew as Private Presley. By week's end, he would be assigned to the Second Armored Division, stationed at Fort Hood, Killeen, Texas.

The Colonel would follow to Fort Chaffee, to cheerfully marshal photographers, share Elvis's first army meal, and try to sneak a Southern string necktie into the army's standard clothing issue. And he would make several visits to Fort Hood, in between planning the release of Elvis's singles during his two-year tour of duty. Though Steve Sholes had fought the Colonel to build up a backlog of recordings, the label had scarcely any material, and now the April release, "Wear My Ring Around Your Neck"/"Doncha Think It's Time," performed poorly in comparison to recent singles. During his two-week furlough, when he returned home to Memphis, Elvis, in regulation khaki uniform, tie, and hat, drove to Nashville for what would be his last studio recording session for two years. Backed by Nashville's crack A-team session players, assembled by Chet Atkins, he cut five steamy, uptempo numbers for a flow of product, including "I Need Your Love Tonight" and "A Big Hunk o' Love," which would help restore his prominence on radio.

But how long, he wondered, would it last? At Fort Hood, Elvis, who had always suffered from sleep disturbance and nightmares, was visited by a haunting dream: when he came out of the army, everything was gone—no songs on the charts, no fans at the Graceland gates, not even a specter of the Colonel. Elvis asked his friend Eddie Fadal, a former deejay who opened his Waco home to him, to help him get some medication— uppers to ease him through the day and downers to let him sleep. It was easy: "My father knew all the doctors in town," says Fadal's daughter, Janice.

Elvis had long pilfered diet pills from his alcoholic mother, Gladys, whom the image-conscious Colonel had encouraged to lose weight for the family publicity photos. Now, nothing a physician might provide eased the pain of their separation. During basic training, Elvis called home, and as Fadal later remembered, "When he got her on the line, all he said was, 'Mama . . . ' And, apparently, she said, 'Elvis . . . ' And from then on, for a whole hour, they were crying and moaning on the tele- phone—hardly a word was spoken."

Soon Elvis installed the family and his pal Lamar Fike in a three- bedroom rental house near the base. But Gladys's health, which had de- clined in the months leading to Elvis's enlistment, grew steadily worse. A doctor in Killeen suspected hepatitis and suggested she return to Ten- nessee at once. On August 8, she boarded a train for Memphis, where she died six days later at Methodist Hospital at the age of forty-six.

Elvis was inconsolable. When Lamar Fike arrived at the hospital shortly after Elvis received the news, "that elevator opened, and I've never heard such crying and screaming and hollering in my life. This wailing. Almost like wolves. It made me shudder. I came around the cor- ner and Elvis was walking towards me, and he said, 'Lamar, Satnin' isn't here.' And I said, 'I know, Elvis, I know.' "

Later that day, Elvis was still in no shape to speak with the funeral director, leaving the task to his father, the Colonel, and Freddy Bienstock.

"When the funeral director came to Graceland," remembers Bienstock, "Vernon was crying and carrying on, and it was mostly bunk, because he was cheating all over the place. Everybody knew it. But he was saying, through these not very convincing tears, 'The best of everything. Give her the best of everything.' The fellow marked it all down and left very quickly, and the moment he walked out the door, the crying stopped. Vernon turned to Colonel Parker and said, 'Don't let him take advantage of me in my hour of grief.'"

Gladys Presley had never made any secret of her dislike of Tom Parker, and he steered clear of her whenever possible. ("I suppose I was never comfortable around her," Parker said, "but I was managing Elvis, not his parents.") Now that she was gone, the Colonel moved to forge a new alliance with Vernon, who shared the Colonel's hunger for money under the table. Parker, who privately complained that Elvis's family was "shit . . . they were awful people," would always work to keep Vernon happy, but it suited him fine that Vernon talked of moving to Germany to keep his son company, taking along his mother, Minnie Mae, who would be a housekeeper for the all-male household. With Gladys out of the way, the Presleys would be easier to control than ever.

The Colonel himself was not going to Europe, he explained to reporters, because he had too much work to do stateside. All the publicity, all the sales, all the films and music came through his office. There were records to promote, motion pictures to negotiate, exhibitors to notify, fan clubs to contact. Even the Elvis merchandising would add an army theme. But first, there would be a grand send-off at the Brooklyn pier.

In early '56, during rehearsals for one of Elvis's *Stage Show* appearances, Anne Fulchino, RCA's national publicity director, was astonished to feel the arms of Tom Parker slipping around her shoulders. Two years earlier, mistakenly believing that Fulchino had discouraged a *Look* magazine photographer from taking his picture on the RCA Country Caravan, he had threatened to have her job. When Chick Crumpacker spoke up, saying that was unfair, Parker, misunderstanding his words, assailed him. "Don't you call me a square!" he bristled, leaving everyone properly stunned.

"I want to apologize, I was wrong," he said of the incident backstage in '56. Fulchino knew that wasn't the Colonel's way ("I thought, good God, what is going on here?") and realized it could only mean one thing:

Parker had few contacts with the New York press and needed help in co-ordinating Elvis's debarkation, already under discussion at the label. Now, with the date upon them, Fulchino spoke with the Colonel. Instead of the army band blasting John Philip Sousa marches, they'd have them play Elvis songs at the pier. And Fulchino would call out 125 members of the media, including photographers Al Wertheimer and Henri Dauman, who would make the most memorable images of the day.

On September 22, 1958, soon after Elvis's troop train pulled into the Brooklyn Army Terminal, Private Presley emerged smiling from a confer-ence with the Colonel and a group of army officials. To a flurry of flash-bulbs, he kissed a WAC, signed autographs, and finally sat down at a table with a gaggle of microphones to answer questions, a prominent bank of recruitment posters behind him. Did he miss show business? "I miss my singing career very much, and at the same time, the army is a pretty good deal, too." Had his music contributed to juvenile delin-quency? "I don't see that," Elvis said, "because I've tried to live a straight, clean life, not set any kind of a bad example."

Steve Sholes beamed, the Aberbachs puffed up with pride, and Fulchino, who two years earlier chided an awkward young singer for greeting RCA executives with a buzzer on his finger ("That may be big in Nashville, but it will never go in New York"), felt a stir of emotion. Parker, standing off to the side, did nothing for a moment but hold tight to a gift from Paramount Studios—a fruit basket, always a prize to the Colonel, a reminder of his visits to the greengrocer as a hungry lad in Holland.

Wertheimer, a German émigré who'd spent considerable time chroni-cling a carefree Presley in '56, was saddened to see what a managed per-sonality Elvis had become. The photographer snapped his shutter as the Colonel, who always surprised him by correctly pronouncing his diffi-cult, Teutonic surname, "pushed his stubby little fist in Elvis's back," guiding him through the well-wishers and out to the pier.

Elvis, carrying a mysterious shoe box that the Colonel had given him, waved to photographers, and struggled to hoist a too-heavy duffle bag to his shoulders, smiling obligingly as he climbed the gangplank of the U.S.S. *Randall* eight times so everyone might get a good shot. The two thousand relatives of his fellow soldiers, there for their own happy send-offs, joined in the waving for the newsreels.

Now the band was into its third rendition of "Tutti Frutti" as Elvis took his place at the rail of the ship and loosened the lid of the shoe box, waiting for the boat to jostle and creak and signal its leave from the harbor. Only then did he empty its contents, fluttering, like so much confetti, hundreds of tiny Elvis images down the side of the boat, onto the pier, and into the scrambling hands of his fans.

Twenty-nine years earlier, Parker had come to this country on a series of ships, and now the man he had built into a symbol of America was leaving it, going to Germany, to a land where the Colonel could not go, a country too close to Holland, where a young woman died violently at the hands of a psychopath in the back of a quiet fruit shop. Twenty-nine years later, her strange murder, marked by a series of dark blows and a baffling trail of pepper, remained to be solved.

Henri Dauman, camera in hand, found the Colonel deep in thought, watching the vessel until it disappeared on the horizon, taking with it both his provision and his protection. Once Elvis joined the army, Parker said in 1980, "I barely saw him for the next two years. There was very little contact, especially after he left for Germany. He called three or four times. I never got any letters. I got one thank-you note one time, but that was all he ever wrote. He did his duty."

Now, except for Diskin, Marie, and Bevo, who sat day after day in the Madison office, pasting sympathy cards for Gladys's death into scrapbooks, the Colonel was alone. Trude would soon be gone, Parker saying he no longer needed a secretary in California, though she would return for a short time in 1960, before her divorce battle. And Byron, fearing he'd turn into Tom Diskin if he stayed, would go back to William Morris. There, he would work in the music and motion picture departments, but after the awful incident with Lenny Hirshan, never advance as an agent. Parker had sacrificed his career.

The Colonel filled his days and nights with thoughts of keeping Elvis's name before the public. No scheme seemed too weird. For a while, he courted the notion of going back out with the Royal American Shows with an Elvis exhibit, deciding instead to have Al Dvorin, his Chicago friend, hire a twenty-five-member "Elvis Presley Midget Fan Club" to carry a banner through the Windy City during Juke Box Convention.

Still, he made numerous trips to Tampa to "cut up jackpots" with his old carny pals, particularly in late January, when the Florida State Fair drew so many of the circus managers, show promoters, and talent buyers who met to plan their summer seasons. One day, he saw that Dale Robertson, the cowboy star, was appearing there and invited him to lunch. Robertson, arriving early at the restaurant, noticed a copy of the

British crown jewels on display under glass. "When we got ready to leave," Robertson remembers, "I took another look at those crown jewels, and there was a card slid up inside the case: LET'S NOT FORGET ELVIS PRESLEY. HE'S FIGHTING FOR OUR COUNTRY."

Soon, the Colonel resumed his own good fight, playing the Hollywood producers off each other for Elvis's next picture.

On such sojourns to Hollywood, Parker sometimes cornered a few business acquaintances and suggested going to dinner at the Luau, where he enjoyed the spicy Indonesian food of his youth. The men usually went for one reason: the Colonel, holding court in his favorite throne-backed chair, had the most unusual party trick—he'd have them lay bets on the amount of hot mustard he could swallow without drinking water.

How he did it they never knew. He didn't even make a face! But what really got them was when he started on the pepper—whole tablespoons of it, straight from the shaker. A spoonful of mustard, alternating with a spoonful of pepper, and back and forth again. Torturous! What was the guy trying to do, punish himself?

13

FRIENDLY PERSUASION: MOGULS,

MILITARY MEN, AND MOBSTERS

DESPITE what Parker would say about the lack of contact with Elvis during his military service, it did not mean the two men were not in communication. Almost every day after Elvis sailed for Germany, the Colonel wrote him long, chatty letters designed to fill him in on his efforts "to keep your name hot over here," and to try to boost the singer's spirits. Immediately, Parker reported spectacular results. The Colonel's hard work, he wrote, combined with his diversity of promotions—$3 million from souvenirs alone—would bring in more revenue for 1958 than for the year before, even as Elvis spent nearly the entire time in the service. And now the crafty manager had finalized the lucrative movie deals he'd spent months negotiating with Paramount and Twentieth Century–Fox. Parker instructed Elvis to send Fox's Buddy Adler a thank-you telegram and wrote out the script for him.

Hal Wallis, determined to produce Elvis's first post-army picture, eventually called *G.I. Blues,* had agreed to pay $175,000 for the film— $75,000 more than Presley's fee for *King Creole,* and $150,000 more than what Elvis was entitled to under the terms of their original contract. Additionally, Wallis and Hazen agreed on options for three more films at $125,000, $150,000, and $175,000 against 7½ percent of gross receipts after the picture earned out. At Twentieth Century–Fox, the Colonel revamped Elvis's existing deal for one picture at $200,000, with an option for a second at $250,000, and a 50–50 split of profits after expenses.

The new contract with Paramount went a long way in neutralizing Parker's acid resentment over the initial agreement. "There was not much I could do . . . except get a little more each time we made a picture," the Colonel wrote in a letter to Elvis and Vernon, who "managed"

Elvis in Germany and was more apt to keep in touch than his soldier son. "The facts are now we do not have to call on Wallis every time with our hat in our hands to ask for a little extra." He added that he had secured a percentage of profits with both deals—something they'd not previously had with either studio—and proudly announced, "This now brings our picture setup in line with a very healthy . . . future. This also will prove to Elvis that he is not backsliding in any way."

In thanking the Colonel for wrapping up the deals with Paramount and Fox, Presley joked, "This sure is a long tour you sent me on," and closed his letter by saying, "I'm sorry the commissions are so small in this engagement."

Parker's new projects seemed to fill him with élan. His correspondence with Wallis and Hazen took on a giddy wit and playfulness, but Hazen had always found the Colonel repugnant, and was barely able to restrain himself from telling him so, at one point writing to congratulate him for his chutzpah in tipping a Las Vegas bellboy with sandwiches pilfered from the Paramount commissary. His disdain for Parker grew immeasurably after the manager snookered him into buying half a million pocket-sized photographs of Elvis in uniform for promotion. The idea was "to give Mr. Presley some additional income," as the Colonel termed it. But in taking the printing to his old Tampa friend Clyde Rinaldi and marking up the job for profit, Parker charged Paramount three cents a picture though the commercial rate elsewhere was half a cent.

When Hazen called him on such shenanigans, the Colonel became churlish and indignant. "I am sure," Parker wrote after one prolonged period of haggling over money, "that both of you will agree that I have endeavored to stay away from . . . you as much as possible in bringing this to its conclusion. In the meantime, I am very happy that my connection with the Salvation Army in the South is strong. As you know, they always have kettles in the street during Christmas . . . it is with great anticipation that I can look forward to not having to share whatever I may get out of these kettles with my associates." He signed it, "You Know Who."

Wallis answered these borderline insults quickly and perfunctorily, as if to say that he feared losing the Colonel, despite their binding contract. Parker, a bloodhound when it came to smelling out human weakness, fed on that fear, and it was Wallis who got the brunt of his teasing, not Hazen. Once, when the producer discouraged Parker's input on a project, repeating, "You've just got to get the big picture, Colonel," Parker took his revenge. A week later, Wallis arrived at his office to find a photo of himself enlarged to the size of a wall and installed behind his desk. The accompanying sign: HERE'S THE BIG PICTURE.

Parker also seemed to have a personal investment in Wallis. In their many letters, the Colonel's tone was categorically different with Wallis than it was with Hazen; it was Wallis's approval he sought in begging for a pat on the back for a favor or a job well done ("This again shows you the little Colonel stays on the ball and follows through"). At times, especially when he sent Wallis such gifts as jars of honey, octopus, and even Texas longhorns, his affection appeared genuine. Each year, the Colonel sent Wallis Valentine's and Father's Day greetings, usually telegrams "from Elvis and myself . . . your two boys" or, once, "your two orphans, Marie and the Colonel." After several such missives, one signed with "love," Wallis responded, "It is nice to be thought of and remembered, even though I am not your father."

Whatever the paternal complexity of his feelings, Parker was unquestionably thinking of his past in December 1958, when he began writing Wallis strange, autobiographical letters offering story ideas for Elvis's motion pictures. In easing into the first, he noted the growing popularity of Hawaiian music and Elvis's "good voice for that type of singing."

A native love story set in Hawaii with "some tough elements" interested him, he said, particularly if Presley were a stowaway on a large steamer bound for the islands. His suggestion was to frame a plot in which Elvis, dressed in disguise and using another name, ran away from all who pursued him, including the fans and the record companies frantic for more product, only to fall into the hands of "a gang of promoters—con artists—that is snowing Elvis into singing with the natives."

These "con artists" would "exploit" Elvis, Parker wrote, making secret tapes of his performances and "selling records like hotcakes." No one would know Presley's true identity until they brought him to Honolulu to do a show, whereupon a frightened Elvis discovered all too late that "he has been promoted into something else."

"I am this far with the story," the Colonel told Wallis, but went on to say he had also been thinking of another plot regarding gypsies. As the "rugged type," Parker said, Elvis would be well cast as a foundling or baby boy stolen "by a bunch of gypsies traveling in wagons [and] sleeping outdoors." Later, he repeated the idea to associate producer Dick Sokolove, changing the focus to "a gypsy boy, traveling with his mother, who gets into trouble with police."

No one at the studio could have known that both plots were illuminating glimpses into Parker's own psyche. His reference to gypsies certainly must have come from memories of his maternal grandfather and the Ponsies' nomadic lifestyle, while "trouble with the police" resurrects the haunting specter of Anna van den Enden. But the Hawaiian story, set in the islands that Parker so loved during his early army years, and its focus on a tramp steamer stowaway and an exploitative promoter who transforms the young artist into "something else," shows how clearly the Colonel identified with Elvis. It also demonstrates how well he understood his own role in the undoing of an artist desperate to shake off the trappings of his fame. Wallis rejected both of Parker's plots, but in responding that he was "definitely interested in a Hawaiian background story for Elvis," inadvertently nurtured the genesis of *Blue Hawaii*.

Parker's scenario of a record company pressuring an artist for more material came straight from the Colonel's dealings with RCA. Only a month before, Bill Bullock had offered to fly Elvis and four of his friends to Nashville for three days of recording, and the Colonel had refused. Similarly, Steve Sholes suggested that the label pay Parker's way to Germany to supervise a session there. The Colonel had never been known to decline a free trip, but now he turned on his heel. Absolutely not! RCA had to learn how to manage the product it had and space out the singles twenty weeks apart to avoid "flooding the market." No one understood sales or promotion as well as he did, he thundered.

The Colonel's refusal to go to Germany at any time during Elvis's stay intensified the rumors at RCA that something was amiss with Parker's citizenship. Even the field reps got to thinking: had he ever gone out of the country for any reason? Yes, after an Eddy Arnold booking in El Paso, Texas, he'd crossed the border into Mexico, but only after insisting that a U.S. marshall accompany him. More suspiciously, when Arnold played Canada's two biggest cities, Parker claimed illness at the last minute and asked Gabe Tucker to take care of things.

But Parker had gone to Canada with Elvis in 1957, as he shows up in the press clippings from Toronto, Ottawa, and Vancouver. However, it was Bitsy Mott and Tom Diskin who surrounded Presley in most of the photographs. Where was the Colonel? His low profile made Byron Raphael remember something startling Parker once told him: "I've got money stashed in places all over the world."

Byron asked him how he did it, and the Colonel explained that there was a pipeline from Canada to the Cayman Islands that bypassed the IRS. His young aide surmised that Parker's promoter friends—Oscar Davis, the advance man on the Canadian dates, and Lee Gordon, the Australian who promoted them—had helped, legally depositing Parker's share of the tour proceeds in foreign bank accounts.

Still, Parker was not about to chance a leap as large as Europe, and when he needed to get what he called "some important papers" to Germany for Elvis's signature, he called upon an unlikely courier—Judy Gay, Connie B. Gay's teenaged daughter. Her father, who knew of Parker's illegality, told her that the Colonel had a fear of flying, and thus couldn't take the papers himself. But Judy, so in love with her boyfriend she couldn't stand the separation, declined, leaving her father's secretary to make the trip instead.

For two years, a helpless Parker—always nervous at the prospect of advice Elvis might be getting from others—watched as some of his most important business partners went to Europe for private meetings with his client. First, Jean Aberbach and Freddy Bienstock visited Elvis on leave in Paris, and then in August '59, Hal Wallis arrived in Germany to begin location shooting for G.I. Blues, calling on Elvis at Bad Nauheim. Wallis had asked the Colonel to accompany him on the steamer, but Parker deflected the invitation in several letters that suggested the producer might have more fun sharing his cabin with the more colorful members of Elvis's entourage. As to his conspicuous absence, "People thought it was strange," Bienstock recalls. "But nobody asked him about it."

In an effort, perhaps, to help Parker rectify his passport problem, Gay, who had been an advisor to several U.S. presidents and organized Special Services shows for the Department of Defense in Europe, invited the Colonel to a number of his famous Vienna, Virginia, barbeques, attended by an array of well-placed politicians.

Parker zeroed in on one in particular—Texas Senator Lyndon Baines Johnson—and in the fall of '59, volunteered Eddy Arnold's services when LBJ honored the president of Mexico, Adolfo Lopez Mateos, at his Johnson City ranch. Ordinarily, Parker, who continued to handle some of Arnold's bookings, would insult anyone who dared ask for a free performance. But he sanctioned this one for a different payoff—a chance to insinuate himself into photographs with Johnson and former president Harry S Truman.

That began a nine-year correspondence between Parker and the future president and his family, including daughter Lynda, who would visit on the set of one of Elvis's films. Almost immediately, Parker inducted John-son into the Snowmen's League, making a supremely useful ally. Two months after the Virginia barbeque, Johnson wrote to Parker using words that must have seemed golden: "I hope our paths cross again in the days ahead, and that you will always feel free to call on me as your friend at any time for anything." Apparently, the Colonel did just that. A mere two weeks later, Johnson told him he was "certainly counting on you to give the office a ring when you get to Washington."

Parker had several reasons to visit the nation's capital in late '59 and early '60. In August, he and Marie had gone to Hawaii for what appeared to be a simple vacation, especially as Marie had nagged him to take her there, only to develop a severe case of diverticulitis from eating raw pineapple. But Parker had more than just sight-seeing on his mind. In 1958, President Dwight D. Eisenhower had approved the creation of a memorial to the U.S.S. *Arizona,* the resting place for 1,177 crewmen who perished on the battleship in the surprise attack at Pearl Harbor. Now the Colonel wanted to see if he might be able to use such a noble cause to his advantage, meeting with the chairman of the *Arizona* Memorial Committee, H. Tucker Grantz, to offer Elvis for a benefit show.

With Grantz's backing, Parker flew to Washington in September '59 for a meeting at the Pentagon. There, he first met with E. J. Cottrell, the army information officer who was Parker's chief liaison in Washington. Cottrell would soon fly to Germany to confer with Elvis about the benefit show. He reported to the Colonel that Elvis was homesick, but in good shape and continuing to do a fine job for his country. He would also arrange for Presley to lend his byline to a recruitment article for *This Week* magazine, later reprinted in *The Army Blue Book* as "What Elvis Presley Learned About the Army." ("If I had only one piece of advice to give to a friend . . . I'd say don't keep your troubles corked up. . . . Work harder, talk to a good friend. . . . Don't jump with all four feet into a mess you'll never be able to wipe away.")

Just what transpired during the Pentagon meeting isn't known, but Parker tantalized Joe Hazen with the barest details in a letter. "My special meeting in Washington Tuesday for lunch was fun and I must tell you about it next time," he wrote. "I did meet a new General and he now wants a snowcard into my club. This I told him would be rather hard to do as we have no way of knowing if he deserves one at this time."

Might the High Potentate have swapped a membership and the promise of an Elvis show for a secret from his past? Was the favor of destroying his own military records—or perhaps any mention of his illegality in the files of the FBI and the INS—too much to ask in return?

There is no proof that he did. But with Parker, who used every ounce of human flesh for even the slightest leverage, it is inconceivable that he did not. What a high he must have had that day, this military deserter and illegal alien, with a general in the U.S. Army groveling to belong to his phantom club and addressing him as Colonel.

Parker's interaction with army officials buoyed Hal Wallis, who hoped Elvis might receive an early release to begin work on *G.I. Blues*. Paul Nathan, Wallis's associate producer, learned in the summer of '59 that the army was willing to accommodate the actor Russ Tamblyn, who had a picture waiting for him at Metro-Goldwyn-Mayer. Nathan apprised Wallis and added in an interoffice memo that Abe Lastfogel "feels they would do the same for Elvis, if we notify them that we are ready to go."

But when Hazen spoke with Parker, the manager was adamant that no such request be made. Elvis must not be seen as shirking even one day of military service. Besides, despite the U.S.S. *Arizona* concert and the movie deals—which included, at Elvis's request, two "serious" pictures at Fox—Parker was still finalizing his plans for Presley's return.

With Lastfogel's help, he had just arranged a splashy television special to be called "Frank Sinatra's Welcome Home Party for Elvis Presley." The appearance would net Elvis $125,000, more than Sinatra would receive as the host, and expose him to an older audience. Cleaned up, tuxedo-clad, and defused of his rock-and-roll passion—in effect, neutered—Elvis would now be safe and palatable for adult consumption. After the Sinatra special, even the pompadour would be gone. What remained was negotiating a new royalty deal with RCA, the endgame to Parker's steady rationing of product.

The Colonel hammered the last nail of the deal in place only two days before Elvis's plane touched down at McGuire Air Force Base near Fort Dix, New Jersey. Under the terms of the contract, any soundtrack recording would count toward Elvis's quota of two LPs and eight single sides each year. Both Elvis and the Colonel would receive a .75 percent recoupable royalty on top of the usual 5 percent royalty. And Parker, who was granted approval on all advertising, promotion, and publicity, would receive an annual $27,000 for supplying photographs for record covers and general "exploitational" support, over and above the cost of postage and materials. The last clause especially rankled RCA's Anne Fulchino, who believed that Bill Bullock had let Parker into her office one

weekend to appropriate all of her picture files and negatives, thus allowing the Colonel to charge RCA for property it already owned.

Elvis's consent on the contract was required but assumed, even as the
overall deal benefited his manager more than him. To Elvis and Vernon,
it didn't matter—what they had was so much more than they'd ever expected. And the Colonel had kept his client's name in the headlines for
the two years he was away, something Elvis never thought possible.
Often, Parker said, he used his own money to do it, all the while turning
down requests to manage other artists as diverse as actress Natalie Wood
and comedian Brother Dave Gardner, with whom the Colonel often
supped in Hollywood. No matter that he had done so because Parker
considered both performers too headstrong to control. All Elvis knew
was that he and his manager were an unbeatable combination. And in the
Colonel's eyes, they were more than a team, more even than a partnership. It was not something either of them could easily explain.

When newly promoted Sergeant Elvis Presley arrived at Fort Dix in the
early morning of March 3, 1960, he was met with the fanfare usually re-
served for returning war heroes. The band played "Auld Lang Syne" as
he walked from the plane in the midst of a late-winter blizzard, beaming
for the fireworks of flashbulbs as snowflakes pelted his uniform. Startlingly handsome, his features lean and chiseled, Elvis looked happy to be
home, even as one reporter noted a suggestion of sadness when he smiled.
"Go get 'em, Elvis!" somebody yelled, and he shot a lopsided grin.

In truth, the nervous flyer was somewhat sedated, having spent a
restless night in the arms of a new girlfriend, this one named Priscilla,
and he had ingested a fair number of pills on the flight to steady his
nerves. The Colonel quickly led him into a press conference, where he
said about the only thing on his mind was to rest up at home for the next
few weeks. The following day, Estes Kefauver, the Tennessee senator who
made his reputation as a crusader against organized crime, now a friend
of Parker, would read his "Tribute to Elvis Presley" into the *Congressional Record,* praising the singer's willingness to become "just another
G.I. Joe."

On hand to greet Elvis that morning at Fort Dix were Steve Sholes;
Jean Aberbach; nineteen-year-old Nancy Sinatra (who brought two lace
shirts as a promotional stunt for Elvis's upcoming TV special with her father); various William Morris representatives; and Hal Wallis, who had
momentarily distracted the Colonel, allowing a *Life* magazine photographer and his assistant to move in and pose Elvis outside the C-in-C bar-

racks for a cover shot. The Colonel, always quick as a cat, suddenly appeared and planted his full girth in front of Elvis, barring the view of the cameraman. Unless they had a check for $25,000, Parker said ("You don't think I'm going to let you put my boy on the cover without us getting paid for it, do you?"), *Life* would have to wait.

Starting at 3:00 A.M., "the Colonel went through that day like a force of nature—just this fierce constructive energy," says Robert Kotlowitz, now a noted novelist, but in 1960 a thirty-five-year-old RCA classical music publicist ready to jump to magazines. He got the nod to accompany Parker to Fort Dix because he was the only one back from lunch when the Colonel came in to arrange the trip, Parker storming through the office, stopping briefly to call an army recruiting officer and float the rumor that Elvis would re-enlist. Kotlowitz had seen how Bill Bullock took orders from him, but even on a military base, the manager was in charge. "None of the relationships I saw were in any way conventional or even normal," he says. "You did what he told you to do, or if you didn't, he was finished with you."

Soon, Kotlowitz would see a very different side of the Colonel, as Elvis spent two days at Fort Dix and then began a welcome-home train trip to Memphis, courtesy of RCA. Parker wanted the pleasant young publicist to come along, and told him to be at the Trenton, New Jersey, station to make sure the train arrived on the right track and to prevent anyone from boarding their private cars. But first he uttered a warning: under no circumstances should Kotlowitz tell anybody what time this train would be stopping in any town—they'd be deluged with reporters and fans, and everything would be a horrible mess. "Of course," Kotlowitz says, "every little village we went through, there were two thousand girls out there at two o'clock in the morning. He'd tipped off every stationmaster by saying, 'Presley's coming through at 2:15 A.M. Do not tell press.'"

Parker, however, hadn't just alerted the press—he'd had his staff call them collect and invite them aboard. One reporter who accepted was David Halberstam, who beautifully captured the freewheeling atmosphere for the Nashville *Tennessean*. Elvis, he wrote, was "like a happy young colt. . . . He wrestled with some of his bodyguards, winked at the girls in the station, and clowned with his ever-faithful manager and merchandiser, Col. Tom Parker. 'Man, it feels good to be going home,' Presley said. 'So good.' Then he put a hand over the Colonel's receding hairline and said, 'Andy Devine [the tubby Hollywood character actor], that's who it is. Andy Devine.' 'Quit pulling my hair out,' the Colonel said. 'I'm just massaging it for you,' Presley said. 'Every time you massage,' [the Colonel countered], 'I have a little less left.'"

When the train reached Memphis, Kotlowitz was ready to fly home to New York. But Parker asked him to stay—Elvis was traveling to Nashville for a recording session, and then he'd take another special railroad car to Miami to do the Frank Sinatra television special. Certainly RCA would want a press representative along, he said, though Kotlowitz's main function was to be an audience for the Colonel, who seemed to have adopted him. "On the train, he would wake me up every morning by standing on my bed, straddling me, and ringing this cowbell. I knew I was 'in' when I saw him doing that, and it was wonderful. I had the time of my life. But we were an unlikely couple, let me tell you."

The next time Kotlowitz heard from Parker, some two months later, the manager invited him to join Elvis and the entourage in Las Vegas, that "sunny place for shady people," as the old-time mob called it. Parker kept his gambling to minor stakes, as far as Kotlowitz could tell, but the Colonel never liked to let any of his young acolytes see him stay too long at the tables.

A year before, he had written to Hal Wallis about his exploits in Vegas and at the dog tracks in Phoenix and Tampa ("One of the dogs may sue us for betting on him while he had piles"), having lost the $50 that Wallis had him place as an "investment." But lately, he had again become preoccupied with the spin of the roulette wheel, the siren call for his favorite diversion, his "road game."

Often, he would get the itch and decide overnight to go, telephoning Freddy Bienstock to fly out from New York. "He would lose fortunes," Bienstock remembers. "Besides the roulette table, he would stand at the craps table and lose and lose. He couldn't stand it. One time I said, 'Come on, let's go.' And he got furious and said, 'Don't you tell me! It's my money!' I never said anything anymore."

"I think the reason for his gambling and going to Vegas was primarily to look like a big shot," says Julian Aberbach. "That's the way they treat the [high rollers], and that is the way they get them."

Undoubtedly, Parker wanted to rub shoulders with all the ruling lords of Vegas, particularly as he began to gamble all around town. George Wood and Hershey Martin of William Morris's variety department were Lastfogel's emissaries to the mob, providing much of the talent for the night clubs and showrooms of the Mafia-owned hotels. The Colonel got to know Martin, a Damon Runyonesque character, during Elvis's ill-fated engagement at the New Frontier in '56. Now he asked Martin to introduce him to Jack Entratter, the co-owner of the Sands Hotel. Entratter booked only the biggest and classiest entertainers for the Copa Room, but with an illegal twist—paying one amount specified under the contract, and another in money meant only for gambling.

By the early '60s, the Sands was known to be controlled by more mobs than any other casino in Nevada, an estimated sixteen from Brooklyn to L.A. Entratter's connections were legendary; he'd been the manager of the Mafia-owned Copacabana in the '40s when it was New York's most popular nightclub. There, Entratter, six foot, portly, and flashing a crooked smile, first became friends with Frank Sinatra, a relationship that ushered in the Rat Pack's dominance at the Sands. Since Parker never dealt with underlings, only the top power people everywhere, it was the syndicate-owned Wilbur Clark he chatted up while gambling at the Desert Inn, and Jack Entratter, known as Mr. Entertainment, that he sought out at the Sands, the hot spot for high rollers from Texas, New York, and Hollywood. On more than one occasion, he dined there with another William Morris client and the host of Presley's "Welcome Home" special, Sinatra himself.

Parker would find more and more reasons to go to the mob paradise of Vegas, which was also becoming a favorite playground for Elvis. But the Colonel was always careful to stop Presley from appearing in photographs with the "wise guys" who wanted to brag about an association. It was one thing for Elvis to be photographed with Prell, who through some kind of arrangement—believed to be only a wink and a handshake—served as Mafia protection, buffering Elvis from the more obvious and frightening mob leaders who would otherwise demand performances, payments, and more. In fact, Elvis would spend his twenty-seventh birthday in Vegas, at one point posing with Prell while cutting a ridiculously tall cake, festooned with two confectionary Hotel Sahara marquees (TO ELVIS FROM MILTON PRELL) to commemorate the occasion. But beyond Prell, whose reputation was cleaner than most, Parker drew the line. He'd seen what the appearance of such friendships had done to Sinatra.

"The Colonel demanded everything to be squeaky clean," says one former RCA employee, "But it would have been impossible for him to do some of the things that he did without the Mafia—in the music business, in television, and in the movies—because until the early '70s, it was as important to have a working relationship with the mob as it was to have a lawyer and accountant."

Elvis had gone back to Las Vegas immediately after completing *G.I. Blues* with Juliet Prowse in June 1960. Prowse, a sometime girlfriend of Sinatra, pursued a career as a dancer in European nightclubs before coming to Hollywood, and her brief sexual trysts with Elvis stirred his fantasies of wicked nights in Paris.

Parker had succeeded in emasculating Elvis's dangerous hooligan image of 1956, but underneath it all, the seemingly conservative, sanitized Elvis had come home from Europe a more licentious man than the boy who'd left. The showgirls of the Lido and the Moulin Rouge in Paris were far more decadent than the Vegas dancers he'd known, and his familiarity with pills, especially uppers, was so educated and obsessive that he talked seriously of buying his own drugstore for a steady supply.

Furthermore, other members of his entourage, especially Lamar Fike, who'd accompanied him to Germany, also shared his fondness and encouraged his indulgence. "He got just wild as a goat in '60, because he was loose from the army, which he hated with a passion," says Fike. "After the service, the biggest change, other than becoming harder, was that he became much more what people thought he should be."

That included playing the good soldier, ad infinitum, beginning with *G.I. Blues,* the first of several pictures in which he wore a military uniform, a plot device that deeply pleased the Colonel. A musical comedy, *G.I. Blues* was light, semiautobiographical fare aimed straight at his hardcore fan base. With Elvis romancing a fräulein, baby-sitting an infant, and crooning "Wooden Heart" to a group of children gathered at a puppet show, the picture would prove a "howling success," in the words of Paul Nathan, ranking the fourteenth highest-grossing film of 1960. Until those numbers came in, the studio would consider Elvis for a version of *The Three Penny Opera* and a remake of *The Rainmaker,* but never again would Paramount put him in a gritty drama like *King Creole.*

To promote Presley's return to Hollywood, Parker rolled out the snow machinery as never before. First he reprised the triumphant cross-country trek—so reminiscent of the great political campaigns—setting Elvis up in a private car of the Southern Pacific's Sunset Limited with a gaggle of reporters, who also witnessed the massive fan turnout on the fifty stops of the three-day trip.

"We feel sure that by the time *G.I. Blues* appears on the screens through the world, some of this effort surely will pay off," Parker wrote Wallis, enclosing a list of plugs he'd secured on TV shows, journalists he'd personally contacted, and even foreign rulers visiting the film set.

But it already had paid off: Elvis's arrival in Los Angeles was the lead story on radio and TV, with newspapers shoving Charles de Gaulle's Canadian visit and the Humphrey-Kennedy debate below the fold on page one. Reporters noted Elvis's attire, which took a nod from his European stay and reflected what he thought was his new level of sophistication—a black silk mohair tux, ruffled white shirt, black silk ascot, and black suede shoes topped with silver buckles. "His be-rhinestoned cuff links," said *Billboard*, "were the size of 50-cent pieces."

With a change of studios, Elvis was optimistic that his next film roles would also present him as a changed man. He had barely a month off before he reported to Twentieth Century–Fox in August to begin work on *Flaming Star*, a dramatic Western in which he played the son of a white father and a Kiowa Indian mother torn between the cultures.

Producer David Weisbart saw the picture as a showcase for Presley's acting skills, and appealed to studio head Buddy Adler to keep the musical numbers to a minimum. Unlike Paramount, which presented Elvis primarily as an entertainer, Twentieth Century–Fox believed that selling Elvis as a dramatic actor could attract an even wider audience.

"I have sweated over the script for the past couple of days trying to find places for Presley to sing," Weisbart wrote two months before filming began. "I cannot see how it is possible for Elvis to break into song without destroying a very good script. . . . Instead of presenting a gimmicked up picture with Elvis Presley, we'd be offering a pretty legitimate picture that represents growth in Presley's career and therefore should be fresh and exciting as far as his fans are concerned."

But at a lunch with the Colonel the following day, Weisbart was overruled. "We want all the best possible results for this picture," Parker said, "including the hundreds of thousands of dollars worth of exploitation represented by a good record release by Elvis Presley." The Colonel had no interest in reading the script, he added, and became paranoid when Weisbart asked his input for selecting a director. "I would not know whether you would need a sensitive director or some other director, even if I had read the script," he followed up in writing, "as this is not one of my qualifications. If someone is using me as a scapegoat, I would like to know the reason. I do not wish to work under any unpleasant conditions over which I have no control."

Parker continued to fight the producer at every turn, even when Weisbart asked Freddy Bienstock to find a good title song and three or four others in keeping with the era. The most important thing, Weisbart said, is that the material be selected purely on Elvis's singing and not be dependent on a modern arrangement and band. The Colonel was quick to balk at those criteria, and at the studio's selection for the title song, insisting it wouldn't be a hit single. Weisbart needed to understand the formula: Elvis's movies would promote the soundtrack albums, and the single from the soundtrack would publicize the film. It was an ideal commercial equation.

"I think Parker is more interested in selling records than he is [in] building a motion picture career for Presley and making fortunes out of his picture reruns," Charles Einfield, Fox's vice president of advertising and publicity, wrote to Weisbart. "It's a helluva way for a partner to act. Too bad."

In the end, only two of the four musical numbers remained in the final cut, which especially pleased Elvis, who found the songs embarrassingly lightweight and inappropriate. Director Don Siegel, later to make his name with Clint Eastwood's *Dirty Harry,* was so impressed with Elvis's dramatic ability that he suggested the picture be advertised with the tag line "Elvis Acts!"—a takeoff on the "Garbo Speaks" campaign for the actress's first talking picture.

Those issues were still being sorted out when the studio began planning its next Presley picture, *Wild in the Country,* with producer Jerry Wald and director Philip Dunne, who had won acclaim for his screenplay of *How Green Was My Valley.* Already Parker was proving difficult, wanting to cut the forty-five-day shooting schedule in half and, over the objections of his client, harping that the picture must have a minimum of four Elvis songs, preferably five or more. On that point, he had the backing of studio head Spyros Skouras.

Fox based the film on J. R. Salamanca's novel *The Lost Country,* with its plot of an innocent farm boy enmeshed in a tragic affair with his older teacher. In casting Hope Lange, with her icy blond beauty, director Dunne added yet another dimension of class discrepancy, though screenwriter Clifford Odets made the relationship even more taboo in altering the boy's character to that of an Appalachian delinquent and transforming the teacher into a court-appointed psychiatrist. Dunne found Elvis "an excellent dramatic actor, a natural actor," and perfect to portray, as Wald said in the story conference, "the gifted individual, the soul born with special wings . . . whose specialness is at once a thing of wonder and beauty and compliment."

Throughout filming, Parker, as before, seemed more preoccupied with his record release schedule than with looking out for Elvis's welfare. He busied himself writing nasty letters complaining about a proposed title change in England—he'd already notified the fan club as to the original title—and about the importance of not leaking any information about the music, as it confused fans about upcoming singles. "I have never advised a studio how to make a picture," he wrote to Wald. "I am always willing to cooperate, but we know our record business!" Indeed, the Colonel was negotiating a new amendment to Elvis's RCA contract, which guaranteed Presley $1,000 per week from an earlier contract, plus an annual payment of $300,000 against royalties. Parker instructed RCA to divert $100,000 of it to All Star Shows for promotion, as per his 75–25 split with Elvis.

Otherwise, the Colonel spent his time at the studio writing press releases, including one with an oddly defensive tone in which he denied being a "Svengali who has hypnotized a country boy into becoming one of the great entertainers of our times." Furthermore, he wrote, "Elvis picks his own songs for all occasions, including motion pictures. The Colonel's control in this area consists only of suggestion and . . . eliminating patently unsuitable songs."

But for whom? Like *Flaming Star,* which initially flopped, appearing only one week on the National Box Office Survey, *Wild in the Country* never found its niche. One faction of the audience came for Elvis's glitz and grind, another for the pathos of Odets. Both were disappointed. "When we previewed," Dunne remembered, the audience laughed when we came to the songs . . . they were going with the story. I shot them so they could be dropped out, and I wish they would drop them out of the prints now. They'd see a good movie."

Without significant box office, *Wild in the Country* would be Elvis's last challenging dramatic role and his final alliance with a serious director. He seemed to sense it, asking Dunne if they might work together again after his next picture for Paramount, *Blue Hawaii.* Dunne declined, knowing the future would hold only more typical vehicles, "the usual bikinis, you know."

Elvis started principal photography on *Blue Hawaii* two days after his much-ballyhooed U.S.S. *Arizona* concert. Apart from a pair of Memphis charity shows in which he warmed up the old magic using elements of "Negro cotton field harmony, camp meeting fervor, Hollywood showmanship, beatnik nonchalance, and some of the manipulations of mass psychology," as the hometown paper raved, the Hawaii concert, produced, like the Memphis charity shows, by Parker's old friend Al Dvorin, would be Elvis's first real return to the stage in more than three years.

While Hawaii always nurtured the Colonel's jovial side—he did a hula dance for Bob Moore when the bass player brought his home movie camera out on the beach—he positively reveled in his opportunity to lord it over the admirals and generals who came to a meeting in Parker's suite at the Hawaiian Village Hotel, and invited two of Hawaii's top radio deejays, Ron Jacobs and Tom Moffatt, to witness his fun. As Parker predicted, the brass arrived full of skepticism about this Tennessee Colonel, whose suite resembled a carnival booth, with Elvis's promotional pictures and movie posters plastered on the walls and RCA Nipper dogs peering out from behind the furniture.

"He started snowing them," recalls Jacobs, "telling them how important they were to the security of the world. After that, he said if they'd just line up, why, he'd give them a little something from Elvis. So all these guys in charge of the military in the Pacific and Asia got in line and stood there anxiously, and Parker went over to a trunk that was full of Elvis memorabilia. Then the Colonel reached in very carefully, almost secretly, and stingily started handing out these tiny Elvis pocket calendars, one to each admiral and general."

As they left, "one of the admirals saluted him!" Moffatt adds. "It was 'yes, sir' to the Colonel."

Yet not everyone was awed. When one high-ranking officer had the temerity to ask for a complimentary pass to the show, Parker refused, barking that ticket sales were to tally nearly $52,000, and, "every penny . . . must go to the fund!" Why, even he and Elvis were buying their own way in. But then the Colonel got a glint in his eye and reconsidered, purposely seating the admiral between the black chauffeur he'd been assigned and a navy seaman who had just joined up. To have such authority figures under his thumb, aggrandizing him and soiling themselves in public in one fell swoop, apparently brought the Colonel supreme joy.

Parker had booked his old friend Minnie Pearl on the bill, and until the moment they arrived at the Honolulu International Airport, she hadn't realized "how encapsulated Elvis was in his fame." With three thousand screaming women scurrying to get to the plane, "I began to get these chilling feelings that maybe I didn't want to be all that close to Elvis—the fans were all along the route he was taking to the hotel, and my husband was afraid that we'd be trampled trying to get inside. I felt myself being lifted completely off my feet by all these people.

"We did the show on a Saturday, and Sunday afternoon, a bunch of us were down on Waikiki Beach, cavorting and kidding and having a big time. We got to talking about how we wished Elvis could come down and be with us, and we turned and looked up at his penthouse, which was facing the ocean. He was standing on the balcony, looking down at us, this solitary figure, lonely looking, watching us have such a good time. He was just getting ready to start making the film, and he literally was a prisoner because of the fans. We sat there on the beach and talked about how it would be—what a price you pay for that sort of fame."

In preparation for *Blue Hawaii,* Wallis wrote Parker with strict orders for Elvis to get into shape. "It is very important that [he] look lean and hard, and well-tanned . . . he should have a good overall coat of tan on his body as well as his face. I will appreciate it if you will talk to him about watching his weight." At the end, Wallis recommended a good sun lamp.

Blue Hawaii, Elvis's first fun-in-the-sun bikini picture, would follow the musical format of *G.I. Blues,* whose success had made it the prototype for all the Wallis-Presley musicals to follow. But now *Blue Hawaii* would surpass it. The 1961 film would easily recoup its $2 million cost and effectively doom Elvis's chances of moving beyond its stultifying structure. It would also mark the first of seven Elvis pictures directed by Norman Taurog.

In wedding an exotic setting and plenty of romance to a fourteen-song framework—three more than even *G.I. Blues* allowed—Wallis perfected his winning Elvis formula. Nearly all the movies Elvis made after 1960 would be assembled around Elvis's personality—or the Hollywood moguls' perception of it—the way larger movies were once fashioned around female stars such as Shirley Temple or Mae West. The Wallis productions, especially, were the last in a series of Hollywood vehicles guaranteed to pull a certain bankable gross just because of who was in them, leading the producer himself to remark, "A Presley picture is the only sure thing in show business."

Couldn't Parker see that such somnambulistic fare would squander his client's talent and suffocate his spirit? Most likely not. As the Colonel indicated to Weisbart, he was woefully aware of his inability to judge either a good script or a fine director. Likewise, he had difficulty discerning a good performance from a mediocre one and relied on the judgment of others to plan Elvis's future in films.

Despite Presley's remarkable portrayal in *King Creole,* Wallis believed that Elvis couldn't carry a picture without music. And Byron Raphael remembers going with Parker to a meeting with producer Joe Pasternak long before he made *Girl Happy* and *Spinout* in the mid-'60s. Pasternak, famous for musicals, had a dramatic property in mind for Elvis, and asked him to do a reading. Afterward, the producer told Parker, "He really can't act. He just doesn't have it." In their four-year association, Raphael says, "the only criticism I ever heard the Colonel make of Elvis was about his acting. He never believed that Elvis was going to be an actor. Not for a second." And nothing he saw changed his mind.

Parker used to tell his staff that the key to successful management was trying different tactics. "It doesn't matter if you do ten stupid things," he'd say, "as long as you do one smart one." Here was his prime example. As long as Elvis made the upbeat musicals that Wallis wanted, he was assured of working in Hollywood. *Blue Hawaii* was the first of a new five-picture deal with Wallis, which paid $175,000 for the first three and $200,000 each for the remaining two.

Elvis was surprised to learn of such a demanding movie schedule. It didn't leave much time for touring—and he wanted to go to Europe—or making records, apart from the movie soundtracks. In Germany, he'd worked on expanding his range and making his voice fuller, and he was eager for more operatic songs, like "It's Now or Never," to show it off.

But after the U.S.S. *Arizona* concert, the Colonel was in no hurry to return Elvis to the concert stage anytime soon. He'd rather people paid to see Presley in the movies, and they might tire of him if Elvis did too many personal appearances. While Parker had been an extraordinary promoter, in time he would turn into an unconscionable manager. In fact, the Colonel no longer thought of his client's needs so much as he did his own.

In Hollywood, Parker was a steel wall of power, something he could never be in representing Presley, the concert artist. Therefore, California was where they would stay, where the Colonel could have almost anything he wanted, free for the asking, with the biggest names in show business at his beck and call. In making or confirming all the big decisions on Presley's pictures, and by refusing to let Wallis or even William Morris have direct access to Elvis, Parker became not only a true power broker, but the "producer" of Presley's pictures. He'd just picked up a two-picture deal with the Mirisch Brothers and United Artists for $500,000 each and 50 percent of the profits; in January 1961, he'd close a four-picture agreement with MGM at a salary of $400,000 per picture, plus $100,000 for expenses, with profit participation equal to the Mirisch deal.

Until the end of his life, Parker told a story that was likely untrue but illuminated his core philosophy. According to the tale, the Colonel, Wallis, and Abe Lastfogel met at the Beverly Wilshire Hotel to discuss a deal for Elvis to play a part in a picture based on what Wallis promised was an Academy Award–winning script.

"That's fine," the Colonel said. "When do you start?" Wallis gave him the date, and the Colonel turned to Lastfogel. "Sounds good, Abe. We get a million dollars, and we'll be there."

Wallis spoke up. "No, Colonel, you don't understand. I said this was an Academy Award–winning script. I only want to pay $500,000, not a million."

"Oh," the Colonel replied, "I didn't get that part of it. Well, tell you what we'll do. You send us the million, and the day Elvis goes up and gets the Academy Award, we'll send you back $500,000."

Parker put little store in industry kudos. "They'll never win any Academy Awards," he said of Elvis's films in 1960. "All they're good for is to make money."

At last, the Colonel had his dancing chicken.

14

"MISTAKES SOME-ONE

MAY HAVE MADE"

W H I L E negotiating the film deals that would carry Elvis through the decade, the Colonel was heavy with worry. Since the late autumn of '60, he had received a series of troubling letters from Holland that threatened to topple the delicate balance of his world.

In the spring of 1960, a Dutch housewife named Nel Dankers–van Kuijk visited her hairdresser in Eindhoven, and thumbed through the new issue of *Rosita,* a Belgian women's magazine. There she saw a photograph that stopped her heart. A young American singing star, Elvis Presley, just home from the army in his handsome dress blues, waved to his fans from the doorway of a train.

But it was the big man standing behind him who caught her eye. He looked so much like her younger brother Jan. Then she saw his name— Tom Parker. Wasn't that the same name scrawled at the bottom of those strange letters from the States some thirty years before?

"My God," the stunned Nel said aloud. "That is our Dries!"

Afterward, Nel had telephoned her brother Ad. First Ad gazed at the face in disbelief, and then he compared it to old family photographs. Now Ad was certain that the famous Colonel Parker was their own long-lost brother.

"It seemed like a fairy tale," he said, but the rest of the family also saw the resemblance. Through the years, they had received the odd postcard, or an envelope containing a miniature American flag, a not so subtle statement of their brother's loyalties. Now several of them began writing, mostly in their native language, which Parker could barely read anymore. They got only Elvis memorabilia in return.

Finally, nineteen-year-old Ad Jr. decided to send a plaintive letter, an

Parker, dressed in his favorite get-up, a Confederate uniform, dances with Marie at a party on the set of *G.I. Blues,* 1960. (The collection of the Bitsy Mott Family)

Parker loved getting the best of Hal Wallis, seen here in the Colonel's Paramount office in 1960, modeling a paper hat stamped "G.I. Blues." (Courtesy of the Academy of Motion Picture Arts and Sciences)

Elvis chuckles at a get well letter the Colonel wrote to Harry Brand, head of publicity for Twentieth Century Fox, during the making of *Flaming Star,* 1960. From left: Bitsy Mott, Tom Diskin, producer David Weisbart, Parker, Elvis, director Don Siegel, and music/sound effects editor Ted Cain. (The collection of the Bitsy Mott family)

"We do it this way, we make money; we do it your way, we don't make money," Parker seems to be telling his client in this undated photograph, probably from the early 1960s. (The collection of the Bitsy Mott family)

A cozy pose with Hal Wallis, probably during the making of *Blue Hawaii,* 1961. (Courtesy of the Academy of Motion Picture Arts and Sciences)

Parker with "Miz Ree," as he jokingly called his wife, on Waikiki, 1961. The picture is inscribed to Bobby Ross's family. (Courtesy of Sandra Polk Ross and Robert Kenneth Ross)

The Colonel valued few gifts as highly as a ham. Here, on behalf of Tennessee governor Buford Ellington, he has Elvis present one of Tennessee's finest to Washington State's first Italian American governor, Albert Rosellini. Elvis was in Seattle filming *It Happened at the World's Fair* in September 1962. From left: Rosellini, director Norman Taurog, Elvis, Parker, and producer Ted Richman. (Museum of History and Industry, Seattle)

A 1960s portrait, signed to Gabe and Sunshine Tucker. (The author's collection/ source unknown)

In his Palm Springs home office, probably late 1960s. (Courtesy of Sandra Polk Ross and Robert Kenneth Ross)

The Colonel's joke button, probably from the 1960s. (Courtesy of Gabe Tucker)

left: Billy Smith sits on the Colonel's knee during the making of *Frankie and Johnny,* 1965. (The collection of Maria Columbus)

Tom Diskin, with Marie, raises a glass at a party to celebrate the Parkers' wedding anniversary, probably in the 1970s. (Courtesy Sandra Polk Ross and Robert Kenneth Ross)

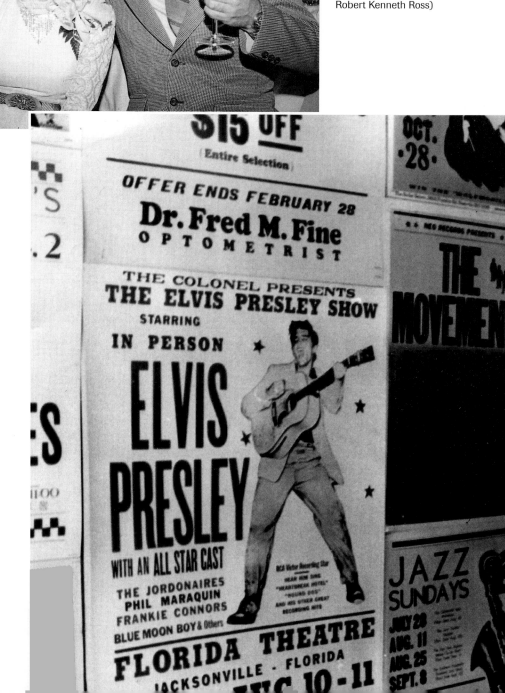

Described as "a combination of con man and Santa Claus" by the *New York Times,* Parker resembles the latter in this undated portrait in a knit cap. (The author's collection/ source unknown)

The Colonel at Hatch Show Print, Nashville, in 1987, with a reproduction of one of his early Elvis concert posters. (Nashville Public Library, The Nashville Room)

With the author, first meeting, Las Vegas, 1992.
(Judy F. May)

The Colonel and Loanne, 1994. (Alanna Nash)

Byron Raphael at
Parker's plaque in
the Walk of Stars,
Palm Springs,
Calif., 1998.
(Alanna Nash)

appeal to the Colonel's heart. He could understand that Parker wasn't interested in relatives he hadn't seen in so many years, he wrote in English, but the family needed to know if at last they had found the brother they had mourned so long. "Are you," he asked, "really my uncle?"

On January 31, 1961, Parker sat down and answered "Master Ad Van Kuyk Jr.," as he addressed the envelope, writing at once the most enigmatic and revealing document of his life. He typed it himself on plain paper, retaining all the odd syntax and spelling ("some-one") that characterized his letters to Hal Wallis.

The letter began in the third person, as if the author were a secretary. Throughout, in guarded self-protection, he showed himself to be deeply disturbed about an episode that he never quite defined. He repeatedly asked in a paranoid tone that all his relatives stop writing until they heard from "Mr. Parker," as the letters were getting mixed in with the fan club mail, and "I am sure you will agree that this matter if it involves Mr. Parker must be handled very carefully and privately."

As for why the family had not heard from him, he assured Ad Jr. that "Mr. Parker has felt the same longing and hopes as all of you but must have had a very good reason and many problems so not to bring them to any of his people at any-time." Then he cryptically referred to "Friends" who might assist them in the future. "We will try to help in some way to at least make-up for any mistakes some-one may have made without meaning to do so."

With that, he bizarrely switched to first person ("Remember me to all of them") as the text hinted of past deeds and secrets. He signed the letter with a signature that only his Dutch family would know—"Andre."

Ad Jr. was proud to have received such a reply but was baffled by its contents. What was Uncle Andre really trying to say, referring to "mistakes some-one may have made without meaning to do so?"

The letter, sent by air and marked "Special Delivery"—useless in Holland, but still communicating a red code of urgency—arrived in Breda on February 4, 1961. Sixteen days later, in a surprise turnabout, Ad Sr. was invited to visit his brother in America. The trip, which Parker paid for, was arranged through a Dutch husband and wife with a similar surname—van Kuijck—living in Hackensack, New Jersey.

Ad Sr. flew to New York on April 9. There he was met by the van Kuijcks, who entertained him for eleven days until the Colonel returned to Los Angeles from the location filming of *Blue Hawaii*. Then the three traveled to California.

Parker, suspicious that his visitor "was a crook from Europe to black-mail him," as Ad Jr. says, asked the man outright if he had come for money. Ad Sr. assured him he had not. Parker stared at his sibling, only four years younger, and then said finally, "Yes, you are my brother."

They spent a week together, with Parker putting him up at his apartment in Los Angeles, conning a William Morris trainee into showing him the sights, even introducing him to a few colleagues as a "business associate." Still, the Colonel kept his distance. He showed no emotion when Ad Sr. told him news of his brothers and sisters.

Ad Sr. had promised the family that he would bring back pictures of himself with their brother, but although Marie obliged, Parker refused to be photographed with him, as if such evidence might somehow be used against him.

Yet it was important that the family understand just how successful he had become. Before Ad went home, Parker did the unthinkable—he took him to Elvis's rented home on Perugia Way and introduced him as his brother. Elvis, watching television with the guys, rose to shake his hand. The Colonel doubtless had a story for why his brother spoke in a thick foreign accent, though according to Ad Jr., Elvis was neither impressed nor especially curious. Lamar Fike believes Presley never understood the connection. "If Elvis had known, he would have said it. He couldn't keep a secret."

When Ad Sr. returned to Holland, the family was eager for news. What was he like? How had he explained his awful absence? Ad Sr. had few answers for them. They hadn't talked much about private matters, he said, other than how Andre had painted sparrows yellow and sold them for canaries, and gypped rube carnival goers with a quarter glued to the side of his ring. Ad Sr. had the distinct impression he shouldn't ask too many questions. But he did meet Elvis Presley, the singer their brother had made the most famous man on earth.

In the following months, Ad Sr. wrote his own story for *Rosita,* and in 1967, as the owner of a drugstore where the jukebox played only Elvis records, he gave an interview to Dineke Dekkers for the Dutch fan club magazine *It's Elvis Time.* Ad Sr. died in 1992 of emphysema, never fully elaborating on the events to his siblings.

"The family connections in Holland were not close at all," says Ad Jr. "To me and my mother, he told a little more." But Ad Jr., a language teacher living in the Dutch village of Oostburg, keeps it to himself.

15

TROUBLE IN THE KINGDOM:

THE COLONEL TIGHTENS HIS GRIP

I N March 1963, Parker worried about the arrival of a different kind of visitor, though there was nothing in her demeanor to indicate that she would become a pivotal figure in anyone's life, let alone the Colonel's. Petite, pretty, empty-headed except for the usual teenage obsessions, and positively gooney-eyed with love, sixteen-year-old Priscilla Ann Beaulieu had captured Elvis's heart in Germany, and now she was moving to Memphis.

The stepdaughter of an American air force captain newly stationed near Friedberg, Priscilla had bragged to a girlfriend back in Texas that she was "going over there to meet Elvis." She achieved her goal in a week and a half. Lamar Fike remembers that she showed up at the house that first night wearing a blue-and-white sailor suit and white socks. "I said, 'God Almighty, Elvis, she's cute as she can be, but she's fourteen years old. We'll end up in prison for life.' I watched that from the very beginning with abject fear."

Parker had long known about her, both from his spies among the entourage, who reported Elvis's every move, and from stories in the press. *Life* magazine had photographed Priscilla at the Rhine-Main air base as she waved Elvis good-bye, captioning their picture "The Girl He Left Behind." Elvis denied that he was smitten ("Not any special one," he told reporters when they asked if he'd "left any hearts" in Europe), but an elaboration ("There was a little girl that I was seeing quite often over there . . .") and a telltale grin said otherwise. It was she he'd spent his last night with in Germany, and he hadn't stopped thinking about her, instructing her to write to him on pink stationery so her letters would stand out in the avalanche of mail. On several occasions, he'd brought her to the States to visit.

Now, Elvis had persuaded Captain Beaulieu to let Priscilla come to Memphis and attend Immaculate Conception High School, where, he told him, the girls wore uniforms and studied under the tutelage of stern-faced nuns. The implication was that Elvis would marry Priscilla when she was old enough, but "he didn't give them a time," she remembered later. "He just said, 'I want her here.'"

The immediate promise was that a chaperoned Priscilla would live on nearby Hermitage Road with Vernon and his new wife, Dee. That arrangement lasted only a matter of weeks, Priscilla slipping back and forth between the houses. With Grandma Minnie Mae Presley serving as lenient watchdog, the teenager soon took up residence at Graceland, sharing Elvis's bed—though chastely, she maintains—and learning the drug protocol that allowed her to participate in his night-for-day world.

During Presley's army years, Parker had steadfastly refused to allow Elvis's most serious girlfriend, Anita Wood, to travel to Germany to see him. ("We had to keep everything so quiet . . . the Colonel said it would hurt his career.") But though the Colonel took an unusual liking to Priscilla, he was furious at such a Lolita-like setup. Elvis was now twenty-eight years old, with twelve years' difference in their ages. Not so long before, in a redneck hormone storm, the piano-pounding Jerry Lee Lewis had ruined his career by marrying his underage cousin. This situation wasn't nearly as dangerous, but if discovered, it would still be a scandal, and Presley's movie contracts had morals clauses in them—a fact, along with paternity suits, that was never far from Parker's mind.

If Elvis insisted on living with Priscilla for any length of time, the Colonel saw, they needed to marry, and Parker told him so. A marriage might calm Elvis down, especially in Hollywood, where the starlets lined up to be admitted to his parties.

After first joining Elvis in California, where he was making *Fun in Acapulco* for Paramount, Priscilla was relegated to Memphis, where she waited impatiently for him to return between pictures. Priscilla was not alone in noticing that his behavior, fueled by a steady stream of uppers, downers, and sleeping pills, was becoming frighteningly erratic. In fact, one night Elvis's temper was so raw he threw a pool cue at a female party guest who had insulted him, injuring her shoulder and collarbone. He was sorry—he broke down and cried and said he hadn't known what had come over him, except he felt increasingly boxed in by the lightweight movies he derisively termed "travelogues" for their quasi-exotic locales. He was doing three and, soon, four a year, rubbed thinner with every picture, and suffering nosebleeds on the set from anxiety.

Fun in Acapulco, Elvis's fifth film since *Blue Hawaii,* was a perfect example of the kind of empty fare that continued to satisfy his fans, if not the actor himself, and is memorable only for a quavering, if coincidental connection to the life of Andreas van Kuijk. In it, Elvis plays an ex–circus performer, an aerialist, who in a moment of fright and misjudgment, allows his brother to fall to his death. Traumatized, he flees the circus world to escape his past and assume a new life in a foreign country.

The film, which at one point has Elvis's character, Mike Windgren, sending a telegram to his hometown of Tampa, Florida, was directed by Richard Thorpe (*Jailhouse Rock*), who again explores the theme of a young man jeopardizing his future through the tragedy of accidental death. As in his earlier film, Thorpe includes the character of a talent manager—a pint-sized Mexican shoe-shine boy ("Are you sure you're not a forty-year-old midget?" Elvis asks)—who takes 50 percent of his client's money, insisting he's not an agent, but a partner. Since Elvis was unable to travel to Mexico, the studio relied on a variety of process shots, mostly background projection, to place him south of the border.

By now, in keeping with the Colonel's cross-promotional synergy, RCA culled most of Elvis's singles from the largely dreadful soundtracks. Since 1961, he'd enjoyed a chart-topper with "Good Luck Charm," and watched a pair of hits, "Can't Help Falling in Love" and "Return to Sender," climb to number two. Yet no Elvis release was a sure bet anymore—some singles failed to crawl out of the thirties—and Parker put the pressure on Bill Bullock in RCA's New York office to make things happen. "I may not type good," Parker joked, a comment on his two-fingered keyboard style, "but they sure do know what I mean up there."

Indeed, they did. A memo went around at RCA with the instructions "always remain friendly with the Colonel," a directive that struck fear in the hearts of those who remembered how he'd gotten one executive fired over an altercation regarding Brother Dave Gardner, whom Parker had brought to the label. Now, if Presley wanted his records mixed one way—with his voice as part of the instrumentation—and Parker wanted Elvis more out front, it was Parker the label obeyed.

In early '62, he worked out a new arrangement with RCA concerning previously released material. The agreement provided both Elvis and the Colonel with substantial new revenue from special side deals, which Parker would later refer to as joint ventures. They would split those monies 50–50.

The contract, which Parker insisted be no longer than one page and contain no legalese, would be renegotiated seven months later. It was changed so often, said one employee, that "RCA has nothing to say about anything Elvis does or anything we do for him." Though the label's lawyers insisted the company back out of promoting a forty-three-city tour in late '62—an artistic disappointment for Elvis and a financial loss of more than $1 million—Parker was regarded as the absolute power.

Consequently, the staff went into a frenzy if he happened to drop by unannounced. Joan Deary, Sholes's secretary, worked out a signal with someone downstairs so she could get the office in order before she met him at the elevator, when Parker would "just explode out into the hall." The first time it happened, she rushed to put out an autographed picture the Colonel had sent her boss for Christmas. "None of us liked it," she remembered, "and we'd put it in a drawer behind the door to Steve's office. I went flying in there to pull it out, and I banged into Steve, who was also trying to get the picture out of the cabinet and on display." Bill Bullock was only half kidding when he sent Parker a large office clock inscribed, "Colonel, it's whatever time you want it to be."

Unlike the men at RCA, ever-present for Parker like dutiful sheep, publicist Anne Fulchino was the only one to contest the Colonel. Concerned about Elvis's morale and the erratic chart placement of his records, she asked Tom Diskin to take her to see Presley on the Paramount lot one day in early '63. "That kid was not only unhappy, he was ashamed for me to see him prostituting himself with those crummy pictures," she remembers. She sat down with him and explained her campaign for promoting his records, "practically drawing him a diagram on how you build a star."

Elvis realized he needed to make major changes in the direction of his music and his movies, and promised Fulchino he would do so. But though she believed Elvis "knew Parker was not the right manager for him—the way the Colonel wanted him to go was not the way Elvis wanted to go"— he allowed himself to be hamstrung with unsuitable projects.

On the set of *Kissin' Cousins,* filmed only months after his talk with Fulchino, Elvis told costar Yvonne Craig that he figured the Colonel would know when the time was right to return him to dramatic pictures. Was Elvis merely saving face? The Colonel's dominance was so strong that Presley may have thought he was incapable of standing up to him, even to demand stronger scripts after Parker turned down his one request to approve them. ("If they're smart enough to pay you all that money, they're smart enough to write a good script.") But Elvis's reticence—his lack of emotional backbone—proved to be his fatal flaw.

Fed by his father—who was beginning to question the Colonel's choices, though still bowing to financial concerns, keeping the books and fretting over every penny—Elvis's constraint found its genesis in the mother-son teachings of Gladys. After her husband went to prison in 1938, it was she who taught her young son to fear authority so that he might survive in a hostile world, never dreaming that he would rise above his social class, where such behavior would become inappropriate.

Elvis made fun of the Colonel to the guys, yet he remained subservient to his face. His refusal to challenge the Colonel factored into the stunting of his personal growth and development, as well as his self-loathing and escalating drug dependency. He turned his anger inward and numbed it with pills.

A turning point came in 1963 with the filming of *Viva Las Vegas*, Elvis's best MGM picture in the post-army years. With the casting of Ann-Margret, the first costar to generate real electricity with Presley on screen, Parker should have seen that *Viva Las Vegas* plugged two live wires together, made a formula musical sizzle, and ensured that future films reconnected such high voltage.

But Parker was threatened by an actress who both competed with his star and engaged Elvis's attention offscreen, as Ann-Margret did from the start. And it's true, as the Colonel complained, that it was difficult to distinguish just whose film it was. Instead of playing up their natural chemistry, he grumbled that Ann-Margret got more close-ups and flattering camera angles, and fought to cut their duets to just one song. Finally, he vetoed special billing for her in the advertisements that MGM hoped would help draw audiences beyond the usual Presley fans. "If someone else should ride on our back," Parker told the studio, "then we should get a better saddle."

Parker was likewise clueless as to how the movie rejuvenated his client's spirits and musical dynamism, particularly with the jumpy title tune. During filming, the Colonel brought his friend Gene Austin to the set and had Elvis rehearse the tunes to the old crooner for comments.

"He was singing one song," recalls Austin's wife, LouCeil, "and the Colonel said, 'Now, Elvis, I don't like about eight bars of that. Call David Houston [Austin's godson, then a hopeful country singer] and sing it to him, and then tell him to give you the Gene Austin licks for those bars.'" Elvis was angry and embarrassed, but kept it to himself, concentrating instead on his banter with Mrs. Austin. "When you'd pay him a compliment," she remembers, "he'd always say, 'Thank you, ma'am, honey.'"

After a string of disappointing flicks, *Viva Las Vegas,* directed by George Sidney (*Annie Get Your Gun*), would topple *Blue Hawaii* as Elvis's highest-grossing film ever—by 1969, revenues would reach $5.5 million, up from Elvis's usual picture gross of $3 million. Its success should have shown Parker that spending money for more alluring costars, creative directors, and imaginative scripts would go a long way to assure his client of longevity. However, at the time, all he saw was that *Viva Las Vegas* had soared over budget.

At MGM, Parker preferred working with men like Sam "King of the Quickies" Katzman and Joe Pasternak, who guaranteed tight shooting schedules and production costs, and welcomed the fact that the Colonel rarely requested story conferences. Katzman nonetheless asked the Colonel to read the screenplay for *Kissin' Cousins,* but Parker told him it would cost him $10,000 and then diffused such an outrageous demand with a vote of confidence similar to what he'd told Elvis: "If you didn't know what you were doing, you wouldn't be here." *Kissin' Cousins* was an embarrassment to Elvis, however, and Katzman would go on to make the worst picture of Elvis's career, *Harum Scarum.*

When Joe Pasternak made the first of his two Elvis pictures (*Girl Happy* and *Spinout*), both shot in thirty-two days, the producer took the Colonel aside and said, "Look, you can't make a picture where the star takes seventy or eighty percent of the cost." Parker was resolute. "He said, 'I'm sending you Elvis Presley.' He didn't want to boost the price up, but he wouldn't budge on Elvis, and he'd want to save on everything else."

Elvis resented the financial shortcuts on his films, as well as the shoddy technical workmanship on *Kissin' Cousins* that prominently showed his stand-in, Lance LeGault, in the finale march. ("Sam Katzman said, 'It's too expensive to shoot it over—no one will even notice,'" remembers Yvonne Craig.) But he was particularly crushed to read an interview with Wallis in the *Las Vegas Desert News and Telegram* in which the producer said it was the profits from the commercially successful Presley pictures that made classy vehicles like Peter O'Toole's *Becket* possible. "That doesn't mean a Presley picture can't have quality, too," Wallis added, but the damage was done.

Still, while Presley usually managed to remain calm and professional on the movie sets, his frustration sometimes poured out in the soundtrack sessions at Radio Recorders, where he could barely hide his discomfort at recording bland and pathetic pop songs like "(There's) No Room to Rhumba in a Sports Car," "Do the Clam," and "Petunia, the Gardener's

Daughter," provided by the Hill and Range writers. One day, anguished at a song put before him, Elvis made a crack about somebody in the business. Everyone laughed, but he quickly recanted. "I didn't mean that, guys," he said. "The Colonel told me to always say nice things."

Freddy Bienstock understood the predicament but was powerless to change it. "Once we started on the MGM contract, with four pictures a year, it was like a factory," he says. "Each producer would send me ten or eleven drafts of the script, and I would mark those scenes where a song could be done without being absolutely ridiculous, and then I would give those scripts to seven or eight songwriting teams. I'd wind up with four or five songs for each spot, and then I would take them to Elvis and he would choose which one to do. But there was no way to have better music, because from the moment one picture was finished, we would have to get started on the next one."

Presley was especially embarrassed to be locked up in Hollywood doing mediocre films while the Beatles—who would visit him at his Perugia Way home in Hollywood in August of '65—threatened his supremacy in musical history, even as his *Roustabout* soundtrack would best their latest album on the charts. But an argument can be made that whatever Parker's intent, Hollywood helped keep Elvis a big star and in the money during a period when his record career might have languished, especially in the protest-and-psychedelic era.

The popular consensus that Parker denied Elvis a significant place in '60s music history comes under fire from several music journalists, including Michael Streissguth, who doubts that Elvis—working strictly in music—would have escaped the fate of other '50s stars. RCA was slow to respond to '60s rock and roll, and since Elvis wrote none of his own material, the label would have had difficulty knowing what do to with Presley during those rapidly changing times.

"By dumb luck," says Streissguth, "the movie years had the effect of preserving Elvis economically while the wild music environment passed over. Elvis was not spent from years of musical rejection, so when the time was right and people were ready to see him in concert, he was fresh and ready to pounce on the opportunity. Inadvertently, Parker's decisions in the early and mid-'60s gave us the great Elvis music of the very late '60s and early '70s."

Starting around 1963, the Colonel, whose physical meetings with Elvis had always been sporadic, became even more remote, spending much of his time in Palm Springs, the hangout for Frank Sinatra and the good ol' boys of Hollywood. For several years, he'd commuted on the weekends, filling the car with weighty bottles of Mountain Valley Spring water and schlepping Marie's favorite houseplants from Los Angeles, staying first at the Spa Hotel, where he enjoyed the baths, and then at a house at 888 Regal Drive, compliments of the William Morris Agency. Then one day in the mid-'60s, he fell over in the driveway with another heart attack—his third—which left him using a cane. Once he grew stronger, he employed it as a prop.

Byron Raphael ran into him at the Tick Tock restaurant in Los Angeles not long after, and he could tell that something awful had happened. "He'd really changed. He had that cane, and he was bent over. It shocked me, because he was like an old man."

To most people, Parker explained he just had a bad back, and pointed to an exercise contraption and the elastic brace he wore around his waist and upper torso for proof. But he was convinced he couldn't survive yet another coronary, casually telling associates, "You don't see any hearses with luggage racks on them," and made the decision to spend the rest of his life as if there were no tomorrow.

Only the biggest and the most would do. First, he wanted a new house in Palm Springs. He went to work on Abe Lastfogel's wife, Frances, paying her a visit while she was in the hospital, hauling in a big vase of flowers and sweet-talking her into letting him have the larger, $250,000 one-floor plan house at 1166 Vista Vespero. There Marie would make everything in the house blue and white, right down to the drapes and bedsheets and even gravel in the driveway. And the Colonel coud relax by the pool and get RCA to install a commercial freezer for the vast amounts of meat he bought and inventoried like gold, even as he struggled to keep his weight in check. Parker didn't mind being fat—as far as he was concerned, his size suited him and added to his psychological heft. But his doctor dictated otherwise.

Sometimes Parker showed up at Elvis's recording sessions and tried to lift his client's mood. On occasion, he ordered lunch in for everyone, and routinely traded jokes with bassist Bob Moore, who had known the Colonel since the Eddy Arnold years and considered Parker "a great, great man," and with Buddy Harman, who drummed on at least nine of the soundtracks and likewise found him to be "a pretty nice old codger, really." It was a sentiment Parker went out of his way to foster with the Nashville musicians, if not necessarily with the L.A. players. Moore, who'd been on nearly all the movie recordings, remembers the time he walked into the control room where Hal Wallis was sitting in the producer's chair. "Boy," the Colonel said to Wallis, "get up and go get me some coffee. Let Bob sit here."

At other times, it was Elvis he humiliated in front of the movie execs. After Wallis sent Parker a letter complaining that Elvis looked "soft, fat, and jowly around the face" in *Viva Las Vegas,* asking the Colonel to have a talk with him about his weight, Parker grilled Marty Lacker about his boss's eating habits at a recording session. "He's just been eating what he always eats," Lacker said, at which point Parker banged his cane on the floor and then raised it in the air, yelling, "Don't lie to me! Tell me!"

But it wasn't so much Presley's eating habits that altered his looks as it was his pharmaceutical habit, according to Lacker, one of the entourage members who alternately carried Presley's black makeup kit, which the singer filled with pills. Often, they dictated his moods.

At the next session, it was Elvis who couldn't contain his rage. "He had this big orchestra in there," remembers Lacker, "and he started singing. He didn't settle for the first take. They were getting ready to do it again, and Elvis reached his breaking point. He started ranting, 'I'm tired of all these fucking songs, and I'm tired of these damn movies! I get in a fight with somebody in one scene, and in the next one I'm kissing the dog. What difference does it make how many times we do this song? I'll tell you what. You just cut the tracks for this next movie, and I'll come in later and put my voice on.'"

Shortly after, the Colonel invited Elvis to join him and Marie and the Tuckers for dinner, but Presley declined, much to Parker's embarrassment. "Colonel just damned near begged him, and he wouldn't do it," Tucker remembers. For years, the Colonel had boasted of never mixing business and pleasure with his client, not even the simple sharing of a meal. ("You do your thing and I'll do my thing, and it'll be beautiful," he had said.) Elvis was in no mood to start now.

With the movie and record deals in place, Parker found himself with plenty of time for something he now considered doubly important: having fun. When he got a call from a promoter about possibly taking Presley out on tour, he'd tell him Elvis was tied up for the next three and a half years, but he'd be happy to rent the gold lamé suit for the weekend for $5,000. Or maybe they'd be interested in Elvis's cars. He had a tour of those going out soon, and he wasn't even kidding about that one.

Parker spent much of the day in his fun-house offices at Paramount and MGM cutting up with the cost-free additions to his staff—Jim

O'Brien, his private secretary, on loan from Hill and Range; Irv Schecter and John Hartmann, supplied by the William Morris office; and Grelun Landon, courtesy of RCA. Soon, Gabe Tucker would also be there on the Morris dime.

On occasion, Parker referred to O'Brien as Sergeant. But as usual, nobody had any real rank except Diskin, whose desk, a third the size of Parker's, was in the Colonel's private office at MGM. The rest were privates who helped Parker carry out his schemes.

Each morning, the staff arrived at the mazelike Elvis Exploitations offices at MGM and prepared a list of VIP birthdays so the Colonel could make his congratulatory calls, the aides lining up in front of a microphone in the office and singing to whomever their boss had on the phone. "I thought it was kind of rank," remembers John Hartmann, who went on to manage David Crosby and Graham Nash, Canned Heat, and the group America, "but I did it anyway."

"We didn't hurt ourselves workin'," says Tucker, whose MGM office was in Clark Gable's old dressing room, and whose duties included tamping down the Colonel's pipe, which replaced the cigars when Parker got upset. Tucker also ran the "cookhouse," a so-called carnival kitchen Parker made by throwing an oilcloth over the conference room table, adding ketchup bottles and kitchen chairs, and promoting a stove and refrigerator from the studio so Parker could cook slumgullion, a boiled stew that hearkened to his hobo days.

Most of the time they ordered food in. But after *Easy Come, Easy Go*, the Colonel would appropriate actor Bob Isenberg from the cast to wear a chef's hat and serve occasional lunch guests like Abe Lastfogel, who choked down the slices of ham the Colonel piled on to watch the little Jewish man squirm. When that grew tiresome, Parker totaled up the free meals he'd gotten in the last month, instructing Tucker to pick a name from the directory of MGM executives and call to say, "The Colonel thinks you ought to invite us to supper."

Soon, the requests grew more elaborate and grand. The president of RCA sent him a check for $1 million without any paperwork when Parker asked for a loan for Vernon Presley, allegedly to buy a Memphis skating rink. The Colonel liked his tests.

He began spending weeks at a time in Palm Springs, where Milton Prell had a house (they both also kept an apartment at the Wilshire Comstock in L.A.), and where he could keep a closer eye on his neighbor, Hal Wallis. The producer continued to humor him, sending him, while on a trip to England, a small dish from the Elephant Club for Parker's collection. Parker wrote him a letter, thanking him for swiping it. "I could tell you that I bought it, but I know that you would have a lot more respect for me if you felt that I had lifted it," Wallis replied.

Their relationship remained cordial but strained, although Wallis succeeded in getting the Colonel to read perhaps his first script, for the carnival-themed *Roustabout,* which Wallis produced in part to honor Parker's colorful past. ("Of course, we want you to be associated with the project, as I know how close this type of life is to you," he wrote.) Afterward, Parker sent Wallis an affectionate letter in which he complimented the producer's ability to make a picture jell. "You have a certain magic wand that makes these things come out even, even if other people don't understand it all the time," he said. "This I respect more than I can put in words."

Parker may have meant the flattery as a kind of balm. "When I was doing *Roustabout,*" recalls the screenwriter Allan Weiss, "I went down to Palm Springs and spent a weekend with the Colonel, interviewing him specifically on his circus background. When I got back, Hal Wallis said, 'How did it go?' I told him it went fairly well, and I thought we had a good subject for Elvis. Then he said, 'It was an expensive weekend.' I thought, 'Oh, my God, is he referring to the hotel I stayed at, or what?' I learned later that the Colonel had billed him for his time."

Wallis took such things in stride, but the two could also go for days and not speak. Afterward, in Palm Springs, it would be as if the incident had never happened, Parker going to dinner and tossing his hat on one of Wallis's priceless Rodin sculptures just to rankle his host, or asking the producer to play golf with Marie's grandson, Tommy, when the boy and his sister, Sharon, came for the summer. Later, the Colonel would throw a black-tie party and invite Wallis, among others, answering the door wearing nothing but Bermuda shorts.

Underneath his various guises, however, the Colonel wrestled with increasingly dark moods of depression. Aside from his concern about his heart and his growing estrangement from Elvis, he was deeply worried about Marie.

In the past, there were times when he'd avoided going to Palm Springs because he didn't want to have to put up with her carrying on about her cats—a dog lover, his ardor barely extended to felines, and he was jealous of her doting on a particular male cat named Midnight.

"I was at the house one day," remembers Lamar Fike, "and Colonel and I were sitting in the den, talking. Marie came in all distraught and said, 'Midnight's on the roof! Midnight's on the roof!' Colonel said, 'He'll come down.'

"She came back in a little while and said, 'Midnight's still on the roof! Do something!' So Colonel went out with a hose about as big as a fireman's, with tremendous pressure, and aimed it at that cat, and blew it over the garage and the porte cochere, and out into the street. It landed on its feet, but boy, was it surprised! Colonel came back in and said, 'Now, *that's* how you get a cat off a roof.'"

Lately, though, he'd demonstrated more compassion. Marie's health had begun to deteriorate. She complained to Gabe Tucker and to her brother, Bitsy, that living with the Colonel was constant stress, and sometimes he got on her nerves so badly she suffered debilitating headaches that left her unable to think straight. But the Colonel believed it was more than that; her mind seemed to be slipping, and sometimes her rantings, he said in off-the-cuff remarks, drove him crazy. Since she was also becoming severely arthritic, after the Tuckers moved out Parker hated to leave her alone, so first he had RCA sales manager Jack Burgess stay up all night with her and play cards. When Burgess grew weary, it was Irv Schecter, one of Marie's favorites, who got the call. Schecter was probably only too glad to be out of Parker's office, where the Colonel thought his William Morris recruit had developed ulcers.

It was during the 1964 making of *Roustabout* that Elvis met Larry Geller, who would become one of the most significant members of the Memphis Mafia and perhaps Presley's purest friend.

A hairdresser in Jay Sebring's tony salon, Geller first showed up at Presley's home on Perugia Way in April '64 at the invitation of entourage member Alan Fortas. Elvis had heard good things about his work, Fortas told him. Affable and expressive, Geller talked at length to Elvis about his dedication to spiritual studies and the metaphysical, which seemed to set the singer's curiosity on fire.

"What you're talking about," Elvis said, hungry for discussion, "is what I secretly think about *all the time.* You don't know what this means to me." They talked of Elvis's purpose in life, and the singer confessed he felt "chosen" but didn't know why. "I've always felt this unseen hand guiding my life ever since I was a little boy," he said. "Why was I plucked out of all of the millions of millions of lives to be Elvis?"

The next day, at Elvis's request, Geller showed up at Paramount with a copy of *The Impersonal Life,* a book he thought would aid Presley in his quest. From then on, Elvis would read such books every day, dedicating himself to the study of Eastern religion and the spiritual path, with Larry as his personal teacher. Almost immediately, the entourage, as well as Parker and Priscilla, viewed Geller with suspicion, seeing him as a disruptive interloper who threatened the status quo.

Toward the end of 1964, however, Parker had much bigger things on his mind than bickering among the Elvis camp. That December, he signed a contract with United Artists for two pictures (*Frankie and Johnny* and *Clambake*) at $650,000 each. But more important, with the help of Abe Lastfogel, who said it couldn't be done, he succeeded in completing a deal with MGM for the benchmark figure of $1 million.

Lastfogel thought Parker was crazy, bringing Gabe Tucker in for some light banter to distract the studio lawyers, and insisting he wouldn't do the deal unless MGM threw in the ashtray that lay on the conference room table. But in the end, he nailed down a deal for three pictures, the first commanding $1 million—$250,000 of which would be paid in $1,000 weekly installments over five years—and the next two drawing $750,000 each. Profit participation was set at 40 percent.

The Colonel couldn't contain his glee. He'd finally gotten the best of them all—Wallis, Hazen, Lastfogel, everyone. By sheer gall and snowmanship, Parker had succeeded in making Elvis the highest-paid actor in Hollywood, and his career total was even more impressive: since the beginning of their relationship, he'd brokered deals that had earned Presley $35 million. But to the Colonel's great disappointment, Elvis didn't seem particularly pleased about the new contract. In fact, since the May departure of Joe Esposito, the foreman of the entourage and the Colonel's chief spy, Parker couldn't even get his client on the phone.

Elvis had picked this time to show a rare spurt of independence. In early October, when he reported to Allied Artists to begin preproduction on *Tickle Me,* he told the Colonel and everyone on the set that it was important to him to be home in Memphis for Thanksgiving. As filming wore on and delays ensued, Elvis realized that the schedule would be tight, but still he kept quiet. Finally, he got his release on Tuesday, November 24, two days before Thanksgiving, with a caravan of cars and a Dodge mobile home yet to transport cross-country.

In late February, Presley went to Nashville to record the soundtrack for *Harum Scarum,* the first of the three MGM pictures, a Sam Katzman quickie with a plot that called for Elvis to wear a turban, be kidnapped by a gang of assassins, and perform with a Middle Eastern dancing troupe— a scenario that seemed to combine Rudolph Valentino's *The Sheik* with the Hawaiian and gypsy stories Parker had suggested to Hal Wallis years before. The session, Presley's first time in a recording studio in eight months, went poorly as the former rocker balked at singing such lyrics as "Come hear my desert serenade." Parker, who had kept tabs on Elvis's mounting dissatisfaction, began sending letters to Marty Lacker, the new Memphis Mafia foreman, stressing the importance of the "caravan superintendent," as he called him, getting Elvis and company to the coast on time to begin filming.

Elvis, however, was in no hurry to report to California, preferring to spend time with Larry Geller in meditation and study. Weeks went by, and Parker's continuous calls went unheeded. "Elvis is not ready to come back," Marty reported, and it did no good for Parker to scream. He was beside himself with anxiety, the studio telephoning night and day and talking breach of contract. To duck their calls, he finally staged an elaborate ruse, having Marie phone Harry Jenkins, who in late 1963 replaced Bill Bullock at RCA in New York.

"My husband is deathly ill," Marie whispered into the phone. "It's a bad situation." She'd just ordered a hospital bed for him, in fact, and she needed Jenkins to get the word to MGM and to Gabe Tucker, relaxing in Houston after months out on the road touring Elvis's cars. Jenkins dutifully reported the grave news: "Gabe, Colonel is bad sick. Marie wants you to come out and take care of him." Tucker, afraid that Parker had suffered another heart attack, caught the first plane, only to find the Colonel himself waiting to pick him up.

"Goddamn, Colonel, you scared the hell out of me. Mr. Jenkins said you was in bad shape."

"Well, I didn't feel good yesterday."

They went home, and Tucker knew there was something wrong after all. "He said, 'Let's sit out by the pool,'" and Parker told him the whole story. Secretly, the Colonel's employee rooted for Elvis. "I thought, well, by God, Elvis showed him this time. For a change he stood up." But Parker was somehow sympathetic, too—craving a kind word and a compliment. No manager had ever accomplished what he had, or taken a star to such heights. Now he'd made a once-in-a-lifetime deal for a client who didn't even care, a client who was surely slipping out of his grasp.

"He asked me, 'Gabe, would you get my bed turned?' And I said, 'Sure.'" Afterward, Tucker rolled it out beside the pool for him, helped him into it, and made him as comfortable as he could. He wondered if Parker wasn't sick after all. Then he plugged in the outside phone.

The two old friends sat there for a minute reminiscing about how far they'd come in twenty-five years. Soon, the phone started ringing non-stop—Elvis still hadn't reported to the studio. "They was on him somethin' awful. I never heard such cussin' and carryin' on, and he didn't usually do that. Finally, I said, 'Colonel, why don't you tell 'em to kiss your ass? You got all the money you need. You can just tell everybody that you managed the highest-paid truck driver in the world.' And he laughed, but he said, 'Goddamn, Gabe, that ain't funny.'"

It was March before Elvis gave in. The caravan left Memphis so late in the day that they needed to drive straight through, without the usual night's rest in Amarillo or Albuquerque. But during a brief stop at a motel for a shower and a change of clothes, Elvis took Larry aside. Intellectually, he understood all the books Larry gave him, but he'd never had the kind of profound spiritual experience they described.

"I explained to him that it had nothing to do with an intellectual perception," Geller says, "that it was more of an emotion, a surrendering of the ego to God." They continued their discussion on the drive, Elvis steering the mobile home and Larry riding shotgun, the other entourage members in the back and following in separate cars.

They drove the rest of the night, and it was well into the next day before Elvis realized he'd gotten separated from the rest of the group. Elvis told Larry he was glad they were lost—"I need to be away from everyone, because I'm really into something important within myself."

By that time, they were in Arizona, near Flagstaff, approaching the famous San Francisco Peaks, in the land of the Hopi Indians. It was coming on dusk when Elvis peered into the electric-blue sky and suddenly said, "Look, man! Do you see what I see? What the hell is Joseph Stalin doing in that cloud?" Larry said he saw it, too, and then the image dissolved back into a fluffy cloud again.

Suddenly, Elvis pulled the mobile home over and, jumping out, yelled, "Follow me, man!" Then he took off into the desert. When Larry caught up with him, Presley had tears rolling down his cheeks. "It happened!" Elvis said, hugging his friend. "I thought God was trying to tell me something about myself, and I remember you saying, 'It's not a thing in your head. It has to do with your heart.' I said, 'God, I surrender my ego. I surrender my whole life to You.' And it happened!" The face of Stalin had turned into the face of Christ.

"It was like a lightning bolt went right through him," Geller recounts. "He said, 'Larry, I know the truth now. I don't *believe* in God anymore. Now I *know* that God is a living reality. He's everywhere. He's within us. He's in everyone's heart.'"

When they returned to California, Elvis took his friend into the den of the rental home on Perugia Way and told him he'd made a decision. After such an intense experience, he couldn't go back to making "teenybopper movies" again. He wanted to quit show business and do something important with his life. "In fact, Larry," he said, "I want you to find me a monastery. I'm not making a move until you tell me what to do."

Geller froze and then, thinking fast, told Elvis he could use his vision to make a difference in his films and in his records. "You've got the greatest career in the history of show business!" Geller told him. "You are the legend of them all! You are Elvis!"

Geller's words found their target. "He got that gorgeous grin on his face, and he said, 'Yeah, well, to tell you the truth, I can't imagine Priscilla next to me in some monastery, raking leaves.'" But Larry knew the conversation meant trouble. At the word *monastery,* collective groans rose from the other side of the louvered doors. Says Geller, "I realized that five minutes later, Colonel Parker would know everything, and the little wheels in his head would start to turn." Soon, Parker would also learn about Elvis's involvement with an ecumenical movement called the Self-Realization Fellowship, based in Pasadena and run by a disciple of Paramahansa Yogananda named Sri Daya Mata. And the Colonel *certainly* wouldn't like that.

The fallout started several weeks afterward on the soundstage of *Harum Scarum.* To keep their relationship strictly business, the Colonel made few appearances on the movie sets, and when he did, he held court, saying, "Where's a chair for the Colonel?" and expecting the Memphis Mafia to snap to attention, bringing him water and lighting his German cigars with the yellow tips. Geller was always uncomfortable when he added, "And bring a chair for Larry . . . You sit with me, Larry."

"He knew that I had Elvis's ear, and that Elvis was changing, and he couldn't figure me out." Sometimes, Parker even asked Geller to give him a haircut or invited him to share the whirlpool bath at the Spa in Palm Springs. It was always tense between them, but this day, Geller knew the Colonel had a different tack, and he wasted no time in getting to it.

"Larry," he began, "I think you've missed your calling. You're tall, and have such a commanding presence. I can see you dressed up in a tuxedo, standing on the stage. You have the quality to hypnotize people."

By now, the Colonel had reinstalled his pipeline, Joe Esposito, who shared co-foreman duties with Marty Lacker. Elvis seemed resigned to the arrangement, telling Geller he knew the Colonel had been taking care of Joe all of those years, and that he didn't care. Several days later, with the picture completed, Esposito reported that Parker had called and wanted his client to come over to MGM right away. Geller was blow-drying Elvis's hair in the bathroom, and they stopped and gathered the rest of the guys and piled into two cars.

"We went over to the lot," Geller says, "and about ten minutes later, Elvis walked out. We knew he was ticked. He got in the car and he said, 'That motherfucker, man. He accused me of being on a religious kick. My life is not a religious kick. I'll show that fat bastard what a kick is.' He fumed for days."

It was as if his resentment about everything had finally boiled over—his embarrassment about the scripts, his frustration at seeing his music reduced to pabulum, and Parker's constant interference. "The Colonel really cares about me? He's supposed to take care of the business end and that's it. He's not a personal friend, he's my manager, and he'd better stay that way!"

Parker never criticized Elvis to any of his acquaintances, but now he drew a radical plan of action. While the Colonel had always directed almost every facet of Elvis's existence, he rationalized that he had involved himself only in Presley's professional affairs. With both his client and their partnership disintegrating, he would rule with an iron fist.

This was the right thing to do, he told himself, since Elvis was incapable of taking care of himself. Besides, they had wrung almost every dollar out of Hollywood; Wallis and Hazen strongly believed the next movie, *Paradise, Hawaiian Style,* would be, as Hazen termed it, "Elvis's last good picture" and would go for only one more, *Easy Come, Easy Go,* once their deal ran out. Charles Boasberg, president of Paramount's distributing company, had sounded the final knell, writing Wallis that *Frankie and Johnny,* a United Artists film, "is dying all over the country, and this is his second poor picture in a row. If it weren't for you lifting him up with some good production in your pictures, Presley would be really dead by now."

Parker fought Joe Hazen on virtually every clause of the new contract, and while Wallis defended him ("I think the Colonel has kept his word with you and has shown fine spirit characteristic of him," he wrote to his partner), Hazen at one point called Parker's changes in the agreement "the height of duplicity . . . he is trying to get his and we *have* ours."

But the Colonel also saw it as a triumph.

"One day," remembers Marty Lacker, "Elvis came up to me and said, 'The Colonel wants you to take him to Palm Springs.' I had never done that before, and I thought it was a very strange request, considering our relationship.

"I went over to his office, and I remember I had on a black pullover sweater. The Colonel looked at me and said, 'You're not dressed right. Let me give you a shirt.' He opened up a closet and pulled out this ugly, old man's yellow-and-white-striped shirt. And it had a cigar burn on the front. I said, 'Colonel, I don't want your shirt.' He said, 'You sure?' And he put it back in the closet.

"We started driving, and we got about a half hour out of Palm Springs, and we hadn't said a word to each other. He was sitting next to me in the front seat. All of a sudden, he started chuckling, and he said, 'Boy, I showed those goddamn Jews, didn't I?' Just out of the blue. Then he chuckled again. Now, I'm saying to myself, You no-good bastard. You've got to know I'm Jewish. I wanted to take that car and head it into a pole, figure out how to kill him without hurting myself."

In 1966, Parker would persist in wooing the producers for another film, issuing a "Snowmen's League Annual Report," a tongue-in-cheek document listing bogus expenses, grosses, and profits. At the end, Parker inserted a photo of Elvis and Wallis shaking hands, onto which he had pasted a bizarre likeness of himself standing behind them and wielding a machete. "If you don't sign a contract," it seemed to say, further suggesting that only he had the power to sever ties, "I'll cut off your arm."

By now, though, the producers were immune to the Colonel's ploys. *Easy Come, Easy Go* would almost not be released, Paramount believing it was doubtful the picture could recoup its cost. After Paramount backed off its advertising campaign and Parker relentlessly complained that he had spent too much of his own money to promote it, Wallis sent him a check for $3,500. But the veteran filmmaker would never do business with him again.

Things were nearly as dismal at MGM. The prefab method by which "the Elvis movie" was assembled had become painfully obvious, with its tiny production budgets and lack of location shots for the films supposedly set in Europe and the Middle East. The grosses were also way down, and the plots had deteriorated to cartoonlike absurdity. *Harum Scarum,* released in late '65, had been so ridiculous, the Colonel suggested, that only a talking camel could save it by making the picture an intentional farce. Parker had always told Elvis never to admit he'd made a mistake, but the manager doubted his own judgment in going along with Sam Katzman's eighteen-day shooting schedule. It would take "a fifty-fifth cousin to P. T. Barnum to sell it," the Colonel said, and the best thing to do was "book it fast, get the money, then try again."

Before long, rumors swirled in Tennessee that Elvis was retiring, or that he was looking to hire another manager, or that the Colonel himself was ready to quit managing his star. In February 1966, the Colonel got on the phone to the Memphis *Commercial Appeal* and explained that there wasn't a word of truth to the rumor, diffusing the situation with bravado, saying, "Heck yes, I would retire and so would my boy—if we received enough money to retire . . . We have contracts for fourteen additional motion pictures to be made over a period of several years."

Still, Parker's judgment remained cloudy. His code of loyalty made him stick with inappropriate directors, including Norman Taurog, a quasi-hack best known for directing *Boys Town* with Spencer Tracy in 1938 and Elvis's own *Blue Hawaii.* Taurog had made a string of Elvis's films, and Parker requested him more often than his talent—or his health—warranted. In meeting with Irwin Wink-ler, who came aboard as the producer of *Double Trouble,* the nearly seventy-year-old Hollywood veteran admitted he was blind in one eye and couldn't see well enough to drive. Taurog would be completely sightless within two years of finishing *Double Trouble,* during which time he would direct two more Presley pictures, *Speedway* and *Live a Little, Love a Little,* which would rank among Elvis's most disappointing efforts.

Even the die-hard fans grumbled that the films weren't opening at the choice suburban movie houses, but at drive-ins. Worse, they relied on the same old formula—Elvis as a virile stock car racer, nightclub singer, or crop duster, saddled with a philandering, bumbling sidekick, and searching for true love through implausible dialogue and hackneyed songs. The president of the Hampshire, England, Elvis Presley Club wrote that the movies were "an insult to Elvis and fans." Another pleaded to Wallis that someone must help Elvis now "when his career is beginning to falter," while an even more prescient voice opined, "I realize that there is not much you can do if Elvis doesn't care, and sometimes I doubt that he does." Despite the fact that exhibitors would soon claim that something must be "radically wrong" with Elvis, judging from his appearance, a lucrative movie offer came from Japan. But Parker turned it down, saying Elvis was booked through 1969.

Byron Raphael used to ask the Colonel how he could be so strong, refusing certain offers and holding out for unprecedented money elsewhere. Parker explained it was because he had a three-tiered client—the real reason he hadn't taken on anyone else to manage. "Byron," he said, "we don't need the movie business. If we couldn't do movies, we could do personal appearances for $50,000 a night. And if we couldn't do personal appearances, we could do records. We have gigantic record sales. I wouldn't do it otherwise."

But in 1966, RCA again refused the Colonel's request to sponsor a big tour of personal appearances. He'd asked for $500,000 this time, and as RCA's Norman Racusin puts it, "I did not know who the $500,000 was going to." The company had also become concerned about slipping sales—as musical tastes changed, an album that might have had a standing order for 2 million copies was down by half—and RCA would soon reduce Elvis's guaranteed advance. But Parker had other plans for Elvis. *If* he could hold him together.

The first order was to get him focused. For that, the Colonel sent a stronger message to Larry Geller.

One Sunday, he invited Geller and his wife and children to come to Palm Springs and spend the day at the house. After a swim, Parker asked Larry inside, where he began to probe him about his spiritual beliefs. The telephone rang, and Geller got the strange feeling from the Colonel's opaque mumbles that the conversation might have been about him.

"He looked at me and he glanced away, and he said 'Yes, yes, right now. Well, yeah, right.' But I dismissed it, because I had no reason to be suspicious."

Parker hung up and suggested they gather the kids and go to Will Wright's Ice Cream Parlor. Afterward, the Gellers made their good-byes and returned to Los Angeles. "The minute I drove into the driveway, I saw the back door open," Larry remembers. "It was a precision strike."

The intruders had not taken items of monetary value, but Geller's files on metaphysical topics—parapsychology, astrology, palmistry, and numerology—along with tapes of music from the Self-Realization church. His clothes, too, were gone. Garbage was dumped upside down in the living room.

Devastated, Geller piled his frightened family in the car and drove to
see Elvis. "He shook his head back and forth a few times and said, 'All
right, we know who did this.'" Though Presley set the Gellers up in a
hotel until they were ready to return home, Elvis downplayed the incident, saying that at least no one was hurt. But it scared them both. Says
Larry, "We just tried to repress it."

With Geller seemingly defused, Parker now attacked the second order
of business: getting Elvis married.

The strange press release that Parker had written for 1961's *Wild in
the Country* shows that the Colonel had been thinking of this for a long
time. "During the making of [the film]," Parker wrote, "Elvis was asked
if the Colonel would object if Elvis married."

"'The Colonel would have nothing to say about it,' Elvis replied with
more than usual emphasis. 'I probably would talk it over with him as a
friend and as a man I respect, but never in the sense of asking his permission.'

"'When the boy wants to marry, I hope he'll ask me to help him do
it,'" Parker said.

"Like a wise father," the press release went on, "Colonel Parker takes
an interest in the girls Elvis escorts, but doesn't interfere. He probably
would step in if he thought Elvis were making some dreadful mistake, but
it would be as a counselor, not as a commanding officer."

In 1966, however, there was another commanding officer to consider.
Priscilla was almost twenty-one now, and her stepfather, the newly promoted Lieutenant Colonel Beaulieu, was sounding off about Elvis's
promise to make her his wife. He'd called in recent months and uttered
what Elvis took to be some mild threats, and Parker didn't know how
long he could hold him off. If Elvis reneged, and Priscilla went to the papers, it could look very bad—the headlines would scream how he'd harbored an underage girl and broken her heart.

Priscilla was beginning to think he was never going to marry her, especially as he was dating Ann-Margret, who told reporters she was in love
with Presley but didn't know if they would marry. A scared Priscilla had
flown out to Hollywood to try to break up the romance, but the Colonel
had sent her home to Memphis so no one would ask questions about
their relationship, too.

Suddenly, everyone was thinking seriously about marriage. The
Colonel figured it would end Elvis's obsession with religion, keep him
away from Ann-Margret and her smart young team of managers, and

stem Elvis's growing fixation with guns and law enforcement. Priscilla hoped it would make him grow up—why did he need all those guys around for slot car races and water balloon fights, anyway? And Vernon, who still pretended to take care of Elvis's personal business ("My daddy doesn't do anything," Elvis had once accurately answered when asked Vernon's profession), would be happy if it quelled his son's incessant spending. At the end of 1966, Elvis would negotiate to buy a $300,000 ranch in Mississippi and blow a fortune on trucks, horses, and trailers for his friends. Parker liked to see Elvis burn through his money—it kept him working—but it made Vernon's head spin.

Yes, they agreed, Elvis must get married. Furthermore, Elvis shouldn't be so remote; he needed to stay in closer touch with the ol' Colonel. And so in September '66, Elvis leased a home in Palm Springs, where he spent Thanksgiving with his manager. But the stress was taking its toll. On the way home to Memphis, Elvis heard "The Green, Green Grass of Home" on the radio and broke down when he arrived at Graceland, telling Marty Lacker, "I walked in the door, and I saw my mama standing there. I saw her, man."

Just before Christmas, Elvis proposed to Priscilla. A vague date was set for the following year. Elvis couldn't find it in him to tell Ann-Margret and simply stopped taking her calls.

With his skewed moral center, Parker believed that forcing Elvis to marry was an honorable move, even if Elvis himself was not emotionally committed. "When I fall deeply in love it will happen," he'd told Hedda Hopper five years earlier. "I'll decide on the spur of the moment, but it won't be an elopement . . . but a church wedding."

When Elvis reported for wardrobe fittings for *Clambake,* his twenty-fifth film, in March of '67, the studio was shocked to discover that he had ballooned to 200 pounds, up 30 from his usual 170. "He ate out of depression," says entourage member Jerry Schilling. "The movies were boring to him, and when he didn't have a challenge, he always got depressed." Parker was furious. Elvis began trying to melt the weight off with diet pills, but on top of the sleeping tablets and his usual arsenal of mood-altering drugs, the medications made him dizzy.

One night at his new rental house on Rocca Place, Elvis got up to use the toilet and tripped over a television cord in the bathroom and hit his head on the sunken tub. By morning, he had a golfball-size lump, and he was woozy when he staggered out of the bedroom and asked the guys to take a look. Esposito phoned the Colonel, thus setting in motion the events that led to Parker's most egregious attachment of Elvis's earnings.

By the time the Colonel arrived at the house, along with several white-uniformed nurses and a doctor carrying portable X-ray equipment, Elvis could barely hold his head up. The diagnosis was a mild concussion, but the start of the movie would have to be delayed by several weeks.

"The Colonel took us out in the hall," Marty Lacker remembers, "and he said, 'Goddamn you guys, why do you let him get this way? He's going to mess up everything! They'll tear up the contract!'"

Then he turned to Larry Geller. "Get those books out of here right now!" he bellowed. "Do you understand me? Right now!"

Afterward, says Lacker, "the Colonel went back in and talked to Elvis, and he said, 'Here's the way it is. From now on, you're going to listen to everything I say. Otherwise, I'm going to leave you, and that will ruin your career, and you'll lose Graceland and you'll lose your fans. And because I'm going to do all this extra work for you, I want fifty percent of your contract.'"

Parker prepared a new agreement, backdating it to January 1. In setting down terms for a joint venture, the Colonel wrote that he would continue to collect a 25 percent commission on Elvis's standard movie salaries and record company advances, but All Star Shows would now receive 50 percent of profits or royalties beyond basic payments from both the film and the record contracts, including "special," or side, deals. The commission would be deducted before any division of royalties and profits. Their merchandising split would remain the same.

Lacker was surprised at how quickly Elvis had okayed such an arrangement, but the foreman didn't know about the clinical depths of Elvis's depression, nor about a conversation that had taken place between Parker and Presley sometime the year before.

They were talking about Sam Cooke, the great soul singer who died in a shooting outside a hooker's seedy motel room in 1964. Cooke had also recorded for RCA—in fact, his live *At the Copa* album was released the month of his death. But it wasn't the manager of L.A.'s Hacienda Motel who killed him, as the press reported, Parker told Elvis. The Mafia got him. Cooke was stepping out of line, the Colonel said, getting involved in civil rights, spouting off about things he shouldn't. He was warned, but he wouldn't shut up. Word came down and the hit was made.

The mob wasn't gangsters in the streets anymore, Parker explained. It was heads of corporations like RCA, the East Coast, Sicilian families—

men whose last names ended in vowels, men with uncles called Jimmy "the Thumb."

"Colonel told Elvis, 'You've got to behave yourself. You can only go so far,'" says Larry Geller. "And Elvis knew the Colonel was a dangerous enemy."

A week or so after the fall, when Presley regained his strength, Parker called a meeting at Rocca Place. Priscilla and Vernon had flown out from Memphis, and along with Elvis and the guys, they sat around the living room as Parker rolled out a list of changes: one, Joe Esposito was to be the lone foreman. Two, no one was to talk about religion to Elvis, and Geller could no longer be alone with him. And three, there was too much money going out. Everyone's salary would be cut back, and several people had better start looking for jobs.

In the end, no one was fired, and only one person left voluntarily, when Larry Geller quit the following month. But the guys had never seen Elvis so docile. He never took his eyes off the floor, and he never spoke up.

At 9:41 on the morning of May 1, 1967, Elvis and Priscilla were married by Nevada Supreme Court Judge David Zenoff in a small, surprise ceremony in Milton Prell's suite at the new Aladdin Hotel in Las Vegas. "She was absolutely petrified, and Elvis was so nervous he was almost bawling," the justice remembers. Afterward, owner Prell laid out a $10,000 champagne breakfast with suckling pig and poached salmon, and then the couple flew to Palm Springs on Frank Sinatra's Learjet to begin their honeymoon.

As if it were the Colonel's own wedding, Parker arranged every detail. "It was the Colonel who got the rings, the room, the judge," Priscilla later said. "We didn't do any of that. It was all through his connections. We wanted it to be *fast,* effortless." Which meant she and Elvis also allowed the Colonel to pick the attendants and the guests, who numbered fewer than twenty. Most of the Memphis Mafia were excluded from the ceremony—a painful slight that would leave bruised feelings for years—but invited to the breakfast, where they mingled with Parker's gambling buddy, the comedian Redd Foxx.

Larry Geller, whom Elvis had once asked to be best man, read about the wedding in the newspaper. Stunned, he thought back to the events of the past month. Parker had taken charge of everything in Elvis's life except the one aspect he should have addressed: Presley's drug use.

Grelun Landon, who worked with the Colonel from 1955 on, first as a vice president of Hill and Range and then as an RCA publicist, says that Parker himself didn't know about the pills during the MGM years, despite Elvis's ever-present "makeup" case. But others insist that can't be true—the Colonel was informed about *everything* that went on—and though their meetings were infrequent, there was no way he couldn't have recognized the erratic behavior and abnormal perspiration of an addict, even one whose dependence was on prescription drugs, not street narcotics.

But just as several of the entourage members were in denial about their own drug use, Parker, according to his friends, refused to believe that Elvis was truly in trouble. A more plausible explanation is that in the days before the Betty Ford Clinic, the Colonel didn't know where to take him for discreet, effective help and loathed risking the loss of work if the truth got out. As a man who spent his whole life covering things up, Parker believed the decent thing was to conceal Elvis's "weakness."

Just as Elvis turned increasingly to drugs in periods of stress, Parker, as his difficulties mounted, visited the gambling tables of Las Vegas for the addictive element of excitement and escape. For many gamblers, the satisfaction—even the thrill—is in losing, not winning, since for pathological gamblers with an impulse control disorder, the game is never about the acquisition of money, but about the action itself. Gambling fed the obsessive twins—Wisdom and Folly—of Parker's personality, which made him by turns calculating and reckless, self-protective and self-destructive.

Parker's losses were now becoming increasingly apparent to his business associates, who saw him as a chronic gambler. Since 1965, he'd been asking for money early on the film contracts, and new RCA president Norman Racusin was well aware that Parker "had a penchant for the tables," as the label had assigned Harry Jenkins to keep the Colonel happy. That meant Jenkins spent an inordinate amount of time sitting at the craps tables with Parker in Vegas, the Colonel intoning, "Let's go down to the office" as his signal for some action.

Jenkins hoped that RCA would reimburse him for the losses he sustained when Parker urged him to throw in a few chips. But the label had no such intention, since it was already occasionally taking care of the Colonel's debts. Though Parker grossed unfathomable sums of money, little of it came in steadily. In between deals, he began calling on Hal Wallis, the Morris agency, and RCA to cover him, the casinos knowing that someone was always going to be good for his money. If not, they gave him credit, or wrote it off as a favor.

"I'm sure there was an awful lot going on," says Parker's acquaintance Dick Contino, the accordionist who was courted by the mob early in his career and remained a favorite of Sinatra. "It would be an obvious thing. If you've got a problem financially, these guys don't write notes—they ask you what you need. If they like you, you got it. Money is nothing, but respect, everything. My guess is that they asked for their favors in return and got them, maybe unbeknown to Elvis. I wouldn't criticize Tom for it. Why not?"

16

BLACK LEATHER BLUES:

THE '68 SPECIAL

SOMETIME in 1965, in near secret, the Colonel started taking meetings with Tom Sarnoff, vice president of NBC's West Coast division. Parker thought Elvis should make a motion picture for television, he told Sarnoff, and after it debuted on the network, he wanted the rights to release it theatrically around the world. The negotiations were long and arduous, and often seemed to stall altogether.

Throughout Elvis's movie years, Parker had fiercely protected the exclusivity to put his client on television, again demonstrating his shrewdness in using the medium. Only once had he had been thwarted. In 1959, he entered into a deal with Irving Kahn, the TelePrompter inventor, for a 100-city closed-circuit television concert to reintroduce Elvis after his return from the army.

Closed-circuit telecasts were commonplace for champion prizefights, but a recording artist had yet to do one, and Parker enjoyed the publicity of the history-making event. But Wallis and Hazen quickly objected, arguing if the paid TV appearance wasn't successful, attendance for Presley's future motion pictures would suffer. Parker scrapped the closed-circuit deal, snippily writing Wallis and Hazen, "I know that both of you must be brokenhearted . . . if there is anything either of you could do to make me feel better, don't hesitate to go to any lengths to achieve this pleasant goal."

From that day, Parker plotted his revenge, drafting long, sabre-rattling letters to the producers whenever they aired one of Presley's films on television. Free showings of any Elvis movie diluted the sales impact of his first-run features, Parker huffed, letting Wallis know that if such practices continued, he "could very well lose the next Presley picture." But what the Colonel really dreaded was interference as he negotiated a big deal with NBC, which, like RCA, was a corporate arm of General Electric.

In October 1967, Sarnoff and the Colonel came together again. This time they talked about a package deal to include Elvis's first TV appearance since the Frank Sinatra special of 1960. Three months later, they agreed on a price: $250,000 for a music special and $850,000 for a feature film plus 50 percent of the profits.

The movie *Charro!*, an offbeat film in the vein of Sergio Leone's so-called spaghetti Westerns, would eventually debut in theaters after all. Though the picture would be a dismal failure, it soothed the actor's ego somewhat. "*Charro!* is the first movie I ever made without singing a song," Presley would tell one of the Colonel's chosen reporters. "I play a gunfighter, and I just couldn't see a singing gunfighter." Ultimately, he would agree to croon the title tune.

For the last year, the Colonel had been rethinking his strategy, trying to find projects to challenge Elvis, to rouse him from his lethargy and depression. With *Easy Come, Easy Go,* Parker had attempted—and failed—to have Wallis cast Elvis in a nonmusical role. And in March of '67, the Colonel wrote to MGM, encouraging the studio to come up with something meaty for the remaining films on Presley's contract—no more bikinis and no more nightclub scenes, "which have been in the last fifteen pictures. . . . I sincerely hope that you are looking in some crystal ball with your people to come up with some good, strong, rugged stories."

Now a televised music special along the lines Sarnoff proposed would let Elvis meet the people eye to eye for his first full-length performance since the U.S.S. *Arizona* concert in 1961. Taped in June 1968, it would air that December for the holiday season.

"Would TV serve to refurbish that old magic, the sort of thing that gave old ladies the vapors and caused young girls to collect the dust from Elvis's car for their memory books?" *TV Guide* asked. Parker thought they would, as did fifty-year-old Bob Finkel, one of four executive producers under exclusive contract to NBC. Sarnoff brought Finkel to the project even before he signed the deal with Parker. Not only had Finkel made his Emmy-winning reputation with variety shows, but more important, Sarnoff believed Finkel might be a match for the High Potentate.

Almost immediately, Parker made him a Snowman—Finkel carried his card in his wallet ("Had to!")—and the two men developed an easy rapport. But Finkel realized that entertaining the Colonel and keeping him distracted from the show would be a full-time job. He also couldn't get past Elvis calling him Mr. Finkel, and needed someone to whom the singer could relate. That's when he placed a call to Binder/Howe Productions, and invited them on board.

Steve Binder was a twenty-one-year-old wise-beyond-his-years producer-director who'd grown up working in his father's Los Angeles gas station. He had a rock-and-roll gut and a primal instinct for what was gold and what was dross, having cut his teeth producing the hip TV music series *Hullabaloo* and *The T.A.M.I. Show,* a 1964 landmark concert film with a virtual who's who of rock, including James Brown and the Rolling Stones. More recently, he'd done a Petula Clark special that spawned a thousand headlines in racially uptight America when Clark exchanged an innocent touch with her guest, Harry Belafonte.

Bones Howe, Binder's business partner and the music supervisor on the shows, was a sound guru, currently producing records for the pop groups the Fifth Dimension and the Association. Years before, he'd worked on a number of Elvis's sessions at Radio Recorders, as the assistant to engineer Thorne Nogar.

Howe remembered what Elvis had been like before Hollywood choked off his ambition, how he produced his own records, listening to stacks of demos over and over, calling for a guitar lick here, a bass thump there, and then danced to his own playbacks turned up loud. He also remembered how much fun Elvis was, flirting with the girls at the stoplight on Sunset Boulevard, rolling down the window just as the light changed, or talking them up the fire escape at the Hollywood Plaza Hotel. Sometimes, he'd flash that crooked grin and invite the teenagers from nearby Hollywood High right into the studio.

Binder and Howe decided the only way to do the special was to create the same relaxed atmosphere in which Elvis made his early records. If they could pull that off, in an interview in which Elvis showed how warm and funny he was, or in a live segment where he just talked about his musical roots, people would see the real Elvis Presley and not the one the Colonel had put on display. Binder told Finkel he was interested only if they could capture the phenomenon of a once-in-a-lifetime personality.

"I wanted Elvis to let the world in on that great big secret," he says, and Finkel agreed.

In May, at Finkel's next meeting with the Colonel, which included representatives of the Singer Sewing Machine Company, the special's only sponsor, Finkel broached the subject of expanding the Christmas theme. He'd like to embrace material from Elvis's long career, he said. Parker approved, as long as a Christmas song closed the program and Elvis controlled the music publishing throughout. Finkel then met with Elvis, and afterward wrote a memo, saying that the singer was excited about the idea, that Elvis would like the "show to depart completely from the pattern of his motion pictures and from everything else he has done. . . . [He] wants everyone to know what he really can do."

Three days later, on May 17, the Colonel invited Binder and Howe for a 7:00 A.M. breakfast at his office at MGM. To stall for time, and to figure how he'd play the relationship (he deliberately mispronounced Binder as "Bindle"), Parker put his staff through the "fire drill" routine—demonstrating how quickly they could pack up the office if the studio heads displeased the Colonel—and showed Howe the scrapbooks he kept as the dogcatcher of Tampa. The trio deliberately steered clear of any conversation about the content of the show, other than Parker's handing Binder an audiotape of a hackneyed Christmas program he routinely supplied to radio.

"This is what I want my boy to do," he said. To Binder, the genius of the Colonel was that he had grown men terrorized all around him. But Binder was emphatic that he needed a one-on-one meeting with Elvis before he committed to the project.

What the producer didn't say was that Elvis was thirty-three years old and no longer the rough-and-ready Hillbilly Cat. In Binder's view, the movies had made Elvis an anachronism in his twenties, as musically relevant to the '60s as Bing Crosby. "There was no blood and guts of this man left." If Elvis could recapture the magnificent essence he once was, he'd enjoy a whole new rejuvenation. Otherwise, with his MGM contract about to expire, he'd be lucky to return to grinding out B movies, this time for second-string studios.

The test came later that day in Binder's office, in what was known as the glass elevator building on Sunset Boulevard in the heart of Hollywood. At first, Binder was caught off-guard by the enormity of Elvis's presence, which he found surprisingly charismatic and unreal. ("You certainly knew . . . that this was a special person . . . his looks were just phenomenally sculptured, without any weak points.") But while he found Elvis dynamic, with a great sense of humor, Binder knew he had to talk straight and find out if the greatest white blues singer could relate to the socially conscious '60s.

To Binder's relief, "we hit it off pretty well. We joked around a lot." Elvis told him he was uncomfortable in television, that he hadn't understood why Steve Allen had made him look silly, singing to a basset hound, and Ed Sullivan had made him seem vulgar, shooting him from the waist up—an idea that Elvis never knew had originated with the Colonel. Binder tried to calm him, saying, "You make a record, and I'll put pictures to it, and you won't have to worry about television." Then the producer eased into the fact that if Elvis didn't do anything else, he would always be remembered as the great rock-and-roll icon of the past. But to the present generation, he was a relic, a man who hadn't placed a record at the top of the record charts in six years. Elvis may have been a highly paid movie star, Binder says in retrospect, but "he was not in the business as far as I was concerned."

If Elvis was nervous that he had been created by the Colonel, Binder saw, "it was my job to let him believe in himself and his talent." Both Binder and Howe knew they couldn't come right out and criticize the Colonel, because Elvis wouldn't have tolerated it. Howe thought, "Elvis probably felt the guy made a pact with the devil, that without the Colonel he would never have gotten there."

On the contrary, the Colonel hadn't been bad for Elvis, Binder allowed. Parker had served his purpose, and he was a marketing genius, though "once he had the stranglehold, he forgot that what he was marketing was built around talent, and manipulated the whole thing with smoke and mirrors." Instead of having somebody pay the Colonel a million dollars to put Elvis in the kind of plastic commercial movies he'd been doing, Binder added, Elvis should give a great director a million dollars to put him in the *right* movie.

"He laughed at that, and said, 'You're right,'" Binder remembers. "He told me he had been burning up inside for years to communicate." But the producer, who knew that Elvis's fear would make him great, also said that television was always a risk—the audience would either see a man who had rediscovered himself or they'd be looking at a has-been. How was Elvis's gut these days? Would he have recorded Jimmy Webb's progressive and poetic "MacArthur Park," for example, if Webb had brought it to him instead of actor Richard Harris?

"Definitely," Elvis said without blinking an eye. That's when Binder knew that Elvis was thinking of the future and not the past. "I felt very, very strongly that the special was Elvis's moment of truth," says Binder, "and that the number-one requirement was honesty." The singer said he was going to Hawaii to get in shape and just relax for a few weeks with his wife and his newborn daugher, Lisa Marie. Binder promised they'd put together a project that they believed in while he was gone.

In the interim, the producers brought in writers Chris Beard and Allan

Blye, who structured the show around the 1909 theater staple *The Blue Bird,* in which a young man leaves home to find happiness, only to return and discover it in his own backyard. Alfred DiScipio, the Singer sewing machine representative, liked the idea and told the Colonel they should go with it, as it was Elvis's story, too, a fact underscored by using snippets of Presley's own music and costume designer Bill Belew's now-famous black leather suit, a brilliant updating of the '50s motorcycle jacket. Elvis never really wore a motorcycle jacket—it was Brando who popularized it in the movie *The Wild One*—but millions of viewers thought he had.

On June 3, Elvis arrived for the start of two weeks of rehearsals at the Binder/Howe offices. "He looked amazing," Binder remembers, suntanned and fourteen pounds lighter from a crash diet. He loved the script, he told them, and then Howe said if they were really going to go in a new direction, he'd like to dispense with Elvis's usual Nashville musicians and bring in some of L.A.'s best session players—guitarists Mike Deasy and Tommy Tedesco and drummer Hal Blaine—who'd enliven him with a fresher sound. No matter what they suggested, Elvis nodded yes, which gave Binder pause: "I wanted him to be not that agreeable and easy to work with—I wanted him to roll up his sleeves and make the show something he contributed to a great deal."

The upbeat mood was shattered barely three days later, when Robert Kennedy was shot in Los Angeles. His murder threw Elvis into an emotional spiral. Already a conspiracy theorist—reinforced, perhaps, by the Colonel's Sam Cooke story—Elvis showed Binder that he was "quite well read" on the subject. "He told me all the books to read—he was convinced it was not Oswald who killed [John] Kennedy, and he was obsessed with the plot to assassinate RFK."

During rehearsals, Binder began to see a dichotomy in Elvis's personality. On his own, or with the guys, Elvis was full of confidence and humor. But in their joint meetings with the Colonel at Burbank's NBC studios, Elvis seemed weak and isolated. He stood with his hands clasped in front of him, his head down. "Elvis was scared to death of the Colonel's power," Binder saw. "He felt shamed. He was very, very submissive." The producer took note of it as he rolled out his ideas to Parker—he'd like to do some choreographed production numbers with a dance troupe, a straight-ahead concert segment in an arena format, and probably a gospel sequence.

Now the Colonel, who had dangled the carrot of naming Binder as the director of Elvis's next motion picture *Charro!,* seemed not so amenable.

"I think what pissed him off more than anything about me is that I wasn't one of his lackeys," Binder remembers.

"Whenever Parker basically told me that I couldn't do what I was doing, the Colonel would look at Elvis and say, 'Right, Elvis?' And Elvis would say, 'Yes, Colonel.' And Parker would say, 'So Steve, we aren't going to do that, are we?' And I'd say, 'If that's what Elvis wants, then we won't do it.' And then we would walk out of the office, and Elvis would lighten up and jab me in the ribs and say, 'We *are* going to do it. To hell with Colonel Parker.' But he never did stand up to him in front of me."

Once the rehearsals shifted to NBC, Bob Finkel, or Finkels, as Parker called him, did his best to keep the Colonel "happy and in tune," playing liar's poker with him, and engaging in a series of pranks. When the Colonel presented Finkel with an autographed photo of himself in a Confederate uniform, Finkel donned a ridiculously large hat and had himself photographed in an Admiral Hornblower outfit, with a sword at his side and a ribbon across his chest. He signed the picture, "To Colonel Tom Parker from Commander Bob Finkel."

The executive producer showed up at work one day to find his office, as well as Parker's, guarded by men from the William Morris office dressed as Buckingham Palace guards, with red jackets and furry hats. "They wouldn't laugh, they wouldn't smile, and they wouldn't let me in my own door," Finkel remembers. "The Colonel was peeping around the corner." A week later, Finkel was preparing to go home when he discovered that his office door had been duct-taped shut from the outside.

Binder and Howe, who were also represented by the Morris agency, were horrified by Parker's humiliation of the young agent-trainees, and at his gall in having himself "guarded" like royalty. But Finkel put up with it all because it kept Parker away from Binder, "who would have died on this show if the Colonel had continued to harass him."

Finkel had also become fond of Parker, whom he called Tom. He'd heard about his immigration problems and knew that the latest movie contracts specified no foreign location shooting. Binder said maybe Interpol was looking for him and the Colonel feared arrest. Finkel couldn't quite imagine that, but he realized Parker was in a quandary. He couldn't take Elvis to Europe because "something prevented him from going through the gate," and he wouldn't let any other promoter take Presley overseas because "he was afraid Elvis would run away."

On the other hand, Finkel believed the Colonel was misunderstood ("I knew a side of him that many people didn't know"), and that he was a better person than he got credit for being. He saw it in the way he cared for his wife, Marie, whom he visited on weekends in Palm Springs. The month before, she had undergone the first of two hip replacement surgeries, and Parker kept nurses at her side around the clock.

"One day, I said, 'Tom, you've been pulling pranks on me all through this escapade,'" Finkel remembers. "'I'm going to do something to you, and I think it'll be the best trick. I'm going to trust you to decide, because you are an honest man. But if you think I topped you, I want your cane.' And he said, 'You've got it.'"

In mid-June, the group faced its first major crisis over the firing of Billy Strange, the one person Elvis had requested on the project. Strange, the show's musical director, had cowritten the song "Memories," a keynote ballad, which set a poignant tone. But his scheduling conflicts kept him from coming up with arrangements in a timely manner. He and Binder argued about it, and when he taunted the producer ("You can't fire me"), Binder replaced him with Billy Goldenberg, Barbra Streisand's former musical accompanist, who had also worked on *Hullabaloo*.

Goldenberg would ultimately change the direction of Elvis's music, creating a sophisticated new sound in moving the singer from a small rhythm section to a thirty-nine-piece orchestra. But at the time, the Colonel was not pleased with Strange's removal, especially as a song he cowrote with Mac Davis, "A Little Less Conversation," would help promote Elvis's movie *Live a Little, Love a Little* when the film was released in late fall. Parker cornered Binder and told him he was going to pull the plug on his job, and furthermore, there could be no special because Elvis would never accept the fact that Strange was gone. Even Finkel's intervention did not cool the Colonel down.

"There was a day of tremendous pressures and tension," Binder remembers. Goldenberg wasn't convinced that he and Elvis could find common musical ground. ("I'm a Jewish kid from New York who grew up on Broadway. What am I doing playing 'Hound Dog'?") And while Elvis accepted the reason for Strange's dismissal, he wasn't sure he wanted anyone tampering with his sound. It scared him nearly senseless when he walked into the studio and saw the horns and the strings, and he called Binder aside and told him he had to promise to send everybody home if he didn't like it. Binder gave him his word, and finally, both Elvis and Goldenberg took a leap of faith.

"When Elvis heard the first note of the session at Western Recorders, he loved it," Binder says. "He had his sunglasses on and was standing next to Billy on the podium, and he looked into the control booth at me and gave me the high sign, like, 'We're going to be okay.' He just fell out, and he never once questioned anything that we did musically. That was the one moment when he knew it would all come together."

By now, Elvis had literally moved into the NBC studios, the staff converting the dressing rooms into sleeping quarters. At the end of each day, Binder and Finkel were fascinated to watch Elvis jam and cut up with his buddies Charlie Hodge, Joe Esposito, and Alan Fortas, an overgrown sweetheart who reminded Binder of the character Lenny in the novel *Of Mice and Men*.

In contrast, Howe found it boring. "Music was [Elvis's] most interesting side—the rest was just a bunch of guys hanging out in a room telling jokes. I mean, how smart were those guys?" But Finkel saw the interaction as comedic: "If Elvis put his hands on his hips, two guys in back of him put their hands on their hips." Binder thought they were all spies for the Colonel, but he also saw something else. "I wanted to capture in almost a documentary what was going on inside the man." If he could sneak a camera into the dressing room and photograph that informality and playfulness, the audience would get a glimpse of an intimate Elvis that no one beyond his family and entourage had ever seen.

"Absolutely not," Parker said, vetoing the idea. But eventually he weakened and gave Binder the right to re-create it, thus inspiring the now-famous "improv" section of the special in which Elvis sits in a boxing ring of a stage with Hodge and musicians Scotty Moore and D. J. Fontana. When Presley balked at the idea of telling stories about his early years ("I'm not sure it's . . . a good idea . . . What if I can't think of anything to say?"), Binder and Allan Blye made a list of topics they'd heard him talk about in private and threw in a question about modern music to update his image. Fortas was also added to help Elvis feel at home.

The Colonel no longer seemed to have dust in his heart, but a larger test came when Binder presented Elvis with a new song, "If I Can Dream." The producer wanted to close the show with something that made a statement about how Elvis felt about the world, youth, and the Vietnam War. For that, he needed a big, idealistic, and emotional ballad that showed the core of the man who had reacted so solemnly to the shootings of Robert Kennedy and Martin Luther King Jr., a man who had grown up in the prejudiced South, "but who was really above all that."

Songwriter Earl Brown stayed up all night conjuring it, and the next day, Binder had Brown and Goldenberg go to Elvis's dressing room and play it for him. "That's a hit song," Howe said. Elvis thought it might be a little too Broadway the way Billy rendered it, and Bones said, "You can do it with a real bluesy feel."

"Let me hear it again," Elvis said. Billy played it seven or eight times, and Elvis looked up. "Okay, I'll do it."

Elsewhere in the building, the Colonel stiffened like a flatiron, telling Finkel, "Over my dead body will Elvis sing an original song at the end of the show! We had a deal for a Christmas song!" Finkel argued that the script had evolved into a different concept, and now there was no need for a Christmas song. "Plus we got Elvis to take a stand. That in itself was a miracle."

Finally, the Colonel said that the song could stay, even though it wasn't "Elvis Presley material." But, Binder recalls, Parker "instantly" had the copyright registered to protect the publishing. "That was all he was interested in." Once recording started, Parker stationed Freddy Bienstock at the studio to make sure no one interfered with song selection, and Bienstock instructed Lamar Fike, by then a Hill and Range employee, to pick up deals on anything he could.

However, the Colonel still lobbied for a Christmas song somewhere in the program. Finkel says Parker's arrogance wasn't exactly carved in stone—he thought a traditional carol would appeal to more conservative viewers, and he was pondering a new holiday album somewhere down the line. Perhaps he'd also argued out of contract obligation—he'd given his word to Tom Sarnoff that this would be a holiday special, something Sarnoff was willing to ignore. But mostly, Binder holds, his insistence lay in splintering spite; Parker savored a taste of victory.

"In my last meeting with the Colonel, Bob and I were asked to go up to Sarnoff's office," he explains. "They said, 'The Colonel's telling us that we cannot air the show unless we have a Christmas song in it.'" Binder listened quietly. All the songs Parker suggested were threadbare standards, tunes Perry Como might have done. The old man glared at the young producer through antediluvian slits, his energy vehement.

"The Colonel just sat there staring at me, and instead of avoiding his eyes, I stared right back at him. I remember our eyes just locked on each other, and I said, 'Are you *ordering* me to put a Christmas song in the show, or are you *asking* me to put a Christmas song in the show?' In essence, it was 'ordering,' and that's how 'Blue Christmas' got added to the improv. His will was so strong that I think he felt in his heart of hearts he could will anybody into anything."

On June 23, Elvis prerecorded "If I Can Dream" in several fervent

takes. To Howe and Binder, it was a staggering moment, an almost religious resurrection. Howe put him out on the floor with a hand mike, and
he sang the song in front of the string section, complete with knee drops.
"The string players were sitting there with their mouths open," Howe remembers. "They had never seen anything like this."

Yet the more extraordinary performance came later, when the producers sent everybody home, and Elvis rerecorded the vocal in the dark, so
engulfed in the emotion he ended up writhing on the cement floor, down
on his side, in a fetal position. After four takes, he went into the control
room, and Binder played the recording back for him fifteen times in a
row. Elvis listened with the fascination of a man who was hearing the
sound of his own rebirth.

Early in the project, the Colonel told Binder he'd never interfere when
things were going well. "On the outside," says Binder, "the Colonel was
very unhappy with what was happening. But being a good businessman,
once he realized that Elvis had bought into what we wanted to do, there's
no doubt that he saw we were on to something special and he shouldn't
rock the boat."

In fact, Parker was more cognizant than Binder imagined. The show
had intrinsic value as a program that would also sell albums. But the
Colonel had all along planned for the event to be a springboard for the
next phase of Elvis's career. Largely on the strength of the television special, Parker would make his client the highest-paid performer in Las
Vegas. "The only way he could set it up was to show how Elvis would
perform with a group behind him," says Lamar Fike. "That's why
Colonel envisioned the special."

On June 25, with an eye toward building Elvis's new public profile,
Parker, in a bright blue sport shirt and Tyrolean hat, presented his refur-
bished attraction to fifty visiting TV editors at an evening press conference on NBC's Rehearsal Stage 3.

One reporter wondered if Elvis's curving sideburns wouldn't be "old
hat in this day of the post-Beatle. . . . He suggests a nice boy trying to be
pleasant." But once the Colonel cracked a few jokes to set the mood, the
singer, making a grand entrance in an electric blue shirt, black pants,
leather wristbands, and "a diamond ring as big as a Ping-Pong ball," captivated the room. Why was Elvis doing TV? "We figured it was about
time—before I grow too old." Had he changed? "No, but I pick my material more carefully." Were small towns the backbone of his audience?
"Yes, ma'am. I've never done well in big cities."

Elvis was smiling, but under his breath, the producers heard him mutter, "Oh, wow! Not that one again." Soon the Colonel sprung him in full pitchman's style—"Right over here, folks, get your picture taken with Elvis"—and then the big man stood aside to avoid the rush.

The following day, June 26, was Parker's fifty-ninth birthday. Finkel arranged a party on the set with a big cake, but the others had a more pointed surprise. Writers Chris Beard and Allan Blye, privy to the Binder-Parker feud, wrote a parody of "It Hurts Me," with lyrics including "The whole town is talking, they're calling me a fool for listening to Binder's same old lies," and ending with the Colonel's rote complaint: "Is it too much to ask for one lousy, tired Christmas song?" Elvis sang it to him amid peals of laughter.

It was a crucial moment, a public humiliation and stunning defeat, delivered in the bright wrappings of celebration. Binder had won his duel with the Colonel, and after wresting control of Elvis away from Parker, the producer had given it back to the artist himself. Now Elvis made a mockery of the man who had guided his every move.

"I have no proof to back it up," says Binder, "but I felt the Colonel had the magic power. And I believe that before Elvis did anything, the Colonel would take him quietly into a room and use his amateur hypnotism talent on him. Elvis was very insecure. But fifteen minutes later, he would come out oozing confidence, convinced that he was the greatest performer who ever walked on the stage."

The problem was that Elvis had now met a better hypnotist.

During the next few days, Billy Goldenberg came in to watch some of the taping, and invariably passed by Parker's broom closet of an office. The arranger was surprised to see the Colonel always sitting alone, leaning on his cane, never joining Elvis and the guys, or huddling with his client except before a performance. In fact, he'd never witnessed one affectionate exchange between them.

"Every time I walked by, the Colonel would say, 'Come on in, boy, and let's talk a little bit,'" Goldenberg remembers. "I'd been told he was the most terrible man in the world, but I liked him. I used to go right in and smile. I wouldn't say that underneath I knew how kind he was, because he never talked about himself. But it didn't seem real, any of it. He always reminded me of the characters that Sidney Greenstreet or Burl Ives or Orson Welles played—he was all those people put together. It was like he was playing a game of some sort, putting on the whole world."

Indeed, Parker had a particularly onerous prank in store for Goldenberg and the rest of the team. On June 27, a day after the Colonel's belittling birthday event, Elvis rehearsed the gospel medley, taped an amusement park scene early in the afternoon, and then retired to his dressing room to rest before his two one-hour sets in front of a live audience that evening. But when show time drew near and only twenty-five people lined up outside, the head of guest relations alerted a frenzied staff. Parker had insisted on receiving all 328 tickets for each show and distributing them to a typical Elvis audience ("You want the blond bouffant hairdo"), flying fans in from all across the country if need be.

Now it was clear he had inexcusably bungled the ticket distribution, and Binder believed it was out of pure malevolence, since the Colonel had made him promise he wouldn't use the improv if he didn't like it. The staff went scrambling, calling a radio station to jump on the air with the news that seats were still available, and running across the street to Bob's Big Boy restaurant to hustle up an audience.

A second crisis fell when Elvis panicked shortly before the six o'clock taping, saying he felt "sheer terror" that he might freeze once he got out on stage. Only once had Binder seen him depressed, when Finkel told him they might need to lighten his hair ("Do you think my hair's too black?" Elvis asked incredulously). But now, "he sat in that makeup chair and literally trembled, just really sweated," Howe recalls. "He said, 'What am I going to do if they don't like me?'" Binder forced him to make the effort as a personal favor: "If you get out there and you have nothing to say, and you can't remember a song, then say 'thank you' and come back. But you've got to go out there."

In his first real performance in seven years, Elvis hit a level he had not found since his seminal Sun recordings. Although visibly nervous—his hand shook at the start—he joked and bantered about the highlights of his career in a way that both revalidated his achievements and rendered him fresh. And when he launched into the rockabilly and blues that fueled the engine of his life, his energy blazed raw, stark, and palpable, his voice showing a tough exuberance, his looks telegraphing a hint of cruelty. By the time he taped the arena segment two days later, he'd summoned such confidence that he resembled not so much a man, but a panther, feral in his sleek black leather suit, growling, groaning, shaking, and strutting across the stage.

The beauty of the special was in watching the metamorphosis take shape. But there may have been more to it. After the first performance, when Howe remembers they had to peel the suit away—"nobody had thought that he'd be so soaking wet you couldn't get it off"—costumer

Bill Belew reported to Binder that they had a problem. Elvis had experienced a sexual emission on stage. "That," says Binder, "is when I really believed that Parker planted the seed through hypnotism that Elvis was the greatest sex symbol who ever existed. I don't think he could have built himself up to have an orgasm unless there was a stimuli there to drive him to do that. I just felt it was not a normal act."

Today, the production numbers—including a bordello scene that a corporate censor ordered cut but was later aired and restored for home video—seem dated. But the live segments still sizzle and stand among the finest music of Elvis's career. His performance of "If I Can Dream," delivered against a backdrop of electric red letters spelling out ELVIS, is a portrait of a man saving his own life.

When the special, "Singer Presents ELVIS," aired on December 3, 1968, the majority of critics raved about the return of an authentic American original, some finding poignancy in the performance. "There is something magical about watching a man who has lost himself find his way back home," Jon Landau wrote in *Eye* magazine. The program was the number-one show of the season, capturing 42 percent of the viewing audience and giving NBC its biggest ratings triumph of the year. Its soundtrack would soar to number eight on *Billboard*'s pop album chart.

Binder and Howe had hoped to have production points on the soundtrack, but no one had provided for potential royalties in the producers' contract because Parker insisted from the beginning that there wouldn't be an album. And when Howe brought it up to Parker while Elvis was in Hawaii, "Diskin started a whole tirade about how we were hired not by them, but by NBC to produce a television special, and 'We're not discussing records at all.' We got calls from NBC saying, 'What are you trying to do, sabotage the show?'"

Parker continued to adamantly deny the existence of a soundtrack album until the day of its release, though late in May, four days after Binder and Howe first proposed the idea to him, he had gotten NBC's agreement to turn over the audiotapes of the show to RCA without charge, a deal that would have amounted to millions of dollars in music rights. In the end, Elvis got a free album—paid for out of the budget of the special—and the producers received credit for the show, if not the recording, on the back of the album.

"That was the only argument I had with Colonel Parker," says Finkel. "He didn't want any of the Elvis mystique to be eroded by a producer." So much so that after the trade magazines posted credits for Binder and

Howe with the first number-one single, their names suddenly disappeared from future listings—a directive, believes Binder, from the Colonel to RCA to threaten to pull its magazine advertising. Binder returned Parker's check for $1,500 for all rights and shook his head in the memory of the Colonel's early promise—"You guys are going to have a million-dollar experience"—his way of compensating for the producer's meager salary of $15,000.

In a sense, the Colonel was right. There was no way for Binder to measure the satisfaction of seeing Elvis come back to life as an artist. When they'd screened the whole show after the first edit—ninety minutes, which Binder pared to an hour for broadcast—Elvis laughed and applauded along with the staff, and then asked if he could see it again, alone with Binder. "He watched it three more times, and he said, 'Steve, I will never sing a song that I don't believe in, and I will never make a movie that I don't believe in. I want to do really great things from your new things.'"

Elvis had always reminded Binder of Hamlet, sequestered in his castle of Graceland, with everyone around him for a purpose. Now he let the words sink in, and offered Elvis a new challenge. "I hear you, Elvis," he said prophetically, "but I don't know if you're strong enough to do that." The singer was taken aback, and Binder explained that Elvis's "sense of loyalty was confused with whether he should or shouldn't do things based on his own integrity," and that he was probably still weak when it came to challenging the Colonel's business machine. Earlier in the day, Binder, who during rehearsals walked Elvis out on Sunset Boulevard to prove it was possible for him to enjoy a degree of normalcy, had invited Elvis to a pizza-and-beer gathering that afternoon at Bill Belew's apartment. "I can't go," Elvis had said, to which Binder replied, "Why not?" Now, as they left the screening room, Elvis told Binder he wanted to go to Belew's after all.

They sped off to Hollywood in Binder's yellow Mustang convertible—the Memphis Mafia following behind in a Lincoln Continental—only to arrive at Belew's apartment and find no one there. It was an awkward moment ("the look on Elvis's face . . ."), and soon they went their separate ways. But back in the screening room, Elvis had scribbled down his private phone number and asked Binder to stay in touch. More than once, the producer called and left messages, but "they were always intercepted. The walls came down immediately. The Colonel wasn't about to let him get out into the real world. It was tragic."

From the beginning of their association, Parker had been afraid that someone younger and more in tune with Elvis's creativity might come along and pose the ultimate threat to his power and control. Always before, the Colonel had been able to huff and puff and stare down an adversary, but Binder had terrified him. Not only could he relate to Presley as Parker never had, but Binder knew what slumbering promise still lay within Elvis ("There's no limit to where he can go if he has the material") and had the psychological leverage to help that talent flourish. Parker saw that he must guard against Binder's interference with the same ferocity he used to keep his dark secrets at bay. Elvis's success was not only his livelihood. It was his life.

Parker would never admit to nearly being toppled, but he would concede to being topped. When the Colonel returned to Palm Springs a day or so after taping ended, he found the towering, electric red letters spelling ELVIS set up and flashing on his front lawn, a generator humming Finkel's glee. The Colonel, always honoring a deal, wrapped up his cane with a note, "To Commander Bob Finkel from Colonel Tom Parker."

The Snowman was melting.

17

LAS VEGAS:

GLITZ, GREED, AND RUINATION

SIXTEEN days after the comeback special aired in December 1968, the Colonel finalized the deal to take Elvis into the soon-to-be-built International Hotel, a $60-million resort palace that owner Kerkor "Kirk" Kerkorian promised would be an oasis of tastefulness on the Vegas desert of glitz and greed.

Kerkorian's ties to the town went back to the postwar years, when he began operating a flying service to scurry gamblers from California to Nevada. Eventually, with a personal fortune of $100 million from the sale of his Trans International Airlines, Kerkorian began buying casinos, acquiring the Flamingo to use as a training ground for the staff that would run his dream hotel, the International.

To book the acts for the International's 2,000-seat showroom—the largest in town—executive vice president Alex Shoofey tapped Bill Miller, the most respected entertainment director since Jack Entratter.

At the Flamingo, where Shoofey and Miller worked hand-in-glove, Miller brought in everyone from Sandler and Young to Tom Jones. Now for a high-profile act to open the International, he presented five names for Shoofey and the department heads to vote on, including Jones, Frank Sinatra, and Barbra Streisand, who had just won an Academy Award for *Funny Girl.*

But Miller had wanted Presley since Parker brought him into the Frontier in '56 ("I made up my mind when I saw him at the time, I'm going to get Elvis") and, through Abe Lastfogel, learned that he might be able to make a deal.

Miller called Parker at his office at MGM and set up a meeting. The Colonel wouldn't hear of his client going into a new room—too many potential problems with sound and lighting and other bugs to work out. So Miller signed Streisand, and then went back to Parker to see about booking Elvis to follow. "He said, 'That's great,'" as the veteran entertainment director remembers, and the wheels were in motion.

Next the Colonel met with Shoofey. During his years at the Sahara and the Flamingo, Shoofey, who brought his team along every time he assumed the head of a new hotel, had earned the nickname "the Cleaver." Knowing full well that he was in line to become president and director of the International, he watched his every step. And every penny. Of course, the hotel wanted Elvis, he told the Colonel, but Presley was unproven as a stage act after so many years in Hollywood, and especially in Vegas, where he hadn't appeared in twelve years.

"Elvis was a question mark, to tell you the truth," remembers Nick Naff, the hotel's former advertising director, who had also come over from the Flamingo. But the Colonel, set on outmaneuvering Shoofey for the best deal, convinced him that the town had never seen the kind of business his client would draw.

"You're going to find out what an opening is like when Elvis comes in," Parker boasted, closing his pitch. "They'll come from all over the world." Shoofey raised a thick eyebrow, pondered the notion, and then nodded.

And so they began to hammer out the details, with the rumor floating through town that Milton Prell, Shoofey's old boss at the Sahara, had really been the one to broker the deal for the Colonel. "Prell got money from the mob for putting the deal together," says one longtime Vegas insider.

In July 1969, Elvis would begin a four-week engagement at the International showroom, performing two shows a night, seven nights a week. No other entertainer had ever committed to such a punishing routine; most usually enjoyed Monday or Tuesday night off. As compensation for such an all-out run, Parker demanded $100,000 a week, out of which Elvis and the Colonel would pay the musicians and backup vocalists. "Mark my words," Parker said. "Elvis will be the first star in Las Vegas to make money for the showroom, apart from whatever his fans drop out in the casino. You'll never have an empty seat," he added. "I can promise you that."

Shoofey, a long-faced Canadian with a degree in business administration from St. John's University, mulled it over and ran the numbers. The International would want an option for a second appearance. But Parker had his needs, too, including complimentary suites at the hotel for both Elvis and him and the right to film a concert documentary. Shoofey agreed. Then the two shook hands, and Parker lined up the publicity pictures, in which Elvis posed signing his "contract" at the International's construction site, with Shoofey and Miller flanking him in hard hats. It was only for show—Elvis would sign the official contract in April. But the photograph was historic. Never again would the Colonel give the hotel such access to his star.

The picture would become a prized possession for Bruce Banke, Nick Naff's assistant and the executive assigned to look after the Colonel. ("Actually, I think I was about the third one, and I was the one that stuck.") Banke would deliver Elvis's weekly paychecks, order the big floral arrangements Parker placed in the hotel foyer each holiday, and be at the Colonel's constant beck and call. In return, Parker treated him with unusual affection. "We were very close. I loved that man. He was like a father to me."

In securing Elvis's comeback in Las Vegas, the greatest carnival midway of all, Parker hoped to achieve two goals: to feed the ferocious beast that had become his gambling habit, and to reinvent and validate Presley to a new generation, building on the entertainer's renewed popularity from the television special. The money from Vegas couldn't touch what Elvis would make on the road, but first Parker needed to generate sizzle about Presley's return to live performance.

Elvis himself was more concerned with following through on his promise to Steve Binder—to restore his credibility as an artist. To that end, he took the advice of Memphis Mafia member Marty Lacker to make his next album not in Nashville, with its factorylike approach to recording, but in Memphis, at Chips Moman's American Studios. Elvis hadn't recorded in his hometown since the Sun years, and Moman was renowned for his soulful cache of studio musicians and his hit-making synthesis of pop and rhythm and blues. The combination, Lacker thought, just might help provide the magic to keep Elvis focused and inspired in the studio. Presley agreed and, during the first two months of 1969, recorded some of his most enduring music, including "Suspicious Minds," "Kentucky Rain," and "In the Ghetto."

However, from the beginning, the project was fraught with tension, as both the label and Hill and Range grumbled at the arrangement. RCA policy dictated that all of its artists record in the company's own studios, using only RCA staff producers. Parker backed Elvis's request to record

in Memphis, but sent Tom Diskin to the session, where RCA producer
Felton Jarvis and label veep Harry Jenkins huddled together. Freddy
Bienstock and Lamar Fike, the gatekeepers for Hill and Range, were
equally watchful, knowing that Chips was also a songwriter and music
publisher and that Lacker, who moonlighted as a song plugger and often
worked with Moman, had been encouraging Presley to reach beyond the
tired Hill and Range repertoire to keep pace with the innovative rockers
of the '60s.

Moman, who had produced more than one hundred hit singles, knew
that his reputation was on the line with the Presley session. And while
"Kentucky Rain," a Hill and Range song by up and coming writer Eddie
Rabbitt, seemed a good choice, Moman found the majority of the songs
that Bienstock and Fike presented sorely lacking. "There were a lot of
bad songs in there," he recalls, "and I told them that if I had to cut all of
those Hill and Range songs, I didn't want to do it."

Only days before the first session, songwriter Mac Davis had brought
Moman a song that mirrored the social consciousness of the times.
Moman knew that Elvis had never recorded anything as controversial as
"In the Ghetto," but the song built on the humanitarian spirit of "If I Can
Dream," and the producer thought it a perfect statement for a man
whose music was rooted in black culture.

"He liked the song," Moman remembers. "But after we cut it, there
was a big discussion about whether it would be right for his image. Of
course, back at that time, the racial thing was still hot and heavy."

Freddy Bienstock had another consideration, since the Aberbachs
didn't control the publishing, and inquired whether Mac Davis would be
willing to give up part of "In the Ghetto" for Elvis to record the song.
Such a practice rankled the producer ("I just thought that was wrong"),
and while Davis conceded, Moman was not about to relinquish even a
fraction of two songs in his own publishing company, "Mama Liked the
Roses" and the spectacular "Suspicious Minds," which Elvis had already
laid down on tape. A confrontation quickly ensued.

"I wasn't angry about it," remembers Freddy Bienstock. "Those sessions were very good. I would become aware of what songs Elvis wanted
to do, and if the publishing rights were available, I would pick them up.
'Suspicious Minds' was more difficult [to obtain] than 'In the Ghetto,'
because 'Suspicious Minds' had been recorded before. [But] Chips and I
became friends."

Moman remembers it differently. "Their deal was that they weren't going to record any song that they didn't have the publishing on. I was ready to erase the tapes and just let it go. I ended the session and sent the musicians home and asked all of the Elvis people to leave my studio."

As tempers flared, Tom Diskin walked over to the phone and dialed his boss. If Moman wouldn't cooperate, Parker told his lieutenant, they'd either go around him or dismiss him altogether. But RCA's Harry Jenkins recognized that "Suspicious Minds" could be a career record for Elvis and took it upon himself to mediate the situation at the next day's session.

"In all the years that I have been involved with Elvis," Jenkins told the group, "I've never opened my mouth about songs or anything else. But that boy [Moman] is right, and we are going to finish this session however he wants to do it."

That August, "Suspicious Minds" became Elvis's first number-one single in seven years, and the last he would ever have. The American Studios sessions would spawn two albums, the first, *From Elvis in Memphis,* garnering a lead review in *Rolling Stone* magazine. But Parker saw only that Chips Moman had challenged his way of doing business, even as Felton Jarvis altered the producer's recording of "Suspicious Minds" by adding "live" horns and a false fadeout at the end. Like Steve Binder, Moman would be banished forever. When Elvis requested that Parker hire Moman's studio band to back him during his upcoming appearance in Vegas, Diskin replied that the group was unavailable.

In July, Elvis flew to Los Angeles to begin working up his show with a small group of handpicked musicians. Later, he would add the International's thirty-eight-piece orchestra, led by Bobby Morris, and two vocal groups—the Sweet Inspirations, a black female vocal quartet that had backed Aretha Franklin and recorded with Moman, and the Imperials, the male gospel quartet Presley had long admired. As he'd done before the TV special, Elvis slacked off the pharmaceuticals and toned his body, hoping to be in peak physical condition for his grueling performance schedule.

Parker, meanwhile, became a constant presence at the hotel. In between readying the advertising blitz for Elvis's engagement, he could usually be found in the hotel's casino, or playing the ponies in the race book.

In fact, Parker operated as if he owned the place. Slipping into the mode of advance man, he commanded complete control of the promotion, with the hotel footing the bill.

"The campaign that he produced was unbelievable," remembers Shoofey. "He had every billboard in the entire city, not only in Vegas, but leading all the way to California."

And while Parker left the print ads to the hotel, he fiercely oversaw every detail of the radio spots, many of which lasted only twenty seconds. "I did the commercials personally under the Colonel's supervision, but [it was really] more the supervision under the Colonel's dictation," says Naff. "He insisted only the word *Elvis* be used in the entire commercial, except to tag it at the end where and when he was appearing. So [it was just] 'Elvis! Elvis! Elvis!' What he tried to do was virtually blanket [Las Vegas] with the fact that Elvis was in town."

Naff was often embarrassed by the Colonel's personal style and found his advertising "schlocky as all hell." Once when Parker requested a particular ad spot that Naff considered beneath the hotel's dignity, he took it upon himself to write a more upscale commercial and planned to sneak on the air. "I would listen to the commercials in my office, and lo and behold, the Colonel was passing by my doorway and heard it. He walked in and made me change the whole thing. He wanted everything to be the Colonel's way."

But no one could dispute that Parker's way worked. "We got calls from all over the world," says Shoofey, whose office was decorated with a gift from Parker, an artificial plant deemed the "snowtree," with cotton balls glued on its branches. "We couldn't accept all the reservations."

"The closing night of Barbra," remembers Bill Miller, "we had a big party. At five or six in the morning, my wife and I went to bed. We went downstairs and the lobby was jam-packed. They were standing three blocks away to get in to see Elvis that night. And that's the way it stayed."

As soon as Streisand ended her engagement, Parker began working into the thin hours of the night to transform the elegant International, with its imported marble walls, into something out of Barnum and Bailey. Though Shoofey held his tongue, Naff was horrified to discover a laddered crew plastering Elvis posters "just all over the goddamned place. Unbelievable."

The Imperials' Joe Moscheo was equally stunned. "There were banners and flags and stand-ups of Elvis in the lobby, and everybody who worked for the hotel was wearing straw hats with an Elvis plaque on the front." Even the casino dealers were ordered to don the promotional chapeaus, as well as red, white, and blue armbands festooned with the word *Elvis*. "They looked like riverboat gamblers," says Moscheo. "Honestly, it was a very strange atmosphere."

Parker considered it one of his most impressive promotional campaigns. But to temper the vulgarity, he promised the money from the souvenirs he sold from a booth in front of the hotel would go to a charity of Naff's choice.

"I don't have to tell you how much went to charity and how much went to the Colonel," says Naff. "It was a profit-making business." What particularly galled the advertising director was the $125 sale of an Elvis portrait in a carved wood frame that bore the label RENALDO OF ITALY. In truth, says Naff, "those frames were made by an employee of ours in the carpenter shop in the basement of the hotel. *He* was the famous Renaldo of Italy."

Still, Naff found Parker to be "a very likable guy, not the kind who irritated people in his demands." One morning, at the height of the Elvis engagement, Naff was delighted to receive a crate of "fresh, gorgeous red strawberries" as a gift. "At the end of the day, I was taking them to my car, and I chanced to pass by the Colonel. He said, 'Hey, Nick, what have you got there?' I said, 'I've got these beautiful strawberries!' And he said, 'Send them up to my room.' Now, he did it in a very smiling way, so I didn't resent it. But I had to stop and think, What's more important, my association with the Colonel, or the strawberries? So I lost them. Oh, he loved strawberries."

While Parker reveled in the merriment of Elvis's opening, the star himself wrestled with a serious case of stage fright and depended on Charlie Hodge to help him with pacing and song selection. Soon Elvis would tell Ray Connolly of *The London Evening Standard,* "I've wanted to perform on the stage again for the last nine years, and it's been building inside of me . . . until the strain became intolerable." But once he moved rehearsals to Las Vegas, Presley began to have his doubts. Catching the end of Barbra Streisand's engagement, he whispered to Hodge that the International looked like a "helluva big stage to fill."

In the days before his July 31 debut, Elvis suffered debilitating panic attacks, one of which lasted until he took the stage at 10:15, following opening sets from the Sweet Inspirations and comedian Sammy Shore. Now thirty-four, Elvis worried if his voice would hold up during such a long engagement. Never had he delivered a full-hour set, and especially not twice a night, though this evening he would be called on to give just one all-important performance.

If he flopped, word would travel fast—not only had fans come in from as far away as Europe and Asia, but the Colonel and Kerkorian had filled the invitation-only audience with such celebrities as Cary Grant, Carol Channing, Wayne Newton, Paul Anka, Fats Domino, and Elvis's old

flame Ann-Margret. In addition, a large contingent of press was in attendance, many of whom Parker had flown in on Kerkorian's private jet.

But when he finally took the stage, Presley hid his nervousness in the
bravado of the rock-and-roll beat. Dressed in a Bill Belew karate-inspired
Cossack costume with macramé belt, he gave the crowd everything he
had, falling to his knees, sliding across the stage, even turning a cartwheel
in a display of boundless energy. The celebrity audience shouted its approval and stayed on its feet for most of the repertoire, which ranged
from early chestnuts like "Blue Suede Shoes" and "Love Me Tender" to
his latest material from the Memphis sessions. Afterward, even hardened
pit bosses commented they'd never seen such excitement.

When the Colonel visited Elvis backstage afterward, he had tears in his
eyes. In the rarest of sights, Parker clasped his arms around his client and
then left to join Alex Shoofey in the coffee shop.

One person who couldn't get back to congratulate the star was Steve
Binder. Parker had excluded him from the guest list, and after the show,
the director went to the stage door guard. "I said, 'Would you please tell
Elvis that Steve Binder's here?' And he got on the phone and [then] said,
'Sorry.'" It would be more than thirty years before Binder would learn
that Elvis had been asking for him.

The Colonel had made a point to invite Bob Finkel, the producer of the
'68 special, who, on the day of the show, was flabbergasted to see Parker
wearing a straw hat and peddling Elvis's albums from under his arm in
the casino. As the Colonel's pal, Finkel rated a special treat—a private
visit with Elvis upstairs in his suite after the performance. Joe Esposito
briefed Presley as to their arrival, and then escorted Finkel and his wife,
Jane, to the private elevator that would deliver them to Elvis's quarters.
The singer, however, had retreated into a world of his own.

"We went up there and the elevator door opened," Finkel remembers,
"and the suite was pitch-black, except for the light from the television
set. There was a Western on, and Elvis was sitting there all alone. After
everything we'd gone through together, all he said was, 'Hi, Bob.' And
then he fired at the television set with a pistol. It scared the shit out of me,
and Jane and I got back in the elevator and went down."

By this time, sitting in the hotel coffee shop, Parker and Shoofey,
now the International's president, had roughed out the terms for a new
contract on a pink tablecloth stained brown with coffee. Foreseeing
that Elvis's would be a record-breaking Vegas engagement (grossing
$1,522,635, with an attendance of 101,500), the hotel, Shoofey said,

would boost Elvis's salary to $125,000 a week and extend its option for two engagements a year for the next five years. Parker asked him to throw in a little present—a trip to Hawaii for Elvis and eight companions. Shoofey smiled, and the two shook hands.

The Colonel had again hit his magic figure of $1 million. But Shoofey was astonished that Parker hadn't asked for a sliding scale, considering how much business Elvis brought to the hotel and its beckoning casinos. In fact, the Colonel had negotiated like a novice.

"He says, 'Now tell me again. You'll give me the same money for the five years?'" remembers Shoofey. "And I said, 'Absolutely.' I mean, this was unheard of that anybody would sign for five years for the same amount of money, no increase. So he took the tablecloth, he wrote the contract on the tablecloth, and he signed it. He was very receptive, very cooperative, and very easy to deal with."

The Colonel soon began bragging that he had gotten the most money for a performer in the history of Las Vegas. But Shoofey and his staff did some gloating of their own. "I heard [they] told someone they had just gotten the biggest name in show business for the least amount of money," says Gordon Stoker of the Jordanaires. "The Colonel could have named any price."

Or certainly more than he demanded, given the showroom's 2,200-seat capacity, even as the top chairs were filled for action in the casino. Parker asked for no bonuses for exceeding certain records, and as the hotel later confirmed, when Elvis played the hotel, all the International's revenue doubled, from the slot machines to the restaurants.

"Just look at the figures," says Marty Lacker. "They had a $15 minimum, and at even two thousand people, that's $30,000 a show. At two shows a night, for twenty-eight consecutive nights, it works out to $1,680,000. But it was really more because fifty percent of the shows were dinner shows, and actually they got even more people in that room. So the hotel was taking in more than $2 million a month on Elvis, twice a year. Now, Vegas knows that most shows lose money, but they book entertainment to get people into the casinos. Elvis was the first act in Vegas history to make a hotel a profit on the show."

Just as Parker promised. So why didn't the Colonel ask for more? Theories abound: that Parker wanted to ensure that Elvis stayed at the hotel out of loyalty to a well-connected and powerful man; that continually sold-out shows in the largest Vegas showroom would translate to filled auditoriums when they went out on the road; and, most important, that

Parker was delirious at being a high roller in the gambling capital of the world, where the hotel showered him with unimaginable perks, from stocking his Palm Springs home with gourmet food—he once demanded prime rib and Dover sole be sent on Frank Sinatra's plane when the hotel forgot to pack it on his own—to forgiving at least a portion of his mounting casino losses.

Joe Delaney, the venerable Las Vegas *Sun* columnist, doesn't believe Parker sold Elvis too cheaply, but likens the Colonel's behavior to that of a double agent. "Was he trying to protect his fifty-two-weeks-a-year relationship with the hotel, or his eight-week-a-year relationship with the artist? If he's going to bleed the hotel for every dollar for Elvis, he's not going to get special treatment, although the way he gambled, I'd give it to him anyway. He had two things going. He had Elvis and he had the gambling."

And increasingly, the two entwined in his mind. Elvis would become, in fact, the Colonel's chit. "He had an open tab [and] nobody ever talked about money," says entrepreneur Joe Shane, who would come to know the Colonel well in the following years. "He had the boy do a lot of free shows just to cover his debt."

Just how reckless was Parker's gambling? "[The] Colonel was one of the best customers we had," Alex Shoofey later reported. "He was good for a million dollars a year."

But others say $1 million is too conservative a figure, that Parker routinely lost between $50,000 and $100,000 a night during Elvis's engagements. Therefore, every penny that Kerkorian and Shoofey paid for Elvis's appearances, they won back on the tables, though most of the time, the Colonel's was marker play. He spread his layouts to make sure he always had money coming back, and each time he won, the casino reduced his bill. Since no money changed hands, Parker developed a lackadaisical attitude about it. Money ceased to be real.

"I never saw anybody who could gamble like that man could gamble," says Lamar Fike. "He used to scare me to death. I was up one night about $75,000 or $100,000. He came and took [my bet] off [one number] and put it on another, and I lost it. I said, 'I ought to kill you for that.' He said, 'Well, you could have won, too.' I saw him lose half a million dollars at a craps table one night between shows. God knows how much money that man lost over a period of years. I'd say an easy forty million."

It was during the first weeks of the engagement that the press began to reference Parker's frequent appearances in the casino, particularly at the roulette table, where the hotel treated him like royalty, security guards roping off a table for his private play, which often went on for twelve or fourteen hours at a time.

Only games of chance, or betting against the house, aroused him. Games of skill, like poker, at which he might have made a living, left him cold. He especially loved the big six wheel, the Wheel of Fortune, so reminiscent of the carnivals, and bet numbers that related to his personal life, such as his birthday, or that of Marie, who brought her friend Maybelle Carter to Vegas for lower-stakes gambling. Always chasing the magic, he tried his best to hypnotize the wheel to deliver the payoff he wanted.

Often, he would wager $1,000 on every number, rationalizing it as betting large sums of money, but losing in small amounts. "If I don't cover a number, and you hit it," he'd bark at the dealer, "you're gonna pay me." A throng usually gathered, but as long as no one approached him directly or tried to muscle in on his table, he instructed that they be left alone—he loved the rush of winning with all eyes upon him. The hotel correctly saw him as a high-rolling shill.

While Parker only rarely tolerated a female onlooker who got too close—he regarded women as bad luck and would light up a cigar to smoke them out or call casino manager Jimmy Newman to remove them—he often requested a woman roulette dealer. "He felt he could intimidate a woman dealer," says Frank Gorrell, a former casino floor man. But with either sex, "he would walk around the table and say to the dealer, 'When I tell you, that's when you spin the ball.' He was also a big craps player, and *he* was going to run the table, not you. He was very sharp—he knew the payoffs better than we did. He'd say, 'Don't you cheat me, I know what I'm getting paid.' And he did." Affirms Gabe Tucker, "He'd stack 'em up all over, and run the men in the club plum crazy. I don't see how they ever kept up with him."

But while Parker loved to win big, tip generously, and watch how the bosses would react, he demonstrated one habit the dealers found peculiar. He was often good-natured when he lost, but when he won at a rough, fast-action game like craps, he liked the box men to curse him, tell him to go fuck himself. "He'd throw you in a couple of hundred if you treated him like shit," says Gorrell. "He loved that atmosphere when he was winning."

Whether the cursing of the croupiers served to reinforce Parker's glee at ripping them off and choreographing their anger into public display— thus garnering Parker greater approval by all gathered at the table—the barking of the gaming dogs echoed the denigration and humiliation he heaped on Elvis's entourage by "hypnotizing" them to "oink" or otherwise behave foolishly in front of authority figures. He treated them all as idiotic, sub-evolved lackeys, exposed under the Colonel's power and control. He also seemed to find solace in reprimand, as if being told he was worthless and undeserving somehow assuaged his guilt.

According to Julian Aberbach, Parker had $7 million in his Madison, Tennessee, bank account in 1969, and had always gambled responsibly. But as he spent more time in Vegas, "everything went haywire" and the Colonel could not control his compulsion, even as he recognized it for what it was. "He told me, 'Don't gamble. There is no way in the world that you can ever win,'" Aberbach remembers. "He lost all his money. It is a tragic story—self-destruction on an unbelievable level, and equal to Elvis's self-destruction. No question about it."

With Elvis's spectacular debut at the International, the Colonel began to receive a myriad of offers and immediately settled on two for 1970, after Presley's four-week return to Vegas in late January. Scrapping a pay-per-view concert film scheduled for March, Parker struck a deal with Kirk Kerkorian, who now headed MGM Studios, to film a concert documentary for theatrical release, called *Elvis: That's the Way It Is*. Filming would begin in July, after a June recording session for RCA in Nashville. But first, as a prelude to a national tour, the Colonel would take Elvis into the Houston Astrodome for six shows in three days in February.

Tom Diskin approached Joe Moscheo, the spokesman of the Imperials, about the group's accompanying Presley in Texas. By now, Moscheo, who had signed the Imperials' Vegas contract for $5,000 a week—or $1,000 per member—had discovered why the Jordanaires, who'd originally been offered the spot, turned down the deal. While the hotel rooms were covered, the group received no per diem, and Moscheo was chagrined to learn that other of the musicians received $2,000 or $3,000 apiece. Moscheo told Diskin they'd go to Houston, but that they needed to renegotiate their fee. Diskin said he'd have to talk to the Colonel, but all of Moscheo's efforts to do so went in vain.

"He just wouldn't see me," Moscheo recalls. "I knew he always gambled after the second show, so about two or three o'clock in the morning, I went looking for him and found him sitting at a table playing roulette with this big crowd around him. He had a stubby little cigar in his mouth, and piles of [chips] everywhere, and a couple guys in his entourage standing behind him.

"My guys were going, 'Just talk to him now . . . go in and tell him what we want,' so I wiggled my way in to Tom Diskin, who was standing right behind the Colonel. The Colonel still wouldn't talk to me directly, so I had to go through Tom.

"I'd say, 'We'd really like for you to pay to get our cleaning done.' And Diskin would go, 'Colonel, Joe said that the Imperials would like you to pay for their cleaning.' Then the Colonel would say, 'Tell them to go to hell. We're not paying.' And Diskin would turn around and tell me, 'The Colonel said to go to hell.' It was a three-way conversation among people standing right next to each other."

In the end, the Imperials got a raise, but the Colonel deftly sidetracked other requests. In October 1969, when Elvis took his Hawaii vacation, largely financed by the International, the Colonel got word from Joe Esposito that his client planned to return to Los Angeles, and with expedited passports for his party, which included Vernon and Dee, the Schillings, and the Espositos, fly on to Europe.

There, Presley hoped to visit some of the cities he'd longed to see since his army days ("Man, I'll put on a disguise . . . I've got to get out of this country just to see the world," he told Larry Geller), and maybe scout locales for a foreign tour. But Parker strongly argued that Elvis's European fans would be insulted if he traveled the Continent before performing there and suggested that the entourage fly to the Bahamas instead. The Colonel had contacts there, he said. Besides, they'd enjoy the gambling. Elvis complied, though once there driving rain and hurricane winds forced him to stay indoors most of the trip, and the couples returned home a week earlier than expected.

Priscilla, who objected to Elvis's long absences and frequent womanizing, hoped a European holiday would smooth out the rougher bumps in the marriage, something Elvis would soon allude to in the press. But neither could have anticipated the Colonel's virulent reaction, or how he interpreted a benign vacation plan as an impulsive and assertive act.

Soon after the couple returned to Memphis, Elvis was visited by two formidable businessmen in suits and ties. The men, who identified themselves as employees of RCA, spoke politely but firmly. "They advised him of the dangers of his desire to travel to Europe because of his status and universal recognition," says Larry Geller, who learned the story from Elvis when he came back into the entourage in 1972. "They told him he would be going eventually, but such things had to be planned out, that they took time and management. Underneath the veneer of cordiality, Elvis felt they were saying, 'Hey, man, what the fuck do you think you're doing?' It made a deep impression upon him—he took it as a threat."

Believing that "Parker obviously manipulated the visit," as Geller puts it, the episode must have reminded Elvis of the Colonel's story of Sam Cooke's fate at the hands of RCA's disgruntled image makers and Mafia hit men. "It was common knowledge that Parker was deeply into the 'people' in Vegas because of his enormous gambling losses," Geller reports. "Elvis became more aware of this as time went by and knew that he was Colonel Parker's bait and ransom, that Parker owned him, and whatever losses Parker incurred, Elvis would ultimately pay off by performing."

When Presley opened his second Vegas engagement in January 1970, he appeared so trim and vibrant, with his cheekbones showing when he smiled, that Lamar Fike found him "damn near gorgeous." But Fike, who had just rejoined the entourage after his stint with Hill and Range, was chagrined to learn that Elvis was now in the second phase of his drug use, with pills in him roughly 60 percent of the time. Fike knew it was only a matter of time before his body would show the effects, particularly as Presley was becoming bolder about what he would take. "Elvis loved downers, and he loved getting totally fucked up," says Fike. "Downers will put weight on you pretty quick." They also added to Elvis's paranoia.

During Presley's next Vegas engagement that summer, an incident occurred that heightened Elvis's fears about his safety, which had grown with Charles Manson's horrific murders of actress Sharon Tate and hairdresser Jay Sebring, in whose Los Angeles shop Larry Geller once worked.

On Wednesday, August 26, the International's security department was notified that Elvis would be kidnapped that evening. The hotel added extra security, and nothing happened, but then the Colonel received a similar call the following day. What shook everyone up was the next message, which came to Joe Esposito in Los Angeles early Friday morning. This time the caller, who dialed Esposito's unpublished home phone number, said that an individual planned to shoot Elvis on stage during his Saturday-night show, and demanded $50,000 in small bills to reveal the name of the assailant. Later, Elvis received a hotel menu with his picture on the front, defaced with a picture of a gun pointed at his head. Written backward were the words "Guess who, and where?"

The Colonel phoned Elvis's Beverly Hills lawyer, Ed Hookstratten, who notified the FBI. Then the attorney hired John O'Grady, a private detective and former L.A. police sergeant to come to Las Vegas to coordinate a ring of defense. Elvis, scared and shaken, called Jerry Schilling, then working as a film cutter at Paramount, and asked him to fly to Vegas to join the other bodyguards and security men who would surround the stage. Downstairs in his dressing room before the show, he told Schilling, "I don't want any son of a bitch running around saying, 'I killed Elvis Presley.' If some guy shoots me, I want you to rip his goddamn eyes out!" Then he tucked a derringer in his boot and went upstairs.

With an ambulance and a Vegas doctor, Thomas "Flash" Newman, standing by, a nervous Presley began his show. The only tense moment came several songs into the performance, when a man yelled out, "Elvis!" The singer dropped to one knee and reached for the pistol. Then the voice continued: "Would you sing 'Don't Be Cruel'?"

Presley was never sure who was behind the hoax, but his mind raced at the possibilities. Maybe it was Parker, playing another trick to keep him in line. Or perhaps the Colonel was really the target. Maybe Parker owed a little bit too much at the tables and needed some incentive to pay up quick. Elvis knew the rumors that Parker borrowed heavily from the mob ("I'd say that Colonel Parker did a lot of stuff with people in this town that nobody is ever going to find out about," echoes Frank Gorrell), and the latest gossip was even more frightening. Talk had it that Parker sold a percentage of Elvis's earnings to the Mafia as payment for his debts.

Whatever the truth, Elvis began to fixate on firearms, cops, and badass effrontery. The following year, inspired by the film *Shaft,* in which a black private eye tangles with a powerful racketeer, he started dressing in black hipster clothing from the wildest racks on Beale Street. In the next months, he would also obtain a badge to allow him to carry a pistol in Memphis, buy an arsenal of weapons—from small handguns to an M16 automatic assault rifle—and customize many of the handles with his TCB ("Taking Care of Business") insignia. Eventually, his fascination would border on the ludicrous. Making friends with policemen throughout the country, he occasionally donned a captain's uniform (a gift from the Denver Police Department) and installed a revolving blue light on the roof of his car, so that he might pull over speeders and offer assistance at accident scenes.

As Elvis slipped deeper into a world of drugs and delusion, he distanced himself from the Colonel. Where earlier in the year Presley had introduced Parker to his Vegas audience, saying he was "not only my manager, but I love him very much," they now spoke mostly through an intermediary, usually Esposito. Presley tried to avoid the Colonel at every turn.

That became easier to arrange in September, when Elvis flew to Phoenix to kick off a six-city tour, his first extended string of road shows since 1957. Tickets for nearly all the dates sold out within hours, especially since Parker kept the price to $10, less than half of what other major performers commanded. On board to promote four of the concerts was a new company called Management III.

The principal partners in the venture were Jerry Weintraub, a thirty-three-year-old former MCA talent agent who was managing the budding singer-songwriter John Denver, and Tom Hulett, whose company, Concerts West, had set the standard for contemporary rock tours with Jimi Hendrix and Led Zeppelin. Management III paid the Colonel $240,000 for the four dates, but Parker insisted on handling all advertising and promotion. The two men had no trouble with that—they'd been writing Parker for nearly two years, wanting to put Elvis into all the big, new arenas that were opening up throughout the country. They met with the Colonel for dinners with their wives and even endured Parker's famous steam room meltdowns ("I make 'em stay until they see things my way") at the Spa in Palm Springs.

"One of the things Jerry said," remembered Denver, who followed his first big hit, 1971's "Take Me Home, Country Roads," with a string of chart-toppers, "was that if he did his job, and I did my job, I would always be able to work in whatever arena I chose, be it television, films, recordings, or concerts. He's a very, very brilliant promoter. He went to the big arenas and said, 'You want Elvis Presley to come play this place? Then I want Concerts West to be involved in every concert that comes into this building.' And as a result of his influence in the concert market, Jerry had an enormous amount of clout with RCA, and also with radio stations."

Just why and how Parker settled on Weintraub and Hulett isn't clear, especially as he had rejected two other concert promoters, Steve Wolf and Jim Rissmiller of Concert Associates, who also attempted to woo the Colonel through a two-year letter-writing campaign, and finally wangled a meeting. The two found Parker charming, but a tough negotiator.

"He wanted us to pay the costs of producing the show," Wolf remembered, "and then he gave us a cushion and a percentage over a certain amount. He threw it out so fast we had to keep asking him over and over, and he kept saying, 'I told you boys, now for the last time this is the deal.' He really hits you. He doesn't sit back and let it sink in. You're sorry you asked a question."

After much back and forth, Parker finally told them Elvis had no plans to tour, as it might hurt business at the hotel. But if he did, he'd need to honor some obligations that went back to the late '50s. Then, in a matter of months, he signed the deal with Weintraub.

"Jerry was very well connected, and a lot went through him," says Joe Delaney. He was a formidable guy—still is."

But Parker made him sweat for his power. The following month, when Weintraub went back to the Colonel to set up another eight-day tour, this time for Concerts West, Parker demanded a $1-million deposit against 65 percent of the gate. Within twenty-four hours. It was a test of both the company's bank account and Weintraub's resolve. "Jerry had to go out and bust his butt," says Joe Shane. The money was late in arriving, though not really through Weintraub's fault, and overall the Colonel's student did not disappoint him.

As reward, Parker gave Weintraub and Hulett a piece of the concessions, though the Colonel later felt a need to wire Weintraub regarding ticket accessibility. In guarding against such stunts as a box office manager pulling free tickets for the city council, he was also looking out for the fans "who made Elvis what he is today." As he told Weintraub in a telegram, "We want our fans to be taken care of. When they wait in line for hours and hours they are privileged customers. They come first."

The Presley road show was now a major business, with huge grosses and attendance records, Elvis taking in more than $300,000 and beating the Rolling Stones' numbers in two shows at the Inglewood Forum in Los Angeles that November. Most of the members of Elvis's entourage traveled with him, Joe Esposito being in top command under Parker, Charlie Hodge acting as stage manager and general assistant, Lamar Fike handling the lighting, and Richard Davis taking care of Elvis's wardrobe. Elvis also added a Memphis physician, Dr. George Nichopoulos, who had personally tended to nearly all of Elvis's medical and pharmaceutical needs since treating him for a cold in 1966.

At the age of sixty-one, Parker still personally advanced the tour, making a promotional trip two months (later cut down to a matter of weeks) ahead of the show. Sonny West, keeping his eyes and ears open for Elvis as Joe Esposito did for the Colonel, traveled with Parker as security chief.

Together, they obtained the hotel rooms—Elvis and the Colonel each oc-cupied a whole floor at a different location from the show group—and figured out which entrance Presley could use to get to his room without going through the lobby. They also worked with the local law enforce-ment, the Colonel picking either a captain or a detective to line up as many as sixty uniformed men to police Elvis's hotel and travel route. The entourage was afforded the same protection as a presidential motorcade.

"He would have it all mapped out, get as many as four limos for de-coys, and time how long it would take to get to the airport, the hotel, and the venue," remembers former RCA rep Gaylen Adams. "He planned such details, it would scare you." By the time Parker's friend Al Dvorin announced, "Elvis has left the building," to calm a frenzied show crowd, Presley was, indeed, already on his way.

Once the tour started, Parker returned to each town the day before the date. He checked on the souvenir sales first—arena rock of the '70s ush-ered in the modern era of merchandising—then tended to the box office and promotion. A sellout was a must, and if ticket sales lagged, Parker counted on a pocketful of tricks to turn the tide. Regularly, he forced RCA to buy a block of tickets as giveaways, but most of the time he relied on carny cunning.

One time in Salt Lake City, Parker remembered in the '80s, "the rest of the auditorium was sold out, and we couldn't sell the last two thousand seats for anything. Then on the Sunday before the show, Elder Stevens [head of the Mormon church] died. The show was set for Wednesday. I called the radio stations and canceled all the ads. We weren't selling tick-ets anyway, and I figured we'd save $1,900.

"What we did," he went on, "was instead of taking the ads, we made an announcement that we were dropping the ads until after Elder Stevens's funeral on Tuesday. Of course, the radio stations gave us all of the announcements free. Then on Wednesday, the ads started again and we sold out all two thousand seats in two hours. It had to be the Mor-mons who bought the tickets."

Another time, much later, in Pittsburgh, they played a 20,000-seat arena and found themselves stuck with 1,100 tickets, all of them "way up in the attic, behind a post. We were selling maybe twelve or fifteen a day. So we pulled all our ads and put in new ones. We said, 'We still have a few seats left. They aren't very good, but it's all we got.' When that hit the air, we sold out right away. People liked the honesty."

For a man who still rose at 5:00 A.M., it was a grueling schedule, one that didn't end until well after sundown. If Elvis was flying in that night after his show, as he always did on the later tours, since he had trouble winding down and falling asleep, Parker would wait for word that he had landed.

The next day, the show plane arrived. "He made life rough for us on the road," says Kathy Westmoreland, Elvis's high harmony singer, "because we were going to bed at four in the morning and getting up at seven-thirty to fly to the next city." Yet the musicians looked out their windows to see the Colonel leaning on his cane on the tarmac, knowing he would always be there to greet them, no matter the weather. Tom Diskin, standing at his side, handed each musician a key as he came off the ramp and boarded the bus to the hotel. Then as the group waved good-bye, Parker took off in his plane for the next town.

Though he met Elvis and the entourage every evening prior to the first show in Vegas, pulling Elvis into another room to talk business if need be, and sometimes staying for the first show, only rarely did the Colonel wait to see Elvis perform on the road. Even if Parker spent the night, he never met with Presley before the concert.

Nonetheless, the man who loved playing Santa Claus at Frank Sinatra's Christmas parties found time to entertain the children whose parents traveled with the show. As "Uncle Colonel," he delighted the kids with stories of "the googala," a giant centipede who resided in the Colonel's imagination, and whose likeness he sketched for the children to take home and tape up on their walls.

It was just as well that Presley and Parker seldom met up on the tours, since Elvis was often furious about his accommodations. In Mobile, Alabama, they'd been booked into the Admiral Semmes Hotel, which may have been luxurious the last time Presley stayed there, in 1955, but was a dump by 1970, a total fleabag, without air-conditioning. The Colonel knew Elvis preferred any modern motel, even a Holiday Inn, to an older place. Hadn't Parker checked it out when he advanced the tour? Presley raved. And why were they playing Mobile, anyway?

Even Concerts West was confused about that one, and as the tours continued, Weintraub and Hulett, who brought the Colonel a list of cities and dates for him to approve, were equally puzzled about a number of towns Parker picked, such as Monroe, Louisiana, and Greensboro, North Carolina, that seemed off the beaten path for a megawatt rock star. Nobody else went there, which, the Colonel said, was precisely the point. Fans in grassroots areas wanted to see Elvis, too, and he was guaranteed a sellout. If Elvis had to perform in basketball gymnasiums, or on three-foot stages—which he sometimes did—it helped pay the expenses between larger dates. Weintraub and Hulett weren't the only promoters out there, and he'd set about proving it to them.

What Parker failed to mention was that he yearned to return to the towns he'd first visited with the carnivals and tent shows, where he still had people in his pocket—from the mayor to the cops—and knew how to control just about anything. He loved going back to the old hotels, too, even if some of the rooms on the floors they stayed on were boarded up. Sometimes he did it to repay a favor. Besides, these old places were dirt cheap. Who could argue with that?

While Elvis had initially been happy to return to live performance, his pill-fueled behavior had become more erratic in recent months. He obsessed about collecting police badges—bugging John O'Grady for how he could get one that would let him carry a gun across state lines—and schemed to get all the guys deputized to pack a weapon in Memphis, Las Vegas, and Palm Springs. Loaded on pharmaceuticals, he shot a .22 automatic at a car one night in Beverly Hills after the driver made a rude gesture, and even terrorized his friends if they mouthed off at him, sticking a loaded .44 Magnum in Lamar Fike's nose one day and threatening to blow his brains out. In December 1970, as best man at Sonny West's wedding, he would stand at the altar wearing five loaded firearms—two gold-plated guns in shoulder holsters, a pair of pearl-handled pistols in his pants, and a derringer in his boot.

When he came off the road that November, Elvis began to fixate on the idea of becoming a federal agent. A federal agent's badge would give him not only ultimate power, but also a feeling of invincibility. No one would dare mess with a federal agent, no matter what controlled substances he carried around with him in a little black bag.

O'Grady, who had headed up the narcotics unit for the L.A. Police Department, was hip to Elvis's habits—he'd done a polygraph test on Presley for an annoying paternity suit—and noticed his pulse and breathing rates were below normal. And Elvis had way too many questions about how to become an agent-at-large for the Bureau of Narcotics and Dangerous Drugs, especially after O'Grady set up a meeting for him with Paul Frees, a voiceover announcer who'd earned just such a badge for undercover work. The unctuous O'Grady liked rubbing shoulders with the famous and told Elvis he might be able to help: he'd get him an introduction to John Finlator, the deputy director of the Narcotics Bureau.

Parker, meanwhile, had grown tired of having to speak to Elvis through his father or Esposito, and early in December, on the same day he completed a deal with RCA to extend his annual $100,000 consulting fee for five years, he wrote to Elvis, expressing his frustration at not being able to get his client on the phone. Using sarcasm to mildly mask his fury, the Colonel cited Elvis's obvious avoidance of him, and reminded him of how hard he had been working in his behalf. "Remember," he concluded, "your slogan TCB . . . only works if you use it."

Vernon Presley was not pleased to see his son at odds with the Colonel and told him so in a blowup in mid-December. The time had come to replace the old bastard, Elvis argued, but Vernon told him he'd never find anybody better. Then Vernon started in on Elvis's lavish spending sprees and produced the bills: $20,000 and $30,000 gun-buying trips, $85,000 worth of Mercedes-Benzes for his friends. Such extravagance had to stop. Priscilla agreed, especially as the couple had just put down a deposit on a new home in Beverly Hills, despite the shakiness of the marriage.

By now, Elvis was so volatile that, as his cousin Billy Smith remembers, "you especially had to be careful of what you said [to him]. He was like a caged animal. He was coming out any way he could. You didn't embarrass him, and you didn't scare him, and you certainly didn't ever humiliate him."

Feeling restricted and hampered by the Colonel, and then by his wife and father, Elvis was about to defy all of them in a demonstration of independence more surprising than they could have imagined. On December 19, 1970, without their knowledge, he slipped out of Graceland, went to the airport alone, and began a journey to Washington to see John Finlator, O'Grady's contact at the Bureau of Narcotics and Dangerous Drugs. Elvis wanted his badge.

Finlator turned him down, but Elvis, by now accompanied by Jerry Schilling and Sonny West, had a backup plan. On the plane, stoned, shaky, and woozy-eyed, he had written a letter to President Richard M. Nixon, declaring himself a concerned American. The country was in bad shape, with the hippies, the drug culture, the Black Panthers, and the Students for a Democratic Society, he wrote. He knew so because he had done "an in-depth study of drug abuse and Communist brainwashing techniques." But if Nixon would make him a federal agent, he could be of service to this great nation, since none of those threats to the American way of life considered him an enemy.

"I would love to meet you just to say hello if you're not too busy," he said in closing, and then dropped the letter off at the White House gates on the way to his hotel. The result: Presley, dressed like Dracula in outlandish garb—a velvet cape topping a black suede suit, a massive gold belt given to him by the International, glittering chains circling his neck, tinted sunglasses, and a cane—got his meeting with Nixon at the White House. And he got the cherished badge, which became, Schilling says, "his most prized physical possession." At last, Elvis was a narc.

The Colonel, who learned about the visit to Washington after the fact, was gravely worried. The president, for God's sake! Elvis was slipping completely out of his control. He would have to find a way to keep Elvis in check and step up his surveillance of his actions.

In March 1971, when Elvis blew up while attempting to record in Nashville—kicking a gun through a guitar and storming out of the session—Parker managed to keep most of it out of the press. The following day, the singer, whose eyesight had been troubling him, was hospitalized for glaucoma. Now Parker saw his act becoming more fractious with each passing month, and realized he had to create new ways to maximize Presley's earning power. Otherwise, the Colonel would find himself in the same sad straits as his friend Oscar Davis—sick, dependent on Parker's handout of $100 a month, and soon to be dead, never again managing a major star nearly twenty years after Hank Williams's self-destructive ways caught up with him on the way to a show date.

Though Parker was constantly renegotiating Elvis's contract with RCA—the latest deal was for the budget Camden label, yet even then he finagled improved royalties—his first foray into new money came in July 1971, when he took Presley into Del Webb's Sahara Tahoe in Stateline, Nevada.

The engagement, where orchestra leader Joe Guercio debuted Richard Strauss's *Also Sprach Zarathustra* as the singer's introduction on stage, was a raging success. Parker had figured out a way to put eight people at a table that normally seated four, which allowed Elvis to break the showroom's attendance record. One month before, the Hilton hotel chain had taken over the International in a 50 percent partnership with Kerkorian and Shoofey, renaming it the Las Vegas Hilton. The Colonel would soon use Elvis's Tahoe numbers, plus the fact that he had negotiated a fee of $300,000 for two weeks, to cut a new deal with Henri Lewin, the Las Vegas Hilton's new executive vice president of hotel and casino operations, and Barron Hilton himself.

Lewin, a German Jew whose family fled the Nazis, already seemed to be in Parker's corner, throwing him a surprise sixty-second birthday party that June. Their first meeting came five hours after Hilton took over the hotel, the Colonel flying in from Palm Springs. Lewin had been nervous: Parker had a clause in his contract that stipulated that if the hotel were sold, he and Elvis were free to go elsewhere.

"The Colonel said, 'I did business with Kerkorian, I liked him, and I have no reason not to trust that you will be as good or better,'" Lewin remembered years later. And, as a measure of honor, the Colonel accepted the same contract. "Elvis was always paid more than we paid anybody else . . . and he was still the cheapest. We made more money paying him more than paying somebody else less. You shake hands with the Colonel, you can forget worry."

But as Parker loved Las Vegas, and he and Elvis were becoming synonymous with the town, Presley was growing tired of the seven-days-a-week, two-shows-a-night grind, so demanding both physically and mentally. At first, remembers Jerry Schilling, "it was great. But going in about the third year, there was no challenge . . . it was the same songs, and the same audience, and we stayed up all night, and slept all day. We didn't see sunlight for a couple months. What was once exciting and fun became dark and angry."

"Elvis was mad," says Lamar Fike. "He didn't want to do it anymore. He said, 'I want out of this place. I don't want to come back.' As a consequence, this seething cauldron of hate built up in Las Vegas."

A month after Tahoe, in August 1971, Elvis opened his summer festival at the Las Vegas Hilton to poor reviews. *The Hollywood Reporter* found Elvis "drawn, tired, and noticeably heavier," and the show "occasionally monotonous, often silly, and haphazardly coordinated." Still the fans came, to the point that Parker added an additional show per day to accommodate the overflow crowds. But the strain was too much—on the sixth day, Elvis cut a show short, complained of the flu, and consulted an ear, nose, and throat specialist, Dr. Sidney Boyer, who, like Thomas "Flash" Newman, would remain in his stable of Vegas physicians.

By the last night, he felt strong enough to close the show wearing a heavy rhinestone-and-jewel-encrusted cape, thrusting his arms in a dramatic stance that would become a hallmark of his performances. But the press preferred to report on Elvis's illness and daily doctors' visits.

"He didn't have breathing room," says Alex Shoofey. "It was a continuous thing. I even said to the Colonel one time, 'Give him a breather, Colonel, gosh! He needs a little rest.' He said, 'Oh, he's young, don't worry. He loves every moment of it.' I think he could have let up a little, given him a little more time off."

"Nobody goes to Vegas and plays four weeks anymore—they do five days, tops," explains Lamar Fike. "And Elvis had such a high-energy show that when he would do an honest hour and fifteen minutes twice a night, he was so tired he was cross-eyed. That's why he took that stuff, to keep him going. And because he was bored. Bored to tears."

According to Henri Lewin, Parker spoke to Vernon about his son's condition. "I was there when Colonel Parker pleaded with Vernon Presley, and then they both pleaded with Elvis to understand the importance of taking care of his personal life."

But Parker continued to weigh his options. With his gambling debts mounting, and Presley becoming more unpredictable, the Colonel apparently, in the fall of 1971, considered selling Elvis's contract to Gordon Mills, the flamboyant manager of Tom Jones. Items to that effect appeared in the American and British press, and an exchange of correspondence between Mills and the Colonel's office concerning a denial of discussions suggests that such talks had, in fact, happened. Later, John Moran, Jones's publicist, confirmed it to Marty Lacker.

The newspapers were more concerned, however, about rumors that Elvis and Priscilla were estranged. As Presley began another tour that November—Elvis replacing the Imperials with J. D. Sumner and the Stamps Quartet, and Parker substituting comedian Jackie Kahane for the alcoholic Sammy Shore—the singer became less guarded about his dalliances with other women. Within months, his marriage would be in tatters.

For quite a while, Presley had been getting reports that Priscilla was dating her karate instructor, Mike Stone. The maid at the Presleys' new house in California told Red West that Stone spent too much time there, and three-year-old Lisa Marie blew the whistle on the pair when she mentioned they'd "wrestled" in a sleeping bag on a camping trip. Then Sonny West caught them in the shower together and told Elvis.

The showdown came during Presley's engagement at the Hilton in February 1972, when Priscilla owned up to the affair, railed against their surreal, life-in-a-bubble existence, and asked for a divorce. Elvis, humiliated and enraged, forced her to have sex in an episode that, according to Priscilla, bordered on rape. Later, he would ask her to reconsider breaking the marriage, but as Priscilla eventually made him understand, it had ended long ago, largely from his own indifference.

Throughout such turmoil, the Colonel had more practical matters on his mind. As Elvis performed in the Hilton showroom, Parker sat in his fourth-floor suite of six rooms and offices and mused about something that the new RCA president Rocco Laginestra had casually mentioned—an innovative technology that allowed for live satellite broadcast around the world. Elvis had again been making noises about wanting to go to Europe to perform, citing the number of letters he got from foreign fans.

"I'm working on it," Parker grumbled. But before long, when the Colonel was offered $500,000 for six concerts in London, he'd repeat that the venues weren't large enough overseas—an unlikely explanation, considering Wimbledon and a myriad of soccer stadiums, though he insisted Elvis himself balked at playing outdoor arenas. Sometimes the Colonel would reiterate that security would be a problem, since European fans were wilder in their adoration, or say simply that the money wasn't right. "[Elvis] wanted to take all of his troupe with him and his own orchestra," Parker offered years later. "When we checked out the possibilities where he could play, he could sell out and [still] lose money."

But, of course, they were never going to Europe, and not just because Parker had no passport. The Colonel was worried about Elvis's stamina; Dr. Nichopoulos had to accompany him on all the tours now. And Parker wasn't sure what kinds of drugs Elvis was taking, lately hearing rumors of cocaine use. If Elvis got sick, or customs found some illegal substance, the Colonel wouldn't be able to keep it out of the papers. The risk was simply too great.

Yet if Parker understood it correctly, with the new satellite, Elvis could "tour" the globe in one concert, without ever leaving the States. Such a coup—the first entertainment special broadcast live around the world—would help keep the boy on top and in the news, and maybe lift him from his funk. The Colonel tore a piece of the old International stationery in half and started making a to-do list ("Clearances needed on songs"). In bold handwriting, with numbers still reminiscent of the European style, he jotted down the costs (backup musicians, rehearsal room) and posed some questions: "RCA makes contracts with talent or do we?"

Laginestra loved the idea of an Elvis satellite tour, especially as Parker had already planned to stage it from Hawaii, the site of so many successful Presley ventures. But Laginestra didn't like dealing with the Colonel personally, and so he handed him off to others in the company, particularly Mel Ilberman, the head of U.S. Operations, who admired Parker ("He was a big friend of mine. . . . He was always honest with me") and tried to keep him happy.

As part of that goodwill endeavor, the label agreed to set up a concert promotion company. That was something the Colonel had been after for years, and a coup RCA's Joe Galante calls "a brilliant move, because he had now taken the company's resources and focused them solely on his act." Though the agreement included Management III, Parker, in effect, controlled everything, with the help of RCA's George Parkhill and Pat Kelleher of the label's promotion department. Their first tour under the new umbrella would begin in April.

The frugal Dutchman pinched every penny—paying a promoter in Tennessee only $1,000 to handle ticket sales—and would continue to do so throughout Elvis's touring years. When keyboardist Tony Brown joined the band two years later, he was surprised to find that the musicians had to buy tickets for their guests, and that the Elvis show had no catering backstage of any kind, in comparison with lesser stars who provided full meals and liquor.

"We finally demanded that we get some soft drinks, and eventually, they started putting a trash can in our dressing room with Cokes and Pepsis and 7UPs, but that was it. Occasionally, the Colonel would get on the bus and walk down the aisle and give everybody a ten-dollar bill for dinner. Of course, once he left, there was all kinds of snickering and sarcastic remarks—'Where you havin' dinner?'—that kind of stuff." Anyone who was late for the bus was fined a dollar a minute.

By now, the Colonel could clearly see that touring was a bigger source of revenue than even Elvis's movies. On February 4, 1972, a week after he signed the joint venture with RCA, he presented a new contract to Elvis. Parker was changing his basic management fee, he explained. After expenses, which included agency commissions, the profits from the tours would now be split two thirds for Elvis and one third for Parker.

"There were a lot of things that maybe the Colonel didn't collect on like he should have," defends Lamar Fike. But only the Colonel really understood what constituted "expenses" and what was "net."

"People talk about the fifty percent and other outrageous splits, but there were times when the Colonel took it all," says Joe Shane. "He was hiding the fact that he was going through Elvis's money. To see him negotiate deals for concerts was just unbelievable. A promoter would say, 'I want to do ten dates in the Midwest,' and the Colonel would say, 'Okay, I'll take a million dollars up front and half of it in cash before you sell the first ticket.' And he'd get it. He always wanted the cash. The truth was, he needed it."

18

GEEK FEVER

L A T E in March 1972, the Colonel told the Las Vegas Hilton that Elvis would soon begin making his second MGM documentary concert film (*Elvis On Tour*) and would therefore be unavailable for the rest of the year. In truth, the movie would be completed in less than two months, and Parker's announcement was little more than a ploy to revise Presley's Vegas contract.

To up the ante, he hinted—by denying rumors to the effect—that in a year or so he might move Elvis to Kirk Kerkorian's MGM Grand Hotel, then under construction. The Hilton caved: in April, the hotel agreed to pay Elvis $130,000 a week for the next two engagements and $150,000 a week for the following three. Parker, as a consultant to the hotel chain, would also be paid $50,000 a year for the next three years.

For Elvis's summer tour, commencing in June, the Colonel engaged the Clanton Ross Advertising Agency of Tampa. The Ross was Bob Ross, Marie's forty-seven-year old son, who suffered from the early stages of multiple sclerosis. A year before, Ross and his wife had divorced, and Bob was now dating Sandra Polk, a spirited Tampa native seventeen years his junior who often flew to Las Vegas with her cousin to attend Elvis's shows. Though Parker's relationship with Ross had always been tentative, the Colonel helped him receive top medical care through friends in Houston. He also continued to throw him business. Bob's agency designed some of Elvis's album covers, posters, and billboards, and before long, Parker would give him lucrative advertising accounts for other big stars whose managers the Colonel befriended.

The advertising for the summer '72 tour held particular sway, as Elvis would play three shows at Madison Square Garden beginning June 9. Parker had deliberately kept his client out of Manhattan, other than for television appearances in the '50s, fearing he might not fill a large arena in such a cosmopolitan area. Now, however, much had changed. Ticket sales for the New York engagement were so brisk that Parker added a fourth appearance, making Elvis the first performer to sell out four consecutive shows at the Garden, with grosses at $730,000.

Elvis had always been anxious about New York, remembering the stinging remarks of a cynical media that had dismissed him so cruelly at the start of his career. But the counterculture rebel of the '50s was now an establishment darling of the '70s, just as Parker had planned. At a press conference between rehearsals, a confident, relaxed Elvis, dressed in a flashy, high-collar blue jacket, bounded out to a bank of microphones and, with quick, good-natured humor, deflected questions as easily as swatting softballs over a fence. When a woman asked about his image as a shy, humble country boy, Elvis smiled. "Ah, I don't know what makes 'em say that," he said with a slight stutter, and then stood and pulled back his jacket to reveal the gaudy gold belt given to him by the International. Elvis won a laugh for his trouble, and Parker, standing by in a rube's straw hat, scanned the reporters' faces and knew the coverage would be good.

Less than a week before the first show, RCA thought to tape the concerts for a live album and scrambled to get the contracts signed and the recording equipment in place. The label kept the plan secret, as not to spook either Elvis or the band, especially as Presley's song selection was so spontaneous that no one ever knew what order he'd choose.

Yet the shows came off without a hitch for everyone except the comic, Jackie Kahane, who was booed off the stage opening night. Elvis heard about it and went to console him in his dressing room. "He said, 'Mr. Kahane, they're animals out there.'" Kahane recalls. "'Don't let them bother you. You go out there tomorrow and you kick ass.'"

When Elvis finally came out to the billowing strains of *Also Sprach Zarathustra,* remembers Joe Guercio, the crowd went into a roar, and "so many flashbulbs went off that the Garden was almost lit for a second."

The *New York Times* described it as a legendary performance, with a headline that likened Presley to "A Prince from Another Planet." Chris Chase, the paper's reviewer, saw Elvis as "a special champion [like] a Joe Louis . . . Joe DiMaggio, someone in whose hands the way a thing is done becomes more important than the thing itself. . . . He stood there at the end, his arms stretched out, the great gold cloak giving him wings . . . the only one in his class."

Yet as Presley's career moved to a new tier of fame and accomplishment, his personal life crumbled around him. On July 26, 1972, Elvis and Priscilla legally separated. Presley's lawyer, Ed Hookstratten, drew up the papers, secured a lawyer for Priscilla, and worked out the amicable terms of the divorce settlement. Priscilla would receive a lump sum of $100,000, plus $1,000 per month for her own expenses and $500 per month child support.

Elvis had already begun seeing the next woman in his life, Linda Thompson, a Memphis beauty queen who babied him and, for the time being, put up with his pharmaceutical habits. Still, Elvis seemed haunted. When he returned to Vegas in August, he received another, though less serious, death threat. One night during the engagement, Wolfman Jack, the popular television and radio personality, came backstage to say hello. "What's it like to be Elvis Presley?" the visitor wanted to know. "I'll tell you what, Jack," Elvis answered, "it's very, very uncomfortable."

Despite Elvis's interest in Linda, the impending divorce seemed to weaken his resolve and usher in his third and final stage of drug use, starting with an increase in sedatives, or downers. Some days the performer was clear, lucid, and seemingly unaffected. But other times, he was so obviously under the influence that Jackie Kahane remembers a child coming up to him after a show and asking, "Was Elvis drunk?"

His usual protocol, says Lamar Fike, was to take a Valium, a Placidyl, a Valmid, some Butabarbital, and codeine—all at the same time. Before long, he would add Percodan and liquid Demerol to his potent cocktail.

On September 4, 1972, Parker and RCA president Laginestra held a press conference in Las Vegas to announce the upcoming satellite broadcast, "Aloha from Hawaii," set for January 1973. The show, staged in Honolulu, would reach 1.4 billion viewers, though not all of them "live," as the ballyhoo maintained, since both Europe and America would receive it on a delayed basis. RCA Record Tours would produce the show—displacing Management III for a year—and the label would also release a double LP of the concert, the first time "in the history of the record business," the company gloated, that an album would be issued simultaneously around the world.

"It's very hard to comprehend," Elvis said over and over, crumpled in a chair at the briefing. But for some, what was harder to understand was why Presley perspired so heavily, with his speech slurred, his eyes dazed and dulled.

As the date of the concert neared, Presley worked hard to get himself in shape, dieting down to a sleek 175 pounds and staying off his drug protocol for two weeks. His entourage hoped that Elvis had turned a corner, that the incentive to clean up might last. But just before he went on stage, he asked for a shot of vitamin B_{12} mixed with amphetamines.

"The next morning," says Marty Lacker, "we were supposed to go to the U.S.S. *Arizona* Memorial. We banged on his door, and nobody answered. Finally, Linda came, and she just made a face and shook her head. Elvis was sitting on the balcony, on the top floor of the hotel, stoned out of his gourd. He was sweating profusely, with a towel around his neck, and he could hardly talk. He'd gone right back into it."

"Aloha from Hawaii" was Elvis's last glorious moment, his final appearance as an undeniable superstar. The resulting album would stay on the *Billboard* charts for thirty-five weeks and climb to number one—his first chart-topping LP in nine years.

But there would be no more.

Parker seemed to sense it. At 3:00 A.M., following the broadcast, the Colonel sat down to write Elvis a congratulatory letter. Filled with sentiment, Parker told his client that they had no need for hugging, since they could tell "from seeing each other on stage and from the floor by the stage" how they felt.

"I always know that when I do my part," he continued, "you always do yours in your own way and in your feeling in how to do it best. That is why you and I are never at each other when we are doing our work in our own best way possible. . . . You above all make all of it work by being the leader and the talent. Without your dedication to your following, it couldn't have been done."

Such emotional display was rare for Parker, but lately he had been under unusual strain. It was around this time that the Colonel, now so large he wore size 3X clothing, suffered yet another heart attack—his fourth. Surely he could not go on much longer. And worse, Marie, whose health had been steadily declining since the mid-'60s, was becoming more and more addled. She complained of worse headaches, and her speech was affected. "She started getting senile, like she was ninety years old instead of sixty-five," recalled her brother, Bitsy Mott. The Colonel phoned her twice a day, and sometimes she didn't recognize his voice or know who he was when he identified himself. Often, she hung up on him.

Parker, who still went home to her in Palm Springs every weekend, suspected her headaches generated from the metal ball and socket she received in hip surgery. Her doctor, however, believed she suffered from degenerative brain disease, or age-related dementia, though her symptoms weren't always consistent with the condition. Whatever the source, Mott remembered, "It just got worse and worse, till finally she was immobile all over."

The Colonel mourned the days when he bought her favorite shoes in every color—an attempt to make up for their impoverished years. But "as the disease progressed," says Sandra Polk Ross, who became her daughter-in-law in 1973, "Colonel started to distance himself from her, keep her home. He would still take her to Vegas, but he would always have someone go with them and be with her."

Within three years, Marie would be so confused she'd think her son was her first husband and, on a trip to Florida to visit Bob and Sandra, would repeatedly rattle the couple's doorknob, trying to crawl into bed with them. The Colonel's monthly nursing bill climbed to $6,000.

Marie, Elvis, himself. It was taking a toll. But Parker couldn't dwell on the negative. The best thing to do was to concentrate on business, think about the new music publishing companies, Aaron Music and Mister Songman Music, he planned to form with Freddy Bienstock, who had earlier been fired by the Aberbachs. Parker had been angered by Bienstock's dismissal, and in August 1972 met with the Aberbach brothers to liquidate the Elvis and Gladys Music firms.

"The Colonel always felt the Aberbachs were part of him," Bienstock explains. "But he had a number of resentments against them, and they stopped all social contact with him after I left the company." In teaming with Bienstock, Parker would show the brothers who really knew the Elvis catalogue.

By now, the Colonel had a new secretary, Loanne Miller, a spinster from Ohio who had previously worked for Nick Naff. When she first interviewed with the advertising director, "she presented me with a little slip of paper listing her personal philosophy of what a secretary should be. Virtually, it said the boss is everything, and you serve him—whether it means washing his feet, or rubbing his back. She reveled in it."

However, Naff wasn't comfortable with such subservience ("I like to get my own coffee"), and while Loanne was splendid in her job, her servility clashed with Naff's hands-on attitude. One day Alex Shoofey called and asked if it would disrupt Naff's office too much if Loanne went to work for the Colonel. "Secretly, I said, 'Great,'" Naff remembers, "but I took the generous posture and said I'd make the sacrifice. He loved that kind of devotion, and [working for him] made her a significant person, so she was ideal for him." Indeed, she had no objections to helping plan Bob and Sandra Ross's wedding and making the arrangements.

Given to airy, New Age beliefs and holistic health practices, Loanne bounced between childlike wonder and tough-cookie tenacity. She thought the Colonel hung the moon, and she defended his every action. "Most people have no idea how much of a genius he was because they weren't with him enough to understand," she maintains.

When she first went to work for the Colonel, he called her one day and said he needed her to fly to Los Angeles to take notes for an important meeting at MGM Studios. Upon her arrival, Parker cautioned her to "really pay attention . . . There are a lot of very important people in this meeting. Please come sit next to me." He then led the nervous secretary back to the conference room, where she found a long table with twelve chairs—each occupied by a huge stuffed teddy bear with a pad and pencil in front of him.

Though Parker got her on the RCA payroll as an executive secretary to George Parkhill, and she had reason to travel with the Colonel, some at the hotel took it for granted that she was his girlfriend. Others discount it, but Bitsy Mott told his family he had caught them in "compromising circumstances" more than once.

Certainly Parker looked after her. Artie Newman, a casino shift boss who also worked the showroom and became one of the Colonel's chief contacts, always let him know when the women's clothing reps came to town, offering apparel in exchange for gambling losses. Soon Newman knew to bring dresses in two sizes—7 for the now-petite Marie, and 12 for the larger-boned Loanne. Since the secretary was lanky, quick with a smile, and every inch the Colonel's puppet, Elvis's entourage wickedly dubbed her Howdy Doody.

When Presley went back into the Hilton showroom for his eighth engagement at the end of January 1973, the singer was tired and lackluster. A week later, he would begin canceling shows, citing a lingering case of the flu. It was a difficult month, made even worse when four South American men jumped on stage near the end of Elvis's performance on February 18. The entourage quickly took control, with Elvis knocking one of the men back into the crowd. "I'm sorry, ladies and gentlemen," Elvis told the audience afterward. "I'm sorry I didn't break his goddamned neck is what I'm sorry about."

The presumed assailants turned out to be no more than exuberant fans, but Presley, paranoid and delusional, convinced himself that Mike

Stone, Priscilla's boyfriend, had sent them to kill him. In the early hours of the morning, high on pills and raging out of control ("Another man has taken my wife! Mike Stone has to die!"), Elvis ordered Red West to hire a hit man to have the karate champion murdered. A week later, he softened.

Priscilla was also on Elvis's mind for another reason. She'd agreed to far too little money in the divorce settlement, she told him, and planned to see a new lawyer about renegotiating the terms.

If it came to that, Parker had a good idea where Elvis could get the money.

Since the fall, RCA's Mel Ilberman had been trying to persuade the Colonel to agree to a deal. Stymied by Parker's long insistence that Presley's records must not be included in the RCA Record Club or repackaged at mid-price, which meant a lower royalty rate, Ilberman wondered if the manager and his client would be interested in selling Presley's master recordings, or back catalogue, for $3 million.

The Colonel was resolute: absolutely not. To do so would mean the label would never again have to pay royalties on records released before 1973, and Elvis would have no control over how those songs would be used. Vernon, however, saw it as an immediate fix to many of the Presleys' financial straits. Parker argued that the material could be worth more in the future, that they shouldn't sell, but added he would go back and see if he could get the record company to up its bid.

Ilberman was now on the spot. "I figured it would take a big check," Ilberman recalls, "but a lot of the people in the company weren't very happy with that, because Elvis's sales had deteriorated dramatically." The Colonel struck what the company saw as a hard bargain, and in the end, Ilberman went out on a limb, paying Elvis $5.4 million for all rights to every song he had ever recorded as of March 1, 1973.

With that, Parker turned to Elvis and demanded a new management agreement. All income from Elvis's recordings would be divided 50–50 from the first dollar, meaning Presley and Parker were now locked into a pure and equal partnership. Money from the tours remained at the two-thirds/one-third split.

But Parker also negotiated a new seven-year contract with RCA. Presley would record two albums and four singles a year for a guaranteed annual payment of at least $500,000. Since the '60s, Parker had an understanding with the label that no pop artist would get a higher royalty than Elvis, but Parker's critics would later call the arrangement too low, considering the success of the "Aloha" special, even as Elvis had been somewhat devalued as a rock act by becoming a Vegas lounge singer. Under the 1973 agreement, they said, Elvis received only half the rate of such major artists as the Rolling Stones, the Beatles, and even Elton John.

The $500,000 sum was subject to Parker and Presley's new 50–50 agreement, of course, and the Colonel would receive extra monies for his side deals of promoting the records and tours, as well as developing merchandising and promotional concepts. At Parker's insistence, Ilberman had to "scream at the lawyers to keep the buyout contract down to three or four pages." As for the Colonel's side deals, says Ilberman, "he always had side deals with everybody. That was the nature of the animal. It was almost a game."

In the end, RCA paid the pair $10.5 million. Of that, $6 million would go to the Colonel, and $4.5 to Elvis. After taxes, Elvis would retain roughly $2 million for his best work—arguably the most valuable recordings in popular music. And now his wife was asking for a large chunk of it.

When the divorce decree was finalized in October 1973, Priscilla would receive a cash payment of $725,000, plus $4,200 a month spousal support for a year (after which the payment would balloon to $6,000 a month for ten years), and $4,000 a month child support. She would also get 5 percent of Elvis's new publishing companies and half the sale of their California house.

The strain of Elvis's emotional and physical fatigue showed in his performance at the Sahara in Tahoe in May 1973. Thirty pounds overweight and lethargic, the singer canceled a number of his shows and went to a local hospital for chest X rays. But according to Marty Lacker, who was present, "He wasn't sick. He was just tired of all that shit. We flew home, and he was fine." The Colonel, who was paid $100,000 for his help with the engagement, returned his fee.

Once Elvis returned to Memphis, an angry Parker contacted Vernon about the open dialogue between Elvis's friends and family concerning his abuse of prescription medications. The fact that Elvis was in grave danger was apparent even to Presley's young daughter, Lisa Marie, who frequently saw him guzzling pills.

"One night when I was about five or six, we were watching TV," she remembers. "I looked up at him and said, 'Daddy, Daddy, I don't want you to die.' And he just looked down at me and said, 'Okay, I won't. Don't worry about it.' I said that to him several times when we were alone together . . . I guess I was picking something up."

According to Dr. Nichopoulos, Elvis was a "hard addict" who already suffered from bladder and bowel trouble, conditions that would soon leave him both incontinent and impotent. Parker didn't like Dr. Nick and suspected he was one of Elvis's main sources for drugs. But where else was he getting them? Through lawyer Ed Hookstratten, the Colonel and Vernon hired John O'Grady to investigate.

Over a period of months, the detective uncovered three physicians and one dentist who kept Elvis supplied with a steady flow of pharmaceuticals. All were summarily threatened, and deliveries occasionally intercepted. But nothing seemed to work. Elvis had no desire to stop using, and there were too many people willing to enable him.

Some of them were part of Presley's own entourage. Another was a friend of the group whose husband was a doctor. "There was more dope in that outfit—you have no idea," remembered Jackie Kahane.

But the FBI thought it knew of a more potent supplier. In a January 31, 1974, informant report about Mafia and drugs in entertainment, an agent noted, "Organized crime reaps profits from the entertainers by receiving kickbacks for obtaining their bookings in popular nightspots and in some cases, furnishing the performers with narcotics. Person contacted stated this is true currently in the case of Elvis Presley. . . . Person contacted stated that Presley is currently psychologically addicted to and a heavy user of cocaine. Because of this, he has turned down an engagement in England, which would have netted him several million dollars."

Larry Geller, whom Parker allowed back into the group in 1972, believing he had hypnotic powers, says that for a short time, Elvis did use liquid cocaine, which he obtained from his California dentist, Dr. Max Shapiro, and administered on Q-Tips stuck up in his nostrils. Soon Presley would begin using Dilaudid, or synthetic heroin. Because only "junkies" shot up, Presley had members of his entourage inject it into his hip. Dilaudid, often prescribed for terminal cancer patients, would become his favorite narcotic.

As Presley's drug use escalated, his relationship with Parker continued to unravel. In the summer of '73, they fought over a variety of issues, from Elvis's insistence on recording again in Memphis—this time, at the legendary Stax studios, where his initial sessions collapsed when Elvis was too slurry of speech—to Presley adding a gospel group, Voice, in Las Vegas. Not only did Parker believe Elvis paid them too much—$100,000 a year—but suspected one of its members helped keep him in drugs.

By now, almost everyone could see that something was wrong with Elvis. *The Hollywood Reporter* was dismayed at the star's August engagement, calling his opening-night show "one of the most ill-prepared, unsteady, and most disheartening performances of his Las Vegas career. . . . It is a tragedy . . . and absolutely depressing to see Elvis in such diminishing stature." The Colonel, who had broken his ankle before going to Vegas, hobbled around on a dark brown bamboo cane, trying to exercise damage control.

Ironically, during that same engagement, Presley accidentally fractured the ankle of one of his female guests while demonstrating a karate hold in his suite. It was this mishap that first brought Elvis into contact with Elias Ghanem, the Hilton's house doctor, who was called to administer aid. The thirty-four-year-old Lebanese immigrant had been born in Israel as one of two sons of a wealthy oil company executive, and after interning at UCLA medical school, came to Vegas as an emergency room physician in 1971. Currently, he was opening the first of a string of twenty-four-hour medical centers on Joe W. Brown Drive near the Las Vegas Hilton. During his off hours, the doctor could be found at the racetrack or hobnobbing with celebrities.

Soon Ghanem would become Presley's favorite Las Vegas physician, the entertainer giving him a Stutz Bearcat and Mercedes. But according to Kathy Westmoreland, "Elvis was worse" after Ghanem came around. Not only was Ghanem lax with a prescription pad, but, says Westmoreland, "he was flaky. He thought he *was* Elvis in a way. He came into Elvis's dressing room wearing one of his jumpsuits a couple of times. Had his hair darkened and everything."

Elvis was not amused, yet he would come to rely on Ghanem for treatment of a variety of ailments. The doctor recognized that Elvis's health was in freefall, that his weight was in the unhealthy range, his liver fatty, and his colon unnaturally sluggish. More and more, Presley seemed to put himself in life-threatening situations.

On October 11, 1973, two days after his divorce was final, Elvis, now addicted to Demerol, had trouble breathing while flying home to Memphis from Los Angeles. Dr. Nichopoulos put him in Baptist Memorial Hospital for tests. Colonel Parker, who did not visit his client during any of his hospital stays, informed the press that the singer suffered from pneumonia, but in truth, the stay amounted to a detox, as the Demerol incident was one of three overdoses that year alone. At Dr. Nick's suggestion, Elvis's next Vegas engagement, in January 1974, would be cut from four weeks to two. Meanwhile, the doctor suggested that Elvis take up racquetball for exercise.

When Presley began rehearsals at RCA Studios in Los Angeles earlier that month, he auditioned a new bass player, Duke Bardwell. The Louisiana native, a lifelong Elvis fan, was "nervous as a chicken in a yard full of roosters." As the first one there, he picked up a few tidbits—Elvis had gained some weight since the last tour and had been put on a diet of 500 calories a day, plus injections of "something that sounded like rabbit urine."

When the double doors swung open, Bardwell caught one glimpse of Elvis and thought he was "watching a Fellini movie. It was all there . . . the funky glasses, the cape, the little black cheroot, the high collar . . . and a big, nickel-plated pistol, which he pulled out of his belt and handed to one of the boys.

"We rocked along for an hour or so, and when they decided to take a break, I found myself standing next to Elvis. I said, 'I know you have a lot of martial arts training, so I was wondering why you carry a gun.' He put that top lip up a little and said, 'That's to handle anything from six feet out. Six feet in, I got it covered.' I was left pondering that while he walked away, and then he spun around and threw a punch that stopped with one of his big rings actually touching my nose. I never saw it coming, but it left me with a red face, a racing heart, and the realization that he could have missed by a half inch and driven my nose bone through my brain."

Elvis's behavior grew even more reckless once he got to Vegas. Shooting out a chandelier. Firing randomly when he couldn't find Dr. Ghanem. Narrowly missing Linda Thompson, indisposed in the bathroom, while aiming at a porcelain owl. Some nights, when the pills dulled the nerves in his esophagus, members of the entourage pulled food from his throat to keep him from choking. More than once, his heart stopped beating, and a frenzied Dr. Nick injected the organ with Ritalin to get it pumping again.

Such rescues became increasingly commonplace. In May 1974, Elvis took a young fan named Paige to Palm Springs after his closing night in Tahoe. Partying on liquid Hycodan, Elvis accidentally overdosed them both, their body temperatures falling dangerously low in Presley's frigid bedroom. The girl, who had frequently attended his Tahoe shows with her mother, suffered permanent effects.

"He said to me one time, 'If I wasn't a celebrity, I'd be put away, because I'm crazy,'" Jackie Kahane recalled. "I saw him wiped out—*wiped out*—crawling on the bloody floor! I couldn't bear to watch him. One time my wife said to him, 'Elvis, you were great tonight.' And he said, 'You saw the best imitation of Elvis Presley that he's ever done.'"

As his client continued deteriorating, the Colonel largely looked away. At least two members of Elvis's band maintain that Parker didn't know the extent of the addiction, or how sick Presley was, even as the singer deliberately cut a festering hole in his hand to get stronger drugs. Others say, in retrospect, that the Colonel still didn't know precisely what to do and hoped Elvis's doctors would find a way to help him manage his habit. The Colonel himself later said that he could complain only when Elvis did a bad show, but as "every performer has good days and bad days," and Presley balanced the off-nights with outstanding performances, he mostly stayed silent.

"I suppose I really began to get concerned at the beginning of 1974," Parker would later tell Larry Hutchinson, chief investigator to the district attorney general for Memphis. "I got worried. He'd gained too much weight and he looked terrible. Now I spoke out . . . told him he did not look well. He said, 'No disrespect, Colonel, but I know what I'm doing. Stay out of my personal life.'"

While most people around Presley were puzzled as to why the Colonel—who had ruled almost every aspect of Elvis's life—stood by as Elvis destroyed himself, Duke Bardwell put it down to Parker's "lack of humanity . . . because Colonel was the only one that could help."

"There's no question in my mind that the Colonel knew Elvis was dying," says Byron Raphael, who had been invited back for one of Elvis's Vegas openings. "And not only did he do nothing to stop it, but in a way, through omission, he was a coconspirator. There was really no strong relationship between the Colonel and Elvis anymore. He had lost his control, and that had to be a terrible thing for him. The real deadliness of Colonel Parker was that he believed the living Elvis had become an impediment to his management style and ambition. He didn't really want him to die, but he knew that was the only way out, and considering the condition Elvis was in, the best thing that could have happened. Because Elvis was easier to control dead than alive. And more valuable, too, from merchandising alone. So he just stepped out of the way and let fate take its course. That way, he and Vernon could continue making the kinds of deals that the Colonel always dreamed of making."

In planning for the inevitable, the Colonel approached Vernon in 1974 about setting up a company to oversee the merchandising of Elvis's non-performance products, as well as Presley's new music publishing companies. Parker called it Boxcar Enterprises, taking the name from the gambling term for double sixes in the game of craps, and had a logo designed with a pair of dice adorning a railroad car.

Boxcar would become the sole entity through which Presley's commercial rights were marketed. But the stock split was distinctly loaded toward the Colonel and his friends, who made up the board of directors and first officers of the corporation. Of the 500 shares issued, Parker owned 200, or 40 percent of the company, with Elvis, Tom Diskin, Freddy Bienstock, and George Parkhill (who was leaving RCA to work for the Colonel) each receiving 75 shares, or 15 percent control.

The salaries were also similarly skewed. At the outset, the Colonel paid himself $27,650 a year, while Elvis received $2,750. Tom Diskin and George Parkhill earned $4,750 each for 1974, though by 1976 the salaries would fluctuate wildly, with Parker earning $36,000, Diskin $46,448, and Elvis $10,500. Just why the star received so little of the company built around his legend was never explained.

Parker intended Boxcar to be a record company as well. George Parkhill, who "actually almost lived with the Colonel," remembered Bruce Banke, was to be in charge of its every-day operation and product distributed through RCA. Yet Boxcar's one and only long-playing album was *Having Fun with Elvis On Stage,* an embarrassing spoken-word recording made up solely of Elvis's between-songs prattle, replete with burps, belches, and bad jokes.

But the label also pressed one single, "Growing Up in a Country Way," by what the Colonel called a "green-grass group," Bodie Mountain Express with Kirk Seeley. While the band hailed from California and regularly played Knott's Berry Farm and Disneyland, the incongruous jacket photo showed four mountaineerish young men in overalls and straw hats holding acoustic instruments. They stood behind the heavier Seeley, who wore a white suit and shoes, and strove mightily to look like Elvis: the Grand Ole Opry meets Vegas.

Parker signed them, says Kathy Westmoreland, because "he knew he had to have other irons in the fire—everyone pretty much knew that Elvis wasn't going to make it very long." Westmoreland, a former beauty contestant, had been picked by the Colonel to be Boxcar Records' premier artist, and he even offered her a management contract. Like others of the Colonel's schemes, however, it didn't fly. Westmoreland balked when she realized that he had no idea how to develop her as a singer. "He knew talent when he saw it, but musically, he didn't know what was professional and what was not."

••

By now, the disease of gambling had become Parker's total rationalization in business, his addiction marshalling his every move. At the Hilton—only one establishment around town that held his markers—his debts reached $6 million. He gambled by phone from Palm Springs on the weekends, and in Vegas, if he didn't feel like going down to the casino, he asked for a roulette wheel to be sent to his rooms.

"He played stupid—they took the limit off when he came to the tables," remembered Bitsy Mott, who watched him play the two, three, seventh, and eleventh spot in craps, which promised big odds but rarely delivered. "He didn't do it with ignorance, but evidently he didn't mind losing so much money." The problem, Mott said, was that Parker had planned on leaving Marie well cared for at his death, with the remainder of his estate going to charity. "Now it looks like charity is the casinos."

During Elvis's August 1974 Vegas engagement, his performances had been riddled with long, rambling, and often painfully embarrassing monologues on a variety of personal subjects, including the rumor that the singer was on drugs. If he ever learned who started such a foul story, he said in a slurry rage that shocked all who heard it, "I'll pull your god-damned tongue out by the *roots!*"

One night, he had attempted to introduce the Colonel, who was not in the showroom. The evening before, comedian Bill Cosby had filled in for Presley, who canceled a show from alleged exhaustion. Now, when Parker was nowhere to be found, Presley again went off. "And my manager, Colonel Tom Parker. Where is he? Is the Colonel around anywhere? No, he's out playing roulette. Don't kid me. I know what he's doin'. Him and Cosby are out there talkin' mash and drinkin' trash, whatever."

The resentment that had built between them in the last several years came to a head the following month. Elvis was blistered about everything, from his indentured slavery to the Colonel's refusal to accept a $1-million offer for a string of Australian dates the previous spring. Now an incident at the hotel would lead to their biggest fight ever.

In late August, Elvis learned that the wife of Mario, the Hilton maître d', was dying of cancer. Presley was fond of Mario, who had served him dinner in his suite every day. At his most delusional, the singer believed he had the power to heal the sick and, with entourage in tow, drove to

Mario's home to treat the woman with the laying on of hands. The hotel didn't tolerate fraternization between staff and stars, however, and believing that Mario had crossed the line, terminated his employment.

Elvis was livid when he learned of Mario's firing in early September and stormed in to confront the Colonel. The hotel had no right to do such a thing, Elvis charged indignantly. But Parker, who disapproved of Mario's habit of accepting $200 tips from fans for front-row tables, told him it was hotel policy and none of Presley's business. That night from the stage, Elvis delivered a furious attack on Barron Hilton: "I think you people ought to know that the big shots at the Hilton are an unfeeling, uncaring group . . . Barron Hilton's . . . not worth a damn."

The Colonel was purple with rage when he appeared in Presley's dressing room after the show. How dare Elvis embarrass the people who had treated them so well! The two got into a shouting match in front of Elvis's guys, and later continued the tirade upstairs in Presley's thirtieth-floor suite. There, Elvis did what he'd been threatening to do for years: he fired the Colonel.

But Parker was not to be outdone. Elvis couldn't fire him, he bellowed, because he quit. "I'll call a press conference in the morning and say I'm leaving!" Presley yelled back that he'd call one that night. And so it went, until Parker, so infuriated that his jowls shook as he pounded the floor with his cane, groused that he wanted only to be paid all the singer owed him, and retired to his offices to draw up the bill. Vernon held his head when he saw it: $2 million, by most estimates, though Billy Smith remembers it at five times that amount.

"How could that be?" Elvis asked his daddy. "Well, he's got it listed here," Vernon moaned. "And he says once we pay him, he'll give up the contract." The Presleys retaliated with their own handwritten letter, informing the Colonel of all their grievances and terminating their relationship.

For a week and a half, Elvis and Parker traded insults and accusations through an intermediary, usually Lamar Fike.

The resolution came when Vernon informed his son that they couldn't afford to buy out the contract. In fact, before long, they'd have to mortgage Graceland to meet the payroll. "I guess I'm gonna have to go make up with the old bastard," Elvis told Joe Esposito.

They met at the Colonel's Palm Springs house, where Parker, realizing what bad financial straits the singer was in, offered to reduce his percentage until Elvis could get on his feet. The singer tore up his list of grievances, forever missing his chance to break free of the servant-master hold. Still, it was a turning point. "It never got better," says Billy Smith. "It got worse."

At the end of September, Elvis started a new tour but seemed in no shape to be on the road. New keyboard man Tony Brown, who'd first joined the show as part of the gospel quartet Voice, saw Presley fall to his knees as he got out of a limousine in Maryland. In Detroit, he cut a show short at thirty minutes. Reviewers expressed puzzlement and dismay over his condition, and both Parker and the doctors agreed that the star needed to take five months off. The Colonel wrote to the Hilton that Elvis would not be able to fulfill his commitment in January.

Elias Ghanem, concerned about Elvis's intestinal problems, ordered a series of colon tests. The results themselves were not alarming, but increasingly, Presley's bowels were becoming so irregular that he would travel with a trunk of Fleet enemas and sleep with a towel fashioned around him like a diaper.

"He would be so damn drugged he couldn't make it to the bathroom," recalls Lamar Fike. "Or he'd get in there and be so groggy he'd fall down on the floor. That's where they'd find him. I used to tell the Colonel, 'You're killing this guy! This guy is sick!' And he'd say, 'Just as long as he can keep doing the dates, we don't have to worry. He'll get himself back together again.'"

But Elvis was only drifting farther from reality. Fearful of odor, yet adverse to frequent bathing, he ingested Nullo deodorant tablets three times a day, believing "they'd kill any type of body odor, from bad breath to butt," says Billy Smith, who with his wife, Jo, moved into a trailer on the Graceland grounds at Elvis's insistence. "We used to con him into the bathtub when he was filthy," adds Fike, "but you didn't physically make him do anything when he wasn't loaded. He'd fight you like a hawk."

Together, Smith, Dr. Nichopoulos, and the physician's office nurse, Tish Henley, would attempt to wean Elvis off prescription drugs, particularly after Presley was again admitted to Baptist Memorial Hospital in January 1975 for breathing difficulties. Vernon, who'd recently split from his wife, Dee, lay in the next room with a heart attack. Elvis was more concerned about his father than about his own health and, before his stay was over, charmed some of the nurses into bringing him whatever drugs he desired.

By the next month, a thinner Elvis was ready to return to Vegas. There, in his dressing room on February 18, he met with Barbra Streisand and Jon Peters, who hoped to interest him in a movie role, a remake of *A Star Is Born*. Jerry Schilling, who was present at the meeting, recalls that Elvis "went for it, definitely." And Gordon Stoker remembers Presley talking about how excited he was at the prospect.

The Colonel, however, had several concerns, starting with billing and money. Streisand's production company, First Artists, offered $500,000, plus 10 percent of profits, but no participation in music or recording rights. Parker responded that Elvis needed $1 million in salary, plus $100,000 in expenses and half of the profits, with a separate deal to be struck for a soundtrack. First Artists balked at the arrangement, and the deal fell apart when Streisand declined to make what Parker considered a suitable counteroffer.

"Mr. Presley has indicated that he would like to make this movie," the Colonel wrote to Roger Davis, a William Morris lawyer, "[but] I advised him not to allow this to become a part of making a cheap deal." Parker would forever be criticized for allowing money to take precedence over revitalizing his client in a challenging film role, something Presley desperately wanted. But he would later shift the blame to Elvis. "There was never no plan for him to do *A Star Is Born*. He told me to make the contract stiff enough where they would turn it down, 'cause he did not want to do it."

Jerry Schilling says that Elvis was disillusioned, "but he knew if negotiations broke down, there was a good reason. He never complained about it that I heard." Lamar Fike believes "deep down, Elvis knew he couldn't play the part [but] laid a lot of the blame on the Colonel."

Yet others saw a deeper malaise, as if Presley, now forty years old and terrified of aging, realized the film had been his last chance to prove himself as an actor. "People aren't going to remember me, because I've never done anything lasting," he said to Kathy Westmoreland in a particularly poignant moment. "I've never made a classic film to show what I can do." His one regret, he told Larry Geller, was that he had never won an Oscar.

To quell his disappointment over *A Star Is Born*, Elvis buoyed himself with new offers to perform in England and Saudi Arabia. The Saudi dates especially thrilled him, says Lamar Fike, as Adnan and Essam Khashoggi offered $5 million for Elvis to play at the pyramids at Giza. But the Colonel turned it down, only to have the arms billionaires double their offer. "Elvis came out to the bus, and he said, 'It's this now,' and he held up ten fingers." When the deal fell through, Billy Smith remembers, "you could almost see the blood drain out of [his] face."

Presley tried to remain hopeful as other offers—including $1 million a night for Germany and Japan—poured in. Still the Colonel refused, even as he bragged about the money to Mel Ilberman and others at RCA, who thought it odd that he didn't take Elvis abroad, considering the vast number of records the singer sold there. Sometimes Parker hinted it would happen, and other times he turned churlish. "I was with the Colonel one time when some people from South America came up and offered him two and a half million dollars for one show," recalls Gaylen Adams, the RCA rep. "And he was just so nonchalant. He said, 'Well, whenever I need two and a half million dollars, I'll call you.' "

Yet not only would Elvis soon borrow $350,000 from a Memphis bank, but the Colonel was so desperate for money that he insisted that concert promoters invest advance ticket funds in certificates of deposit under his name. Such profitable foreign dates could have easily solved the pair's financial problems, and Parker could have gotten around the passport dilemma by having Weintraub and Hulett take Elvis abroad. But the Colonel, fearing loss of control, was too paranoid for that. Lately, he'd heard rumblings that Elvis asked Tom Hulett to manage him if Presley and Parker reached another impasse.

For now, the performer was trying to make amends. In July, hearing that Elton John had given his manager a $40,000 Rolls-Royce, he bought the Colonel an airplane, a $1.2-million G-1 turboprop—a kind of companion to his own recent acquisition, a Convair 880 jet to be named the *Lisa Marie,* which he settled on after first attempting to buy exiled financier Robert Vesco's impounded Boeing 707.

Parker understood such impetuous and spontaneous shopping, and refused Presley's gift of the twelve-seat plane, saying he couldn't afford the taxes. That left Elvis angry, embarrassed, and more determined than ever to dismiss the Colonel for Hulett.

The talks with Hulett got far enough along, according to David Briggs, Presley's piano player at the time, that "we all thought it was going to happen." In fact, the men had already discussed going to Europe.

Loanne Miller cites two more reasons why Parker balked at going to Europe—his own bad health and the difficulties of doing business with foreign promoters. "Colonel was adamant that the fans not be taken advantage of with extremely high priced tickets, and everyone who wanted [to bring] Elvis overseas wanted to charge the equivalent of $100.

Colonel knew that most of the fans didn't begin to have that kind of money."

Whatever the reasons, the fact remains, says Duke Bardwell, that Elvis never realized his dream. "To deny him that was the last nail in the coffin. He didn't have anything to look forward to, and so he just went deeper and deeper into the things that let him hide."

Yet more and more there was no hiding much of anything. On July 20, Elvis embarrassed his backup singers, Kathy Westmoreland and the Sweet Inspirations, with racial and sexual insults on stage in Norfolk, Virginia. Two days later, in North Carolina, he angrily waved a Baretta pistol at Dr. Nichopoulos when the physician tried to control his medications, the gun discharging, and a bullet ricocheting off a chair and striking Dr. Nick in the chest, wounding him only slightly. By the time Elvis arrived in Vegas in August, he was so loopy that he sat down for most of one performance, and finally lay flat on the stage, prompting yet another hospital stay.

After the Norfolk incident, the Colonel got Vernon on the telephone, according to Mike Crowley, who had just gone to work for Concerts West. "I was there," says Crowley, the company's liaison to the Colonel. "He said, 'You're going to have to take him off the road for at least six months to clean himself up. He can't do this to the fans or himself.'" Vernon replied that Elvis had to work, Crowley says, and if Parker didn't want to take him out on the road, they'd find someone else who would.

"I hate that old man," Elvis told Billy Smith shortly afterward. His cousin asked him why. Elvis mumbled something about Parker being senile and rude, and Smith pumped him for more. "He said, 'The Colonel is too concerned with my drug use. I'm tired of the old son of a bitch threatening me, saying he's not going to book me anymore. Goddamn it, I've done performances that I didn't want to. They booked me in places that I didn't want to be. We need to stick to our old agreement, where Colonel takes care of the business part, and I take care of the performing. It'll work a hell of a lot better.'"

Despite such friction, the Colonel still pondered ways to boost his client to new heights. For New Year's Eve 1975, Parker let Jerry Weintraub take Elvis into the huge Pontiac, Michigan, Silverdome as a substitute for the Rolling Stones, who canceled due to illness. But Elvis made a poor showing, hampered by drugs, mediocre pickup musicians, and weather so frigid that one of the players plugged in an electric blanket. Presley was so late getting to the stage that intermission, following several opening acts, including Parker's "green-grass" group, lasted more than an hour.

"He's really screwed up," conductor Joe Guercio told Jackie Kahane, who emceed the show. Kahane saw for himself, as the star said he was "scared shitless" as he passed him on the stairs.

Within minutes, Elvis split his pants and left the stage to change, and when he returned, he was so discombobulated that he kept on singing once the orchestra stopped for the countdown to midnight and the playing of "Auld Lang Syne." Then when the band went into "Happy Days Are Here Again," Elvis launched into a hymn, and segued into "I Can't Help Falling in Love with You," the last song of the show. "He didn't do twenty minutes," Kahane recalled. "I figured they'd kill him." But the Silverdome booked him back before he even left town, says the comic. "That was the magic of Elvis."

The Colonel would tout the appearance as another Elvis "first." With 62,500 fans in attendance, the show grossed more than $800,000—the biggest sum ever generated by a single artist in a one-night performance. After expenses, Presley and Parker divided $300,000 by their two-thirds/ one-third agreement for the night's work.

However, twenty-three days later, the Colonel presented Elvis with a document that called for Parker to receive a larger share of such profits, or a 50–50 split on all live appearances.

"It is hereby understood by both parties," the contract read, "that these [tours] are a joint venture and that Elvis Presley is responsible for the presentation of his stage performance and Colonel Tom Parker and his representatives [for the] advertising and promotion of the show. . . . This authorization and agreement will run for seven years from [January 22, 1976.]" Elvis signed without hesitation, though he was so strapped for cash that Parker took his old one-third commission for a time, Presley agreeing to pay him back when finances weren't so tight.

Now Parker turned his attentions to fulfilling Elvis's recording obligations, the source of much rancor between the label and the star. Neither the Colonel nor Felton Jarvis had been able to get Elvis into the studio for nearly a year. Finally, in early 1976, the record company saw it had no choice but to take the studio to him.

On February 2, engineers from RCA Nashville pulled up at Graceland in the big red recording van, which amounted to a mobile studio. Elvis's guys helped move the hideous Polynesian future out of the den, and the crew rolled the baby grand piano in from the music room. Then they did their best to blunt the acoustics, draping the walls with heavy blankets, nailing plywood sheets together to set up partitions, and bringing in extra carpeting to try to isolate each musician's sound—a necessity, since Elvis held fast to the old way of recording, where everyone played at once.

Jarvis had hoped to glean twenty new masters from the sessions, and budgeted more than $74,000 for six nights of recording. But Elvis, popping pills, wearing his cop's uniform, and ranting about his plot to rub out all the drug dealers in Memphis, gave everyone fits, stretching Felton's budget by another $30,000. One night, he stopped everything to fly off to Denver for a peanut butter sandwich.

"Felton would come back and say, 'It just wasn't good,'" remembers RCA's Joe Galante. "The company was at the point where it wasn't a matter of control or direction anymore, but just containment."

On the fourth day, as if to police the goings-on, the Colonel himself made an uncustomary appearance, historic both for his showing up at a recording session, and even more for visiting Graceland. David Briggs, who played electric keyboard, flinched as Parker walked in during the playback of a pornographic version of "Hurt," which Elvis had recorded as a joke for the players. "The Colonel almost shit when he heard it. He said, 'Get rid of that tape!'" though by then too many people already had copies to keep it out of circulation. On the last day, Elvis refused to come downstairs, and the session was canceled.

Eventually, Presley would lay down enough tracks for the *Moody Blue* album, though it would require additional recording in October to get just enough songs to pad out an LP. Even then, the sessions dragged on as Elvis played pool and ate chicken.

"We'd come to the house and wait all day long, sitting in the living room," remembers Tony Brown, who played piano on the fall sessions. "One night he was singing a track, and he excused himself. We were all there, J.D. [Sumner] and the Stamps, the Sweet Inspirations. Maybe two hours later, he comes downstairs with a hat and a trench coat on and a shotgun, pretending to blow everything up with it. For the next four hours, he explained that gun to us and told us how many guns he owned. And then the session was over." Another time, he abruptly ended rehearsals when a truck arrived with a delivery of motorcycles.

To some, Elvis appeared to simply want company. One particularly difficult night, unable to shake the loneliness, he disappeared, and Felton went looking for him, eventually finding him outside in the dark. "Why are you sitting out here, Elvis?" The singer let out a weary sigh. "I'm just so tired of playing Elvis Presley."

Things were no better when Elvis went back on tour in the spring. "There was a lot of dissension [in the band] there at the end," says Tony Brown, "and I think it was frustration over Elvis not being at the top of his game. Some nights it just sounded awful, and we were all looking like fools. We were always thinking, Is he going to be on or off tonight? Ninety percent of the time, he was pretty much off." Backup singer Sherrill Nielsen was instructed to double Presley on the high notes in case he couldn't sustain them.

By now, Elvis's drug regimen for the road was so specific that Dr. Nichopoulos prescribed it in six stages. Stage one, administered at 3:00 P.M., when Presley arose, consisted of a "voice shot" that Dr. Ghanem concocted, three appetite suppressants, medication for dizziness, a laxative, vitamins and herbs, and testosterone. Stage two, delivered an hour before he went on stage, was made up of another voice shot, a decongestant with codeine, an amphetamine, a pill for vertigo, and Dilaudid. Stage three, timed just before his performance, included more Dilaudid, Dexedrine, and caffeine. And stage four, designed to bring him down after the show, included a pill to lower his blood pressure, some diluted Demerol, a sedative, and an antihistamine.

At bedtime, Elvis received stage five, a Placidyl, a Quaalude, three additional sedatives, an amphetamine, a blood-pressure pill, and a laxative. If Elvis couldn't sleep, he advanced to stage six, made up of Amytal, a hypnotic sleeping pill, and more Quaaludes.

These extreme ups and downs were taking their toll. When private investigator John O'Grady caught Presley's show in Tahoe that April, "he had locomotive attacks where he couldn't walk . . . I really thought he was going to die." O'Grady reported what he'd seen to attorney Ed Hookstratten in L.A. In June, "Hookstratten, Priscilla, and I did everything to get him in the hospital for three or four months," O'Grady recalled, referring to the drug-treatment program at the Scripps Clinic in San Diego. They also considered taking him to a private hospital on Maui and one in the mid-South.

By now, Elvis suffered a host of physical problems, from blood clots, to hypoglycemia, to an enlarged heart. His liver was three times its normal size, his colon twisted. In three years, his weight, on a diet of junk food and downers, had zoomed from 175 to 245, something he tried to camouflage with darker jumpsuits and an elastic corset that held in his girth. Secretly, Presley told Kathy Westmoreland he had bone cancer, ask-ing her to keep it quiet: "I don't want anybody to know how sick I am . . . I don't want people coming to see a dying man." But Elton John, visiting him backstage in Maryland in June, saw it anyway. "He had dozens of people around him, supposedly looking after him," the Englishman later said, "but he already seemed like a corpse."

In July, Dr. Ghanem moved Elvis into a wing of his house for one of several "sleep diets," a kind of rapid detox in which the patient ingests only liquid nourishment and sedatives, slumbering through withdrawal. Elvis's feces had lately been as white as chalk, a certain sign of liver trou-ble, probably from ingesting massive amounts of pills. While a host of physicians contributed to Elvis's problem, Tennessee records would later show that Dr. Nichopoulos alone had supplied a staggering 1,296 am-phetamines, 1,891 sedatives, and 910 narcotics for the year 1975. That number would escalate dramatically for each of the next two years.

When Elvis returned to Memphis, he was withdrawn, sullen, de-pressed. Nothing became of the plan to hospitalize Presley because no one enforced it. Certainly not his manager, who couldn't forget his own institutionalization forty-three years before, nor the spineless Vernon, and least of all the Memphis Mafia, which was powerless to do much of anything.

The entourage was largely made up of younger men now—Dean Nichopoulos, son of Dr. Nick, and Elvis's stepbrothers David, Billy, and Rick Stanley, the latter of whom had been arrested in August 1975 at Methodist Hospital in Memphis, trying to use a forged prescription for Demerol. Too often, they looked at the job as a paycheck and reflected glory. Joe Esposito lived in California. Jerry Schilling, also on the West Coast, had little contact with Elvis anymore. And Presley was somewhat estranged from Red and Sonny West for, among other reasons, their rough handling of fans, one of whom was bringing a lawsuit against the star.

Parker himself felt shut out of Elvis's life, and complained about it in a letter to him on June 16, more than a week after the singer ended an eleven-day tour.

"As I told Vernon today, I have not heard from anyone since I got back, neither from Sonny or from any other member of your staff. I just wanted you to know in the event you feel that they are in contact with me, but they are not."

Still, on the whole, whether out of depression or compulsion, the

Colonel seemed less concerned with managerial vision than continuing to play the numbers.

"I was gambling at the Las Vegas Hilton," remembers Mike Growney, general manager of the Gold Coast Casino, "and there was one man sitting there, and I noticed that a security guard would keep coming over and bringing a stack of $100 chips. He would put the whole pile down and bet the number, and then they would spin the wheel. Then the security guard would bring over another stack of chips. And it's $10,000 at a time. I said to the floor man, 'What's going on?' And he said, 'That's Colonel Parker . . . He's lost a million dollars.' "

Despite such willful extravagance, the Colonel kept an eye peeled for anyone who tried to fleece him out of a dollar. Which was how he met Joe Shane, then a twenty-six-year-old merchandiser from Paducah, Kentucky, who'd sold thousands of Elvis Presley "Aloha from Hawaii" T-shirts by running ads in *TV Guide* and *The National Enquirer*. Shane was just about to close a deal with JC Penney's 1,900 stores when he ran into a snag: he didn't own the licensing rights.

"I understand you're trying to sell some merchandise of my boy," Parker rasped into the phone.

"Yes, sir, I am."

"Do you pay me any money for that?"

"No, sir, I do not."

"Well," the manager said evenly, "I think you'd better start."

If the young merchandiser wanted to continue selling Elvis shirts, he needed to give the Colonel 25 percent of retail. Shane gulped—the usual fee was 10 percent of wholesale—and agreed. "Then you'd better get out here," Parker beckoned from California. "Let's put this deal together."

"The Colonel prefers to give his contracts to people who're hungry, people on the way up fast but still not at the top, people stretched a little thin and willing to take a smaller piece of the pie," as one of the Colonel's former associates explains.

Shane fit the bill. "We had a nice camaraderie because he saw some carny in me," he says. And Parker, who never attempted mass merchandising through magazines, was fascinated that Shane had been able to sell 1,500 shirts a day from an ad. But his big concern was why he didn't sell *more*. A few days after they struck their deal, Parker took him to the William Morris Agency and signed the papers to make Shane the only other licensed Elvis merchandiser in the world.

As Parker forged a new alliance in California, an old one was breaking up in Memphis. On the morning of July 13, 1976, Vernon placed three phone calls—the first to Red West, the second to Sonny West, and the third to Dave Hebler, one of Elvis's newer bodyguards, who'd been hired mainly for his karate expertise. All three were being terminated with one week's pay. Vernon explained that it had been a difficult year and he needed to trim the payroll, but the real reasons ran more to the pending lawsuit and the Wests' tendency to cause friction among the group. Red, who had been Elvis's friend and protector since high school, was particularly stunned not to have received the news from Elvis himself. Presley, too, was upset but, not knowing what to do or say, remained silent.

Ten days later, as Elvis began his fifth tour of the year, his stage moves were little more than perfunctory, his voice worn and tired. The Colonel, distraught at reports of a string of bad shows, confronted Elvis in Hartford and again bellowed that if Elvis didn't shape up fast, he was in danger of losing not only his fans, but his Vegas contract and recording deal. Presley, shaken by the encounter, sought out Tom Hulett for solace. "You are the biggest entertainer there is, and everybody loves you," Hulett said reassuringly. But Hulett, too, knew that Elvis couldn't go on much longer.

In Houston, on August 28, Elvis gave such a dismaying show that critic Bob Claypool described it as a "depressingly incoherent, amateurish mess served up by a bloated, stumbling and mumbling figure who didn't act like 'the King' of anything, least of all rock 'n' roll." For more than twenty years, Claypool wrote, Elvis had been breaking hearts. "Saturday afternoon in the Summit—in a completely new and unexpected way—he broke mine."

"It was really bad," says Lamar Fike, who'd replaced Sonny West as security chief. "We almost lost him in Houston. But nobody would say it, even though it was just tearing us up, ripping us to shreds. I felt like some sort of voice in the wilderness. I said, 'God almighty, guys, look what's happening here! He's going on us!' "

Larry Geller was equally disturbed but, like Fike, found most of the people around Elvis in denial. "It took him more and more time to get ready for the show. I would go to people's rooms and literally cry. I'd say, 'Look at him. He's sick and something's got to be done.' And they'd say, 'No, man, in twenty years Elvis is going to look better than he does today. He's going to pull out of it.' "

But Dr. Nichopoulos knew better and, with the help of Billy Smith, stepped up the efforts to quell Elvis's craving, diluting his shots, draining his capsules, and substituting placebos for the harder pills, delivered as "attack packets" at appointed hours by Elvis's stepbrothers. Like any drug addict, Presley caught on quick, demanding more and stronger stuff. If Nichopoulos refused, he'd fly to Vegas or L.A. to find another source.

Despite Elvis's physical condition and faltering shows, the public had no knowledge of the extent of Presley's drug habit, believing he was simply ill. All that was about to change.

In September, rumors swirled that Red, Sonny, and Dave Hebler were writing a book about their life with Elvis, intending to reveal his terrible deterioration as a kind of wake-up call. Jackie Kahane had encouraged members of the group to go to the newspapers months before. "What would the point be?" Joe Guercio asked him. "To save his life! He's on dope, he's on everything!" Kahane said. "Forget it," Guercio told him. "You'd look like an ass."

"When Elvis found out about the book," Larry Geller remembers, "he was so hurt. We were in Mobile, Alabama. I can still see him, sitting in bed, with tears running down his cheeks. He said, 'How could these guys do this to me? They could have anything they want.' He wasn't so worried about how it would impact him, but rather his family. He kept saying, 'How is it going to affect my father and my little girl? When she grows up, what is she going to think about her daddy?'"

Through Vernon, Elvis asked Parker to have the book stopped. The manager hired John O'Grady, who learned that the tell-all was being cowritten by Steve Dunleavy of the tabloid *Star*, and offered the Wests and Hebler $50,000 to cancel the project. But the bodyguards refused. Nothing more was ever done.

Geller believes the Colonel didn't find a way to stop the book because he wanted it to be published. Fike says that Parker tried to halt it, but by the time he learned of its existence, the authors had already signed their contracts. Elvis, however, believed the matter had been taken care of, though his obsession with the book caused him to overindulge his love of fattening foods, his weight ballooning even higher.

When he returned to Las Vegas that December, Elvis was so large that Bruce Banke couldn't believe his appearance ("I said, 'He's putting us on. That's got to be padding in there.' His belt buckle was down below his belly"). He injured his ankle on stage, railed about his frustrations, cursed the "tinny" microphone, and one night, told a perplexed audience, "I hate Las Vegas." Bill Burk of the *Memphis Press-Scimitar* wrote what everyone was thinking but few would say: "One walks away wondering how much longer it can be before the end comes."

By the last months of '76, Linda Thompson, tired of watching Elvis self-destruct and "feeling that I wasn't worth anything without him," had all but phased herself out of his life. In November, he met twenty-year-old Ginger Alden, another dark-haired Memphis beauty queen who currently held the title of Miss Mid-South Fair. Ginger reminded Elvis of a young Priscilla, but several factors hampered the courtship, including Elvis's physical condition, the twenty-two-year difference in their ages, and Ginger's feisty independence.

Unlike other of Elvis's girlfriends, Ginger refused to build her life around Presley's, preferring to be with her friends much of the time instead of spending the night at Graceland or going on tours. In January 1977, when she was to accompany Elvis to Nashville for a recording session, she changed her mind at the last minute and refused to go. Elvis, moody and angry, checked in to a Nashville hotel, but never made an appearance at the studio, complaining of a sore throat.

He returned to Memphis the next day, prompting the Colonel to once more lay down the law: "Get off your tail [and] fulfill your commitment, or there will be no more tours."

The canceled recording session made its way into the *Nashville Banner,* where a columnist reported Presley's aides "contend the singer's new girlfriend . . . [is] absolutely running him ragged." Later that month, Elvis presented Ginger with an 11.5-karat diamond engagement ring. Then in March, he took her family on vacation in Hawaii, bringing along several of the guys.

Larry Geller was among them. When the men were alone, Geller spoke to Elvis about his health, advising him on his diet and suggesting foods and vitamins to strengthen his immune system. Elvis needed rest, he told him, and the singer vowed to take off six months to a year and come back to the islands to relax and restore his well-being. He also pledged to make other changes.

"He was adamant about firing the Colonel," says Geller. "I'd never heard him so resolute, and I'm convinced he was going to get rid of him." In several conversations, Presley brought up the '74 incident, saying he was sorry he hadn't gone through with it then. "He even had the time picked out when he was going to make his move, and he was certain he wanted Tom Hulett to manage his career. He said, 'Larry, I promise you, this is exactly what I'm going to do.'" He would see to it after the last tour wound down in August.

Several days later, Elvis cut his vacation short after suffering an eye infection, and when he went back on the road at the end of the month, he did not appear well. Billy Smith could barely get him on the plane. In Alexandria, Louisiana, on March 30, he stumbled through "Can't Help Falling in Love," and finally improvised his own prophetic lyric: "Wise men know/ When it's time to go . . ."

The next day, in Baton Rouge, Elvis woke up feeling ill, and summoned Dr. Nick, Joe Esposito, and Larry Geller to his suite. "I told Daddy and Nick I'm sick, man, I can't go on tonight," he moaned. "I'm canceling the rest of the tour." But Geller had obtained galley sheets of the West and Hebler book through a fan, and knew that the tabloids would see a cancellation as verification of the story. The awful details were already beginning to appear in the British press.

Presley's entourage had kept the news from the star, but now Geller thought he should hear it. Elvis exploded in anger ("Get me the Colonel!") and was so traumatized that Dr. Nick felt the need to sedate him. When he awakened, he insisted on flying back to Memphis and going into the hospital, as much for insurance reasons as health.

The Colonel would add the canceled dates on to a later tour, but the crowd in Baton Rouge would never forget the bizarre way Parker handled the last-minute cancellation. "He had us go on stage and take our places as if Elvis was coming out," remembers Kathy Westmoreland. "Then he faked a blackout, and whisked us out of the building into police cars. Tom Hulett said they were trying to get everybody out without getting hurt. In fact, there was a riot afterwards."

Three weeks later, with Ginger in tow, Elvis was back on the road for his third tour of the year. One review described the performer as "seeming not to care." A Detroit columnist wrote, "He stunk the joint out."

Although a few industry insiders knew the relationship between Parker and Presley had broken down, perhaps irretrievably, a story in the *Nashville Banner* in late April came as a surprise to most. The Colonel had put Elvis's management contract up for sale, and a group of West Coast businessmen had expressed interest, the paper reported, quoting sources in Nashville, Memphis, and Los Angeles.

The reasons were said to be the Colonel's failing health and financial problems, particularly his high-rolling habits. Parker and Presley had reportedly "not spoken in two years," wrote columnist Bill Hance.

By the next day, Parker, in St. Paul to advance the singer's concert, was on the phone to dispute the story, telling Nashville's morning paper, the *Tennessean,* he had "absolutely no plans to sell Elvis Presley. . . . I'm here working with Elvis, I'm in good health, and I don't have any debts—at least none that I can't pay." Joe Esposito, who parroted the Colonel's words, also dismissed the report that the two men didn't talk. "They're on the road together all the time, and the Colonel just spoke to Elvis yesterday."

What prompted the story isn't known, but clearly Parker was exploring new directions, including one he had shied away from for so long. Around this same time, he contacted Peter Grant, the corpulent manager of the British rock group Led Zeppelin, whose U.S. dates were handled through Concerts West. Could Grant promote a European tour for Elvis, since Parker was too busy stateside to accompany his star? They made plans to talk about it after Presley's last shows of the summer.

But in truth, Elvis was not up to performing. By May, on his fourth tour of 1977, he wore the same white, Aztec-calendared jumpsuit thirteen days in a row. It was the only one that fit him.

In Knoxville, a doctor who saw Elvis backstage reported that "he was pale, swollen—he had no stamina." Then in Landover, Maryland, he left the stage, tossing two microphones to the floor, to answer "nature's call." A week later, in Baltimore, he again walked off for thirty minutes. "At the finale," *Variety* wrote, "there was no ovation, and patrons exited shaking their heads and speculating on what was wrong with him."

Presley himself knew the signs. Not long before, he'd invited the songwriter Ben Weisman to come up to the suite in Vegas. Elvis, his face puffy, sat down at the piano. "Ben," he said, "there's a song I love, called 'Softly As I Leave You.' But it's not about a man leaving a lady. It's about a man who's going to die."

Before the taping of a CBS-TV concert special in Rapid City, South Dakota, Elvis showed Kathy Westmoreland a blue jumpsuit he planned to wear that evening. "I'm going to look fat in that faggy little suit," he told her, "but I'll look good in my coffin." Westmoreland found herself unable to say a word, "because I knew that it was inevitable and could come at any moment. He wanted me to wear white, not black, at the funeral."

Westmoreland consoled herself with the news that after the fifth tour ended in June, Elvis would have the entire month of July to himself. Though the Colonel often gave the band very little notice, the next dates weren't scheduled to start until August 17, and Lisa Marie was coming for a two-week visit. Ordinarily, Elvis liked to work, and other than the times he was ill, he never thought of Parker as pushing him to tour, even asking him to book more shows when the Colonel suggested he slow down. But now he knew he needed time off.

"I'm so tired," he told Westmoreland. "I don't want to go out on this next tour, but I have to. The Colonel owes $8 million."

Elvis, too, was feeling the pinch. Recently, he had issued Priscilla a deed of trust to Graceland, guaranteeing her nearly half a million dollars still owed on the divorce settlement.

Lamar Fike also looked forward to Elvis's last show before the midsummer break, which fell in Indianapolis on June 26, the Colonel's sixty-eighth birthday. Like Geller, Fike had encouraged the singer to go to Hawaii and change everything he hated about his life. Now Fike wondered if it might be too late. On stage, Elvis had summoned new strength, giving his best performance in months, and ending his eighty-minute show with impassioned renditions of "Hurt" and "Bridge over Troubled Water." But moments before, he'd looked so fatigued, as if the life had already drained out of him.

"He'll never see the snow fly," Fike told the entourage. "I promise you."

The Colonel had seen irrefutable evidence of Elvis's dire condition himself as late as May 21, in Louisville. Larry Geller was in the anteroom of Elvis's hotel suite, waiting for Dr. Nick to finish administering the drugs that would transform Presley from a sick, lethargic man to an energized performer. Suddenly, Geller heard a loud knock at the door. He answered it to find an angry Parker leaning on his cane. Geller was shocked—never had he known the Colonel to come to Elvis's room on tour.

"Where is he?" Parker demanded.

Geller said he would let Elvis know he was there. "No, I'm going in," the Colonel said curtly, brushing Geller as he passed.

The Colonel opened the door to a devastating sight—Elvis, semiconscious and moaning, with Dr. Nick working frantically to revive him, kneeling at his bedside, dunking the singer's head into a bucket of ice water.

The Colonel banged the door behind him. For a moment, Geller's heart sank. Then he felt relieved. Finally, the Colonel had seen Elvis at his worst. Surely now he would talk to him, pull him off the road, take steps to get him help. Yet ninety seconds later, the manager thundered out.

Larry rose. "You listen to me!" Parker shouted, stabbing the air with his cane. "The only thing that's important is that he's on that stage tonight! Nothing else matters!"

And then the Colonel was gone.

"I thought, Oh my God!," Geller remembers. "What about Elvis? Doesn't Colonel understand that this man is in dire straits? I was horrified. I can only surmise he acted out of stupidity and denial. But still, how could he be so callous?"

The answer to that question was one that almost no one knew, with origins deep in Parker's carny past. As a young man on the circuit, one of his jobs had been to befriend the geek, the pathetic dipsomaniac who sat in a pit and bit the heads off live chickens in exchange for a daily bottle. Periodically, the poor soul would run off and hide in the fields, unable to face another bloody performance. Parker would find him, shuddering and desperate, then wave the bottle as bait and reward, and bring him back to do the show.

"Parker and Presley represent the convergence of two characters from carnival culture: the poor country boy who grabs the brass ring and the mysterious stranger who fleeces the innocent," Richard Harrington wrote in *The Washington Post*.

But Parker's gambling had morphed him into a combination of the two, and then some. As Elvis prepared for his next tour in August 1977, the Colonel's gambling debts at the Las Vegas Hilton reached a staggering $30 million.

It is in that sad fact that the lines begin to blur between the geek, his keeper, and the chicken, dancing or otherwise.

In the late 1950s, Parker invited Byron Raphael to Grauman's Chinese Theater for a showing of his favorite movie. Produced in 1947 as gritty and disturbing film noir, *Nightmare Alley* perfectly captured the sordid netherworld of the small-time carnival. In the picture's evocative opening, Tyrone Power, as the ambitious young sideshow hustler Stanton Carlisle, encounters his first gloaming geek. At the sound of frenzied squawking, the crowd gasps, and a shaken Carlisle asks the show owner: "How does a guy get so low? Is he born a geek?"

By the end of the film, after relying on fakery and illusion to climb to Chicago's supper-club-and-society level, Carlisle learns the horrific answer firsthand. The inevitable fall of "Stanton the Great" results from his unyielding need to manipulate and mislead, and from his inability to separate himself from the marks he deceives.

"The fascination Colonel had with that picture was unbelievable," remembers Raphael. "He sat there so engrossed that he never moved, though God knows how many times he'd seen it. He talked about it all the time, for years."

Parker identified with the dark morality tale not just for the haunting, vulgar realism of the sideshow milieu, with its depictions of mitt camps and Tarot card readings, but because the character was very nearly him.

As drawn in William Lindsay Gresham's potent novel, Stanton Carlisle began life with a too-strict father, a deep love for animals, and the knowledge that he's a bit too fond of his mother. As he slips into a life of deception and fraud, he causes the accidental death of a friend and, later, in a miracle worker "spook" scam gone wrong, brings on the stroke of a client he's bilked out of a fortune. Lost and desperate, with the police on his trail, Carlisle sinks into the violent underworld of the fugitive, riding the rails and living with hobos. But in his eventual return to the carnival, he sentences himself to a living damnation he could not have imagined, as the most debased of the sideshow freaks.

"I never thought Colonel would wind up as the geek," says Raphael. "But in becoming the most horrendous of compulsive gamblers in his later years, that's exactly what he did. He turned into the very thing he despised. All those years, nobody could touch him, and so he destroyed himself."

In the movie's frightening finale, Carlisle, wild-eyed, screaming, and deep in the grips of psychosis ("The geek's gone nuts!" yells an onlooker), finds himself chased by a mob with a straightjacket. McGraw, the carny boss who'd hired him only that morning, stops with a roustabout to watch. For the first time, the boss recognizes his new geek as the famed "mentalist" of old.

"Well, he certainly fooled me," mutters McGraw. "Stanton. Stanton the Great."

"How can a guy get so low?" asks the roustabout, echoing what the young Carlisle said long ago.

McGraw, who's seen it all, shakes his head. "He just reached too high."

19

"WE THINK HE OD'D":

THE DEATH OF ELVIS

O N the sweltering evening of August 15, 1977, Elvis Presley slipped out of his blue silk lounging pajamas and, with the help of his cousin Billy Smith, climbed into a black sweat suit emblazoned with a Drug Enforcement Agency patch, a white silk shirt, and a pair of black patent boots, which he wore unzipped due to the puffy buildup of fluid in his ankles.

At 10:30, after a night of motorcycle riding with girlfriend Ginger Alden, the singer stuffed two .45-caliber automatic pistols in the waistband of his sweatpants. Then he donned his blue-tinted, chrome sunglasses to slide behind the wheel of his Stutz automobile. With Alden, Smith, and Smith's wife, Jo, in tow, Elvis steered his way to the office of his dentist, Dr. Lester Hofman, in East Memphis. A crown on Presley's back tooth needed fixing, and he wanted to tend to it before he left the following evening for Portland, Maine, the first date of a twelve-day tour.

When the couples returned to Graceland around midnight, Elvis and Ginger went upstairs, and the Smiths retired to their trailer. Sometime around 2:00 A.M., Elvis spoke with Larry Geller. Geller recalls his friend was "in a very good mood, looking forward to the tour, and making plans for the future." Around 4:00 A.M., Elvis still felt energetic enough for a game of racquetball, and phoned Billy and Jo to join him and Ginger. As the foursome went out the back door and down the concrete walkway to Elvis's racquetball building, a light rain began to fall.

"Ain't no problem," Elvis said, and put out his hands as if to stop it. Miraculously, Smith remembers, the rain let up. "See, I told you," Elvis said. "If you've got a little faith, you can stop the rain."

Despite his sudden burst of energy, Elvis was exhausted from several days of a Jell-O diet, the latest in a series of desperate attempts to trim him down enough to fit into his stage costumes. He tired quickly on the court, and the couples resorted more to cutting up than concentrating on their game. After ten minutes, they took a break, then returned to the court. But they quit a second time when Elvis misjudged a serve and hit himself hard in the shin with his racquet.

Limping into the lounge, Presley fixed himself a glass of ice water and then moved to the piano and began singing softly, ending with "Blue Eyes Crying in the Rain."

Afterward, upstairs in the house, Smith washed and dried his cousin's hair. Presley again obsessed about the bodyguard book, *Elvis: What Happened?*, which had hit the stands two weeks before. Yelling wildly, out of his head, Elvis fumed he'd bring Red, Sonny, and Dave Hebler to Graceland, where he'd kill them himself and dispose of their bodies. Then his mood dimmed, and he rehearsed a speech he planned to give from the stage if his fans, shocked to learn their idol spent $1 million a year on drugs and doctors, turned on him in concert. "They've never beat me before," he said, "and they won't beat me now." Billy knew what he meant: "Even if I have to get up there and admit to everything."

Numb, frightened, and weary from dread, he cried pitifully, shaking. Billy petted him, cooed baby talk to him. "It's okay," Billy soothed. "It's going to be all right." As Smith went out the door, Elvis, the cousin who was more like a big brother, turned to him. "Billy . . . son . . . this is going to be my best tour ever." At 7:45 A.M., the singer took his second "attack packet" of four or five sleeping pills within two hours. The third would come shortly afterward. He'd had no food since the day before.

Sometime around 8:00 A.M., Elvis climbed into bed with Ginger. As she recalled, she awakened in the tomblike room—always kept at a chilly sixty degrees—to find her aging boyfriend too keyed up to sleep, preoccupied with the tour. "Precious," he said, "I'm going to go in the bathroom and read for a while." Ginger stirred. "Okay, but don't fall asleep."

"Don't worry," he called back. "I won't."

Behind the bathroom door, Elvis picked up *A Scientific Search for the Face of Jesus*, a book about the Shroud of Turin, and waited for his pharmaceutical escort to slumber.

As Elvis's day was ending in Memphis, the Colonel's was already in full swing in Portland, the big man holed up in the Dunfey Sheraton and riding herd on Tom Hulett, Lamar Fike, George Parkhill, and Tom Diskin to oversee every detail of Elvis's two-day engagement there. Fike had flown in from Los Angeles on the red-eye and immediately went to work setting up the security and arranging the hotel rooms for the band and crew. Then he grabbed a quick bite to eat and went to bed.

Just before noon, Billy Smith walked over to Graceland and spoke with entourage member Al Strada, who was packing Elvis's wardrobe cases. Smith inquired as to whether anyone had seen the boss. Al said no, that Elvis wasn't to be awakened until 4:00 P.M. Billy wondered aloud if one of the Stanley brothers had checked on Elvis and started up the stairs to do so himself. No, if they ain't heard from him, God, let him rest, he thought. He needs it.

At 2:20, Ginger turned over in Elvis's huge bed and found it empty. Had he never come back to sleep? She noticed his reading light was still on and thought it odd. Ginger knocked on the bathroom door. "Elvis, honey?" No response. She turned the knob and went inside. Elvis was slumped on the floor, angled slightly to the left. He was on his knees, his hands beneath his face, in a near praying position, his silk pajama bottoms bunched at his feet. Inexplicably, he had fallen off the toilet and somehow twisted himself into the grotesque form. But why hadn't he answered? Ginger called again. "Elvis?" He lay so still, so unnaturally still.

Now Ginger bent down to touch him. He was cold, his swollen face buried in the red shag carpet, blood dotting the nostrils of his flattened nose, his tongue, nearly severed in two, protruding from clenched teeth. His skin was mottled purple-black. She forced open an eye. A cloudy blue pupil stared back at her lifelessly.

Elvis Presley was dead at the age of forty-two.

Not wanting to believe the worst, a frightened Ginger pressed the intercom, which rang in the kitchen. Mary Jenkins, the cook and maid, took the call. Breathless, Ginger asked, "Who's on duty?"

"Al is here," Mary answered, and passed the phone to Strada. "Al, come upstairs!" Ginger said. "I need you! Elvis has fainted!" Strada rushed upstairs, took one look, and with fear in his voice, called downstairs for Joe Esposito. Joe bounded up the stairs and turned the body, stiff with rigor mortis, on its side.

Already Esposito knew the awful truth, but still he called for an ambulance. Then, after some delay, he got Dr. Nick on the phone with the news that Elvis had suffered a heart attack. With the ambulance screaming through Whitehaven, Joe called down to Vernon's office. Suddenly, the upstairs was filled with people: Charlie Hodge crying and begging

Elvis not to die; Vernon, recuperating from his own heart attack six months earlier, collapsing on the floor; nine-year-old Lisa Marie, visiting from California, peering wide-eyed into the scene.

"What happened to him?" asked Ulysses Jones, one of the emergency medical techs. Al blurted out the truth. "We think he OD'd."

The paramedics were puzzled. Why was everyone so emphatic that they bring back a man who was so obviously dead, and who had *been* dead for hours? Who was he, anyway? Jones was shocked to learn the answer. The body was so discolored, he later said, he thought he'd been working on a black man.

At Baptist Memorial Hospital, the emergency team did its best. But no measure, whether frantic or heroic, could save Graceland's master. Finally, Dr. Nick, his face orchid white, entered the private waiting room, where Esposito sat with Hodge, Strada, Smith, and David Stanley. "He's gone," said the doctor who had prescribed 19,000 pills for Elvis in less than three years. "He's no longer here."

The men cried shamelessly and held on to each other for support. Dr. Nick asked Maurice Elliott, the hospital spokesman, not to make the announcement until he'd given Vernon the terrible truth. Worrying that the old man's heart might not be able to take such a shock, Dr. Nick immediately left for Graceland to perform the crushing duty.

Vernon, suspecting that his son would not be coming home, had already prepared Lisa Marie. When the final news came, Elvis's daughter dialed her father's old girlfriend. "It's Lisa," she said into the phone. Linda Thompson cooed. "I know who it is, you goobernickel." Then came the words that Thompson had dreaded so long: "Linda," said the small voice, "Daddy's dead."

As Dr. Nick left the hospital, Joe asked Maurice Elliott for a private line. The public relations man led him into a conference room off the ER. There, Esposito called the Colonel in Maine. George Parkhill answered, and gave the phone to his boss.

"I have something terrible to tell you," Joe began, his voice wavering. "Elvis is dead."

Thirty seconds, maybe more, passed before Parker spoke.

"Okay, Joe," he said, his voice flat, devoid of emotion. "We'll be there as soon as we can. You just do what you have to do. Tell Vernon we'll be there. We have a lot of work." Esposito sensed that beneath the calm, the Colonel was shaken. "Like me," Joe later wrote, "he would do whatever had to be done: cancel the tour and let everyone know it was all over."

Lamar Fike was still sleeping when Tom Hulett banged on his door. "Lamar!" he called. "The Colonel wants to see you right now." Fike was groggy and spent. "Fuck him," he yelled back. "I'm tired. I'm sleepy." Hulett persisted. "Lamar, answer the door!"

Fike slipped the chain off. Hulett had his head down. "I said, 'What's the matter with you, Tom?'" he remembers. "Hulett said, 'You need to come down to the room and talk to the Colonel right now.'"

The hotel was built in the round. "I remember walking around the circle to Colonel's room. I went in, and he was sitting on the side of the bed, hanging up the phone from Joe. Everybody was looking down at the floor.

"I said, 'What the hell is going on here?' I had my arm on the television set. Colonel got up and walked over to me, and stood maybe ten inches away from my face. He said, 'Lamar, you need to go to Memphis and meet with Mr. Vernon. Elvis is dead.'"

Fike was shattered but hardly surprised. Only the coldness of Parker's attitude shocked the aide.

"I said, 'That's it?' Colonel said, 'Yeah, that's it.' I said, 'Well, it took you awhile, but you finally ran him into the ground, didn't you?'" Parker challenged him: "What did you say?" And Fike was resolute. "I said, 'You heard what I said. He couldn't run anymore, could he?'" Lamar looked around the room, searching the faces of the others, his anger building. "'I kept telling you guys, man. None of you listened to me.'"

That night, the advance team would go downstairs to dinner as planned, though no one felt like eating. "I don't want anyone making any scenes," Parker ordered. "We're going to show respect, and we're going to put on the best face possible."

In Las Vegas, Parker's Hilton contact, Bruce Banke, was in his office when he got a call from Robert Macy, a friend at the Associated Press. Macy told him he'd just gotten a bulletin that Banke needed to hear. The PR man recognized the background sounds—four bells on the Teletype machine, to signal a major news story—and said, "Bob, I hope to hell World War III has just broken out." Macy told him no, it was worse.

Banke found Barron Hilton meeting with the hotel's senior officers. "I must have been just pale as a sheet, because I walked in and the entire meeting stopped and everybody turned around and stared at me." Hilton said, "What is it, Bruce?" Banke had just stopped speaking when the phone rang. It was the Colonel calling from Portland.

The show plane, which had departed from Los Angeles, having

stopped in Las Vegas to pick up Joe Guercio, was en route to the East Coast. Suddenly, the pilot announced that the plane would land in Pueblo, Colorado. Jackie Kahane remembers how puzzled everyone was.

Marty Harrell, the trombone player and Guercio's assistant, got off in Pueblo and went inside the terminal, where he found a note to call the Colonel. Parker minced no words and gave him his orders to make the announcement and fly back to Vegas. Drawn, Harrell put down the receiver and reboarded the aircraft. "Would everybody get off the plane?" he asked. Only the Sweet Inspirations' Myrna Smith refused. "Please," Harrell begged. "I have something to say, and I can only say it once."

Smith obliged, and Harrell, standing on the runway, cleared his throat. "I hate to tell you guys this, but Elvis is dead."

Several of the men began softly crying. Myrna Smith took off running around the airfield in a wild frenzy of grief, only to be caught and sedated with Valium. Kahane tried to call his wife. Both his phone lines were busy, so he dialed the operator to break through for an emergency. "The operator was crying," he remembers. "She said, 'Do you know that Elvis Presley died?' The people in the show were the last to know."

While the most devoted of Presley's fans began a pilgrimage to Memphis, the Colonel booked a flight not to Tennessee, but New York. "I can't waste time mourning," he explained later. "There's plenty of people ready to come in and cut the ground from under our feet."

After canceling the tour, Parker flew to New York to meet with RCA, for whom his client had sold more tapes and records than any other performer in recording history. The old carny rightly expected that every store in the country would sell out of Presley product within twenty-four hours. Now he put the squeeze on RCA to keep a rich river of Elvis records churning.

Next he met with Harry "the Bear" Geisler, a forty-eight-year-old former steelworker and third-grade dropout who had just made a fortune overnight with Farrah Fawcett posters and T-shirts, putting up $300,000 for the rights in early 1977 and paying out some $400,000 in royalties to Fawcett's agent that summer. His company, Factors Etc., Inc., had also acquired the merchandising licenses for tie-ins for the movies *Star Wars* and *Rocky*. The Bear was a hustler to be reckoned with.

In preparing a likeness of an artist and selling it, from Eddy Arnold on, Parker may have innovated concert merchandising, but mass merchandising was beyond him, which is why he'd brought Hank Saperstein into the split in 1956. Now he needed Geisler to do the same.

But the Colonel also wanted to include his young friend Joe Shane, the Kentucky merchandiser he'd taken under his wing and given the exclusive worldwide rights for the name of Elvis Presley. "He knew exactly what was going to transpire," Shane recalls, "and he was wise enough to know that he couldn't stop it. I got him on the phone as soon as I heard Elvis was gone, and he said, 'Joe, this thing is gonna get out of control. You better get protected.' And I said, 'Yes, sir.'"

Shane played tough with all the fly-by-night companies that called, but he knew scaring off Geisler was out of the question.

"The Bear said, 'We're not asking you, we're *telling* you that starting tonight, we're gonna put out a line of Elvis Presley posters and iron-on transfers,'" Shane remembers. "We got into a little shouting match, and I said, 'I hope you sell a billion, because I've got the rights.'" And he said, 'I *will* sell a billion, and you won't get anything.' He was really gruff."

On August 17, as tens of thousands of fans from around the world lined up in front of Graceland and down Elvis Presley Boulevard, snaking up the driveway for a last look at the famous face laid out in the huge copper casket in Graceland's foyer, Shane and the Colonel talked again. They agreed to meet at the William Morris office in Los Angeles in the days following Elvis's funeral to finalize the contract with Geissler. Shane would assign his rights to Factors for a one percent royalty. "I couldn't police the industry, and he could, and that was his big selling point." But as part of the deal, the twenty-seven-year-old Shane would take over the merchandising of Factors' rock-and-roll contracts for *Grease, Saturday Night Fever,* and the Bee Gees. "The Bear said, 'Son, you are going to be one of the richest men in the country.'"

Their contract included a provision that Factors, Etc., Inc., would sue the bootleggers who horned in on the territory, thus giving both Shane and Presley a percentage of the illicit sales without Parker having to dirty his own hands.

"The Colonel really looked after me. He said, 'Whatever you do, don't give up your rights to the boy.' Of course, once I had assigned my rights to Factors for a royalty, I wasn't really in control anymore. But the Colonel felt as long as I had an association with him, I was okay. He paged me at an airport between flights and said, 'Are the people treating you right? Let me know if they are or not.' Because anybody who wanted to sublicense had to have the Presley estate's approval, and it wasn't Vernon or Lisa Marie or anybody else. It was the Colonel. He was calling all of the shots."

Without question, Shane says, "He was like, 'The boy's dead, and how much money can I make?'" But in doing what he did, when he did it, Parker "legitimized the value of merchandising after an artist is no longer living. The industry owes him a debt of gratitude for doing that, because the numbers became overwhelming."

But the Colonel didn't strictly have the right to negotiate such deals until after he arrived in Memphis for Presley's service, along with celebrities Ann-Margret and husband Roger Smith, James Brown, and Caroline Kennedy, who covered the event for the New York *Daily News*. With the tabloids' helicopters circling overhead, and the droning screech of cicadas hanging heavy in the Memphis humidity, Parker cornered Vernon in the Graceland foyer. He explained that pirates and scam artists would come out of the woodwork to cash in on Elvis's memory now, and that Vernon, the executor of Elvis's estate, was in no physical or emotional shape to deal with them, especially as he had other worries on his mind.

The estate would eventually be valued at $7.6 million, but that was before taxes, and lately Elvis had been in the habit of mortgaging Graceland to make his payroll. Shouldn't they just continue business as usual? The Colonel could advance the estate $1 million to pay off debts and make it look as if Elvis had some cash in his depleted checking account. Besides, "Elvis didn't die. The body did," Parker said—and would repeat for days on end whenever reporters got close. "It don't mean a damned thing. It's just like when he was away in the army. . . . This changes nothing."

The Colonel would go on managing Presley's memory, and on August 23, Vernon signed the official letter, drafted, one suspects, by Parker himself. "I am deeply grateful that you have offered to carry on in the same old way, assisting me in any way possible with the many problems facing us," Vernon allegedly wrote. "I hereby would appreciate if you will carry on according to the same terms and conditions as stated in the contractual agreement you had with Elvis dated January 22, 1976, and I hereby authorize you to speak and sign for me in all these matters pertaining to this agreement."

While the Colonel had business on his mind the day of the funeral, several of the mourners gathered in Graceland's music, dining, and living rooms for the 2:00 P.M. service on August 18 found his behavior more peculiar than ever, beginning with his dress: a Hawaiian shirt and a baseball cap, from which protruded unruly tufts of gray-brown hair.

"If Elvis looks down and he sees the Colonel all dressed up, he's gonna say, 'What the hell is that?'" Parker explained later. "This is the way I always dress. Informal. No point putting on airs now." When he saw Tom Hulett dressed appropriately in a tie and black suit, the Colonel told him to go change into his usual jeans and loafers.

But what galled everyone was that Parker refused to be a pallbearer, and, as Jackie Kahane remembers, "every time he would go past the coffin, he would avert his eyes." Larry Geller also found it strange. He remembers the Colonel being stoic.

"He didn't talk to many people, and he was way in the back. He certainly wasn't sitting in the front room, and he could have been right down there with Grandma [Minnie Mae Presley] and Vernon if he'd wanted." Afterward, Geller expected Parker to have a private moment at the casket before the lid came down for the last time and a white hearse trailed by seventeen white limousines carried the body to Forest Hill Cemetery. "But it never happened. He wouldn't walk up. He didn't even look. You could almost see him struggling *not* to look."

Kathy Westmoreland was upset with the Colonel for the way he was dressed, but rationalized his actions. "I could see there was pain in his eyes, and he didn't want to show it."

Years later, Parker boasted that he never once wept at the funeral. "No, sir. If anybody had seen my eyes mist up for a second they must have had their hands in my pockets."

And if Parker wondered just what killed his client, he spoke of it to no one in Presley's camp. Jackie Kahane thought he had a fairly good idea. "Elvis committed suicide for want of another term. It saddened me to see such a big talent kill himself." On the plane, the comedian wrote a eulogy, which he read at the service between performances by gospel groups and remarks by evangelist Rex Humbard.

"When I joined the TCB group seven years ago," Kahane began, "I was given simple instructions by Colonel Parker. He said, 'Jack, keep it clean.' As an entertainer, Elvis was the embodiment of clean, wholesome entertainment."

But as a private citizen, he was something else, a prescription drug addict, not much different from a gutter junkie, except in his drugs of choice. Yet what *had* killed Elvis Presley? Dr. Elias Ghanem told friends he was certain Elvis had fallen off the toilet and suffocated in the shag carpet, and pointed to his lolling tongue as proof. Others speculated that Elvis had mistaken the codeine tablets given to him by his dentist for Demerol and had ingested all ten, suffering an allergic reaction.

But a grief-stricken Vernon believed his son had been murdered, either by a member of the entourage or, he suspected, by Parker himself, especially in light of Elvis's growing interest in finding another manager and the Colonel's monumental gaming debts, his association with nefarious circles, and his inability to sell Elvis's contract in California. For that reason, Vernon authorized both a private investigation and an autopsy.

On October 18, Dr. Eric Muirhead, chief of pathology at Baptist Memorial Hospital, took a team to Graceland to explain the autopsy report to Elvis's father.

According to *The Death of Elvis: What Really Happened*, by Charles C. Thompson II and James P. Cole, the toxicology report showed that Elvis died of a drug overdose, or polypharmacy, the lethal interaction of a number of drugs taken concurrently. Vernon was told that at the meeting, the authors contend.

The following day, October 19, the Memphis *Commercial Appeal* ran a story by an enterprising staff journalist named Beth Tamke, who reported that Vernon had been told that tests ordered by Baptist Memorial Hospital showed at least ten different drugs in the singer's system. Tamke's story went on to speculate that the interaction of the drugs might have affected Elvis's heart and caused his death.

But to reporters who contacted him later, Vernon insisted it was too early to say whether drugs played a role in his son's demise, and added a baffling statement: "I can't straighten it out by telling another lie."

On October 21, Dr. Jerry Francisco, Shelby County medical examiner, appeared at a news conference and passed out a press release that said Elvis Presley died of "hypertensive heart disease, with coronary artery disease as a contributing factor." According to Francisco, who had signed the death certificate the day before, Elvis died of cardiac arrhythmia, although he conceded that no fewer than eight drugs had been present in Presley's body. "Prescription drugs found in his blood were not a contributing factor," Francisco said. "Had these drugs not been there, he still would have died."

Earlier that month, CBS-TV aired "Elvis in Concert," which had been taped in Omaha, Nebraska, on June 19, and in Rapid City, South Dakota, on June 21. The special, which many fans and entourage members say never should have been broadcast, revealed a legend colliding with myth, too fat to move and too often short of breath. Big and bloated, Elvis stumbled through his lyrics, slurred his speech, and sweated like a man on fire. In the end, he was all chins, gut, and gospel singer hair, a shocking caricature of a once brilliant talent.

Three years after Elvis's death, Parker told Larry Hutchinson, chief in-

vestigator to the district attorney general for Memphis, that he first noticed Elvis's drugs in the late '60s, "not that it specially concerned me," as
Elvis always showed up to do his work in the movies. But other than their
confrontation in 1974, when Presley told his manager to stay out of his
personal life, "I couldn't get involved," the Colonel said.

After that, Parker insisted, he was oblivious of any real problem. "I
was aware he was treated by physicians in Las Vegas and Palm Springs,
but I had no personal experience of his visits. Sonny West told me one
time that he was getting prescriptions in other people's names, but I
didn't know about that."

Yet while he knew that Dr. Nick was often in the dressing room before
a performance, Parker testified, "I never saw Elvis being given drugs,
though I know that Dr. Nick has said he prepared medications for Elvis
before he went on stage and when he came off." Likewise, "I never heard
of him being admitted to the hospital for an overdose of drugs. I was concerned sometimes, but I couldn't talk to him about it . . . It's a sad situation. I had no control over him. That was Elvis's choice."

In September 1978, the Colonel staged a fan festival, Always Elvis, at
the Las Vegas Hilton, where he, Vernon, and Priscilla would dedicate a
life-size bronze statue of the singer in the lobby. The convention was
booked into the hotel's new Pavilion, where Elvis was to have performed
that year. Always Elvis, which offered, for a price separate from the $15
general admission, a multimedia show that Jerry Weintraub later took on
the road, was the first of many events that would prove the Colonel right:
Elvis didn't die after all.

"It was just like when Elvis would be there at the Hilton for the summer festival," says Presley collector Robin Rosaaen. "Banners hung outside the Hilton and from the roof tops—carnival was the atmosphere,
and money was the name of the game."

The Colonel was in his glory, working the crowd as the Memphis Mafia
mingled with the fans. When the statue was unveiled, fans packed the
showroom, and a throng of entertainers, including Robert Goulet and
Sammy Davis Jr., sat in the plush booths, as if waiting to see Elvis himself.

Indeed, his clothes were already there, on ghoulish display and draped
on mannequins, inspiring a now-famous *Saturday Night Live* sketch in
which Elvis's coat toured the nation. Nothing was too outlandish. Charlie Hodge charged $5 to have his picture taken with fans, and the
Colonel, sitting in a vendor's booth with a cigar clinched between yel-
lowed teeth, hawked and signed his own Elvis poem for a buck.

Robert Hilburn, rock critic for the *Los Angeles Times,* happened upon the Colonel that day and drew the old man out. "We made a hell of a team," Parker said once the crowd cleared. "I thought we'd go on forever, but . . ." He stared out into the huge room, leaning on the pearl-handled cane that had become his favorite, and paused as if trying to think of something more to say. "Sure," he finally added, answering a question that Hilburn never asked. "Sure, I loved him."

"I sat with him there for a week, signing autographs," says Jackie Kahane, who emceed the event. "And in the course of talking, he referred to Elvis as being like a son. But I don't think Colonel was capable of demonstrating love. That was always the problem."

A larger test of Parker's fatherly affection came closer to home in the months just after Presley's death. Suddenly and without warning, the Colonel inexplicably pulled all his advertising accounts from his stepson, Bob Ross and, according to Ross's widow, Sandra, gave the business to Jerry Weintraub.

By that time, through the Colonel's influence, the Rosses had handled accounts for Rick Nelson, Tom Jones, Engelbert Humperdinck, Frank Sinatra, and Olivia Newton-John. It all dried up, and the couple sustained huge financial losses just as Bob's multiple sclerosis worsened. With the added stress of the economic strain, Ross suffered a fatal heart attack and died ten days after his fifty-third birthday, in July 1978.

"You could say the Colonel killed him," Sandra offers. "But when Bobby was dying, Colonel called him three times in one day to see how he was. Bobby said in amazement, 'Three times in one day. He really does care.' And I think he did. He just didn't understand the ramifications of what he did."

Parker sent Tom Diskin to the funeral. Marie, now lost to the ravages of her disease, never knew her son was dead.

A matter of weeks after Bob Ross's death, his widow opened the door to see a ghost. Billy Ross, Bobby's fifty-one-year-old clubfooted brother, whom Marie had given to the Florida Children's Home as an infant, stood in the transom. "I thought I would die. He looked so much like Bobby, and even sounded like him." Sandra found his story heartbreaking, but the visit upset her terribly. "It was just too much, too soon. And I didn't know what he wanted out of me."

What he wanted was his heritage. Adopted by a Plant City dirt-farming family, Billy had endured a difficult life. They had worked him like a mule in the fields, and their natural children had never accepted him, even barring him from sitting with them at their mother's funeral.

For years, he had tried to discover his real identity. Once he had gotten his birth records unsealed, his search led him to Bitsy Mott, who referred him to Sandra and the Colonel. Billy was bitter that his real mother had lived a luxurious life as the wife of a famous entertainment manager, and resentful that his brother, Bob, had led such a grandiose existence, mixing and mingling with starlets in Hollywood and hanging out with Elvis Presley.

Now he demanded two things: a meeting with Marie and his share of the pie. Otherwise, he would write a book about his story; he had, in fact, begun a manuscript. He intended to petition the courts to restore his name to Ross.

Both Sandra and the Colonel explained that Marie was in no shape to see him, and that if by some miracle she did understand who he was, the shock might kill her. But Billy persisted, hoping he could somehow restore his mother's mind and win her heart.

Parker, who remembered the importance of a mother's love, wrestled with the problem for a time and finally acquiesced, flying Billy and his wife and children to Palm Springs to see Marie, who had no idea why this stranger had come to meet her. Billy's book never appeared. Sandra Ross believes the Colonel simply bought him off to protect Marie's reputation, the way he'd handled so many problems before.

However, the Colonel was to realize a new set of problems in the events that began on June 26, 1979, when Vernon died on Parker's seventieth birthday. Elvis's father had resisted naming Priscilla the new executor to his son's estate, but she had cajoled him into it, citing the interest of Lisa Marie, Elvis's sole beneficiary. To keep the money straight, Vernon named Joe Hanks, Elvis's certified public accountant, and the National Bank of Commerce in Memphis, as co-executors.

Immediately after Vernon's death, Parker approached Priscilla about carrying on his arrangement with the estate. By now, she and the co-executors had put together an impressive board of directors to maximize income from one of the most famous names on the planet.

In 1979, the estate's income would be $1.2 million, much of it from the 160 licenses the Colonel had arranged. Parker would get half of the money. And sometimes more.

That year, Dennis Roberts, Elvis's optician, got a call from the Colonel about designing a line of eyeglasses to be licensed through Boxcar. Roberts met Parker at his office at the RCA Building in Los Angeles and, in the course of conversation, made a casual inquiry.

"I said, 'You know I made 488 pairs of eyeglasses for Elvis,'" as Roberts remembers. "He went, 'Yeah.'" I said, 'What happened to all of them?' The Colonel said, 'I don't know. I was never social with the man.' I said, 'Colonel, Elvis spent over a quarter of a million dollars on glasses. The EPs and the TCBs that I designed are fourteen-karat gold. Some of them have diamonds and sapphires in them.' He said, 'You gotta be kidding.' And he picked up the phone and buzzed some aide to call Graceland, and when he got 'em on the phone, he said, 'I want you to round up all of Elvis's glasses and overnight 'em to me immediately.' And that was the last anybody ever saw of Elvis Presley's eyeglasses, except the very few that have shown up at auction."

Roberts wasn't thrilled with the way his Boxcar deal turned out. "It cost me about $135,000 for licensing and inventory, but it never really jelled because the Colonel didn't come through with his promise to promote them. He was more consumed with his Elvis musical whiskey decanters. He thought those were the rip-off of the century. He said, 'We're getting $200 for these things!'"

But if Roberts wasn't pleased with Parker's efforts, the co-executors were, even as Priscilla admits "it was a shock to all of us" that Elvis had left so little money. Three days after Vernon's death, on June 29, 1979, they wrote the Colonel a letter directing him to carry on pursuant to his agreement with Vernon. All income for the estate would be forwarded to Parker, who would then deduct his 25 percent to 50 percent and forward the balance to the estate.

In May 1980, the co-executors filed a petition to approve Parker's compensation agreement and ratify all payments of commission, even as the estate's lawyers raised an eyebrow. "We weren't aware of the extent of Parker's commissions until Vernon died," says D. Beecher Smith II, one of the Memphis attorneys who helped settle Presley's estate. "Vernon had been relatively secretive about it. We filed a petition with the probate court to rule on the propriety of the commissions."

That decision would alter the Colonel's saga in ways no one could have imagined.

20

LIVING TOO LONG:

LITIGATION AND LONELINESS

W H E N Priscilla and the co-executors petitioned Shelby County, Tennessee, probate court to allow Parker to continue representing the estate, they expected a quick rubber-stamping of the agreement. But Judge Joseph Evans was astonished to discover that the Colonel had been guaranteed half of Presley's income while the singer was alive, and even more amazed that the estate would sanction such an arrangement now that Parker had no artist to manage.

As such, in a move that stunned the executors, he appointed a thirty-eight-year-old Memphis attorney, Blanchard E. Tual, to investigate Parker's compensation agreement and to "represent and defend the interests of Lisa Marie Presley." In legal terms, Tual was to act as the twelve-year-old's guardian *ad litem*.

Tual spent four months looking into Parker's financial dealings with the estate. On September 30, 1980, he filed a three-hundred-page report that concluded that it was inappropriate for the executors to rely on the January 22, 1976, agreement as a basis to continue a full relationship with the Colonel, and argued that "all agreements with Elvis Presley terminated on his death." He recommended that the court not approve the 50 percent commission Parker received for administration, as it was "excessive, imprudent, unfair to the estate, and beyond all reasonable bounds of industry standards." And he implored the court to immediately order all monies due the estate be paid directly to the executors and not to Parker, and to enjoin the executors from paying the Colonel any further commissions pending the conclusion of his investigation.

Finally, in what would become the most infamous part of the report, the lawyer, who had conferred with three nationally recognized music business attorneys, charged that Parker had been guilty of "self-dealing and overreaching" and that he had "violated his duty both to Elvis . . . and to the estate." As proof, Tual cited the Boxcar agreement, which gave Parker 56 percent control of the company, apart from the 50 percent individual commission.

But the Colonel was not the only one who came under fire. The guardian *ad litem* also found fault in Parker's handling of the royalty revenue from Presley's publishing agreements. Tual chided the executors for not giving the Colonel definite guidelines and limits in writing, and for refusing to challenge Parker's statements, which the guardian *ad litem* found "unsatisfactory" in failing to clarify if the figures were gross or net. Such reports, he said, were "totally unreliable in determining what actual monies passed through Parker's hands." He asked that the Colonel provide a statement of his present net worth as well as his past income tax returns, and he demanded that the executors secure a full audit from RCA, since Parker's agreements did not contain the standard auditing clause customary in every recording contract. Additionally, Tual called for accountings from all of the entertainment companies with which Parker did business—from the William Morris Agency to Factors to the movie studios to Concerts West.

Tual's findings rocked the music world and shocked Presley's fans, as, rumors notwithstanding, no manager-client dealings had been as veiled as those of Colonel Tom Parker and Elvis Presley. Most agreed that the 50 percent commission was particularly egregious, since the majority of personal managers received 10 percent or 15 percent, and only rarely 25 percent. But the ratio was more complicated than it appeared. "I'm sure a lot of people see him as just this money-grubbing curmudgeon," points out Parker's friend Mike Crowley, "but it wasn't fifty percent of everything."

The Colonel, who reacted to the report with anger, was not without sympathy beyond his circle. Says music attorney and author Stan Soocher, "You can't paint Parker as an angel, because the overreaching was clear. However, the particularities of the Elvis-Parker-RCA situation may not fully apply to the industrywide standard. A lot of this was a very tough call."

"Most people would say [the 50 percent commission is] highway robbery," concurs David Skepner, the manager who built country singer Loretta Lynn into a national figure. "But he was working under very abnormal conditions, including the drugs, so getting anything accomplished was a miracle." And, points out RCA's Joe Galante, "While he kept getting a higher proportion of the take, he was bringing in more revenues than other managers."

Indeed, then, if Presley's gross earnings totaled an estimated $200 million, why shouldn't the man who wrangled such huge sums receive more than the industry standard, if not 50 percent? In 1968, the British journalist Chris Hutchins asked Parker about a wild rumor floating through the industry. "Is it true," he ventured, "that you take fifty percent of everything Elvis earns?" For a moment, Parker seemed speechless. "No," he finally answered. "That's not true at all. He takes fifty percent of everything I earn." And that's the way he saw it. The Colonel spent many more hours plying the Elvis trade than Elvis did. And even though he had side deals with the very companies with whom Elvis did business—from RCA to the Hilton to Management III—Parker gave Presley undiluted attention in refusing to represent other acts on a grand scale.

Elvis himself never balked at the arrangement, and, echoes Barry Coburn, the manager who brought country singer Alan Jackson to prominence, the practices of the industry of the '60s shouldn't be compared to the business ethics of today. "How can you argue with the legacy that remains?" he asks, especially one that continues to influence managers and music executives alike.

In short, the Colonel was all the things that he appeared to be, both good and bad, and if Parker was the very definition of shrewd, the morality of his decisions was not always discernible as black or white.

Surprisingly, the estate itself had difficulty making that assessment. Less than three months after Tual delivered his first report and began gathering information for a second, the executors balked at the guardian's requests. They argued that he had overstepped his authority and should be removed. They attempted to prevent Tual from continuing his investigation, a move the judge quickly quashed.

Dr. Beecher Smith III, one of the estate's Memphis attorneys, denounced Parker as a "shaman" but also praised his doggedness ("When he was working for Elvis, he could negotiate the gold out of people's teeth"). Furthermore, Smith cited "contractual barriers" to the recommendation that Parker no longer be a conduit for all of Presley's income.

"I'm not prepared to paint Parker black," Smith said some years later. "There were villainous elements, but . . . [he] was instrumental in establishing many of the things the estate benefits from today. His greatest sin was not being savvy about the state of the industry during the last five or ten years of Elvis's life."

In late 1980, as the investigation continued, Parker received what some considered fateful retribution when he suffered a fall at the RCA Building in Los Angeles, where he continued to keep an office on the seventh floor. Tripping at the entrance to the elevator, the old man lay beneath his own weight as the automatic door opened and shut repeatedly, breaking and slamming his right shoulder in relentless assault. The injury would forever limit the mobility of his arm and neck, and age him, in the opinion of friends, by ten years. Until he healed, he insisted that George Parkhill accompany him to the casinos to pull the handles on the slot machines; subsequently, he referred to the one-armed bandits as his "exercise."

Shortly after the accident, Tual flew to California, where he held a meeting with Parker and the estate in the Colonel's hospital room. In a newspaper interview in December 1980, the lawyer said he felt strange during the visit, expressing his surprise at how the executors "sandbagged" him and refused to question Parker's 50 percent commission.

"I got the feeling the executors and the attorneys were afraid of Colonel Parker," he said. "Every time he would laugh, they would laugh. Every time he said yes, they said yes." Tual was stunned at the hold Parker seemed to have over the very people he had defrauded out of a fortune—$7 million or $8 million in the last three years alone, he estimated. But still he admired his cunning: "He had it from the eyebrows up."

The guardian *ad litem*'s second report, delivered July 31, 1981, was even more damning than the first and elaborated on what Tual considered Parker's poor management. Foremost was the RCA buyout ("the worst decision ever made in the history of rock 'n' roll"), motivated, Tual charged, by Parker's gambling debts and recent heart attack, and "the conscious decision to make as much money as he could from Elvis before his inevitable premature death." Tual also hammered on the surprisingly low figure for which Elvis played Las Vegas and Parker's failure to register Presley with BMI for performance royalties as a songwriter.

The latter discovery was a sweet victory for Joe Moscheo, the leader of the Imperials, whom Parker had treated so shabbily in Las Vegas. In 1978, the singer had left the road to go to work for BMI, where, in learning the system, he routinely checked up on royalties for his songwriter friends. Moscheo was bewildered when he typed in Presley's name and saw "NA," not affiliated.

"Elvis had thirty-three songs that he was credited as either writing or cowriting, including some big ones, like 'All Shook Up,' and he never received any writer performance royalties from BMI from 1955 to 1978," says Moscheo. In investigating, he learned that "the Colonel would not allow Elvis to sign anything that Parker didn't understand or agree to, and evidently, he didn't understand what all of this performance thing meant. It was just an oversight, but there were hundreds of thousands of dollars that Elvis never received as a songwriter. Priscilla was furious."

Tual was likewise enraged, but saved his knockout punch for Parker's rampant "self-dealing." He boldly charged the Colonel and RCA with "collusion, conspiracy, fraud, misrepresentation, bad faith, and over-reaching," asserting the record company paid off Parker to keep Elvis quiet and obedient while the label cheated "the most popular American folk hero of this century."

The manager's side deals with the company constituted a clear conflict of interest, Tual said, as "Colonel Parker could not possibly deal with RCA at arm's length on Elvis's behalf when he was receiving that much money from [the label]." As late as February 1980, RCA paid Parker $50,000 for "services with respect to promotion, merchandising concepts, and packaging suggestions."

On August 14, 1981, when thousands of fans gathered in Memphis to pay tribute to Presley on the fourth anniversary of his death, Judge Evans ordered attorneys for the estate to halt further payments to the manager, as "the compensation received by Colonel Parker is excessive and shocks the conscience of the court," the judge wrote in a heated opinion. Additionally, he required the executors to file suit against Parker for alleged fraudulent business practices and ordered an investigation into RCA Records' dealings with Presley and the estate. Finally, the judge admonished the executors not to "enter into any future agreements with Parker" without the court's approval.

The Colonel was not in attendance, and his attorney, Jack Magids, denied all allegations of impropriety leveled against his client. Parker's allies, speaking out in his favor, wondered if Tual's report would have been different if the Colonel, then seventy-two years of age, were younger and healthier.

But Parker was fully capable of defending himself, he said in interviews with newspaper reporters. Courting the press where he'd once put a price on his time—$25,000 for small talk, $100,000 for a long conversation—he began to lift the curtain, if only slightly, around the great "Elvis and the Colonel" construct. Parker was shocked, he said in a written broadside, at what occurred in the probate proceedings, as he had made "every effort to honor [Elvis's] name and preserve his memory and dignity." Such allegations not only attacked Parker's reputation, "but also are unfair and insulting to the memory of Elvis and his father, Vernon." The fact that their relationship lasted twenty-one years "should say it all," he added, and insisted "Elvis knew that I provided services for others. He was satisfied with our arrangement, and it worked."

Yet within a month, as lawyers closed in and public sentiment turned vicious, Parker felt the need to speak again. The man with the hide of a rhinoceros had "nervous energy" in his voice as he talked with a reporter from the Memphis *Press-Scimitar,* insisting that Tual hadn't given the whole picture of his relationship with the late singer. And for the first time, he criticized his client.

Far from being malleable and easily controlled, Elvis was "moody" and "headstrong," Parker said, and had to be forced to honor his commitments. Though he refused to discuss Elvis's drug problem, the Colonel hinted that theirs was not an easy relationship, and that Presley, lacking self-motivation, was often desultory, his actions unpredictable. "Sometimes," he told the reporter in an uncharacteristic display of emotion, "it was such a heartache to keep [him] going."

But what the Colonel really hoped to convey revolved around the issue of fiduciary trust. According to Parker, Elvis frequently refused his advice on important business deals. "He wanted to always make the final decision," Parker said. "That's the way it was. He had a mind of his own."

At the heart of his argument was the RCA buyout, which the Colonel claimed was greatly misunderstood. "Keep in mind," he said, "that Elvis approved all of the contracts with RCA. Elvis was fully aware of the entire transaction, and it was his decision. I had absolutely nothing to hide."

Despite the fact that Presley's older songs "weren't selling" and earned very little, he said, "when [RCA] approached us about the buyout, I was not interested. I thought it was a stupid idea to even consider it." However, both Elvis and Vernon "really pushed" for the deal and instructed Parker to counter the offer of $3 million. In getting the price to $5 million he ended the uncertainty of regular income from royalties. As a result, "Elvis's decisions in 1973 were correct," he maintained, adding that the agreement was "the best deal under the circumstances."

The Colonel also patted himself on the back. Though he negotiated a new recording contract at the same time as the buyout, Parker said, Elvis failed to produce the required albums every year. To prevent the label from balking on the guaranteed royalty, the Colonel assembled tape recordings of live concerts, which RCA accepted in lieu of studio recordings. Thus, Parker argued, he kept Presley from violating his contract. As for having no auditing clause, most of the artists of the day didn't have one, but he had been smart to insist on dollars and cents per unit protection.

Still, the accusations flew, and soon the executors took a different legal tack, asserting Parker never had a permit to act as Elvis's manager. Yet with its limited resources—less than $5 million in real cash—the estate was on the brink of bankruptcy and loathe to tie itself up in expensive litigation, especially as the Internal Revenue Service had recently demanded payment of $14.6 million in additional taxes. The estate had undervalued Graceland itself, the IRS charged, as well as the worth of Elvis's royalty rights for films, records, and television specials.

And, executors knew, Parker would fight back. In March 1982, he filed suit, calling his relationship with Elvis a partnership and citing the January 2, 1967, agreement as proof. ("I never saw anything to indicate it was a partnership," says Tual.) The Colonel maintained he was due $1.6 million that he advanced Elvis in the months before his death, and asked a Nevada court to order the Presley estate liquidated. In the meantime, he sought the right to promote Presley's name and to gain full control of the business that he and Elvis shared, the profits to be divided between him and Lisa Marie.

With litigation already stretching from California to Tennessee, in May 1982, RCA Records filed suit in U.S. District Court in New York against the executors, Tual, and Parker.

That's when the Colonel played his toughest card.

Flushed out by Albert Goldman's book *Elvis,* which in 1981 reported that Parker had been born Andreas van Kuijk in Breda, Holland, Parker spoke publicly for the first time about his European origins and forfeiture of his Dutch citizenship. In legal papers filed in response to the suit, he claimed that he could not be sued under federal law because "I am advised by my attorneys that the Court lacks jurisdiction over the subject matter of the complaint and the cross-claims herein, since I am not a citizen of the United States or any foreign country for purposes of diversity jurisdiction."

Or, as Parker told *Variety,* "Yes, I am a man without a country."

The revelation drew gasps from Parker's acquaintances and spawned additional newspaper headlines. But still it failed to trigger an INS or

FBI check. "That old son of a bitch was some kind of magician," his foes whispered, "unless someone like Lyndon Johnson fixed things for him."

But either Johnson acted in secrecy—a well-placed phone call, a discreet note on private stationery—or the oversight at the immigration service was exactly that. There is nothing in the Parker-Johnson correspondence to indicate the former president was cognizant of Parker's citizenship problems.

Blanchard Tual likewise found no proof that Parker had been befriended by government leaders, and believed that Parker could still be sued in federal court, despite his claims to the contrary. But in June 1982, the estate, acting on the order from Judge Evans and following the directives of the Tual report, formally brought suit against the Colonel in Memphis Chancery Court. Charging contract manipulations and exploitation for personal gain—duping Presley out of more than $1 million—the executors asked that Parker's rights to any contract with Presley and the estate be forfeited.

To bolster its claim, the estate cited six interrelated documents dated March 1, 1973, which paid Parker $6.2 million over a seven-year period, while Presley received $4.6 million. The agreements, all related to the RCA buyout, collectively provided the Colonel with 57 percent of all income, plus another 10 percent of RCA's net profits from tours. ("I did not receive more than Elvis did from the music or the motion pictures, only for the extra deals I made," Parker later insisted.) The lawsuit, which sought to negate Parker's claim of a joint venture, also criticized the manager for failing to instigate tax and estate planning, and for refusing to set up foreign concert tours, presumably because Parker never obtained an American passport nor attempted to become a U.S. citizen.

But with the estate groaning under the weight of mounting legal fees, Tual and the executors reached an out-of-court settlement with Parker and RCA in November 1982, though full resolution wouldn't be reached until the following June. Tual, who was well aware of Parker's heart condition, had considered the Colonel's ill health in making the decision. "We figured the Colonel might die before we finished litigation, and we would have to deal with his estate," he says. But "if Elvis had lived and we tried a case against the Colonel, Elvis would have won."

And yet in a nearly mythological display of fortitude to withstand any tide or torrent, Parker not only prevailed with another slick deal, but again succeeded in finding someone else to pick up his tab.

The settlement eliminated the Colonel's future share of income and prohibited him from commercially exploiting the Presley name for five years. But in exchange for turning over master copies of Elvis's audio recordings and 350 concert, movie, and TV clips to the estate, RCA would give Parker $2 million, doled out in payments of $40,000 a month—$60,000 each June—until May 1987. In addition, the Colonel collected $225,000 from the estate for his shares in Boxcar Enterprises, and agreed to provide it with a sampling of his vast Elvis memorabilia, including costumes, personal items, and stage paraphernalia. Now he felt vindicated. As he told his brother-in-law, "Bitsy, if I was doing something wrong, why are they trying to buy me out? Does that make sense?"

By the time the final documents were signed in 1983, the estate had undergone profound changes. Priscilla Presley and the board of directors were about to turn Elvis's memory into a profitable business through the licensing of souvenirs, just as Parker had envisioned with Boxcar. They would also make Graceland a top tourist spot. Of the nation's famous private residences, only the White House would receive more visitors each year.

Though the settlement demanded Parker sever ties with Priscilla and Lisa Marie, the Colonel had no such intent. Since the lawsuit began, he finagled a way to resume a relationship with both of them, sending Elvis's daughter a toy, found in storage, that she had treasured as a child.

"A couple of weeks after we opened Graceland [in June 1982], someone walked into my office and said that a man is on the phone who says he's Colonel Parker," remembers Jack Soden, CEO of Elvis Presley Enterprises. "I got on . . . and he said, 'You've got a big challenge ahead. Call me anytime. This battle isn't between you and me. You don't have anything to do with it.'"

As Graceland developed into a $15-million-a-year business—sales of all things Elvis would top $37 million a year by 2002—the Colonel formulated his own strategy for cashing in on the legend. In the late '80s, he began telling Elvis fans that he was opening his own museum, the Wonderful World of Show Business Exhibit, in his Madison home. Friends say he never really planned such a thing and simply hyped it as a bluff to sell Graceland the remainder of his memorabilia.

Still, he put up a convincing ruse, obtaining an occupancy permit, paving his front yard for a parking lot, and installing chain-link fencing and security lights. He also insisted that he had a Japanese bidder who offered top dollar. Though the negotiations would drag on for years, the estate would eventually cough up his $2-million asking price, the Graceland movers arriving in the dead of night to load an estimated thirty-five tons of material—business records, photographs, newsreels, telegrams, letters, artwork, acetate recordings, and Elvis's famous gold lamé suit—into seven semi-trucks for their secret move to Memphis.

With the lawsuit resolved, the Colonel's old friends rallied around him to help boost his reputation. In 1984, Janelle McComb, a Tupelo, Mississippi, friend of the estate who had spearheaded the building of the non-denominational chapel on the land behind the house where Presley was born, staged a private banquet for him in conjunction with a fund-raiser for the Elvis Presley Foundation. Rick Nelson—whom Parker casually counseled through his manager, Greg McDonald, a Palm Springs–based promoter and another of his "adopted" sons—performed a benefit concert. And the Colonel "signed" photographs of himself with a rubber stamp held in his left hand, leading the attendant members of Presley's British fan club to wonder if the seventy-five-year-old had suffered a stroke.

At the same time the Colonel worked to redeem himself with the estate and Elvis's fan base, he tried hard to mend his image in the industry. Since Elvis's death, he had continued as a "consultant" for Barron Hilton, though he had worked without a contract since 1978. As he explained it, "I didn't hear from them when the time was up, so I wrote them a nice thank-you letter and said, 'If you ever need me,' [and] I got a letter back [that] said, 'Perish the thought of you ever leaving my team.' "

Many thought it was an arrangement by which Parker worked off a fraction of his gambling debts, as that same year, 1984, *People* magazine would report that the Colonel's $30-million tab had been paid in full. The Colonel insisted his employment was anything but a way to write off his losses. "I've had offers far more financially better since those new [hotels] went up, but . . . [Barron] knows that I do a job."

Despite his lofty title, Parker's tasks harkened to those he performed as an advance man for the carnivals. While someone else booked the acts into the showroom, the Colonel handled promotions—arranging billboard rentals, finishing posters, and buying radio spots. He successfully teamed country singer George Strait with Jerry Weintraub to make the movie *Pure Country* after Strait broke Presley's attendance record at the hotel. But Vegas old-timers saw him as little more than a public relations figure, a walking Elvis souvenir, the live companion to the Presley statue in the foyer. "Any time the Colonel came into view, it was the old Elvis picture from way back, even if he was just there in the casino," says *Variety*'s Bill Willard.

Yet despite the enduring stardust of the Colonel's name, by 1984 Barron Hilton had had enough of Parker's escalating gambling tab. The rumor circulated that the hotel casino, like other places around town, had cut off Parker's credit at the tables and relegated him to the $25 slot machines. It was a humiliating comedown.

While the Colonel was welcome to a small office in the hotel, the suite of rooms on the fourth floor was also no longer at his disposal, so Parker leased apartment 23G in Regency Towers, a high-rise located on the golf course in the Las Vegas Country Club Estates on Bel Air Drive behind the Hilton. Marie, a bedridden invalid from 1975 on, remained at the couple's home in Palm Springs. In 1982, mute but still alert, she was operated on, and found to have a massive, benign brain tumor, undetected for perhaps twenty years. She would die in November 1986 of "chronic brain syndrome."

"Marie's a vegetable," Parker would say point blank when anyone asked about her. "You wouldn't want to see her now."

And so Loanne moved to the high-rise with him and made it look like a home, replete with the Colonel's vast elephant collection, which he proudly showed to visitors. Residents regarded the duo as wonderful neighbors.

On the surface, nothing had changed between Parker and the Hilton. In 1987, on the tenth anniversary of Presley's death, the old entrepreneur brought Wayne Newton into the showroom for a tribute to Elvis, and the hotel opened Presley's thirtieth-floor suite to the public. There, the Colonel set up a mini-museum of his life together with Elvis, plastering the walls with memorabilia and photos, and taking fans on guided tours of Presley's bedroom. Though Parker was adamant that nothing be sold ("To me, that's not a real tribute when you sell a lot of merchandise"), fans were given a free poster of the Colonel on the way out. The gesture did little to assuage the majority of Elvis's faithful supporters, who still saw him as a black-hearted villain who traded the singer's soul for the demon dollar.

To publicize the event, Parker appeared on Ted Koppel's *Nightline*. ("He wanted me to come to New York—I said, 'No, you bring a satellite to me.'") From the start, the Colonel was combative, correcting the host and lambasting critics who charged that he stunted Elvis as an actor with a steady diet of beach 'n' bikini movies. "If they know so much, they ought to go into the management business," he huffed. "[Elvis] knew that he could do whatever he wanted."

But at a Vegas press conference, he mostly waxed nostalgic. "I'll never manage anyone again. After Elvis, where do you go?" It wasn't true that the two never shared a meal, he said ("We may have had dinner three times a year"), and while Elvis had been the highest-paid performer in Vegas, "I feel ashamed to tell you what Elvis made for his shows back then."

Still, he denied that he booked Presley for overlong engagements ("Elvis worked two-hour shows for two hundred nights a year. If you add that up, he worked about four months a year"), and insisted his client had only one goal that he never accomplished, and that was to "stay alive." The Colonel feigned deafness when questions turned to drug use. "We're here to honor his memory. I think I didn't hear you very well."

Parker steadfastly maintained that his only concern was to keep Elvis's name before the fans. But others say the estrangement from the estate weighed heavily on his mind. When Alex Shoofey's ex-wife visited him in the Elvis suite, he confided his dismay. "He thought he had been given the shaft, that the family had done him wrong, and Priscilla should have lived up to the deal," says Joan Shoofey Richardson. "It was the only time I ever saw him angry."

And so it was an emotional Parker who accepted Jack Soden's invitation to come to Graceland for two days in June of '87, both to talk about selling the remainder of his memorabilia (the estate would finally announce the acquisition in 1990) and to be welcomed back for special projects. Shortly after, a reporter asked if the visit held special memories. "None of 'em are memories for me," the Colonel said. "You relive it every day."

Seven months later, Parker was back in Memphis for the observance of what would have been Presley's fifty-third birthday. Fierce snowstorms crippled the country, and although canceled flights turned his trip into a grueling two-day ordeal, Parker appeared humbled and on his best behavior at a gathering of media and fan club members. "Why did you come this year, Colonel?" someone shouted. "Well, it's been too long," Parker answered, casting an eager glance at Soden. "But things are working out." Soden nodded his head. "Yes, they are, Colonel. Yes, they are."

Wearing a round fur hat and a heavy camel's hair coat, Parker resembled a friendly Khrushchev as he settled into a jovial mood. A woman from Arkansas cornered him, he joked, and told him of an Elvis séance. "I said, 'I'll give you my new phone number. Tell Elvis to call me.'"

"Colonel," a woman chirped, "why did you decide to be Elvis's manager?"

"I didn't decide. I received a telegram from his father and mother asking if I could get Elvis a record contract. It just happened, that's all."

"Do you think if Elvis were living today," called another voice, "he'd still be playing the same style of music?"

"Well," Parker shot back, "let's ask him that when I talk to that lady in Arkansas!"

And then it was over. "Okay," he shouted off mike. "If you want a picture with the Colonel, no charge." A woman stepped up. "Just don't kiss me," he said. "I got the measles."

But when Parker appeared that evening at a Graceland-sponsored banquet, the fans greeted him with no more than polite applause, saving their enthusiasm for Steve Binder, the man who rejuvenated Presley's career and spirit with the 1968 television special.

The Colonel poked fun at himself as he took the podium, and then made his peace with the producer he'd fought with years before. ("I don't think there was any producer [who] could ever . . . get the talent out of Elvis like Steve.") But when he quipped that his plaque should be larger than Binder's ("Colonel, we'll send it out and get you a bigger one," he was assured), an undertow of disgust roiled through the crowd. "I think," says Soden, "that Colonel Parker hoped history would treat him kinder."

Certainly Priscilla Presley extended herself to him in ways that made many wonder if their legal settlement had amounted to an armed truce. Both Priscilla and Lisa Marie made a video to be played at the banquet, in which they said a "special hello to an old friend of ours" and lauded the manager-singer duo, one Priscilla guessed would never be duplicated "in the history of show business."

Suddenly, the estate began spinning a revisionist take on the Presley-Parker past and planning an Elvis and the Colonel Museum. The two men "shared an abiding friendship that is often overlooked and misunderstood by the press and the general public," as Soden later put it.

That stance put Soden and company in an awkward position when author Chet Flippo came down hard on the Colonel in the introduction to an estate-sanctioned book, *Graceland: The Living Legacy of Elvis Presley*. No one at Elvis Presley Enterprises read Flippo's manuscript before it went to press, and Priscilla unsuccessfully put pressure on the publisher to pull the volume from distribution.

"As I recall," says Flippo, "Parker read the book, blew up, and called Priscilla, who . . . demanded to have [it] killed." The work was immediately removed from the Graceland gift shops, and the estate soon set up the Colonel Parker Tribute Committee to issue a thirty-two-page magazine, *Elvis & Colonel Tom Parker: The Partnership Behind the Legend.*

Like the estate, Barron Hilton was publicly loyal to the end. In June 1989, the hotel staged a gala dinner for the Colonel's eightieth birthday, with former Tennessee lieutenant governor Frank Gorrell, who had long handled Parker's charitable contributions, as master of ceremonies. Celebrities winged in on the Hilton's tab, RCA executives hovered and fawned, and scores of others, including President George Bush, Bob Hope, and Bill Cosby sent cheery telegrams of congratulations. "They window-dressed it pretty nicely," says Joe Delaney, the *Las Vegas Sun* columnist. "The Colonel held court."

Two months earlier, the Colonel and Loanne ("a single man and a single woman," as the deed read) jointly bought a town house in the Spanish Oaks area, an old, upgraded neighborhood. While $300,000 homes were not uncommon in the gated community, the residence was modest by comparison. They lived simply, shopping at Von's grocery at Decatur and Sahara, where Parker often waited outside on a bench and talked to passersby while Loanne did the marketing. She bought his clothes off the rack at JC Penney.

By all accounts, Loanne was good for him. She hung on his every word, laughed at his stories, and bragged on him to others, seeking not so much respect for herself, but for him. More important, she served as an indispensable nurse, doling out his daily medications, watching his cholesterol and his diet to stave off the gout that swelled his extremities, and driving him to Elias Ghanem's medical clinic for the slightest ailment, even as Parker's loyalty to the doctor who gave his client so many drugs seemed to some perverse.

They made an odd couple—she tall and angular, towering over him; he, squat and shorter than anyone remembered, balancing his bulky body on a bamboo cane and leaning heavily on her arm in his increasingly unsteady walk. She was also his most vigilant watchdog. When Merilyn Potters, a reporter for the *Sun,* visited the house for an upbeat story to mark Parker's birthday, she found the couple guarded, insisting on conducting the interview in the front courtyard instead of in their home. "He wouldn't answer certain questions regarding Elvis," Potters remembers. "And often, when he began to ramble, [Loanne] put the lid on." Her usual technique: Glancing over and raising an index finger to halt him if she thought he revealed too much.

"I think the Colonel was sharp enough to realize that he needed a guardian," offers Joe Delaney. "Loanne was a completely faithful servant."

And so, at the urging of Mae Axton, Parker married Loanne at the home of lawyer John O'Reilly on October 26, 1990. The Colonel was then eighty-one; Loanne, who took on the unofficial title of Mrs. Colonel, fifty-five.

A month after the ceremony, Parker signed a will that established a trust for talented youngsters, left monetary gifts to friends, and provided for his new wife. What few people knew was that in relative terms, the Colonel was no longer a wealthy man.

While he remained a loyal contributor to the *Sun* camp fund for needy children, donating $14,000 in the last six years of his life ("buying his soul out of hell," charged one wag), he largely lived off U.S. Treasury bonds, which he'd let mature and roll over. Occasionally, he put in appearances at fund-raisers around town (including one for presidential candidate Bill Clinton, whose mother, Virginia Kelley, became a gambling buddy), but the invitations were gratis, and Loanne kept her eye on every penny. Though he still sent cash to treasured acolytes at Christmas, twice in coming years Parker would add codicils to his will to reduce or rescind his financial gifts.

"Loanne hoarded money to keep him from pissing it away at the tables," as Jackie Kahane recalled. While the Colonel gambled, she sat quietly, reading a book.

Privately Loanne told people Parker was often cold to her, but in public their interaction was playful and childlike. "He said, 'Without her, I wouldn't be living,'" remembers a friend. "And when she'd try to give him his pills, they would just fuss, but that was part of the game. They were like two little kittens. She added those extra years to his life."

In the early '90s, the Colonel suffered what some said was his second stroke. Milder than the first, it was still an ominous sign, given the correlation between strokes and heart disease, the twin harbingers of the death that was beginning to take the lives of so many of his family members in Holland. Josephus, the eldest boy, had died in 1984, and then Adriana, the eldest girl, succumbed in 1989, eight years after she had written her estranged brother in America, begging to hear word of him. Her letter had been hand-carried by the Colonel's onetime compatriot, Lamar Fike, who, working with the Dutch reporter Dirk Vellenga, helped Albert Goldman uncover Parker's European past.

"When his sister walked into that room in Breda, I almost had a heart attack—she looked like a twin of Tom Parker. It was like finding out your daddy wasn't who he said he was." The Colonel just stared at Fike when he put the letter in his hand and "didn't make a comment either way." Adriana received no reply.

Now Engelina was ill with cancer and wanted to tell her brother good-bye. In November 1989, her daughter, Mieke Dons-Maas, introduced herself to Bill Burk, the American publisher of *Elvis World* magazine, at a meeting of the Dutch Elvis Presley fan club. She asked his help. Burk directed her to the Las Vegas Hilton, and for months, she faxed Parker letters and left phone messages, but all went unanswered.

Finally, Burk gave her Parker's private number. Mieke got Loanne on the line and explained she was the Colonel's niece. In halting English, she told her of her mother's last request, and of how the other family members loved their brother Dries and cried at the mention of his name. Loanne listened patiently, went to deliver the message, and returned with one curt sentence: "The Colonel said he doesn't wish to speak with anyone from Holland."

The family remains mystified as to why Parker refused contact. "I suppose he just wanted to cut those ties and any information about Holland muddied the history he had created for himself," says Mieke.

Unless, that is, his fate had become entwined with that of Anna van den Enden sixty years before. If so, a second tragedy for Parker, his family, and his famous client may have been the Colonel's ignorance of the fact that he was never named in the police report for the murdered woman. Under Dutch law, the longest any suspect would have been wanted for questioning was thirty years, and then only if he had been sought or accused. After 1959, whoever knew the ultimate truth about the death of Anna van den Enden was a free man, able to travel the world without restrictions.

Loanne insists Parker was proud of being a Dutchman, and "spoke with great love and affection about his country. He never forgot his roots." Certainly they were often on his mind. He made his charitable contributions on his birthday, a European custom. And in casual conversation, he told acquaintances that he and Loanne had adopted a son, poignantly producing a picture of a large, clubfooted rag doll. Its name: Andre.

Still, he remained diffident about all old-world contacts. When a young Dutch couple, Angelo Somers and Hanneke Neutkens, sent him a $100 box of cigars with a letter explaining their wishes to establish a Colonel Tom Parker Foundation in Breda, he returned their carefully decorated gift unopened. Dutch newsmen fared no better. Constant Meijers tracked him down at a slot machine in the Hilton casino and explained his plans to make a documentary film about Parker's integral role in the history of rock music. The man who'd once threatened to have a publicist's job because she had not included him in photographs now wanted nothing to do with the media in his native country.

"He talked a little bit of Dutch to me, and then he held on to the coins with one hand, and he waved me away with the other, saying, 'You're from Holland? Thank you, no, bye-bye. I know about Holland, I've been there.'"

Freelance videographer Jorrit van der Kooi had a similar experience, approaching Parker at the slots on his birthday. Van der Kooi spoke to him in Dutch, and after a brief exchange about Parker's heritage, delivered the news that Ad van Kuijk, the brother who had visited Parker in the States, had died. The Dutch journalist was rebuffed in his attempt to snag an interview, but captured chilling footage of his angry subject. As van der Kooi's camera whirred on, the Colonel, wearing dark cotton gloves to keep the handle from sullying his hands, continually poured what was left of his fortune into the eager slots, his face contorted with rage.

Though his stroke had left him weak, he still went out for lunch every day, and then on to the Hilton—nothing kept him from the twilight world of the Las Vegas casinos, where the ringing of the slot machines sounded like so many old-time carnival bells, and the croupiers called out like pitchmen. Loanne helped him into a wheelchair and pushed him through the crowds to the high-roller section.

"He continued to gamble until the day he died," remembers Nick Naff. "But it's awful hard to play roulette from a wheelchair, so he would sit and have two or three people pull the slot machines for him." Usually, he insisted on feeding the machines himself—sometimes four at once—but often he was so feeble or stiff that he dropped the tokens, attendants scrambling to pick them up for him as they skittered across the floor.

When the occasion called for it, however, he could rally, as he did at a ribbon-cutting ceremony for the Elvis Presley commemorative postage stamp at the Hilton in January 1993.

Inside Edition reporter Craig Rivera covered the event, mostly to corner Parker for comments on *Elvis and the Colonel: The Untold Story,* a made-for-TV movie set to air later that month, starring Beau Bridges in a dismally unflattering portrait of the man who made the King.

Parker denied he was upset by the portrayal ("Now, when they've done all they could with [Elvis], they're pickin' on me a little"), but found himself in his toughest interview yet. He denied trading Elvis's services for gambling debts ("My gambling has never had anything to do with Elvis"), and laid the blame on Presley for never playing overseas ("I had a whole staff that could go to Europe with him. He didn't want to go, because he didn't want to play outdoors, and if you don't play outdoors, you can't make it").

Finally, Rivera skewered him on the 50 percent commission, which Parker still defended as a partnership arrangement. "I know of four or five big stars that have a deal like that. But my deal was not fifty percent of the profit. My deal was fifty percent of work I created where he did not have to perform . . . On the motion pictures, the hotel, and the music business, twenty-five percent. Never no more. I sleep very good at night. And Elvis and I were friends."

The Colonel would be uncharacteristically sentimental about his client in latter years, telling reporters, "Every once in a while I sit by myself in my old rocking chair and talk to myself about Elvis . . . Some of the best deals we made were when we argued together [because] we came up with a better solution . . . It's hard to convince people how close you can be to someone."

And with reason. When Chris Hutchins visited Parker at home in 1993 for a book he was writing on Elvis and the Beatles, he was surprised to find the Colonel's "secret shrine" to Presley, made up of letters, telegrams, and photographs. Yet he found Parker as emotionally hard-shelled as ever.

"Do you miss him?" Hutchins asked. "Frankly no" came the reply. "There's no point missing what you haven't got." The reporter gazed at the vast collection of gold records lining Parker's hallway. "Which of these records do you play the most?" he inquired. "None of them," Parker said. "The only records I keep are business records. That's what he paid me for." In fact, the manager was fond of relating, he never took the time to listen to Elvis's last three albums or watch his final movies.

But down deep, Hutchins probed, wasn't Elvis the son the Colonel never had? The bulbous body leaned forward. "I have to be honest,"

Parker answered. "I can't say yes to that one either. I never looked on him as a son, but he was the success I always wanted."

Normally, Parker told interviewers, he was saving his Elvis stories for his autobiography, which he planned to call *How Much Does It Cost If It's Free?* His would be only a favorable account. "I've turned down more books for big money . . . a $2-million advance . . . because my story, they will not print. They said, 'No, we want the dirt.' I said, 'Well, I'm not a dirt farmer.' "

Parker had been claiming the autobiography was under way since 1957, of course, leading one journalist to muse that the book "seemed designed more to intimidate a number of lifelong business acquaintances than to herald a switch to the world of letters." The Colonel waved off such critics. "I got the book right up here," he would say, tapping his forehead. "I don't know if a guy should put out a book too soon if he's still alive . . . if I were to expire before completing it, Mrs. Parker here has all the information to finish it." But as late as 1994, he privately admitted he had yet to write the first word. "He freezes," Loanne said, "when I take out a tape recorder."

"I teased him about it a couple of times," remembers Bill Willard. "I saw him at breakfast over at Leo's Celebrity Deli and I said, 'How's the book coming along?' And he grumbled and grumped and turned away. [Loanne] looked at me and just shook her head."

By then, most of Parker's oldest friends were dead or dying, unable to confirm or deny the Colonel's mythology. When he wasn't in the casino or working for Barron Hilton, he said, he spent his time reading. "I've got plenty to do . . . I think a lot . . . People take up exercise, you know, but I exercise my brain."

To do so, he wrote doggerel poetry and sent it to friends such as Jerry Weintraub. And even though he still got up at five A.M., he watched Elvis's movies on late-night TV. But he was more entranced by the television evangelists, particularly Pat Robertson, who built a $20-million studio with viewers' contributions, Parker told one visitor, a gleam in his eye. And he never quit dreaming up promotions, entering into a business deal with Vegas entrepreneur Hank Cartwright to sell back-to-the-'50s memorabilia via catalogue.

Mostly, he stayed on the telephone and dictated letters to Loanne, who wondered why there were no Colonel fan clubs in Europe, considering the amount of overseas mail he received.

"He just got lost after Elvis died," says June Carter Cash, whom

Parker represented in the early '50s. "He would send me little notes say-ing he was still thinking about me and still loved me—anything to make him feel like he was close to the old days and to the things that really started it all."

While he took great pride in boasting how many old pals like Gene Autry and others kept in touch ("Eddy [Arnold] calls me probably at least once a month"), the truth was that he often did the calling, greeting familiar voices with his usual "kid, how you doin'?" He particularly made comforting calls to the sick, phoning the cancer-riddled Alan For-tas every Sunday, and keeping in daily contact with British fan club pres-ident Todd Slaughter after Slaughter's heart transplant in 1994.

"He was a lonely old man who came over from a foreign country alone and terrified," says a friend of thirty years, "and he didn't know how to accept somebody who loved him for just being the Colonel. But he wanted to be loved more than anybody I ever knew."

Others saw it, too. Elvis's piano player, Tony Brown, thought Parker had mellowed in old age, finding him surprisingly "very nice" when the two met again in the Colonel's last years. To some extent, it seemed to be true. Though he never forgave Byron Raphael for leaving the fold and largely cast him out "like a king would banish you from the court," as one observer notes, he made up with a number of people he had cast aside—the still-infatuated Trude Forsher, for example—or whose feathers he had ruffled, including Julian Aberbach and Lamar Fike. "We hadn't spoken in probably ten years," says Fike. "He said, 'Do you still love me?' And I said, 'Yeah, I still love you. How could I not, for crying out loud? You're part of my life.' He acted like nothing ever happened."

But he never lost his paranoia. When psychologist-author Peter Whit-mer contacted him for an interview for his book *The Inner Elvis: A Psy-chological Biography of Elvis Aaron Presley,* Parker felt so threatened he telephoned Joe Esposito and Henri Lewin, the retired president of the Hilton, and "warned them about what to say." And after the publication of *Elvis Meets the Beatles,* author Chris Hutchins was shocked to get an irate phone call, Parker "shouting very loudly" because Hutchins had written about the Colonel's secret shrine. "It wasn't like a manager lec-turing an errant journalist. It was more like a father telling off his son— he was quite a bitter old boy."

The real problem, says Lamar Fike, is that Parker expected to die by age seventy and never thought he'd outlast his enemies. And if living to old age was his punishment, Parker began wearing every day of it on his face and on his body. His eyes still snapped, but his skin—so thin it seemed translucent—was speckled with liver spots, the backs of his hands mottled to an almost solid brown. His flesh hung in crepe-like folds at his neck; his eyes sank into bottomless blue wells. Plagued by congestive heart disease and a recurring bronchitis that often slipped into pneumonia, he looked not old, but ancient. His arthritis was so painful that he sometimes canceled engagements, and it took all his strength to hoist his weight off a chair. But, he insisted, "I'm healthy up in my mind."

For the most part, he pretended all was well, keeping secret his hospital stays and appointments with several cardiologists. If people asked why he'd given up his beloved cigars, he claimed they cost too much and never mentioned his persistent cough or difficulty breathing. When he insisted on going to Los Angeles to take the children of one of his favorite vendors to the circus, he faltered, out of breath and ghostly pale, on the walk to the top of the arena.

He made his last two major public appearances in 1994. In March, he returned to Palm Springs for the ceremony to unveil three stars in the sidewalk at the corner of Palm Canyon Drive and Tahquitz Canyon Way—one for Elvis, one for Rick Nelson, and the last for Parker, an honor arranged by the Colonel's former protégé and Nelson's manager, Greg McDonald. That June, the Hilton threw a sumptuous bash for his eighty-fifth birthday, and Priscilla Presley, among others, flew in from Los Angeles.

Only a month before, Parker had spoken brazenly of Lisa Marie's marriage to Michael Jackson, spewing disdainfully that Elvis would not have approved. And he had taken other jabs at the estate, insisting he had never "exploited Elvis as much as he's being exploited today." Yet at the party, all seemed well. Jack Soden testified to his help and suggestions in running Graceland since it opened to the public, and Priscilla dutifully hugged and kissed the Colonel and Loanne. "I'm still working for you, Elvis," an emotional Parker said, wiping his eyes and pointing a finger skyward. He'd arrived in a golf cart, not wishing to use his wheelchair. Everyone knew this was the last of the big birthdays.

Throughout 1995, his health continued to deteriorate. When his old friend Gabe Tucker saw him the following year, "he knew he was dyin'. He never said nothin' about it, but he didn't want us to go. God, he was in bad shape. I seen him breakin' fast." By September 1996, he was essentially housebound. But still potent and quick with advice. He entertained a few visitors such as Jimmie Dale Gilmore, the Texas singer managed by Parker acolyte Mike Crowley. Gilmore was enchanted: "He said Elvis was as hard a worker as he ever knew, and it looked like tears were coming to his eyes." Anyone who demonized the Colonel, Gilmore said, "will never convince me."

Such visits buoyed him. "In the last years," Freddy Bienstock offers, "he had hardly any business. People had shunned him, or he shunned them. He would tell me I was the closest friend he had." The two last spoke in November 1996. "I was supposed to go out that fall, and I told him I couldn't make it, but I'd definitely be there in February. And he said, 'I'll be here. I'm not going anywhere.' "

But by December, the Colonel could barely speak. When friends called, Loanne had to talk for him and relay messages back and forth. Still, at eighty-seven, he clung to his entrepreneurial dreams. In one of his last visits with Jerry Weintraub, they schemed about putting their own relationship on film.

"He was my mentor, my teacher, my father figure," says Weintraub. "He told me he loved me, and I said, 'I love you, too,' and I kissed him, and he kissed me. I'm glad we had that moment."

On Monday afternoon, January 20, 1997, Parker was at home in his living room, perusing a pile of Christmas cards and letters. Loanne, in another room, suddenly heard a thud. She called out to no answer, and found him slumped in his chair. The Colonel had suffered a stroke.

At Valley Hospital, Loanne got on the phone and called her husband's circle. Bruce Banke, Parker's loyal contact at the Hilton, arrived to find the Colonel still in the emergency room. Banke leaned over and took his hand. "Colonel, it's Bruce." The old man opened his eyes, squeezed his friend's finger, and then faded. "I was the last person he saw," Banke says. "He never regained consciousness." The following morning, just before ten, he died. Loanne arranged for his cremation, though the final resting place of his ashes—not in Palm Cemetery, as reported—would become as mysterious as the rest of his peculiar life. His death certificate would list his birthplace as Holland but his citizenship as American.

Four days later, the invitation-only guests who filtered into the service at the Hilton were a predictable lot, a few famous faces—Eddy Arnold, Sam Phillips—mixed in with hotel honchos, record company execs, highbrow carnies, and swarthy men in dark, monied suits. Elvis-ographers large and small paid their respects, as did Phyllis McGuire, once Sam

Giancana's girlfriend. Ron Jacobs, the radio personality Parker had be-friended in Hawaii so long ago, draped a fresh maile lei around a giant picture of the Colonel.

Almost no one noticed Tom Diskin, who after leaving Parker's employ upon Elvis's death, had finally made a life for himself, marrying a French Elvis fan and producing a daughter. Scrimping through the years, he had nonetheless invested his stock and bonuses wisely, buying a luxurious California mansion before moving back to Nashville. He would die the following year in a traffic accident, leaving a multimillion-dollar estate, much of it in property and land.

As with the classic ant-and-grasshopper tale, the boss Diskin had come to mourn this January afternoon—a man who had earned an esti-mated $100 million from Elvis Presley alone—left behind only $913,000 in savings bonds, securities, and memorabilia. Much of that would go to Marie's grandchildren, Parker's secretary Jim O'Brien, and Mary, Patti, and Tom Diskin—hush money, some would say. The charitable trust dis-appeared in probate.

"How and where do you begin to celebrate the memories of a man who's been so dear to us?" asked Parker's Las Vegas lawyer and master of ceremonies, John O'Reilly.

Speaker after speaker sobbed in eulogizing "a very emotional man," whose eyes "were but windows to the world of kindness and love." Jerry Schilling read a letter from Tommy Sands, who thanked the Colonel for making all his dreams come true, and Henri Lewin remembered that "to work with him was actually working for him." "You and Elvis are to-gether again," Lewin mourned in his heavy German accent. "I know you both looked forward to this moment."

Of those who lauded the man who had promoted his client's name into the consciousness of two generations, only Priscilla Presley was matter-of-fact. "Elvis and the Colonel made history together, and the world is richer, better, and far more interesting because of their collaboration. And now I need to locate my wallet, because I noticed there was no ticket booth on the way in here, but I'm sure that Colonel must have arranged for some sort of toll on the way out."

Loanne, who announced she hoped one day to erect a monument to such a great man, had planned carefully for this day, accenting her simple dress with a glittering diamanté brooch fashioned in the shape of a snow-man. But Mrs. Colonel had none of her late husband's power.

The new head potentate was Priscilla Presley, who, in a year's time, would send her late ex-husband back out on the road to fulfill his dream to tour abroad. "Elvis: The Concert" would pair live performance from fifty of Presley's former instrumentalists and singers with video of their old boss on stage. For two hours, a virtual Elvis, circa 1970–1973, would sing, strut the stage, show off his karate moves, and mumble to the band, all on a twenty-foot screen.

Colonel Parker's idea for the satellite-beamed "Aloha from Hawaii" had been brilliant—Presley traveled the world without ever having to leave the States. But now Elvis wasn't even required to be alive. His jump-suited specter would sell out shows and earn rave reviews in America, Europe, Australia, and Japan, many fans reporting the event was as good or better than seeing him in the flesh.

Such bodacious sleight of hand was a weird and wonderful bit of hum-buggery, a tribute befitting the greatest carny con man of them all.

NOTES

The following abbreviations are used in the notes:

DWC/USC   David Weisbert Collection, University of Southern California Film Library Archives

HWC/MPAS   Hal Wallis Collection, Margaret Herrick Library, Academy of Motion Picture Arts and Sciences Library, Beverly Hills

JHC/UM   Jerry Hopkins Collection, Special Collections, University of Memphis

JWC/USC   Jerry Wald Collection, University of Southern California Film Archives

MPAS/OHP   Margaret Herrick Library, Academy of Motion Pictures Arts and Sciences, Beverly Hills, Oral History Project

TCFC/USC   Twentieth Century–Fox Correspondence, University of Southern California Film Archives

Acknowledgments

v   *"a haunting, an act of deliberate psychological trespass"*: New York Times Book Review, October 17, 1999.

v   *"was waiting for the recognizer—"*: New York Times Book Review, October 17, 1999.

Preface

2   *"It's so strange"*: Larry Geller in the documentary *Mr. Rock & Roll*, 1999.

Introduction

3   *"Did you see it?"*: Colonel Tom Parker to author, June 18, 1994.

4   *"Cooked the Colonel's Way"*: Serene Dominic, *Phoenix New Times*, January 30–February 5, 1997.

4   *"I want to leave you with just one thought"*: Loanne Miller Parker at Colonel Tom Parker's Memorial Service, Las Vegas, January 25, 1997.

5   *"He was so immense"*: Robert Kotlowitz to author, 1998.

5   *"the most overrated person"*: Dave Marsh, *USA Today*, January 22, 1997.

5   *"a nobody who needed a somebody to be anybody"*: Constant Meijers to author, 1997.

5   *"the best manager I ever saw"*: Chet Atkins to author, 1998.

5   *"Whatever he cost Elvis"*: Chet Atkins quoted in *Tennessean*, January 28, 1997.

5   *"Nobody killed Elvis except Elvis"*: Mike Crowley to author, 1998.

6   *"I sleep good at night"*: Colonel Tom Parker to author, 1994.

6   *"Elvis is my only client and my life"*: Colonel Tom Parker quoted in Audrey West, *Memphis Press-Scimitar*, February 22, 1974.

6   *"That man's a mystery"*: Bitsy Mott quoted in Goldman, *Elvis*.

6   *"when the Colonel's stepson, Bobby Ross, died"*: Sandra Polk Ross to author, 1998.

CHAPTER 1: THE LITTLE DUTCH BOY

14   *"Dries was very keen on his looks"*: Marie van Gort–van Kuijk to author, 1997.

15   *"When they had done serious wrong"*: Marie van Gort–van Kuijk to author, 1997.

16   *"I was never happy at the convent"*: Marie van Gort–van Kuijk, to author, 1997.

17   *"I worked for a gypsy"*: Colonel Tom Parker quoted in Merilyn Potters, "Birthday Bash for Colonel Parker," *Las Vegas Sun*, June 24, 1994.

18   *"the orphans stood in a row of twelve"*: Engelina Maas–van Kuijk to Hanneke Neutkens, 1996.

18   *"He would scheme, but always in a good way"*: Mieke Dons-Maas to author, 1997.

18   *"They all slept in the loft"*: Mieke Dons-Maas to author, 1997.

19   *"He never hurt anyone"*: Nel Dankers–van Kuijk quoted in Vellenga, "Breda Family Wants to Get in Touch."

19   *"even on the back of the meanest horse"*: Mieke Dons-Maas to author, 1997.

21   *"You could close the drawer"*: Engelina Maas–van Kuijk to Hanneke Neutkens, 1996.

21   *"our mother was clever"*: Marie van Gort–van Kuijk to author, 1997.

23   *"Possessing money"*: Marie van Gort–van Kuijk to author, 1997.

23   *"he was very conscious about how he looked"*: Engelina Maas–van Kuijk to Hanneke Neutkens, 1996.

23   *"if Mother didn't iron his collar properly"*: Marie van Gort–van Kuijk to author, 1997.

23   *"He would never drink a complete beer"*: Joe Esposito, *Elvis International Forum*, February 1997; also Peter Guralnick, *Careless Love*, p. 272.

24   *"I'm sure that by the time"*: Marie van Gort–van Kuijk to author, 1997.

25   *"He came to say hello and good-bye"*: Marie van Gort–van Kuijk to author, 1997.

CHAPTER 2: BEHAVIOR MOST STRANGE

27   *"He never told me"*: Marie Cornelisse-Ponsie quoted in Vellenga and Farren, *Elvis and the Colonel.*

31   *"Dries must have been talking about me"*: Marie Cornelisse-Ponsie quoted in Vellenga and Farren, *Elvis and the Colonel.*

35   *"I remember it like yesterday"*: Adriana van Gurp–van Kuijk quoted in Vellenga, "Breda Family Wants to Get in Touch."

35   *"He just changed identity"*: Marie van Gort–van Kuijk to author, 1997.

CHAPTER 3: "ALL GREAT NEPTUNE'S OCEAN"

36   *"We were driving through Hobbs, New Mexico"*: Byron Raphael to author, 1998. All quotes from Byron Raphael come from the author's extensive interviews with Mr. Raphael, 1998–2002.

37   *Parker himself said he gained entry:* Lloyd Shearer, "Presley vs. Parker," *Parade,* August 1, 1982.

38   *"The Smith Act, or the Alien Registration Act":* Marian Smith to author, 1998.

38   *"And I am curious":* Smith to author, 1998.

38   *"knifing a man to death in a fairgrounds brawl":* The People, January 26, 1997.

39   *"no recollection of such a story":* Chris Hutchins to author, 1998.

39   *"Do you know that Colonel Tom Parker comes from Breda?":* Dirk Vellenga, *De Stem,* September 20, 1977.

39   *"Did something serious happen":* Dirk Vellenga, *De Stem,* October 15, 1981.

39   *"Gentlemen: At last, I want to say":* De Stem, August 9, 1997.

41   *"fancy costume . . . a dark fantasy jacket costume":* Breda Police Report: The Murder of Anna van den Enden.

41   *"in a gray-colored overcoat":* Breda Police Report: The Murder of Anna van den Enden.

42   *"conflict of words":* Breda Police Report: The Murder of Anna van den Enden.

42   *"pretty chubby around the hips":* Breda Police Report: The Murder of Anna van den Enden.

42   *"very thin layer":* Breda Police Report: The Murder of Anna van den Enden.

43   *"part of the brain":* Breda Police Report: The Murder of Anna van den Enden.

43   *"I really don't think there was a murder in him":* Todd Slaughter to author, 2002.

43   *"I don't think there's any doubt":* Lamar Fike to author, 2001.

CHAPTER 4: MISSING IN ACTION

45   *"When he got off that boat":* Gabe Tucker to author, 1997.

46   *"working in a circus":* Ad van Kuijk quoted in *It's Elvis Time,* April 1967, May 1968, and June 1968.

46   *"about two years when I was sixteen years old":* Colonel Tom Parker on private audiotape recording of Elvis Presley Birthday Banquet, Memphis, January 8, 1988.

46   *"Please tell [Garth]":* Colonel Tom Parker in letter to Pam Lewis, 1994.

47   *"Colonel never invited questions":* Byron Raphael to author, 1998.

47   *"The story I heard":* Mac Wiseman to Beverly Keel for author, 1998.

47   *"Colonel was very loyal":* Sandra Polk Ross to author, 1997.

47   *"He was like a giant elephant":* Beecher Smith quoted in Soocher, *They Fought the Law.*

48   *"The place looked like a carnival midway":* Alan Fortas to author, 1985.

49   *"After I left the Netherlands":* Thomas A. Parker, affidavit in response to lawsuit, *RCA Records v. Joseph A. Hanks, National Bank of Commerce of Memphis, and Priscilla Presley, co-executors of the Estate of Elvis A. Presley, Thomas A. Parker, individually and d/b/a All Star Shows, and Blanchard E. Tual, Jr., guardian ad litem for Lisa Marie Presley,* May 18, 1982.

During Elvis's movie days, he routinely obtained costumes from Western Costumers and in them struck dramatic poses for photographs of himself wearing everything from a Confederate colonel's uniform and fake mustache to elaborate women's garb and wig.

"The Colonel was always disguising himself with props—a hat, a costume, or buttons—so people would look at the prop instead of the man," says Al Wertheimer, who photographed Elvis extensively at the outset of his career.

49   *"I had ten or twelve pictures"*: Cees Frijters quoted in Vellenga and Farren, *Elvis and the Colonel.*

50   *Parker never reminisced:* "I never have heard Colonel speaking of his army activities." Bitsy Mott to Dirk Vellenga, raw interview transcript, 1983.

51   *"Looking back from 1982":* Constant Meijers to author, 1997.

52   *"We didn't have much to do":* Earl Kilgus to author, 1998.

52   *Yet Jerry Goodson:* "There's just no reference for this guy." Jerry Goodson to author, 1998.

53   *"We should also be entitled":* Peter A. Herbert in letter to Dirk Vellenga, 1982.

53   *"We were never successful":* Blanchard E. Tual to author, 1998.

54   *"The men who served here":* David Ogden to author, 1999.

54   *A week later:* Based on information in official U.S. Army unit rosters and morning reports.

54   *"50 big and little elephants":* " 'Greatest Show' Here," *Pensacola Journal,* September 27, 1932.

55   *when he returned:* Based on information in official U.S. Army unit rosters and finance statements.

55   *Records show that:* Based on official U.S. Army finance statements.

56   *"Psychosis, Psychogenic Depression":* Discharge on certificate of disability, official U.S. Army records, Army Medical Center, Office of the Detachment Commander.

56   *On August 19, 1933:* Based on official U.S. Army records, Army Medical Center, Office of the Detachment Commander.

In its manic form, bipolar disorder is a cyclical disease occurring in spontaneous episodes with periods of remission or depression in between. Mood disturbances severe enough to damage job or social functioning, or requiring almost continual supervision or hospitalization to prevent suicidal actions or violence to others are also common, as are outbursts of suspicion and persecutory delusions.

Today, several avenues of therapy are available to the bipolar patient, primarily with controlling drugs such as lithium. But in 1933, the severely disturbed were treated with nonsensical methods that ranged from barbaric to violent—placing the straightjacketed patient in a spinning chair for lengthy periods, for example, or dunking him in ice water baths for extensive hydrotherapy.

What was thought to be the most effective treatment for psychosis in the 1930s was also the most dangerous and controversial—insulin shock. Administered by intravenous injection, insulin shock dropped the patient's blood sugar low enough to send him into diabetic coma and often convulsions. Intense treatment involved up to ninety tortuous injections and, not surprisingly, resulted in a high mortality rate. While the treatment had some marked therapeutic effect in reducing psychotic behavior, it also created confusion and memory loss in individuals who were already fragmented. After treatment, patients were often left with their same symptoms of delusions, hallucinations, and thought disorders, and were now sometimes brain damaged as well. The treatment was considered so perilous that electric shock—considerably safer—was developed to replace it in the late 1930s. Exactly how Private Parker was treated is unknown.

56   *In his pocket:* Based on official U.S. Army finance statements.

58   *"She was for me":* Mieke Dons-Maas to author, 1997.

CHAPTER 5: TURNING THE DUKE

59 *"He started out in a candy stand"*: Larry Davis to Constant Meijers, raw interview transcript from the documentary *Looking for Colonel Parker*, 1999.

60 *"I knew him"*: Joe McKennon to author, 1997.

60 *"he just didn't make an impression"*: Joe McKennon to author, 1997.

60 *"I used to know"*: Joe McKennon to author, 1997.

60 *"You could know a guy"*: John Campi to author, 1998.

61 *"in 1933, he was"*: Jack Kaplan to Dirk Vellenga, raw interview transcript, 1983.

61 *"He did a lot"*: John Campi to author, 1998.

61 *"I think that everyone"*: Larry Davis to Constant Meijers, raw interview transcript from the documentary *Looking for Colonel Parker*, 1999.

63 *"You could say"*: Joey Hoffman to author, 1997.

63 *"He always had quick ideas"*: Jack Kaplan to Dirk Vellenga, raw interview transcript, 1983.

CHAPTER 6: DANCING CHICKENS, TOOTHLESS LIONS, AND RODEO COWBOYS

66 *"The Colonel told me"*: Larry Davis to Constant Meijers, raw interview transcript from the documentary *Looking for Colonel Parker*, 1999.

66 *As someone who often treated animals with more dignity*: "If he saw one hurt, it would really touch him." Gabe Tucker to author, 1997.

67 *"I'd start each week"*: Hutchins and Thompson, *Elvis & Lennon*, p. 118.

67 *"He used to come"*: Ernie Wenzik to author, 1998.

68 *"Mr. Velare," he began*: Jack Kaplan to Dirk Vellenga, raw interview transcript, 1983.

68 *"One time, Colonel produced"*: Alan Fortas to author, 1988.

68 *"always intrigued by cowboys and cowboy stars"*: Oscar Davis to Jerry Hopkins, JHC/UM.

CHAPTER 7: ONE BORN EVERY MINUTE

70 *"a pussy pulls stronger than an elephant"*: Feiler, *Under the Big Top*.

71 *"She was a piss cutter"*: Sandra Polk Ross to author, 1997.

71 *"Colonel fell in love with Marie"*: Sandra Polk Ross to author, 1997.

71 *"I knew he had a girl"*: Jack Kaplan to Dirk Vellenga, raw interview transcript, 1983.

71 *"She had two children"*: Bitsy Mott to Dirk Vellenga, raw interview transcript, 1983.

71 *a startlingly beautiful child*: "My husband always told me this was the prettiest baby he had ever seen." Sandra Polk Ross to author, 1997.

71 *he was adopted two years later*: "It took two years for him to be adopted." Sandra Polk Ross to author, 1997.

71 *"play toy"*: Billy Ross, unpublished manuscript.

71 *"She said she was"*: Official divorce records.

71 *"willful, continuous and obstinate desertion of the complainant"*: Official divorce records.

72 *"I believe they were in love"*: Sandra Polk Ross to author, 1997.

73 *"I guess they went"*: Bitsy Mott to Dirk Vellenga, raw interview transcript, 1983.

74 *"by morning"*: Sandra Polk Ross quoting Bobby Ross to author, 1998.

74 *"Look what I won!"*: Sandra Polk Ross quoting Bobby Ross to author, 1998.

75 *"He made Mr. Rinaldi rich"*: Gabe Tucker to author, 1997.

76   *"the big, wise white man"*: Rosita, 1961.
76   *"I didn't want you all to know"*: Rosita, 1961.
76   *sometimes spoke in a foreign language:* "Spoke something in a language that sounded foreign to me—could have been Yiddish." Bitsy Mott to Dirk Vellenga, raw interview transcript, 1983.
77   *"The truth is"*: Sandra Polk Ross to author, 1997.

CHAPTER 8: DEEPER INTO AMERICA
79   *"Starting as a boy with his family"*: Austin and Pabst, *Gene Austin's Ol' Buddy.*
79   *"a great salesman"*: Austin and Pabst, *Ol' Buddy.*
80   *"It was obvious"*: Austin and Pabst, *Ol' Buddy.*
81   *"The stars come and go"*: Gabe Tucker to author, 1997.
81   *as he later claimed:* "I managed him for two or three years." Colonel Tom Parker to Ralph Emery, raw interview transcript, April 7, 1993.
81   *"proud, bulging bank account"*: Austin and Pabst, *Ol' Buddy.*
81   *"We sold out and made enough money"*: Colonel Tom Parker quoted in *Memphis Commercial Appeal,* September 14, 1984.
82   *"as an overstayed crewman"*: Marian Smith to author, 1998.
85   *in regarding Parker:* "He thought Colonel hung the damn moon, and he wanted to be like him so bad." Gabe Tucker to author, 1997.
85   *"As you know, Mr. Bevis"*: Crumbaker with Tucker, *Up and Down with Elvis Presley.*
86   *castoffs he got free:* "He made friends with two or three florists around there in the neighborhood." Gabe Tucker to author, 1997.
86   *"I wish you could have been here yesterday"*: Colonel Tom Parker quoted in Crumbaker and Tucker, *Up and Down with Elvis Presley.*
86   *"Colonel took care of Bevo"*: Al Dvorin to author, 1998.
87   *"He was always so crazy"*: Buddy Killen to Beverly Keel for author, 1998.
87   *"Marie yelled, 'Hey Buddy!'"*: Buddy Killen to Beverly Keel for author, 1998.
87   *"I know he and Marie"*: Gabe Tucker to author, 1997.
87   *"As for kids"*: Gabe Tucker to author, 1997.
88   *"and be there long enough"*: Sandra Polk Ross to author, 1997.

CHAPTER 9: NASHVILLE'S NASAL WHINE: JAMUP AND HONEY, EDDY ARNOLD, AND HANK SNOW
90   *"Minnie, you'll have to leave off that last part"*: Hall, *Hell-Bent for Music.*
90   *"When I came along"*: Minnie Pearl to author, 1975.
90   *"It was the first time"*: Minnie Pearl to Jerry Hopkins, JHC/UM.
91   *"could charm the warts off a hog's back"*: *Time,* date unknown.
92   *"Tom said the guy"*: Gabe Tucker to author, 1997.
93   *"When I heard that Mother was dead"*: Colonel Tom Parker to Ad van Kuijk, *Rosita.*
94   *"Regardless of how big"*: Pee Wee King to author, 1995.
95   *"He introduced himself to me"*: Eddy Arnold to Mike Streissguth, raw interview transcript, 1995.
96   *"Tom was obviously interested"*: Eddy Arnold to Mike Streissguth, raw interview transcript, 1995.
96   *"I was a hungry boy"*: Eddy Arnold at Colonel Tom Parker's Memorial Service, Las Vegas, January 25, 1997.

96 *"he'd constantly try"*: Justin Tubb to author, 1997.

97 *"We performed barefooted"*: Gabe Tucker to author, 1999.

97 *"Everybody said we were crazy"*: Hurst, *Nashville's Grand Ole Opry.*

98 *"Even with the tent shows"*: Pee Wee King to author, 1977.

98 *"and oh God, that truck smelled awful"*: Gabe Tucker to author, 1997.

99 *"He was trying"*: Gabe Tucker to author, 1998.

99 *"little wasp-nest hotels"*: Hurst, *Nashville's Grand Ole Opry.*

100 *"I was with him"*: Minnie Pearl to Jerry Hopkins, JHC/UM.

100 *"Southern people talk"*: Minnie Pearl to Jerry Hopkins, JHC/UM.

100 *"right out of that dog pound"*: Honey Wilds to Jack Hurst, raw interview transcript, 1974.

100 *"what each did"*: David Wilds to author, 1998.

101 *"He used to tell people in New York"*: Jack Kaplan to Dirk Vellenga, raw interview transcript, 1983.

101 *"He'd take a chance on anything"*: Gabe Tucker to author, 1999.

102 *"He would always wear"*: Nelle Poe to author, 1998.

102 *"As soon as Ernest"*: Nelle Poe to author, 1998.

102 *"He always said to me"*: Nelle Poe to author, 1998.

103 *"It's free today"*: Colonel Tom Parker quoted by Joey Hoffman to author, 1997.

103 *"He was a ball of fire"*: Eddy Arnold quoted in *Atlanta Journal,* January 22, 1997. See also *The Life and Times of Eddy Arnold* (Nashville Network) and Eddy Arnold to Constant Meijers, raw interview transcript from the documentary *Looking for Colonel Parker,* 1999.

104 *"When he was settin' up a tour"*: Gabe Tucker to author, 1997.

104 *"We got somebody"*: Colonel Tom Parker quoted by Gabe Tucker to author, 1997.

104 *"It was really too much"*: Roy Wiggins to author, 1998.

105 *"Tom came back backstage"*: Eddy Arnold at Colonel Tom Parker's Memorial Service, Las Vegas, January 25, 1997.

105 *"We used to play"*: Bitsy Mott to Dirk Vellenga, raw interview transcript, 1983.

106 *"Tommy told him, 'Plowboy' "*: Gabe Tucker to author, 1997.

106 *"I said to him once"*: Arnold, *It's a Long Way from Chester County.*

107 best-selling *"folk" music*: "Folk" in the chart name was changed to "Country & Western" in 1949.

108 *"You like your room?"*: Roy Wiggins to author, 1998.

108 *"He turned around"*: Gabe Tucker to author, 1997.

108 *"The specter of Tom"*: Bob McCluskey in e-mail to author, 1999.

108 *"all of us would run"*: Gabe Tucker to author, 1997.

109 *"Where do you think you're going"*: Tom Diskin to Roy Wiggins, quoted by Michael Streissguth, "I'd Trade All of My Tomorrows (for Just One Yesterday): The Ting-a-Ling and Tears of Little Roy Wiggins," *Journal of Country Music,* vol. 21 (no. 2), 2000.

109 *"Well, fuck the Coinnal!"*: Bob Moore to author, 1998.

109 *"I'll kill that big, fat, sloppy mother"*: Roy Wiggins quoted in Streissguth, "I'd Trade All of My Tomorrows."

109 *"It's one of the things"*: Roy Wiggins to author, 1998.

109 *"Don't you know about insurance?"*: Colonel Tom Parker quoted in Streissguth, "I'd Trade All of My Tomorrows."

109 *"Don't run that 'snowplow' at me"*: Roy Wiggins to author, 1998.

109   *"I want to talk to you"*: Colonel Tom Parker quoted in Streissguth, "I'd Trade All of My Tomorrows."

109   *"Did you say, 'Fuck the Coinnal?'"*: Colonel Tom Parker quoted by Bob Moore to author, 1998.

109   *"I had embarrassed him"*: Roy Wiggins quoted in Streissguth, "I'd Trade All of My Tomorrows."

110   *"It was really for nothing"*: Julian Aberbach to author, 1997.

110   *"almost every release of any importance was a Hill and Range song"*: Bob Mc-Cluskey in e-mail to author, 1999.

Hill and Range would come to represent a staggering number of classic songs, from "Frosty the Snowman" to "Arrivederci Roma."

Steve Sholes was thirty-four years old in 1945, the year he assumed the head of RCA's country and R&B divisions, which the company quietly referred to as "hillbilly and race," without either prejudice or hopes for spectacular sales. The real power and prestige belonged to the pop division, and hardly anyone paid the folk, or "hillbilly," category any mind. Sholes was born in Washington, D.C., grew up in Camden, New Jersey, where his father worked in the Victor Talking Machine Company plant. At Rutgers University, he wangled a part-time job with the record company, mostly as a messenger boy, and played saxophone and clarinet in regional dance bands. After graduation, Sholes went to work in the factory storeroom of RCA's radio department, and drifted into a clerk's job in the record department. Soon, Frank Walker, learning of Sholes's musical background, had him producing jazz, pop, and ethnic acts, first out of New York, and later in Chicago and Atlanta, where country acts lined up to make "field recordings" in a rented hotel room.

To Sholes, country music was an essential and important part of cultural America. While privately he was not above doing dead-on imitations of Southern dialects ("Well, I guess I'll go out and plow the back forty now"), the big fat fellow whose eyes squinted when he grinned formed an affinity for the country people. His mild-mannered and diplomatic demeanor quieted the mistrust of those Southerners who still regarded Yankees with disdain. Universally liked and viewed by many as a workaholic who neglected his own health for the sake of his artists ("He was one of the greatest men I ever knew," says his protégé, Chet Atkins), Sholes saw himself merely as a hard worker who dedicated himself to turning around Victor's struggling status in the early '40s.

Sholes had signed Arnold to a new one-year contract at the end of 1945, just as Tom Parker took over Eddy's management. Parker's opposite in nearly every way, the quiet executive, two years younger, listened to Parker's demands for his artist and put up with his rude bluster, but refused to be intimidated by any of it. Sholes had managed to negotiate his career without playing corporate politics—a move that earned him the respect of the men in his employ—and he wasn't about to start kowtowing to a singer's manager, even if he represented the division's biggest star.

"I don't think Steve could have been intimidated by Parker, because he understood him," says Charles Grean, Sholes's assistant from 1947 to 1952 who also doubled as an A&R man and studio bass player, building on his background as a copyist for the Glenn Miller Band. "We all knew what he was—a pusher and a blowhard. He made a lot of noise, but that was his way of doing the job. Half of the time we didn't pay any attention to him."

111   *"If Eddy got the twenty grand"*: Bob McCluskey in e-mail to author, 1999.

111   *"which was more than justified"*: Julian Aberbach to author, 1997.

111   *"All Eddy takes care of"*: Colonel Tom Parker quoted by Bill Kimbro to author, 1997.

111   *"Which one of our planes"*: Roy Wiggins to author, 1998.

112   *"Tell the Colonel"*: Roy Wiggins to author, 1998. Arnold denied to biographer Michael Streissguth that he was about to hit Parker, but in interviews with both Streissguth and the author, Wiggins was adamant about what he saw. "They were about to have fisticuffs, I think," he told the author, "and Marie stepped up and said, 'Don't hit him.' She kind of stopped it."

112   *"treated him like a flea-bitten alley dog"*: Gabe Tucker to author, 1997.

112   *"as he'd already gotten a reputation"*: Bob McCluskey in e-mail to author, January 13, 1999.

113   *"He got the money up front"*: Bob McCluskey in e-mail to author, January 9, 1999.

113   *"Plowboy"*: Colonel Tom Parker quoted by Gabe Tucker to author, 1997.

114   *"Colonel Tom got me out"*: Marty Robbins to author, 1997.

CHAPTER 10: THE MAN IN THE SHADOWS

116   *'Bob, this guy is incredible'*: Oscar Davis to Jerry Hopkins, JHC/UM.

117   *"It was really Oscar who found Elvis"*: Charlie Lamb on tape made for author, 1998.

117   *"We would see him"*: D. J. Fontana to author, 1998.

117   *"razzle, dazzle character"*: Bob Neal to author, 1977.

117   *"one of the big resort hotels in Nevada"*: Bob Neal in letter to Ed McLemore, quoted in Guralnick and Jorgensen, *Elvis Day by Day*.

117   *"I always felt that Elvis"*: Bob Neal to author, 1977.

117   *"Oscar lived high, wide, and handsome"*: Richard H. Frank Sr. to Charlene Blevins for author, 1999.

118   *"He was a deserter, plain and simple"*: Oscar Davis Jr. to author, 1999.

118   *"I became completely discouraged"*: Oscar Davis to Jerry Hopkins, JHC/UM.

118   *"I thought, hey"*: Sam Phillips in the documentary *Mr. Rock & Roll*, 1999.

118   *"We must have met"*: Norman Racusin to author, 1997.

118   *"Did I buy the wrong boy?"*: Steve Sholes to Sam Phillips, quoted by Chet Atkins to author, 1981.

119   *"Girls, I'll see you all backstage"*: Elvis quoted in Cotton, *All Shook Up*.

119   *"He was on top"*: Marty Robbins to author, 1977.

119   *"Perhaps it is to lighten our burdens"*: *Look* November 13, 1956.

120   *"He really was tone deaf"*: Joan Deary in the documentary *Mr. Rock & Roll*, 1999.

121   *"My boy"*: Colonel Tom Parker quoted by Tommy Sands to author, 1998.

121   *"I thought I'd have to be Mr. Clean"*: Tommy Sands to author, 1998.

121   *"Since Elvis Presley is pretty securely tied up"*: Stephen H. Sholes in letter to Tom Diskin, pictured in Guralnick and Jorgensen, *Elvis Day by Day. The Definitive Record of His Life and Music* (New York: Ballantine Books, 1999).

121   offered the *"possibility that we could record Tommy"*: Stephen H. Sholes in letter to Tom Diskin, pictured in Guralnick and Jorgensen, *Elvis Day by Day*.

121   *"but my voice hadn't changed"*: Tommy Sands to author, 1998.

121   *"He was just one of those pretty faces"*: Chet Atkins to author, 1998.

121   *"The fact that"*: Gabe Tucker to author, 1997.

121 *"priming me for whatever the next move was going to be"*: Tommy Sands to author, 1998.

122 *"That really made him"*: Cliffie Stone to Jerry Hopkins, JHC/UM.

122 *"the actor who is going to play me"*: Colonel Tom Parker quoted in Edward Linn, "Colonel Tom Parker, Pitchman Extraordinary," *Saga,* January 1958.

122 *"a very special type of voice"*: Harry Kalcheim in letter to Colonel Tom Parker, quoted in Guralnick and Jorgensen, *Elvis Day by Day.*

122 *"exploited properly"*: Colonel Tom Parker in letter to Harry Kalcheim, quoted in Guralnick and Jorgensen, *Elvis Day by Day.*

122 *"interested in making a picture with this boy"*: Colonel Tom Parker in letter to Harry Kalcheim, quoted in Guralnick and Jorgensen, *Elvis Day by Day.*

123 *"if you ever follow one of my hunches"*: Colonel Tom Parker in letter to Harry Kalcheim, quoted in Guralnick and Jorgensen, *Elvis Day by Day.*

123 *"just tied up a youngster, Elvis Presley"*: Harry Kalcheim in letter to Sam Fuller, quoted in Guernsey's, *Official Auction Catalogue.*

124 *"I don't think this artist"*: Colonel Tom Parker in letter to Harry Kalcheim, December 16, 1955, pictured in Guralnick and Jorgensen, *Elvis Day by Day.*

124 *"You know as well as I do"*: Colonel Tom Parker in letter to Harry Kalcheim, December 16, 1955, pictured in Guralnick and Jorgensen, *Elvis Day by Day.*

124 *"final approval of all contracts"*: Nat Lefkowitz of the William Morris Agency in memo to Colonel Tom Parker, January 31, 1956, pictured in Butterfield's auction on eBay, December 19, 2000.

125 *"idiot savant"*: Jerry Leiber and Mike Stoller, quoted in Jorgensen, *Elvis Presley.*

125 *"why buy a cow"*: Elvis Presley quoted in Guralnick and Jorgensen, *Elvis Day by Day.*

125 *Yet it was nothing for him:* "He was, for all his talent and sensitivity, this goof who would sit and laugh like a retarded person." Anonymous source, 1999.

125 *"There was absolutely no access"*: Bob Schulman to author, 1997.

125 *"did they spell his name right?"*: Colonel Tom Parker quoted by Gabe Tucker to author, 1997.

126 *"If it's a question"*: Colonel Tom Parker to Red Robinson, *From the Bottom of My Heart,* vol. 2, Savanah Records, 1997.

126 *"I don't think the Colonel is going to like this"*: Colonel Tom Parker quoted by Freddy Bienstock to author, 1997.

126 *the cost of an Elvis Presley appearance:* The money paid for television appearances escalated. In a 1997 letter to the author, Steve Allen recalled his dealings with the Colonel and how the *Sullivan Show* appearance came about: "I don't recall ever having any problems with Colonel Parker myself. As you probably know, the generally agreed upon top price on television shows in the '50s—regardless of the stature of the performer involved—was $7,500. That's why it produced repercussions when Ed Sullivan, apparently out of the desperation caused by his realizing he'd made a serious mistake in publicly criticizing Elvis, not only changed his mind on that point—so much for principle—but actually called the Colonel backstage at our theater the night his client appeared and broke his own and the industry's price-ceiling, which, for all I know, may have been actionable price-fixing.

"When the Colonel told us about the matter after our show was off the air, he said, 'I've talked to Elvis about this and we want to be fair to you guys. After all, you hired Elvis when Sullivan wouldn't, so if you want to keep us with you, we'll be happy to go along with that decision.' I'm only about 97 percent certain that he added something like, 'Of course, we would have to agree to accept the fee from you that Sullivan is offering.' I'm pretty sure that that fee was $10,000.

"When our producer, Bill Harbach, told me about what the Colonel had said, I thought the matter over for about thirty seconds and then decided not to accept it although the Colonel's thought about the $10,000 price had nothing whatever to do with my decision. I said to Bill, 'Tell the Colonel that I really do appreciate the way he's handling this, but it's okay with me if Elvis now accepts Sullivan's offer.'

"The reason was that while Sullivan's was a typical vaudeville variety show—and quite a good one—ours was something else altogether, a comedy show. I didn't want to have to figure out ways to make Elvis funny for four or five more appearances. It may be argued that I made a mistake in not keeping Elvis as part of our guest-family because of his enormous ratings potential."

126 *"you put a lump in my throat"*: Quoted in *TV Guide*, November 30, 1968.

126 *"Elvis was still standing there"*: Norman Racusin to author, 1997.

127 *"Elvis is just one"*: Carolyn Asmus in letter to Kay Wheeler, October 25, 1955, quoted in Harbinson and Wheeler, *Growing Up with the Memphis Flash*.

127 *"a couple of times a day"*: Bill Denny to author, 1998.

127 *mostly by assembly line*: "We had a sort of assembly line." Bill Denny to author, 1998.

128 *"this thing became a beautiful, successful nightmare"*: Charlie Lamb to author, 1998.

128 *"a real stroke of genius"*: Sam Phillips in the documentary *Mr. Rock & Roll*, 1999.

128 *"You don't have to be"*: Colonel Tom Parker quoted by Minnie Pearl to Jerry Hopkins, JHC/UM.

128 *"As long as Elvis"*: Colonel Tom Parker quoted by Byron Raphael to author, 1998.

129 *"Dear Colonel, Words can never tell you"*: Elvis Presley, telegram to Colonel Tom Parker, quoted in Guralnick and Jorgensen, *Elvis Day by Day*.

129 *"When someone would ask"*: Bill Denny to author, 1998.

130 *"I don't want to end up with cider in my ear"*: Colonel Tom Parker quoted by Byron Raphael to author, 1998.

130 *"Let's say she wasn't"*: Anne Fulchino to author, 1998.

130 *"She had a twelve-foot closet just for coats"*: Sandra Polk Ross to author, 1997.

130 *"She was the only person I knew"*: Ann Dodelin to author, 1999.

131 *She was happiest, some say*: June Carter Cash to author, 1998.

131 *"the Colonel's stable base"*: Hubert Long to Jerry Hopkins, JHC/UM.

131 *"a goner, just a pile of shit mixed with alcohol and pills"*: Connie B. Gay quoted in Joe Sasfy, *Regardie's*, March 1987.

131 *"It was the only time"*: Connie B. Gay quoted in Joe Sasfy, *Regardie's*.

131 *"Later, Mother said"*: Judy Gay Burkley to author, 1997.

131 *"an old, fat, nice guy"*: Judy Gay Burkley to author, 1997.

132 *"One reason Tom always stayed with us"*: Jan Gay to author, 1997.

132 *"was getting a little belligerent"*: Bitsy Mott to Dirk Vellenga, raw interview transcript, 1983.

132 *"I didn't want people comin' knockin' on the door, you know"*: Colonel Tom Parker to author, 1994.

133 *"$20,000 or $30,000 worth"*: Colonel Tom Parker to author, 1994.

133   *"a small truckload of Elvis memorabilia"*: Monsignor George Rohling to author, 1997.
134   *"I thought it was rather unusual"*: Monsignor George Rohling to author, 1997.
134   *"pictures of family members"*: Monsignor George Rohling to author, 1997.

CHAPTER 11: "ELVIS MAKES PITCHAS"
135   *"look at this fellow"*: Harriet Ames quoted by Joseph Hazen to Peter Whitmer, raw interview transcript, February 18, 1994.
135   *"We chatted"*: Joseph Hazen to Peter Whitmer, raw interview transcript, February 18, 1994.
135   *"There was something about his eyes"*: HWC/MPAS.
135   *"I knew instinctively"*: Wallis with Higham, *Starmaker.*
136   *"nothing would stop me"*: Wallis with Higham, *Starmaker.*
137   *"we were agog"*: Chick Crumpacker in letter to author, February 16, 1998.
137   *"It was the talk of the place"*: Crumpacker to author, 1998.
137   *"meteoric rise is unquestionably a freak situation"*: Joe Hazen to Hal Wallis, June 11, 1956, HWC/MPAS.
137   *"but his dramatic abilities and talents"*: Joe Hazen in letter to Colonel Tom Parker, quoted in Guernsey's, *Official Auction Catalogue.*
137   *"My ambition has always been"*: Elvis Presley to Hal Wallis, HWC/MPAS.
137   *"The idea of tailoring"*: Hal Wallis in the documentary *Elvis: The Echo Will Never Die,* 1986.
138   *"No check is good"*: Colonel Tom Parker quoted in *Time,* May 16, 1960.
139   *"full shadow of a real blue beard"*: "You could see the full shadow of a real blue beard, one that she would have to shave twice a day." Bob McCluskey in e-mail to author, 1999.
139   *Parker, who had demanded early*: Abe Lastfogel in letter to Hal Wallis, May 3, 1956, HWC/MPAS. "Dear Hal: Am quoting an excerpt of a memorandum from Ann Rosenthal re ELVIS PRESLEY: 'In talking to Joe Hazen you might also tell him that if he or Hal Wallis have anything to discuss with respect to Presley they should not contact him direct but channel all of these matters through Colonel Parker or through us. The Colonel is most sensitive about this.' "
140   *"Parker has a peeve about neglect"*: Joe Hazen in interoffice memo to Hal Wallis, October 2, 1956, HWC/MPAS.
140   *"I wouldn't be a hundred feet"*: Joe Hazen to Peter Whitmer, raw interview transcript, February 18, 1994.
140   *"very confidentially—and as man to man"*: Joe Hazen in interoffice memo to Hal Wallis, October 26, 1956, HWC/MPAS.
140   *"crap"*: Joe Hazen in interoffice memo to Hal Wallis, September 6, 1957, HWC/MPAS.
140   *"methods that have been very helpful"*: Colonel Tom Parker in letter to Buddy Adler, September 25, 1956, TCFC/USC.
140   *"I was in his office when the call came"*: Freddy Bienstock to author, 1997.
141   *"maybe he needs a new manager"*: Colonel Tom Parker to Buddy Adler, quoted in John Semien, "Graceland Magazine Honors Parker," *Memphis Commercial Appeal,* June 23, 1994.
141   *"Better take this, Tom"*: Abe Lastfogel quoted in Linn, "Pitchman Extraordinary."
141   *"Go back to 'em"*: Colonel Tom Parker quoted by Byron Raphael to author, 1998.

142   *"in getting the most"*: Leonard Hirshan to author, 1998.
143   *"If anybody laughs"*: Colonel Tom Parker quoted by Byron Raphael to author, 1998.
143   *"a familiar face will help keep this fellow settled down"*: David Weisbart in memo to Harry Brand, August 22, 1956, DWC/USC.
144   *"He's been so cooperative with us"*: David Weisbart in memo to Buddy Adler, September 24, 1956, DWC/USC.
145   *"because I was developing too much of a relationship with Elvis"*: Leonard Hirshan to author, 1999.
145   *"You can't trust people in this town"*: Colonel Tom Parker quoted by Byron Raphael to author, 1998.
145   *"possessed him"*: Joseph Hazen to Peter Whitmer, raw interview transcript, February 18, 1994.
146   *"I want to be the kind of actor"*: Elvis Presley in the documentary *Elvis in Hollywood*, 1993.
146   *"I'd sooner cut my throat"*: Elvis Presley quoted in Lloyd Shearer, *Parade*, September 30, 1956.
146   *"it's pretty easy"*: Colonel Tom Parker quoted by Byron Raphael to author, 1998.
146   *Presley, who as a small child:* "Seems we was always in debt. Can't hardly remember when we wasn't. We used to sit on the doorstep talkin' about our debts. After a while Elvis'd look up, he was just a little fella, an' he'd say, 'Don't worry none. One of these days things will change.' Well, Elvis changed 'em." Gladys Presley quoted in Lloyd Shearer, *Parade*, September 30, 1956.
146   *"For the first twelve years"*: Freddy Bienstock to author, 1997.
147   *"a very rough way"*: David Weisbart in memo to Harry Brand, August 22, 1956, DWC/USC.
147   *"a beginner who had"*: Mildred Dunnock to Jerry Hopkins, JHC/UM.
147   *"He has magnetism"*: Trude Forsher to author, 1997.
148   *"Spread the news"*: TCFC/USC.
148   *"as to how much money"*: Joe Hazen in interoffice memo to Hal Wallis, October 26, 1957, HWC/MPAS.
149   *"divided among them according to their own desires"*: Joe Hazen in interoffice memo to Hal Wallis, January 17, 1957, HWC/MPAS.
149   *"could not or would not keep any of it personally"*: Abe Lastfogel, quoted in Joe Hazen in interoffice memo to Hal Wallis, December 3, 1956, HWC/MPAS.
149   *"your paying Elvis Presley and Colonel Parker the additional $50,000"*: Abe Lastfogel in letter to Joe Hazen and Hal Wallis, February 7, 1957, HWC/MPAS.
149   *"for the cooperation of Colonel Tom Parker"*: Contract quoted in Guernsey's *Official Auction Catalogue.*
150   *"You want to tell me"*: Colonel Tom Parker to Oscar Davis, quoted in *Rosita*, 1960.
150   *"the only Jewish fella in Madison"*: Colonel Tom Parker to Ralph Emery, raw interview transcript, April 7, 1993.

CHAPTER 12: DIRECTIONAL SNOWING
152   *"a lot of people hated him"*: Hal Kanter to Barbara Hall, MPAS/OHP, July 5, 1994.
152   *"a nasty little boy"*: Hal Kanter to Barbara Hall, MPAS/OHP, July 5, 1994.

152 *"orchid-pretty"*: Kanter, *So Far, So Funny*.

152 *"There were some things"*: Hal Kanter to Barbara Hall, MPAS/OHP, July 5, 1994.

152 *"I thought the colorful Colonel"*: Kanter, *So Far, So Funny*.

153 *"Trude, if you come with me now"*: Colonel Tom Parker quoted by Trude Forsher to author, 1997.

153 *"Speak German for me, Trude"*: Colonel Tom Parker quoted by Trude Forsher to author, 1997.

153 *"this bombastic, driving, one-man minstrel show"*: A. C. Lyles to author, 1997.

155 *"My induction was given to me over dinner"*: Charlie Boyd to author, 1997.

156 *"how much, not who, where, when, or why"*: Hal Kanter to Barbara Hall, MPAS/OHP, July 5, 1994.

156 *"I would never know"*: Hal Kanter to Barbara Hall, MPAS/OHP, July 5, 1994.

156 *"was happier fleecing the world"*: Kanter, *So Far, So Funny*.

156 *"pink face turned magenta"*: Kanter, *So Far, So Funny*.

157 *"Now I see why you have the police there"*: Hal Kanter to Barbara Hall, MPAS/OHP, July 5, 1994, and Kanter, *So Far, So Funny*.

157 *"eight doors removed from the donniker"*: Colonel Parker in letter to Hal Wallis and Joseph Hazen, May 5, 1959, HWC/MPAS.

158 *"I consider it my patriotic duty"*: Colonel Tom Parker quoted in Jerry Hopkins, unpublished magazine article, JHC/UM.

158 *"I love to pay taxes"*: Colonel Tom Parker to Boots Randolph, quoted in Peter Cronin, Scott Isler, and Mark Rowland, "An Oral Biography: Elvis Presley," *Musician*, October 1992.

159 *"just scared him to death"*: Bitsy Mott to Dirk Vellenga, raw interview transcript, 1983.

161 *"What he told me"*: Anne Fulchino to author, 1998.

161 *"He was an angel"*: Sam Esgro to author, 1998.

163 *"my people listen to me"*: Gabe Tucker to author, 1997.

163 *"I'll know about it"*: Linn, "Pitchman Extraordinary."

163 *"I know the inside of the Colonel"*: Trude Forsher to author, 1997.

164 *"just scares me"*: Guralnick and Jorgensen, *Elvis Day by Day*.

164 *"I am the most miserable"*: Elvis Presley quoted by James Hamill to author, 1977.

165 *"After the break"*: Freddy Bienstock to author, 1997.

165 *"Oh my God, Cole Porter"*: Jean Aberbach quoted by Byron Raphael to author, 1997.

166 *"pushed a chair in front of the door"*: Mike Stoller to Jerry Hopkins, JHC/UM.

166 *"I called [the Colonel] and said"*: Jerry Leiber to Jerry Hopkins, JHC/UM.

166 *"a necessary evil"*: Gordon Stoker to author, 1998.

167 *"The Colonel had a grip"*: D. J. Fontana quoted in Cronin, Isler, and Rowland, "An Oral Biography."

167 *"He just wants to use your name"*: The Jordanaires to Chris Clark, WTVF-TV, Nashville, May 2000.

167 One day, the Colonel found: The Mike Stoller anecdote comes from his quotes in Cronin, Isler, and Rowland, "An Oral Biography."

167 *"was trapped by his dependency"*: Jerry Leiber quoted in Cronin, Isler, and Rowland, "An Oral Biography."

168 *"Elvis, Trude's here"*: Colonel Tom Parker quoted by Byron Raphael to author, 1998.

168   *"It's better to be feared than liked"*: Colonel Tom Parker quoted by Byron Raphael to author, 1998.

168   Don't Push Me Too Far, *or* Trouble Is My Name: Colonel Parker letter to Pandro Berman, March 23, 1957, quoted in Guernsey's *Official Auction Catalogue*.

169   *"deathly afraid to be alone"*: Mardy Baum to author, 1997.

169   *"Don't you know"*: Colonel Tom Parker quoted by Byron Raphael to author, 1998.

169   *"Like he was going to call roll"*: Gordon Stoker to author, 1998.

169   *"If we would go out for a meal"*: Byron Raphael to author, 1998. Parker's obsessive-compulsive traits, including excessive neatness, fear of germs, preoccupation with feces, and repeated washing, were likely the result of abnormally low serotonin levels in the brain. Studies show that low serotonin activity also increases aggressive behavior. Violent criminal offenders—particularly those who act impulsively in predatory attacks such as the one on Anna van den Enden—are often found to suffer from this condition. As children, in keeping with the antics of the young Dries van Kuijk, who also bit his teacher on the ankle, these subjects are usually disruptive in school; as young adults, they can show particularly aggressive and/or violent behavior while intoxicated. Parker is on record for having reported impaired impulse control while drinking in his own young adult life, and gave it as his reason for avoiding alcohol. The level of serotonin in the brain is also affected by the consumption of carbohydrates—typical of the starchy food Parker loved.

171   *"They paid the sheriff"*: Frank Bogert to author, 2001.

171   *"I kept hearing stories"*: Eddy Arnold quoted in Streissguth, *Eddy Arnold*.

171   *"The times when I was there"*: Gabe Tucker to author, 1997.

172   *The Sahara was built*: Denton and Morris, *The Money and the Power*.

172   *"Bitsy, I trust you more than anyone else"*: Bitsy Mott to Dirk Vellenga, raw interview transcript, 1983.

173   *"mental telepathy and perpetual perception motors"*: Colonel Tom Parker in letter to Hal Wallis, June 19, 1963, HWC/MPAS.

174   *"There's no war going on"*: George Klein in the documentary *Elvis in Hollywood*, 1993.

175   *"What's going to happen to me?"*: Freddy Bienstock to author, 1997.

176   *"Is it in the [Production] Code?"*: Hal Wallis in memo to Paul Nathan, January 7, 1958, HWC/MPAS.

176   *"That crooked son of a bitch"*: Anonymous source, 1998.

176   *"a ton of balloons"*: Lenny Hirshan to author, 1998.

177   *"For the first time, I know what a director is"*: Elvis Presley quoted by Jan Shepherd in the documentary *Elvis in Hollywood*, 1993.

177   *"Just like in his music"*: Michael Curtiz quoted in Guernsey's *Official Auction Catalogue*.

177   *"Colonel Parker," a reporter scribbled*: *Life*, February 10, 1995.

177   *"Good-bye, you long, black son of a bitch"*: Elvis Presley quoted in *Life*, February 10, 1995.

178   *"My father knew all the doctors in town"*: Janice Fadal quoted in Michael Hall, "Viva Fort Hood," *Texas Monthly*, December 2000.

178   *"that elevator opened"*: Lamar Fike to author, 1995.

179   *"When the funeral director"*: Freddy Bienstock to author, 1997.

179   *"I suppose I was never"*: Colonel Tom Parker quoted in Hutchins and Thompson, *Elvis & Lennon*.

179   *"shit . . . they were awful people"*: "The Colonel said to me at one time, 'The problem with Elvis was his family was shit. They were awful people.'" Colonel Tom Parker quoted by Todd Slaughter to author, 2002.

179   *"Don't you call me a square!"*: Colonel Tom Parker quoted by Chick Crumpacker in letter to author, 1998.

179   *"I want to apologize, I was wrong"*: Conversation recounted by Anne Fulchino to author, 1998.

180   *"I miss my singing career very much"*: Elvas Presley quoted in Peter Guralnick, *Last Train to Memphis*.

180   *"That may be big in Nashville"*: Anne Fulchino to author, 1998.

180   *"pushed his stubby little fist in Elvis's back"*: Al Wertheimer to author, 1998.

180   *"I barely saw him"*: Colonel Tom Parker to Larry Hutchinson, chief investigator to the district attorney general, Memphis, 1980.

182   *"When we got ready to leave"*: Dale Robertson to author, 1999.

182   *going to dinner at the Luau*: Byron Raphael to author, 1997.

CHAPTER 13: FRIENDLY PERSUASION: MOGULS, MILITARY MEN, AND MOBSTERS

183   *"to keep your name hot over here"*: Colonel Tom Parker in undated letter to Elvis Presley quoted in Guralnick and Jorgensen, *Elvis Day by Day*.

183   *$3 million from souvenirs alone*: Hedda Hopper, *Motion Picture*, May 1961.

183   *"There was not much I could do"*: Colonel Tom Parker in letter to Vernon and Elvis Presley, November 18, 1958, pictured in Guralnick and Jorgensen, *Elvis Day by Day*.

184   *"This sure is a long tour"*: Elvis Presley in undated letter to Colonel Tom Parker, quoted by Sean O'Neal, raw interview transcript from the documentary *Looking for Colonel Parker*, 1999.

184   *tipping a Las Vegas bellboy with sandwiches*: "We thought that using our sandwiches for a tip to the bellboy in Las Vegas was pretty good." Joe Hazen in letter to Colonel Tom Parker, February 16, 1959, HWC/MPAS.

184   *"to give Mr. Presley some additional income"*: Joe Hazen in undated letter to the William Morris Agency, HWC/MPAS.

184   *"I am sure,"*: Colonel Tom Parker in letter to Hal Wallis and Joe Hazen, April 28, 1959, HWC/MPAS.

184   *"You've just got to get the big picture, Colonel"*: Colonel Tom Parker quoted by Byron Raphael to author, 1998.

185   *"This again shows you"*: Colonel Tom Parker in letter to Hal Wallis, February 19, 1964, HWC/MPAS.

185   *"from Elvis and myself"*: Colonel Tom Parker in telegram to Hal Wallis, June 21, 1959, HWC/MPAS.

185   *"your two orphans, Marie and the Colonel"*: Colonel Tom Parker in telegram to Hal Wallis, June 15, 1968, HWC/MPAS.

185   *"It is nice"*: Hal Wallis in letter to Colonel Tom Parker, June 17, 1968, HWC/MPAS.

185   *"good voice for that type of singing"*: Colonel Tom Parker in letter to Hal Wallis, December 13, 1958, HWC/MPAS.

185   *"a gang of promoters"*: Movie-plot ideas, Colonel Tom Parker in letter to Hal Wallis, December 18, 1958, HWC/MPAS.

185   *"a gypsy boy"*: Dick Sokolove in interoffice memo to Hal Wallis, June 5, 1961, HWC/MPAS.

186   *"flooding the market"*: Colonel Tom Parker to Steve Sholes, quoted in Guralnick and Jorgensen, *Elvis Day by Day*.

186 *"I've got money stashed in places all over the world"*: Colonel Tom Parker quoted by Byron Raphael to author, 1998. According to two other people close to the Colonel, he occasionally traveled out of the country with a fake passport. This has not been documented.

187 *"some important papers"*: Judy Gay Burkley to author, 1997.

187 *"People thought it was strange,"*: Freddy Bienstock to author, 1997

188 *"I hope our paths cross again"*: Lyndon Baines Johnson in letter to Colonel Tom Parker, December 29, 1959, Senate Masters Collection, Lyndon Baines Johnson Library.

188 *"certainly counting on you"*: Lyndon Baines Johnson in letter to Colonel Tom Parker, January 13, 1960, Senate Masters Collection, Lyndon Baines Johnson Library.

188 *"My special meeting in Washington"*: Colonel Tom Parker in letter to Joe Hazen, September 30, 1959, HWC/MPAS.

189 *"feels they would do the same"*: Paul Nathan in interoffice memo to Hal Wallis, July 21, 1959, HWC/MPAS.

190 *Often, Parker said:* "Then Elvis went to the army for two years and I spent my money keeping Elvis's name alive for the two years until he came out." Colonel Tom Parker to Ralph Emery, phone conversation quoted in raw interview transcript, April 1993.

190 *"just another G.I. Joe"*: Estes Kefauver, "Tribute to Elvis Presley," *Congressional Record,* Friday, March 4, 1960, no. 40, pp. 4151–4152.

191 *"You don't think"*: Colonel Tom Parker quoted by Steve Sholes to Jerry Hopkins, JHC/UM.

191 *"the Colonel went through"*: Account of Kotlowitz's time with the Colonel, Robert Kotlowitz to author, 1999.

191 *to call an army recruiting officer"*: Norman Racusin to author, 1997.

191 *"like a happy young colt"*: David Halberstam, *Tennessean,* March 7, 1960.

192 *"One of the dogs may sue us"*: Colonel Tom Parker in letter to Hal Wallis, February 23, 1959, HWC/MPAS.

192 *"He would lose fortunes"*: Freddy Bienstock to author, 1997.

192 *"I think the reason for his gambling"*: Julian Aberbach to author, 1997.

193 *"controlled by more mobs than any other casino in Nevada"*: Reid and Demaris, *The Green Felt Jungle.*

193 *known as Mr. Entertainment:* Information on Jack Entratter comes from Berman, *Lady Las Vegas; The Agency;* and the author's interviews with Byron Raphael and with Art Nadler of the *Las Vegas Sun.*

193 *for Elvis to be photographed with Prell:* The information about Parker's relationship with Milton Prell comes from Goldman, *Elvis,* and from sources who wish to remain anonymous.

193 *"The Colonel demanded everything"*: Anonymous source, 1998.

194 *"He got just wild"*: Lamar Fike to author, 1994.

194 *"We feel sure"*: Colonel Tom Parker in letter to Hal Wallis, June 30, 1960, HWC/MPAS.

195 *"His be-rhinestoned cuff links"*: *Billboard,* April 25, 1960.

195 *With a change of studios:* Twentieth Century–Fox believed that selling Elvis as a dramatic actor as well as a singer could attract an ever wider audience than before. Charles Einfeld letter to David Weisbart, November 7, 1960, DWC/USC.

195 *"I have sweated over the script"*: David Weisbart in letter to Buddy Adler, June 6, 1960, DWC/USC.

195   *"We want all the best":* Colonel Tom Parker quoted by David Weisbart to Ted Cain, August 10, 1960, DWC/USC.

195   *"I would not know":* Colonel Tom Parker in letter to David Weisbart, July 12, 1960, DWC/USC.

196   *"I think Parker":* Charles Einfeld in letter to David Weisbart, November 10, 1960, DWC/USC.

196   *"Elvis Acts!":* Don Siegel in letter to Harry Brand, October 12, 1960, DWC/USC.

196   *"an excellent dramatic actor, a natural actor":* Philip Dunne, MPAS/OHP.

196   *"the gifted individual":* From story conference with Joseph Stefano and Jerry Wald, April 29, 1958, JWC/USC.

197   *"I have never advised":* Colonel Tom Parker in night letter to Jerry Wald, November, 1960, JWC/USC

197   *"Svengali who has hypnotized":* Twentieth Century–Fox, unpublished press release for *Wild in the Country,* 1960, JHC/UM.

197   *"When we previewed":* Philip Dunne, MPAS/OHP.

197   *"Negro cotton field harmony":* Memphis *Commercial Appeal* quoted in Guralnick and Jorgenson, *Elvis Day by Day.*

198   *"He started snowing them":* Ron Jacobs to Jerry Hopkins, quoted in Hopkins, unpublished magazine article, JHC/UM.

198   *"one of the admirals":* Tom Moffatt to Jerry Hopkins, JHC/UM.

198   *"every penny . . . must go to the fund!":* Music Reporter, February 20, 1961.

198   *"how encapsulated Elvis was in his fame":* Minnie Pearl to author, 1981.

199   *"It is very important":* Hal Wallis in letter to Colonel Tom Parker, January 30, 1961, HWC/MPAS.

199   *"A Presley picture":* Hal Wallis in the documentary *Elvis in Hollywood.*

200   *"He really can't":* Joe Pasternak quoted by Byron Raphael to author, 1998.

201   *"That's fine":* Colonel Tom Parker quoted by Jerry Weintraub at Colonel Tom Parker's Memorial Service, Las Vegas, January 25, 1997.

201   *"They'll never win":* Colonel Tom Parker quoted by Jean Bosquet in Guralnick and Jorgensen, *Elvis Day by Day.*

CHAPTER 14: "MISTAKES SOME-ONE MAY HAVE MADE"

202   *"It seemed like a fairy tale":* Adam van Kuijk quoted in *Rosita,* see below.

203   *"Master Ad van Kuyk Jr.":* A copy of the letter from "Andre" to Master Ad Van Kuyk Jr. was obtained from Mr. Van Kuyk. The original remains in his possession. The quotes from Ad Sr. are from articles in *Rosita,* July 1, 8, and 15, 1961. All quotes from Ad Jr. are from the author's interview, and from letters to the author dated May 4, 1998, and February 21, 1999. I also relied on Dineke Dekkers, "Tom Parker . . . American or Dutchman?" *It's Elvis Time,* April 1967.

204   *"If Elvis had known":* Lamar Fike to author, 2001.

CHAPTER 15: TROUBLE IN THE KINGDOM: THE COLONEL TIGHTENS HIS GRIP

205   *"going over there to meet Elvis":* Presley and Harman, *Elvis and Me.*

205   *"I said, 'God Almighty' ":* Lamar Fike to author, 1994.

205   *"Not any special one":* Elvis Presley, press conference, Memphis, March 7, 1960.

206   *"he didn't give them a time":* Priscilla Presley quoted in Finstad, *Child Bride.*

206   *"We had to keep everything":* Anita Wood quoted in Finstad, *Child Bride.*

207   *"I may not type good":* Colonel Tom Parker quoted by Al Wertheimer to author, 1998.

207 *"always remain friendly with the Colonel"*: Constant Meijers to author, 1998.

208 *"RCA has nothing to say"*: Jerry Hopkins, unpublished magazine article, JHC/UM.

208 *"just explode out into the hall"*: Joan Deary in the documentary *Mr. Rock & Roll,* 1999.

208 *"None of us liked it"*: Joan Deary to Constant Meijers, raw interview transcript from the documentary *Looking for Colonel Parker,* 1999.

208 *"That kid was not only unhappy"*: Anne Fulchino to author, 1998.

208 *"If they're smart enough"*: Colonel Tom Parker quoted by Byron Raphael to author, 1998.

209 *After her husband went to prison:* The author is grateful to Virginia Overholt, whose letter provided the central thesis of this argument.

209 *"If someone else"*: Colonel Tom Parker to MGM, April 15, 1964, quoted in Guralnick and Jorgensen, *Elvis Day by Day.*

209 *"He was singing one song"*: LouCeil Austin to author, 1998.

210 *"If you didn't know"*: Colonel Tom Parker quoted Sam Katzman to Jerry Hopkins, JHC/UM.

210 *"Look, you can't"*: Joe Pasternak to Jerry Hopkins, JHC/UM.

210 *"Sam Katzman said"*: Yvonne Craig to Jerry Hopkins, JHC/UM.

210 *"That doesn't mean"*: Interview with Hal Wallis in *Las Vegas Desert News and Telegram,* April 1964.

211 *"I didn't mean that, guys"*: Elvis Presley quoted by Bob Moore to author, 1998.

211 *"Once we started on the MGM contract"*: Freddy Bienstock to author, 1997.

211 *"By dumb luck"*: Michael Streissguth to author, 1999.

212 *"a great, great man"*: Bob Moore quoted in Cronin, Isler, and Rowland, "An Oral Biography."

212 *"a pretty nice old codger, really"*: Buddy Harman to author, 1997.

213 *"Boy," the Colonel said:* Colonel Tom Parker to Hal Wallis quoted by Bob Moore to author, 1998.

213 *"soft, fat, and jowly around the face"*: Hal Wallis in letter to Colonel Tom Parker, December 10, 1963, HWC/MPAS.

213 *"He's just been eating what he always eats"*: Marty Lacker to author, 1994.

213 *"He had this big orchestra in there"*: Marty Lacker to author, 1994.

213 *"Colonel just damned near"*: Gabe Tucker to author, 1997.

213 *"You do your thing"*: Colonel Tom Parker quoted by Gordon Stoker to Chris Clark, WTVF-TV, Nashville, May 2000.

214 *"I thought it was kind of rank"*: John Hartmann to Jerry Hopkins, JHC/UM.

214 *"We didn't hurt ourselves workin' "*: Gabe Tucker to author, 1997.

214 *"The Colonel thinks you ought to invite us to supper"*: Gabe Tucker to author, 1997.

215 *thanking him for swiping it:* "Thanks for the little dish you swiped from the Elephant Club." Colonel Tom Parker in letter to Hal Wallis, June 4, 1963, HWC/MPAS.

215 *"I could tell you"*: Hal Wallis in letter to Colonel Tom Parker, June 10, 1963, HWC/MPAS.

215 *"Of course, we want"*: Hal Wallis in letter to Colonel Tom Parker, August 19, 1963, HWC/MPAS.

215 *"You have a certain magic wand"*: Colonel Tom Parker in letter to Hal Wallis, June 17, 1963, HWC/MPAS.

215 *"When I was doing* Roustabout*"*: Allan Weiss to author, 2001.

215 *"I was at the house one day"*: Lamar Fike to author, 1994.

216   *"What you're talking about"*: Elvis Presley quoted by Larry Geller to author, 1998. All quotes from Larry Geller come from the author's extensive interviews and e-mails with Mr. Geller, 1998–2002.

217   *he'd brokered deals that had earned Presley $35 million*: *People,* February 3, 1997.

218   *"My husband is deathly ill"*: Marie Parker to Henry Jenkins as recounted by Gabe Tucker to author, 1997.

218   *"Gabe, Colonel is bad sick"*: Henry Jenkins quoted by Gabe Tucker to author, 1997.

218   *"Goddamn, Colonel, you scared"*: Conversation between Colonel Tom Parker and Gabe Tucker quoted by Gabe Tucker to author, 1997.

221   *"Elvis's last good picture"*: Joe Hazen in letter to Hal Wallis, October 23, 1965, HWC/MPAS.

221   *"is dying all over the country"*: Charles Boasberg in letter to Hal Wallis, May 11, 1966, HWC/MPAS.

222   *"I think the Colonel"*: Hal Wallis in interoffice memo to Joe Hazen, September 13, 1965, HWC/MPAS.

222   *"the height of duplicity"*: Joe Hazen in letter to Hal Wallis, October 23, 1965, HWC/MPAS.

222   *"Elvis came up to me"*: Marty Lacker to author, 1994.

222   *wielding a machete*: The machete photograph appears in the *1966 Annual Report for Colonel Hal Wallis, Picture Producer,* HWC/MPAS.

223   *"a fifty-fifth cousin to P. T. Barnum"*: Colonel Tom Parker quoted in Guralnick and Jorgensen, *Elvis Day by Day.*

223   *"Heck yes, I would retire"*: Colonel Tom Parker quoted in James Kingsley, *Memphis Commercial Appeal,* February 6, 1966.

223   *"an insult to Elvis and fans"*: Janet White, president of the Hampshire, England, fan club, in letter to Hal Wallis, 1966, HWC/MPAS.

223   *"when his career is beginning to falter"*: "Concerned Fan" in letter to Hal Wallis, July 5, 1966, HWC/MPAS.

223   *"I realize that there is"*: Marjorie Reep in letter to Hal Wallis, 1964, HWC/MPAS.

224   *"radically wrong"*: Hal Wallis in letter to Colonel Tom Parker, September 6, 1966, HWC/MPAS.

224   *"I did not know who"*: Norman Racusin to author, 1997.

225   *"During the making of [the film]"*: Twentieth Century–Fox, unpublished press release for *Wild in the Country,* 1960, JHC/UM.

226   *"My daddy doesn't do anything"*: Elvis Presley quoted by Bones Howe in Cronin, Isler, and Rowland, "An Oral Biography."

226   *"I walked in the door"*: Elvis Presley quoted by Marty Lacker to author, 1994.

226   *"When I fall deeply in love it will happen"*: Elvis Presley quoted by Hedda Hopper, *Motion Picture,* May 1961.

226   *"He ate out of depression"*: Jerry Schilling to Jerry Hopkins, JHC/UM.

227   *"The Colonel took us out in the hall"*: Marty Lacker to author, 1994.

227   *"The Colonel went back in"*: Marty Lacker to author, 1994.

228   *"She was absolutely petrified"*: Judge David Zenoff, *Life,* February 10, 1995.

228   *"It was the Colonel"*: Priscilla Presley quoted in Finstad, *Child Bride.*

229   *"had a penchant for the tables"*: Norman Racusin to author, 1997.

230   *"I'm sure there was an awful lot going on"*: Dick Contino to author, 1998

CHAPTER 16: BLACK LEATHER BLUES: THE '68 SPECIAL

231   *"I know that both of you"*: Colonel Tom Parker in letter to Hal Wallis and Joe Hazen, May 5, 1959, HWC/MPAS.

231   *"could very well lose"*: Colonel Tom Parker quoted by Hal Wallis in letter to Joe Hazen, September 27, 1965, HWC/MPAS.

232   "Charro! *is the first movie"*: Elvis Presley quoted in Susan Doll, *The Films of Elvis Presley.*

232   *"which have been in"*: Colonel Tom Parker quoted in Guralnick and Jorgensen, *Elvis Day by Day.*

232   *"Would TV serve to refurbish"*: TV Guide, November 30, 1968.

233   *"I wanted Elvis to let the world in"*: Steve Binder to Jerry Hopkins, JHC/UM.

234   *"show to depart completely from the pattern"*: Bob Finkelin in memo, quoted in Guralnick and Jorgensen, *Elvis Day by Day.*

234   *"This is what I want my boy to do"*: Colonel Tom Parker quoted by Steve Binder to Peter Whitmer, raw interview transcript, 1993.

234   *the genius of the Colonel:* "To me, the genius of the Colonel is that he had grown men terrorized all around him." Steve Binder to Peter Whitmer, raw interview transcript, 1993.

234   *"There was no blood and guts of this man left"*: Steve Binder to Jerry Hopkins, JHC/UM.

234   *"You certainly knew"*: Steve Binder to Peter Whitmer, raw interview transcript, 1993.

234   *"without any weak points"*: Steve Binder to author, 2001.

234   *"We hit it off pretty well"*: Steve Binder to Constant Meijers, raw interview transcript from the documentary *Looking for Colonel Parker,* 1999.

234   *Steve Allen had made him look silly:* In a 1997 letter to the author, Allen made it clear he did not mean to humiliate Presley, and in fact, while Allen received much criticism for the stunt through the years, he believed it enhanced Presley's performance. "I had personally come up with the two ideas that made Elvis look so good that night," he wrote, "the singing 'Hound Dog' to an actual dog, and the Range Roundup sketch with Andy Griffith and Imogene Coca."

235   *"You make a record"*: Steve Binder to author, 2001.

235   *"he was not in the business as far as I was concerned"*: Steve Binder to Peter Whitmer, raw interview transcript, 1993.

235   *"it was my job"*: Steve Binder to Peter Whitmer, raw interview transcript, 1993.

235   *Howe thought, "Elvis probably felt"*: Bones Howe quoted in Cronin, Isler, and Rowland, "An Oral Biography."

235   *"once he had the stranglehold"*: Steve Binder to author, 2001.

235   *"He laughed at that"*: Steve Binder to Constant Meijers, raw interview transcript from the documentary *Looking for Colonel Parker,* 1999.

235   *"He told me he had been burning up"*: Steve Binder to Jerry Hopkins, JHC/UM.

235   *"I felt very, very strongly"*: Steve Binder to Jerry Hopkins, JHC/UM.

236   *"He looked amazing"*: Steve Binder to author, 2001.

236   *"I wanted him to be not that agreeable"*: Steve Binder to Jerry Hopkins, JHC/UM.

236   *"quite well read"*: Steve Binder to Peter Whitmer, raw interview transcript, 1993.

236   *"Elvis was scared to death of the Colonel's power"*: Steve Binder to author, 2001.

236 *"He felt shamed"*: Steve Binder to Peter Whitmer, raw interview transcript, 1993.

237 *"I think what pissed him off"*: Steve Binder to Peter Whitmer, raw interview transcript, 1993.

237 *"Whenever Parker basically told me"*: Steve Binder to Constant Meijers, raw interview transcript from the documentary *Looking for Colonel Parker,* 1999.

237 *Binder said maybe Interpol:* "Because Interpol was looking for him and he didn't want to leave the United States for fear of being arrested." Steve Binder to Peter Whitmer, raw interview transcript, 1993.

238 *"You can't fire me"*: Bill Strange quoted by Steve Binder to author, 2001.

238 *"There was a day of tremendous pressures and tension"*: Steve Binder to Jerry Hopkins, JHC/UM.

238 *"I'm a Jewish kid from New York"*: Billy Goldenberg quoted by Steve Binder to author, 2001.

238 *"When Elvis heard the first note"*: This paragraph is a combination of quotes from Steve Binder to Jerry Hopkins, JHC/UM, and Peter Whitmer, raw interview transcript, 1993.

239 *an overgrown sweetheart who reminded Binder:* Steve Binder to author, 1998.

239 *"Music was [Elvis's] most interesting side"*: Bones Howe, quoted in Cronin, Isler, and Rowland, "An Oral Biography."

239 *"I wanted to capture"*: Steve Binder to Jerry Hopkins, JHC/UM.

239 *"I'm not sure it's . . . a good idea"*: Elvis Presley quoted in Jorgensen, *Elvis Presley.*

239 *"but who was really above all that"*: Guralnick and Jorgensen, *Elvis Day by Day.*

240 *"That's a hit song"*: Bones Howe to Jerry Hopkins, JHC/UM.

240 *"That was all he was interested in"*: Steve Binder to Jerry Hopkins, JHC/UM.

240 *"In my last meeting with the Colonel"*: Steve Binder to Peter Whitmer, raw interview transcript, 1993.

240 *"They said, 'The Colonel's telling us' "*: Steve Binder to author, 2001.

240 *"The Colonel just sat there staring at me"*: Steve Binder to Peter Whitmer, raw interview transcript, 1993.

241 *"The string players"*: Bones Howe quoted in booklet accompanying *Elvis: From Nashville to Memphis: The Essential '60s Masters* (RCA Records, 1994).

241 *"On the outside"*: Steve Binder to Constant Meijers, raw interview transcript from the documentary *Looking for Colonel Parker,* 1999.

241 *"The only way he could set it up"*: Lamar Fike to Constant Meijers, raw interview transcript from the documentary *Looking for Colonel Parker,* 1999.

241 *"old hat in this day of the post-Beatle"*: Material on NBC press conference from *TV Guide,* November 30, 1968.

242 *"I have no proof to back it up"*: Steve Binder to Peter Whitmer, raw interview transcript, 1993, supplemented with quotes from Binder to author, 2001.

242 *"Every time I walked by"*: Billy Goldenberg to Jerry Hopkins, JHC/UM.

243 *"You want the blond bouffant hairdo"*: Colonel Tom Parker quoted by Steve Binder to Peter Whitmer, raw interview transcript, 1993.

243 *"Do you think my hair's too black?"*: Elvis Presley quoted by Steve Binder to author, 2001.

243 *"he sat in that makeup chair"*: Bones Howe to Jerry Hopkins, JHC/UM.

243 *forced him to make the effort:* "Forced him to go out there as a favor to me." Steve Binder to author, 2001.

243 *"nobody had thought that he'd be so soaking wet"*: Bones Howe quoted in Cronin, Isler, and Rowland, "An Oral Biography."
244 *"when I really believed"*: Steve Binder to author, 2001.
244 *"There is something magical"*: Jon Landau, *Eye,* date unknown.
244 *"Diskin started a whole tirade"*: Bones Howe to Jerry Hopkins, JHC/UM.
245 *"You guys are going to have a million-dollar experience"*: Guralnick and Jorgensen, *Elvis Day by Day.*
245 *"He watched it three more times"*: Steve Binder to Constant Meijers, raw interview transcript from the documentary *Looking for Colonel Parker,* 1999.
245 *"I hear you, Elvis"*: Steve Binder to author, 2001.
245 *"sense of loyalty was confused"*: Steve Binder to Peter Whitmer, raw interview transcript, 1993.
245 *"the look on Elvis's face"*: Steve Binder to Peter Whitmer, raw interview transcript, 1993.
245 *"they were always intercepted"*: Steve Binder to Peter Whitmer, raw interview transcript, 1993.
246 *"There's no limit"*: Steve Binder to Jerry Hopkins, JHC/UM.

CHAPTER 17: LAS VEGAS: GLITZ, GREED, AND RUINATION
247 *"I made up my mind"*: Bill Miller quoted in *Desert Sun,* May 3, 1998.
248 *"Elvis was a question mark"*: Nick Naff to Art Nadler for author, 1997.
248 *"Prell got money"*: Anonymous source, 2001.
249 *"Actually, I think I was about the third one"*: Bruce Banke to Karen Schoemer, raw interview transcript, 1997.
250 *"There were a lot of bad songs"*: All quotes from Chips Moman come from the author's interview, 2001.
250 *"I wasn't angry about it"*: Freddy Bienstock to author, 1997.
251 *"In all the years"*: Harry Jenkins quoted by Chips Moman to author, 2001.
251 *"The campaign that he produced was unbelievable"*: Alex Shoofey in the documentary *Mr. Rock & Roll,* 1999.
252 *"I did the commercials"*: Nick Naff to Art Nadler for author, 1997.
252 *"He insisted only the word* Elvis*"*: Nick Naff in the documentary film *Mr. Rock & Roll,* 1999.
252 *"schlocky as all hell"*: Nick Naff to Art Nadler for author, 1997.
252 *"We got calls from all over the world"*: Alex Shoofey in the documentary *Mr. Rock & Roll,* 1999.
252 *"The closing night of Barbra"*: Bill Miller quoted in *Desert Sun,* May 3, 1998.
252 *"just all over the goddammed place"*: Nick Naff to Art Nadler for author, 1997.
252 *"There were banners and flags"*: Joe Moscheo to Beverly Keel for author, 1998.
253 *"I don't have to tell you"*: Nick Naff to Art Nadler for author, 1997.
253 *"a very likable guy"*: Nick Naff to Art Nadler for author, 1997.
253 *"I've wanted to perform on the stage again"*: Elvis Presley quoted by Ray Connolly in Guralnick and Jorgensen, *Elvis Day by Day.*
253 *"helluva big stage to fill"*: Elvis Presley quoted by Charlie Hodge in Guralnick and Jorgensen, *Elvis Day by Day.*
254 *"I said, 'Would you please tell"*: Steve Binder to author, 2001.
254 *"We went up there"*: Bob Finkel to author, 1999.
255 *"He says, 'Now tell me again' "*: Alex Shoofey in the documentary *Mr. Rock & Roll,* 1999.
255 *"I heard"*: Gordon Stoker in the documentary *Mr. Rock & Roll,* 1999.

255   *"Just look at the figures"*: Marty Lacker to author, 1994.

256   *"Was he trying to protect"*: Joe Delaney to author, 1997.

256   *"He had an open tab"*: Joe Shane to Constant Meijers, raw interview transcript from the documentary *Looking for Colonel Parker,* 1999.

256   *"He had the boy"*: Joe Shane to author, 1998.

256   *"[The] Colonel was one of the best customers we had"*: Alex Shoofey in Amended Report of Guardian *ad litem,* July 31, 1981.

256   *"I never saw anybody"*: Lamar Fike to author, 2001.

257   *"He'd stack 'em up all over"*: Gabe Tucker to author, 1997.

258   *"everything went haywire"*: Julian Aberbach to author, 1997.

258   *"He just wouldn't see me"*: Joe Moscheo to Beverly Keel for author, 1998.

259   *"Man, I'll put on a disguise"*: Elvis Presley quoted by Larry Geller to author, 1999.

260   *"damn near gorgeous"*: Lamar Fike to author, 1994.

260   *"Elvis loved downers"*: Lamar Fike to author, 1994.

261   *"I don't want any son of a bitch"*: Elvis Presley quoted by Jerry Schilling to Jerry Hopkins, JHC/UM.

262   *"not only my manager"*: Elvis Presley quoted in Guralnick and Jorgensen, *Elvis Day by Day.*

262   *"One of the things Jerry said"*: John Denver to author, 1991.

262   *"He wanted us to pay"*: Steve Wolf to Jerry Hopkins, JHC/UM.

263   *"Jerry was very well connected"*: Joe Delaney to author, 1997.

263   *"Jerry had to go out and bust his butt"*: Joe Shane to Constant Meijers, raw interview transcript from the documentary *Looking for Colonel Parker,* 1999.

263   *"who made Elvis what he is today"*: Colonel Tom Parker in telegram to Jerry Weintraub, October 12, 1970 quoted in Guernsey's *Official Auction Catalogue.*

264   *"He would have it all mapped out"*: Gaylen Adams to author, 1998.

264   *"the rest of the auditorium"*: Colonel Tom Parker quoted in Jerry Hopkins, unpublished magazine article, JHC/UM.

265   *"He made life rough"*: Kathy Westmoreland to author, 1997.

267   *"Remember," he concluded*: Colonel Tom Parker in letter to Elvis Presley, quoted in Guralnick and Jorgensen, *Elvis Day by Day.*

267   *"you especially had to be careful"*: Billy Smith to author, 1993.

267   *"I would love to meet you"*: Elvis Presley in letter to Richard M. Nixon, reproduced in Worth and Tamerius, *Elvis.*

268   *"his most prized physical possession"*: Jerry Schilling to Jerry Hopkins, JHC/UM.

269   *"The Colonel said"*: Henri Lewin to Jerry Hopkins, JHC/UM.

269   *"it was great"*: Jerry Schilling in the documentary *Mr. Rock & Roll,* 1999.

269   *"Elvis was mad"*: Lamar Fike in the documentary *Mr. Rock & Roll,* 1999.

269   *"drawn, tired, and noticeably heavier"*: The Hollywood Reporter quoted in Guralnick and Jorgensen, *Elvis Day by Day.*

269   *"He didn't have breathing room"*: Alex Shoofey in the documentary *Mr. Rock & Roll,* 1999.

270   *"Nobody goes to Vegas"*: Lamar Fike to author, 1993.

270   *"I was there"*: Henri Lewin quoted in *Las Vegas Style,* 1994.

271   *"[Elvis] wanted to take all of his troupe with him"*: Colonel Tom Parker quoted in Woody Baird, "Couldn't Have Saved Elvis, Manager Says," *Tennessean,* December 7, 1990.

271 *lately hearing rumors of cocaine use:* Informant report, FBI file, January 31, 1974.

271 *"Clearances needed on songs":* Colonel Tom Parker's private notes, pictured in *Elvis: The Official Auction Catalogue* on Guernsey's Web site (www.guernsey's. com) [no longer available].

271 *"RCA makes contracts with talent or do we?":* Colonel Tom Parker in private notes, quoted in Guernsey's *Official Auction Catalogue.*

271 *"He was a big friend of mine":* Mel Ilberman to author, 1998.

272 *"a brilliant move":* Joe Galante to author, 1998.

272 *"We finally demanded":* Tony Brown to author, 1998.

272 *"There were a lot of things":* Lamar Fike to author, 1993.

272 *"People talk about the fifty percent":* Joe Shane to author, 1998.

CHAPTER 18: GEEK FEVER

274 *"Ah, I don't know what makes 'em say that":* Elvis Presley, press conference, New York City, June 9, 1972.

274 *"He said, 'Mr. Kahane, they're animals out there'":* Elvis Presley quoted by Jackie Kahane to Peter Whitmer, raw interview transcript, 1994.

274 *"so many flashbulbs":* Joe Guercio to Karen Schoemer, raw interview transcript, 1997.

274 *"A Prince from Another Planet":* Chris Chase, *New York Times,* June 18, 1972.

275 *"His usual protocol":* Lamar Fike to author, 1993.

275 *"in the history of the record business":* RCA press release quoted in Guralnick and Jorgensen, *Elvis Day by Day.*

275 *"It's very hard to comprehend":* Elvis Presley quoted in Guralnick and Jorgensen, *Elvis Day by Day.*

276 *"The next morning":* Marty Lacker to author, 1993.

276 *"from seeing each other on stage":* Colonel Tom Parker in letter to Elvis Presley quoted in Guralnick and Jorgensen, *Elvis Day by Day.*

277 *"as the disease progressed":* Sandra Polk Ross to author, 1997.

277 *"The Colonel always felt":* Freddy Bienstock to author, 1997.

277 *"she presented me":* Nick Naff to Art Nadler for author, 1997.

278 *"Most people have no idea":* Loanne Miller Parker to Constant Meijers, raw interview transcript from the documentary *Looking for Colonel Parker,* 1999.

278 *"really pay attention":* Colonel Tom Parker quoted by Joe Esposito at Colonel Tom Parker's Memorial Service, Las Vegas, January 25, 1997.

278 *"compromising circumstances":* John Mott in e-mail to author, 2002.

278 *"I'm sorry, ladies and gentlemen":* Elvis Presley quoted in Guralnick and Jorgensen, *Elvis Day by Day.*

279 *"I figured it would take a big check":* Mel Ilberman to author, 1998.

280 *"He wasn't sick":* Marty Lacker to author, 1994.

280 *"One night when I was about five or six":* Lisa Marie Presley quoted in *Life,* December 1988.

281 *"hard addict":* Dr. George Nichopoulos quoted by Marty Lacker to author, 1994.

281 *"There was more dope in that outfit":* Jackie Kahane to Peter Whitmer, raw interview transcript, 1994.

281 *"Organized crime":* Informant report, FBI file, January 31, 1974.

282 *"one of the most ill-prepared":* The *Hollywood Reporter* quoted in Guralnick and Jorgensen, *Elvis Day by Day.*

282 *"Elvis was worse"*: Kathy Westmoreland to author, 1997.

283 *"nervous as a chicken"*: Duke Bardwell to author, 2002.

283 *"He said to me one time"*: Jackie Kahane to Peter Whitmer, raw interview transcript, 1994.

284 *"every performer has good days and bad days"*: Colonel Tom Parker to Larry Hutchinson, chief investigator to the district attorney general for Memphis, 1980.

284 *"lack of humanity"*: Duke Bardwell to author, 1999.

285 *Boxcar would become:* Corporate reports, Boxcar Enterprises, Report to Guardian *ad litem,* September 30, 1980.

285 *"actually almost lived"*: Bruce Banke to Karen Schoemer, raw interview transcript, 1997.

285 *"he knew he had to have other irons"*: Kathy Westmoreland to author, 1997.

285 *"He knew talent"*: Kathy Westmoreland to author, 1997.

286 *"He played stupid"*: Bitsy Mott to Dirk Vellenga, raw interview transcript, 1983.

286 *"I'll pull your goddamned tongue"*: Bootleg tape, Elvis Presley live in Vegas, 1974.

286 *"And my manager, Colonel Tom Parker"*: Bootleg tape, Elvis Presley live in Vegas, 1974.

288 *"It never got better"*: Billy Smith to author, 1994.

288 *"He would be so damn drugged"*: Lamar Fike to author, 1994.

288 *"they'd kill any type of body odor"*: Billy Smith to author, 1994.

288 *"We used to con him into the bathtub"*: Lamar Fike to author, 1994.

289 *"went for it, definitely"*: Jerry Schilling to Jerry Hopkins, JHC/UM.

289 *"Mr. Presley has indicated"*: Colonel Tom Parker quoted in Guralnick and Jorgensen, *Elvis Day by Day.*

289 *"There was never no plan"*: Colonel Tom Parker to Craig Rivera, *Inside Edition,* January 1993.

289 *"but he knew if negotiations broke down"*: Jerry Schilling to Jerry Hopkins, JHC/UM.

289 *"deep down"*: Lamar Fike to author, 1994.

289 *"People aren't going to remember me"*: Elvis Presley quoted by Kathy Westmoreland to author, 1997.

289 *"Elvis came out to the bus"*: Lamar Fike to author, 1994.

290 *"you could almost"*: Billy Smith to author, 1993.

290 *"I was with the Colonel"*: Gaylen Adams to author, 1998.

290 *"we all thought it was going to happen"*: David Briggs to author, 1998.

290 *"Colonel was adamant"*: Loanne Miller Parker to Constant Meijers, raw interview transcript from the documentary *Looking for Colonel Parker,* 1999.

291 *"To deny him that"*: Duke Bardwell to author, 1999.

291 *"I was there"*: Mike Crowley to author, 1997.

291 *"I hate that old man"*: Elvis Presley quoted by Billy Smith to author, 1993.

292 *"He's really screwed up"*: Joe Guercio quoted by Jackie Kahane to Peter Whitmer, raw interview transcript, 1994.

292 *"scared shitless"*: Jackie Kahane to Peter Whitmer, raw interview transcript, 1994.

292 *"He didn't do twenty minutes"*: Jackie Kahane to Peter Whitmer, raw interview transcript, 1994.

292 *"It is hereby understood"*: Agreement between Colonel Tom Parker and Elvis Presley quoted in Guralnick and Jorgensen, *Elvis Day by Day.*

293   *"Felton would come back"*: Joe Galante to author, 1998.

293   *"The Colonel almost shit"*: David Briggs to author, 1998.

293   *"We'd come to the house"*: Tony Brown quoted in Cronin, Isler, and Rowland, "An Oral Biography."

293   *"Why are you sitting out here, Elvis?"*: Felton Jarvis quoted by Ray Walker to author, 1977.

294   *"There was a lot of dissension"*: Tony Brown to author, 1998.

294   *"he had locomotive attacks"*: John O'Grady quoted in Guralnick and Jorgensen, *Elvis Day By Day*

294   *"Hookstratten, Priscilla, and I"*: John O'Grady to Jerry Hopkins, JHC/UM.

295   *"I don't want anybody to know"*: Elvis Presley quoted by Kathy Westmoreland to author, 1997.

295   *"As I told Vernon today"*: Colonel Tom Parker in letter to Elvis Presley, June 16, 1976, quoted in Guralnick and Jorgensen, *Elvis Day by Day.*

296   *"I was gambling"*: Mike Growney in the documentary *Mr. Rock & Roll,* 1999.

296   *"I understand you're trying to sell"*: Colonel Tom Parker quoted by Joe Shane to author, 1998.

296   *"We had a nice camaraderie"*: Joe Shane to Constant Meijers, raw interview transcript from the documentary *Looking for Colonel Parker,* 1999.

297   *"You are the biggest entertainer"*: Tom Hulett quoted in Guralnick and Jorgensen, *Elvis Day by Day.*

297   *"depressingly incoherent"*: Bob Claypool, quoted in Guralnick and Jorgensen, *Elvis Day by Day.*

297   *"It was really bad"*: Lamar Fike to author, 1994.

298   *"What would the point be?"*: Joe Guercio quoted by Jackie Kahane to Peter Whitmer, raw interview transcript, 1994.

298   *"I said, 'He's putting us on' "*: Bruce Banke to Karen Schoemer, raw interview transcript, 1997.

299   *"One walks away"*: Bill Burk quoted in Guralnick and Jorgensen, *Elvis Day by Day.*

299   *"feeling that I wasn't worth anything"*: Linda Thompson to author, 1977.

299   *"Get off your tail"*: Colonel Tom Parker quoted in Guralnick and Jorgensen, *Elvis Day by Day.*

299   *"contend the singer's new girlfriend"*: Quoted in Guralnick and Jorgensen, *Elvis Day by Day.*

300   *"He had us go on stage"*: Kathy Westmoreland to author, 1997.

300   *"seeming not to care"*: Quoted in Guralnick and Jorgensen, *Elvis Day by Day.*

300   *"He stunk the joint out"*: Quoted in Guralnick and Jorgensen, *Elvis Day by Day.*

301   *"absolutely no plans"*: Laura Eipper, "Manager Denies Presley or Sale," *Tennessean,* April 30, 1977.

301   *"he was pale, swollen—he had no stamina"*: Quoted in Guralnick and Jorgensen, *Elvis Day by Day.*

301   *"At the finale"*: *Variety* quoted in Guralnick and Jorgensen, *Elvis Day by Day.*

301   *"I'm going to look fat"*: Elvis Presley quoted by Kathy Westmoreland to author, 1997.

302   *"I'm so tired"*: Elvis Presley quoted by Kathy Westmoreland to author, 1997.

302   *"He'll never see"*: Lamar Fike to author, 1994

303   *"Parker and Presley"*: Richard Harrington, *Washington Post,* January 24, 1997.

303   a staggering $30 million: *People,* March 5, 1984.

CHAPTER 19: "WE THINK HE OD'D": THE DEATH OF ELVIS

305 *"in a very good mood"*: Larry Geller to author, 2001.

305 *"Ain't no problem"*: Elvis Presley quoted by Billy Smith to author, 1994.

306 *"They've never beat me before"*: Billy Smith to author, 1994.

306 *"It's okay"*: Billy Smith to author, 1994.

306 *"Billy . . . son . . . this is going to be my best tour ever"*: Elvis Presley quoted by Billy Smith to author, 1994.

306 *"I'm going to go in the bathroom"*: Elvis Presley quoted by Billy Smith to author, 1994.

307 *No, if they ain't heard from him*: Billy Smith to author, 1994.

307 *"Who's on duty?"* Ginger Alden quoted in Esposito and Oumano, *Good Rockin' Tonight*.

308 *"What happened to him?"*: Ulysses Jones quoted by Marty Lacker to author, 1994.

308 *"He's gone"*: Dr. George Nichopoulos quoted in Esposito and Oumano, *Good Rockin' Tonight*.

308 *"It's Lisa"*: Lisa Marie Presley quoted by Linda Thompson, *Life,* February 10, 1995.

308 *"I have something terrible to tell you"*: Esposito and Oumano, *Good Rockin' Tonight.* Loanne Miller Parker says the news came in two phone calls, the first alerting the Colonel that something awful had happened, and it was unclear whether Elvis was dead or alive.

308 *"Okay, Joe"*: Colonel Tom Parker quoted in Esposito, *Good Rockin' Tonight.*

309 *"The Colonel wants to see you right now"*: Tom Hulett quoted by Lamar Fike to author, 1994.

309 *"I don't want"*: Colonel Tom Parker as quoted by Loanne Miller Parker to Ken Vrana, 2002.

309 *"Bob, I hope to hell"*: Bruce Banke to Karen Schoemer, raw interview transcript, 1997.

309 *"I must have been"*: Bruce Banke to Karen Schoemer, raw interview transcript, 1997.

310 *"Would everybody get off the plane?"*: Marty Harrell quoted by Jackie Kahane to Peter Whitmer, raw interview transcript, 1994.

310 *"The operator was crying"*: Jackie Kahane to Peter Whitmer, raw interview transcript, 1994.

310 *"I can't waste time mourning"*: Colonel Tom Parker to Chris Hutchins, *The People,* January 26, 1997.

311 *"He knew exactly what was going to transpire"*: Joe Shane to author, 1998.

311 *"He was like, 'The boy's dead"*: Joe Shane to Constant Meijers, raw interview transcript from the documentary *Looking for Colonel Parker* 1999.

312 *The estate would eventually be valued at $7.6 million*: Sources differ as to the estimate. See *People,* December 1, 1980, *Tennessean,* December 7, 1990; and Woody Baird, "Graceland Earns Millions for Heir," Associated Press, August 14, 2002.

312 *The Colonel could advance the estate*: At his death, Elvis had $1.4 million in a non-interest-bearing checking account and about $750,000 in savings, though sources close to Presley believe that Parker advanced the bulk of the money to the estate.

312 *"Elvis didn't die"*: Colonel Tom Parker quoted in Jerry Hopkins, "Playing the Elvis Presley Game," unpublished manuscript, JHC/UM.

312 *"It don't mean a damned thing"*: Colonel Tom Parker quoted in Tosches, *Country.*

312 *"This changes nothing"*: Colonel Tom Parker quoted in *Irish Times*, January 24, 1997.

312 *"I am deeply grateful that you have offered"*: Vernon Presley in letter to Colonel Tom Parker, August 23, 1977.

312 *"If Elvis looks down"*: Colonel Tom Parker quoted in Jerry Hopkins, "Playing the Elvis Presley Game," unpublished manuscript, JHC/UM.

312 *"every time he would go past the coffin"*: Jackie Kahane to Peter Whitmer, raw interview transcript, 1994.

312 *"He didn't talk to many people"*: Larry Geller to author, 2001.

313 *"I could see there was pain"*: Kathy Westmoreland to author, 1997.

313 *"No sir"*: Colonel Tom Parker to Chris Hutchins, *The People*, January 26, 1997.

313 *"Elvis committed suicide"*: Jackie Kahane to Peter Whitmer, raw interview transcript, 1994.

313 *"When I joined the TCB group"*: Jackie Kahane to Peter Whitmer, raw interview transcript, 1994.

314 *"I can't straighten it out by telling another lie"*: Vernon Presley to author, 1977.

314 *"hypertensive heart disease"*: Dr. Jerry Francisco, press conference, Memphis, 1977, quoted in Thompson and Cole, *The Death of Elvis*.

314 *"not that it specially concerned me"*: Colonel Tom Parker to Larry Hutchinson, chief investigator to the district attorney general, Memphis, 1980.

315 *"It was just like"*: Robin Rosaaen in e-mail to author, 2001.

315 *"We made a hell of a team"*: Colonel Tom Parker to Robert Hilburn, *Los Angeles Times*, 1978, quoted in "Colonel Tom Parker," *Journal of Country Music*, vol. 19 (no. 1).

315 *"I sat with him there"*: Jackie Kahane to Peter Whitmer, raw interview transcript, 1994.

316 *"You could say the Colonel killed him"*: Sandra Polk Ross to author, 1998.

316 *"I thought I would die"*: Sandra Polk Ross to author, 1998.

317 *"I said, 'You know I made 488 pairs'"*: Dennis Roberts to author, 2000.

318 *"It cost me about $135,000"*: Dennis Roberts to author, 2000.

318 *"it was a shock to all of us"*: Priscilla Presley to Katie Couric, *Dateline*, August 13, 2002.

318 *"We weren't aware"*: D. Beecher Smith II, in Soocher, *They Fought the Law.*

CHAPTER 20: LIVING TOO LONG: LITIGATION AND LONELINESS

319 *"represent and defend the interests of Lisa Marie Presley"*: Amended Report of Guardian *ad litem,* July 31, 1981.

319 *"all agreements with Elvis Presley terminated on his death"*: Amended Report of Guardian *ad litem,* September 30, 1980.

320 *"I'm sure a lot of people see him"*: Mike Crowley to author, 1998.

320 *"You can't paint Parker as an angel"*: Stan Soocher to author, 1999.

320 *"Most people would say"*: David Skepner to author, 1997.

320 *"While he kept getting a higher proportion"*: Joe Galante to author, 1998.

321 *"How can you argue"*: Barry Coburn to author, 1997.

321 *"When he was working for Elvis"*: D. Beecher Smith II quoted in *People* February 3, 1997.

321 *"contractual barriers"*: D. Beecher Smith II quoted in *Tennessean,* December 11, 1980.

321 *"I'm not prepared to paint Parker black"*: D. Beecher Smith II quoted in Soocher, *They Fought the Law.*

322   *"I got the feeling":* Blanchard E. Tual quoted in *Tennessean,* December 11, 1980.

322   *$7 or $8 million:* Blanchard E. Tual in Soocher, *They Fought the Law.*

322   *"He had it from the eyebrows up":* Blanchard E. Tual to Constant Meijers, raw interview transcript from the documentary *Looking for Colonel Parker,* 1999.

322   *"the worst decision ever made in the history of rock 'n' roll":* Blanchard E. Tual quoted in Soocher, *They Fought the Law.*

322   *"the conscious decision to make as much money":* Amended Report of Guardian *ad litem,* July 31, 1981.

322   *"Elvis had thirty-three songs":* Joe Moscheo to Beverly Keel for author, 1998.

323   *"collusion, conspiracy, fraud":* Amended Report of Guardian *ad litem,* July 31, 1981.

323   *"the compensation received by Colonel Parker":* Judge Joseph W. Evans quoted in *People,* August 31, 1981.

323   *"enter into any future agreements with Parker":* Randell Beck and Richard Powelson, "Judge Halts Payments to Col. Parker," *Memphis Press-Scimitar,* August 14, 1981.

323   *$25,000 for small talk, $100,000 for a long conversation:* Richard Harrington, "One for the Money: Elvis Presley Paid a High Price for His Fame," *Washington Post,* January 24, 1997.

324   *"every effort to honor [Elvis's] name":* "Elvis's Manager Promises Defense of Fraud Charges," *Nashville Banner,* August 17, 1981.

324   *"but also are unfair and insulting":* "Col. Tom Parker Denies He Ever Cheated Elvis," *Tennessean,* August 16, 1981.

324   *"Elvis knew that I provided services":* Colonel Tom Parker quoted in *People,* August 31, 1981.

324   *"nervous energy":* "Parker Calls Elvis Headstrong Client," *Memphis Press-Scimitar,* September 9, 1981.

324   *"moody" and "headstrong":* Quotations in this and the next two paragraphs from "Parker Calls Elvis Headstrong Client."

324   *"weren't selling":* "Parker Calls Elvis Headstrong Client."

324   *"really pushed":* "Parker Says Elvis Accusations 'Insulting,'" *Nashville Banner,* August 31, 1981.

324   *"Elvis's decisions in 1973 were correct":* "Parker Says Elvis Accusations 'Insulting,'" *Nashville Banner,* August 31, 1981.

325   *"I never saw anything to indicate it was a partnership":* Blanchard E. Tual to author, 1998.

325   *"I am advised by my attorneys":* Affidavit of Thomas A. Parker, U.S. District Court, Southern District of New York.

325   *"Yes, I am a man without a country":* Colonel Tom Parker quoted in *Variety,* June 24, 1983.

326   *"I did not receive more than Elvis did":* Colonel Tom Parker quoted in Baird, "Couldn't Have Saved Elvis."

326   *"We figured the Colonel might die":* Blanchard E. Tual to Constant Meijers, raw interview transcript from the documentary *Looking for Colonel Parker,* 1999.

326   *"if Elvis had lived":* Blanchard E. Tual quoted in Soocher, *They Fought the Law.*

327   *"Bitsy, if I was doing something wrong":* Colonel Tom Parker quoted by Bitsy Mott to Dirk Vellenga, raw interview transcript, 1983.

327   *"A couple of weeks after we opened Graceland"*: Jack Soden quoted in Soocher, *They Fought the Law.*

327   *sales of all things Elvis:* Baird, "Graceland Earns Millions for Heir," citing *Forbes.*

328   *"I didn't hear from them"*: Colonel Tom Parker to Ralph Emery, raw interview transcript, 1993.

328   *the Colonel's $30-million tab: People,* March 5, 1984.

328   *"I've had offers"*: Colonel Tom Parker to Ralph Emery, raw interview transcripts, 1993.

328   *"Any time the Colonel came into view"*: Bill Willard to author, 1998.

329   *"chronic brain syndrome"*: Marie Parker, certificate of death, November 25, 1986.

329   *"To me, that's not a real tribute"*: Colonel Tom Parker quoted by Pat Embry, "The Colonel: In a Rare Interview, Elvis' Promoter More Teddy Bear Than All Shook Up," *Nashville Banner,* June 12, 1987.

329   *a black-hearted villain:* A 1994 article in the San Diego *Union-Tribune* noted that Elvis purists view Parker as "the devil who traded the singer's rock 'n' roll soul for the demon Hollywood dollar."

329   *"He wanted me to come to New York"*: Colonel Tom Parker to author, 1993.

329   *"If they know so much"*: Colonel Tom Parker to Ted Koppel, *Nightline,* August 16, 1987.

330   *"I'll never manage anyone again"*: Colonel Tom Parker quoted by Ed Koch, "Where Do You Go After Elvis? Parker Won't Manage Again," *Las Vegas Sun,* August 15, 1987.

330   *"We may have had dinner"*: Colonel Tom Parker quoted in *Las Vegas Sun,* August 11, 1987.

330   *"We're here to honor his memory"*: Colonel Tom Parker quoted in Las Vegas *Review-Journal,* January 22, 1997.

330   *estrangement from the estate weighed heavily:* "He never recovered." Gordon Stoker to Constant Meijers, raw interview transcript from the documentary *Looking for Colonel Parker,* 1999.

330   *"He thought"*: Joan Shoofey Richardson to Art Nadler for author, 1997.

330   *"None of 'em are memories for me"*: Colonel Tom Parker quoted in *Nashville Banner,* June 12, 1987.

330   *"Well, it's been too long"*: Colonel Tom Parker, private videotape recording of press conference, January 8, 1988.

331   *"I don't think there was any producer"*: Colonel Tom Parker on private audiotape recording of Elvis Presley Birthday Banquet, Memphis, January 8, 1988.

331   *"I think"*: Jack Soden quoted in Soocher, *They Fought the Law.*

331   *"special hello to an old friend of ours"*: Priscilla Presley on private audiotape recording of Elvis Presley Birthday Banquet, Memphis, January 8, 1988.

331   *"shared an abiding friendship"*: Jack Soden quoted in *Memphis Commercial-Appeal,* December 25, 1993.

331   *"As I recall"*: Chet Flippo in e-mail to author, 1998.

332   *"They window-dressed it pretty nicely"*: Joe Delaney to author, 1997.

332   *"He wouldn't answer certain questions"*: Merilyn Potters in e-mail to author, 1997.

333   *"I think the Colonel was sharp enough"*: Joe Delaney to author, 1997.

333   *"Loanne hoarded money"*: Jackie Kahane to Peter Whitmer, raw interview transcript, 1994.

333 *"He said, 'Without her, I wouldn't be living"*: Author's anonymous source, 1997.
334 *"When his sister walked into that room"*: Lamar Fike to author, 2001.
334 *"The Colonel said he doesn't wish"*: Loanne Miller Parker to Mieke Dons-Maas, 1990, quoted to author, 1997.
334 *"I suppose he just wanted"*: Mieke Dons-Maas to author, 1997.
334 *"spoke with great love and affection"*: Loanne Miller Parker to Constant Meijers, raw interview transcript from the documentary *Looking for Colonel Parker*, 1999.
335 *"He talked a little bit of Dutch to me"*: Constant Meijers to author, 1997.
335 *"He continued to gamble until the day he died"*: Nick Naff to Art Nadler for author, 1997.
336 *"Now, when they've done all they could with [Elvis]"*: Colonel Tom Parker to Craig Rivera, *Inside Edition*, January 1993.
336 *"Every once in a while"*: Colonel Tom Parker quoted in Mike Weatherford, "Colonel Recalls King," Las Vegas *Review-Journal*, January 8, 1995.
336 *"It's hard to convince people"*: Colonel Tom Parker quoted in Woody Baird, "Col. Tom Speaks Out on Elvis' Drugs, Rock 'n' Roll," Associated Press, December 7, 1990.
336 *"Do you miss him?"*: Chris Hutchins conversation with Colonel Tom Parker quoted in *The People*, January 25, 1997.
337 *"I've turned down more books for big money"*: Colonel Tom Parker to Craig Rivera, *Inside Edition*, January 1993. See also *The People*, January 25, 1997.
337 *"seemed designed more to intimidate a number"*: Michael Gray, "25 Percent of the King," *Guardian*, January 23, 1997.
337 *"I got the book right up here"*: Colonel Tom Parker to author, 1994.
337 *"I don't know if a guy should put out a book"*: Colonel Tom Parker quoted in Embry, "The Colonel."
337 *"if I were to expire before completing it"*: *The People*, January 25, 1997.
337 *"He freezes"*: Loanne Miller Parker to author, 1994.
337 *"I teased him about it a couple of times"*: Bill Willard to author, 1998.
337 *"I've got plenty to do"*: Colonel Tom Parker to Ralph Emery, raw interview transcript, 1993.
337 *"People take up exercise, you know"*: Colonel Tom Parker quoted in Embry, "The Colonel."
338 *"Eddy [Arnold] calls me"*: Colonel Tom Parker to Ralph Emery, raw interview transcript, 1993.
338 *"He was a lonely old man"*: Author's anonymous source, 1997.
338 *"very nice"*: Tony Brown quoted in Rob Tannenbaum, "Rock and Roll to Colonel Tom: Tom Parker, 1909–1997," *Village Voice*, February 4, 1997.
338 *"like a king would banish you from the court"*: Lamar Fike to author, 2001.
338 *"warned them about what to say"*: Peter Whitmer in e-mail to author, 2001.
338 *"shouting very loudly"*: Chris Hutchins to author, 1998.
339 *"I'm healthy up in my mind"*: Colonel Tom Parker quoted in Weathersford, "Colonel Recalls King."
339 *"exploited Elvis as much as he's being exploited today"*: Colonel Tom Parker to Craig Rivera, *Inside Edition*, January 1993.
339 *"I'm still working for you, Elvis"*: Colonel Tom Parker quoted in James Kingsley, "Col. Parker Honored in Nevada," *Memphis Commercial Appeal*, June 27, 1994.
339 *"he knew he was dyin'"*: Gabe Tucker to author, 1997.

340 *"He said Elvis was as hard a worker"*: Jimmie Dale Gilmore quoted in Tannenbaum, "Rock and Roll to Colonel Tom."

340 *"In the last years"*: Freddy Bienstock to author, 1997.

340 *"Loanne had to talk for him"*: Author's anonymous source, 1997.

340 *"He was my mentor, my teacher"*: Jerry Weintraub quoted in Michael Fleming, "Weintraub, Shelton Team," *Variety,* December 2, 1997.

340 *"He told me he loved me"*: Jerry Weintraub at Colonel Tom Parker's Memorial Service, Las Vegas, January 25, 1997.

340 *"Colonel, it's Bruce"*: Bruce Banke to Karen Schoemer, raw interview transcript, 1997.

341 *$913,000 in savings bonds, securities, and memorabilia:* Petition for probate of will and codicils and for letters testamentary for the estate of Tom Parker, Las Vegas, February 5, 1997.

341 *"How and where do you begin"*: John O'Reilly at Colonel Tom Parker's Memorial Service, Las Vegas, January 25, 1997

341 *"a very emotional man"*: John O'Reilly at Colonel Tom Parker's Memorial Service, Las Vegas, January 25, 1997

341 *"to work with him"*: Henri Lewin at Colonel Tom Parker's Memorial Service, Las Vegas, January 25, 1997.

341 *"Elvis and the Colonel made history together"*: Priscilla Presley at Colonel Tom Parker's Memorial Service, Las Vegas, January 25, 1997.

BIBLIOGRAPHY

Arnold, Eddy. *It's a Long Way from Chester County*. Old Tappan, NJ: Hewitt House, 1969.

Austin, Gene, and R. M. Pabst, *Gene Austin's Ol' Buddy*. Phoenix, AZ: Augury Press, 1984.

Axton, Mae Boren. *Country Singers As I Know 'Em*. Austin, TX: Sweet Publishing, 1973.

Bashe, Philip. *Teenage Idol, Travelin' Man: The Complete Biography of Rick Nelson*. New York: Hyperion, 1992.

Berman, Susan. *Lady Las Vegas: The Inside Story Behind America's Neon Oasis*. New York: TV Books, 1996.

Cotton, Lee. *All Shook Up: Elvis Day-by-Day, 1954–1977*. Ann Arbor, MI: Pierian Press, 1985.

Crime Novels: American Noir of the 1930s & 40s (including *Nightmare Alley* by William Lindsay Gresham). New York: Library of America, Literary Classics of the United States, 1997.

Crumbaker, Marge, with Gabe Tucker. *Up and Down with Elvis Presley*. New York: G. P. Putnam's Sons, 1981.

Cusic, Don. *Eddy Arnold: I'll Hold You in My Heart*. Nashville, TN: Rutledge Hill Press, 1997.

Davis, Skeeter. *Bus Fare to Kentucky: The Autobiography of Skeeter Davis*. New York: Birch Lane Press, 1993.

Delmore, Alton. *Truth Is Stranger Than Publicity: Alton Delmore's Autobiography*. Nashville, TN: Country Music Foundation Press, 1977.

Denton, Sally, and Roger Morris. *The Money and the Power: The Making of Las Vegas and Its Hold on America, 1947–2000*. New York: Alfred A. Knopf, 2001.

Doll, Susan. *The Films of Elvis Presley*. Lincolnwood, IL: Publications International, 1991.

Dunn, Hampton. *Tampa: A Pictorial History*. Virginia Beach, VA: Donning Company Publishers, 1985.

Emery, Ralph, with Patsi Cox. *The View from Nashville*. New York: William Morrow, 1998.

Esposito, Joe, with Elena Oumano. *Good Rockin' Tonight*. New York: Simon & Schuster, 1994.

Feiler, Bruce. *Under the Big Top*. New York: Scribner, 1995.

Finstad, Suzanne. *Child Bride: The Untold Story of Priscilla Beaulieu Presley.* New York: Berkley Boulevard, 1997.

Geller, Larry, and Joel Spector with Patricia Romanowski. *If I Can Dream: Elvis' Own Story.* New York: Avon Books, 1989.

Goldman, Albert. *Elvis: The Last 24 Hours.* New York: St. Martin's Press, 1991.

Griffis, Ken. *Hear My Song: The Story of the Celebrated Sons of the Pioneers.* Northglenn, CO: Norken, 1998.

Guernsey's. *Elvis: The Official Auction Catalogue.* New York: Harry N. Abrams, 1999.

Guralnick, Peter. *Last Train to Memphis: The Rise of Elvis Presley.* Boston: Little, Brown, 1994.

———. *Careless Love: The Unmaking of Elvis Presley.* Boston: Little, Brown, 1999.

Guralnick, Peter, and Ernst Jorgensen: *Elvis Day by Day: The Definitive Record of His Life and Music.* New York: Ballantine Books, 1999.

Haley, John W., and John J. von Hoelle. *Sound and Glory: The Incredible Story of Bill Haley, the Father of Rock 'n' Roll and the Music That Shook the World.* Wilmington, DE: Dyne-American Publishing, 1989/1990.

Hall, Wade. *Hell-Bent for Music: The Life of Pee Wee King.* Lexington, KY: University Press of Kentucky, 1996.

Harbinson, W. A., and Kay Wheeler. *Growing Up with the Memphis Flash.* Amsterdam, Holland: Tutti Frutti Productions, 1994.

Hopkins, Jerry. *Elvis: A Biography.* New York: Warner Books, 1972.

Hurst, Jack. *Nashville's Grand Ole Opry.* New York: Harry N. Abrams, 1975.

Hutchins, Chris, and Peter Thompson. *Elvis & Lennon.* London: Smith Gryphon Publishers, 1996.

Irwin, Will. *The Confessions of a Con Man.* New York: B. W. Huebsch, 1909.

Jorgensen, Ernst. *Elvis Presley: A Life in Music.* New York: St. Martin's Press, 1998.

Kanter, Hal. *So Far, So Funny.* Jefferson, NC: McFarland & Company, 1999.

Lewin, Henri. *Be a Mensch.* Mt. Royal, NJ: Vector Press, 1990.

Malone, Bill C. *Country Music, U.S.A.* Austin, TX: University of Texas Press, 1985.

McKennon, Joe. *A Pictorial History of the American Carnival,* vols. 1 & 2. Sarasota, FL: Carnival Publishers, 1971, 1972.

———. *Circus Lingo.* Sarasota, FL: Carnival Publishers, 1970.

Morris, Charles G. *Understanding Psychology,* 3d ed. Upper Saddle River, NJ: Prentice Hall, 1996.

Nash, Alanna, with Billy Smith, Marty Lacker, and Lamar Fike. *Elvis Aaron Presley: Revelations from the Memphis Mafia.* New York: HarperCollins, 1995.

Neese, Chuck, et al., ed. *Country Music Who's Who—1972.* Nashville, TN: Record World Publications, 1972.

Ogden, David P. *Frontline on the Home Front: The 13th Coast Artillery at Pensacola, 1930–1947.* Eastern National Park and Monument Association, 1991.

Pearl, Minnie, with Joan Dew. *Minnie Pearl: A Biography.* New York: Simon & Schuster, 1980.

Presley, Priscilla Beaulieu, and Sandra Harmon. *Elvis and Me.* New York: G. P. Putnam's Sons, 1985.

Pugh, Ronnie. *Ernest Tubb: The Texas Troubadour.* Durham, NC: Duke University Press, 1996.

Reid, Ed, and Ovid Demaris. *The Green Felt Jungle*. New York: Trident Press, 1963.

Rose, Frank. *The Agency: William Morris and the Hidden History of Show Business*. New York: HarperBusiness, 1995.

Schlappi, Elizabeth. *Roy Acuff: The Smoky Mountain Boy*. Gretna, LA: Pelican Publishing Company, 1978.

Shaw, Arnold. *The Rockin' '50s*. New York: Hawthorn Books, 1974.

Snow, Hank, with Jack Owenby and Bob Burris. *The Hank Snow Story*. Urbana, IL: University of Illinois Press, 1994.

Snyder, Robert E., and Jack B. Moore. *Pioneer Commercial Photography: The Burgert Brothers, Tampa, Florida*. Gainesville, FL: University Press of Florida, 1992.

Soocher, Stan. *They Fought the Law: Rock Music Goes to Court*. New York: Schirmer Books, 1998.

Streissguth, Michael. *Eddy Arnold: Pioneer of the Nashville Sound*. New York: Schirmer Books, 1997.

Swenson, John. *Bill Haley*. London: W. H. Allen, 1982.

Thompson, Charles C., II, and James P. Cole. *The Death of Elvis: What Really Happened*. New York: Delacorte, 1991.

Tosches, Nick. *Country: Living Legends and Dying Metaphors in America's Biggest Music*. New York: Charles Scribner's Sons, 1985.

Vellenga, Dirk, with Mick Farren. *Elvis and the Colonel*. New York: Delacorte Press, 1988.

Wallis, Hal, with Charles Higham. *Starmaker: The Autobiography of Hal Wallis*. New York: Macmillan, 1980.

Westmoreland, Kathy, and William G. Quinn. *Elvis and Kathy*. Glendale, CA: Glendale House Publishing, 1987.

Worth, Fred L., and Steve D. Tamerius. *Elvis: His Life from A to Z*. Chicago: Contemporary Books, 1992.

INDEX